Historical Perspectives on Modern Economics

English historical economics, 1870 – 1926

Historical Perspectives on Modern Economics

General Editor: Professor Craufurd D. Goodwin, Duke University

This series contains original works that challenge and enlighten historians of economics. For the profession as a whole it promotes a better understanding of the origin and content of modern economics.

English historical economics, 1870 – 1926

The rise of economic history and neomercantilism

Gerard M. Koot
Southeastern Massachusetts University

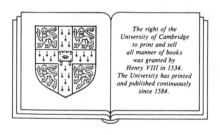

*The right of the
University of Cambridge
to print and sell
all manner of books
was granted by
Henry VIII in 1534.
The University has printed
and published continuously
since 1584.*

CAMBRIDGE UNIVERSITY PRESS

Cambridge
New York   New Rochelle
Melbourne   Sydney

Published by the Press Syndicate of the University of Cambridge
The Pitt Building, Trumpington Street, Cambridge CB2 1RP
32 East 57th Street, New York, NY 10022, USA
10 Stamford Road, Oakleigh, Melbourne 3166, Australia

First published 1987

Printed in the United States of America

Library of Congress Cataloging in Publication Data

Koot, Gerard M.
  English historical economics, 1870–1926.

  (Historical perspectives on modern economics)
  Bibliography: p.
  1. Economics—Great Britain—History. 2. Economic
history. I. Title. II. Title: Neomercantilism.
III. Series.
HB103.A2K65   1987   330′.0941   87–11592

British Library Cataloguing in Publication Data

Koot, Gerard M.
  English historical economics, 1870–1926 :
  the rise of economic history and
  neomercantilism – (Historical perspectives
  on modern economics).
  1. Economic history – England – History
  I. Title   II. Series
  330.9   HC28.5.G7
  ISBN 0–521–32854–3

Contents

Acknowledgments

This study would not have reached fruition if it had not been for the encouragement and advice I received from Professor Bernard Semmel, State University of New York at Stony Brook, and Professor A.W. Coats, the University of Nottingham. Professor Semmel first suggested the subject to me and encouraged my work in the history of economic thought. The intellectual framework of this work owes much to his insights in British intellectual and social history. Professor Coats urged me to pay greater attention to the institutional framework in which the historical economists found themselves. Both have read several versions of the manuscript, made many valuable suggestions, and saved me from many errors. Without their advice and friendship, this study would not have been completed. I also owe a special debt to Professor Elizabeth Durbin of New York University. Her painstaking review of the manuscript has done much to strengthen its argument.

Thanks is also due to the kind critics, especially the members of the Society for the History of Economic Thought on both sides of the Atlantic and in Australia, who have helped formulate my ideas. I am especially grateful to Mr. Paul Sturgis, Loughborough University, who pointed me to manuscript material early in the project. My colleague, Professor James Hijiya, in the History Department at Southeastern Massachusetts University kindly helped with matters of style. Archivists and librarians in the United States and the United Kingdom have not only allowed me to use material in their stewardship, but have also pointed me in new directions. I am particularly grateful to those at the British Library of Political and Economic Science, the Kress Library of Business and Economics at Harvard University, the Marshall Library in Cambridge, as well as the many others who permitted me to use the manuscript collections listed in the bibliography.

Various drafts of the manuscript were typed by Ms. Cheryl Phillips and Ms. Judy Veiga of Southeastern Massachusetts University. They performed an often difficult task with efficiency and good humor. Financial aid for various parts of the study was received from the Kress Library of Business and Economics at Harvard University, the National

Endowment for the Humanities, and Southeastern Massachusetts University.

Finally, I owe the greatest debt to my family. My parents, to whose memory the work is dedicated, made the sacrifices and provided the inspiration which allowed their son to attend a University. My wife, Sheila, whose confidence, support, and affection encouraged me to pursue my interests. My sons, Michael and Christian, who watched its progress with a bemused interest and enjoyed the travel it entailed.

G.M.K.

August 1987

Southeastern Massachusetts University

North Dartmouth, MA.

Introduction

As the first president of the Economic History Society in 1926 William James Ashley, the most original of the English historical economists, warned economic historians: "the theoretical economists are ready to keep us quiet by giving us a little garden plot of our own; and we humble historians are so thankful for a little undisputed territory that we are inclined to leave the economists to their own devices."[1] Ashley's comment was symbolic of the relationship between economics, economic history, and historical economics. Ashley had set out fifty years earlier not only to promote the study of economic history, but also to replace deductive economic theory with a new historical economics erected on a foundation of inductive research. Ashley was unwilling to acquiesce in the compartmentalization of economic studies into economic theory, applied economics, and economic history.[2] In this study the term "economic history" is used to describe the study of past economic phenomena, that is, it is used primarily to describe a category of history. "Applied economics" is here characterized as the study of contemporary economic issues for the formulation of policy. Finally, the term "economic theory" will be employed to describe the derivation of abstract principles from economic phenomena. Between the 1870s and 1920s, economic theory and economic history began to be recognized as separate, though related, disciplines in British universities. The historical economists were those who began their careers before this division became enshrined in the examinations of the universities. They wrote and taught economic theory, applied economics and economic history. Their ovewhelming emphasis, however, was upon economic history and applied economics.

With the partial exception of Ashley, the English historical economists, unlike the better known German historical school, did not aim to construct a systematic historicist economics upon their inductive research. The historicist program was an effort to derive general laws from inductive and historical research and thus create a new system of social theory. Instead, the English historical economists hoped to remind economic theorists and the wider public of the limitations of theory, and

1

to promote the inductive studies of economic history and applied economics in the service of social reform. Further, although the English
historical economists shared a broadly similar research program, that
included a common teleological and evolutionary view of history as
process, their specific interests and personal circumstances did not allow
for the creation of a "school" of historical economics in England, such
as the German historical school of economics or Alfred Marshall's neoclassical school of economics.[3] As A. W. Coats suggested, English historical economics constituted a primarily historical criticism of orthodox
English political economy. In short, English historical economics was a
historist critique rather than a historicist effort of building a new system
of economic theory.[4]

During the 1870s the dominant school of English political economy
was still primarily deductive in method and Ricardian in its theoretical
structure. Its intellectual prestige was due not only to its brilliant, if
narrow, theoretical structure, but also to the fact that classical economics
had basked in the glory of being identified as the creed that had accompanied Britain's rise to industrial supremacy during the first half of the
nineteenth century. With the unification of Germany and the American
recovery from the Civil War, and, especially between 1873 and 1886, a
sluggish rate of growth and technical innovation in Britain, the classical
economic prescription of free trade, theoretical opposition to the combination of labor, and faith in unrestrained competition came under
increasingly serious attack. At the same time, theoretical criticism by
both the historical economists and those associated with the marginal
revolution questioned its very method, its theory of value, its scheme
of distribution, and its underlying assumptions of perfect competition
and omniscience. The historical economists were much more successful
in their first goal of laying low the old than they were in their second
of building a new edifice. The latter task was completed by the neoclassical economists. They not only participated in the destruction of
the old theories, but also, first under Jevons and then under Marshall,
established a new orthodoxy in Britain. Neoclassical economics remained true in spirit to a deductive methodology, though tempered by
historical criticism, as it rebuilt its theoretical structure upon the sounder
foundation of marginal utility analysis. Moreover, it was far more cautious in its claims of the relations between science and application than
classical economics had been.

The failure of the English historical economists to become a dominant
school of economics in Britain, to say nothing of the dominant one,
should not lead us to conclude that they were of little or no importance
in the history of economic thought or to history in general. Even in the

history of economic thought, in which Whiggish interpretations of history often still flourish, their importance has been acknowledged. Their chief historical significance lies in three areas. First, they helped destroy the overconfidence, the insularity, and even the dogmatism that often characterized English classical economics. They continually reminded neoclassical economists of the hypothetical nature of their conclusions, the need for empirical research, and the relativity of economic theory and policy to a particular time and place. Second, in the field of economic policy, the historical economists generally expounded the need for a national, and even an imperial, scheme of economic policy and social reform that has become so characteristic of the twentieth century. Third, they played a major role in the development of economic history as a recognized field of study. This became their most lasting and specific legacy.

The foundation of the Economic History Society in 1926 demonstrated that the academic discipline of economic history had achieved professional status. By this time the discipline could point to its inclusion in university examinations, a nucleus of university posts, a growing number of works in economic history produced by professional economic historians, and a wide popularity as evidence for its claim that it constituted a recognized discipline.[5] Despite the fact that the impetus for the creation of the society came from historians,[6] the historical economists had, during the last quarter of the nineteenth century, played the major role in laying the intellectual, as well as the institutional, foundation for the new discipline.

Before economic history became a recognized discipline in England, a good many historical tracts, monographs, treatises, and pamphlets had already been written on a variety of subjects in the field.[7] What distinguished the late nineteenth century from the earlier period was the increasing role assigned to such subjects in academic teaching and writing, in both history and economics, and the emergence of an intellectual and social framework that gave coherence to these writings and the underlying interests they reflected. There were positive and negative sides to these factors. The negative side was primarily an attack upon the established methodology and principles of classical economics in particular and of utilitarian social theory in general. These principles reflected the social ideals of individualism and cosmopolitanism current during the first half of the nineteenth century. By contrast, social thought during the second half of the nineteenth century placed a greater emphasis upon evolutionary, historical, and collectivist patterns of ideas than the relatively mechanistic conceptions derived from the eighteenth century.[8] On the positive side, the late nineteenth century saw the development of a "scientific" historical method, especially in legal studies and history; the introduction of examinations in history at both Oxford and Cambridge; a greater emphasis upon the economic aspects of history;[9] calls for the creation of a general science of society; and an increasing public demand for an historical understanding of contemporary problems. Alongside this, and linked with the negative aspects, was the growing feeling by some that the reigning body of economic ideas, however adapted, was largely inappropriate for the circumstances of the time, and was, moreover, associated with distasteful policies and attitudes. The historical economists asserted that the study of economic history and applied economics would serve as a more appropriate guide to the formulation of public policy than either classical or neoclassical economic theory.

The social ideals and policy recommendations of the historical economists differed significantly from those of the orthodox school. The conflicts between the historical economists, on the one hand, and the classical and the neoclassical economists, on the other, should not be interpreted as a pale reflection of the German *Methodenstreit*, a celebrated methodological debate between the deductive Austrian economic theorists, led by Carl Menger, and the inductive German historical school, led by Gustav Schmoller. The English *Methodenstreit* was a dispute over the appropriate use of an inductive or deductive methodology in economic study, the role of the scientist in society, competition over academic posts and intellectual territory within the universities, and, perhaps most importantly, broadly dissimilar social and political ideals. Taken as a whole, the writings of the English historical economists can be characterized as neomercantilist. They not only insisted that the more inductive and practical methodology of the mercantilist writers was superior to the abstractions of the classical economists, but also believed that mercantilism's nationalist concerns, its faith in corporate responsibility for the welfare of the people, and some aspects of its scheme of state regulation were more desirable than what they called the system of laissez faire. In addition to reflecting these ideals in their writings, the historical economists were also variously active on behalf of such causes as Irish social reform, the condition of agricultural and industrial workers, recognition of the labor unions, and, especially, tariff reform. As historical economists, they saw no conflict between their political advocacy and academic activity; indeed, such action expressed the very essence of their aims.

The historical economists – particularly Arnold Toynbee, W. J. Ashley, H. S. Foxwell, William Cunningham, and W. A. S. Hewins – sought a middle way between socialism and unregulated capitalism. Although they moved from Liberal to Unionist and Conservative politics, they, like J. M. Keynes after them, hoped to manage capitalism. Their program might be called "corporatist" or, more persuasively, "social-imperialist." The term "neomercantilist," however, seems superior for several reasons. First, the historical economists rehabilitated the history of mercantilism in England. Second, they themselves constantly reiterated the proposition that mercantilist economics, however imperfect, was at least a political economy that sought to deal with pressing issues of the day. Third, they argued that mercantilism's concern for the welfare of the community was a superior mental and moral framework to that of classical and neoclassical economics, which emphasized the welfare of the individual and the firm. Fourth, while orthodox economics, except in its more popular and dogmatic form, had never exclusively championed laissez faire or free trade, the historical economists frontally attacked these ideals between 1870 and 1914. Fifth, the very term "neomercantilism" was coined in reference to English historical economics.

The term is used here in its broadest sense as illustrated, for example, by L. L. Price in a 1902 article on tariff reform. Price argued that a tide of national feeling was sweeping the world: "This national feeling will be allowed by the candid observer to harmonize more evidently with the ideas of the Mercantile System than with those of Free Trade." Despite many qualifications, Price concluded: "Free Trade is 'cosmopolitan' and Protection is 'national.' "[10] As the large literature on English mercantilism suggests, the mercantilists hoped to achieve both power and plenty. This tradition was what most English historical economists wished to adapt to the twentieth century. Keynes's famous 1924 statement on the end of laissez faire and his more spectacular call for national self-sufficiency in 1930 have frequently been noted as prophetic comments for our time. But the politicians, businessmen, and civil servants who were slowly eroding free trade during the 1920s were not yet listening to Keynes. Instead, they could seek justification, if intellectual justification seemed useful, for their protectionist and interventionist schemes in the academic writing and public pronouncements of English historical economists.

The transformation of English classical economics and the rise of historical economics were contemporaneous with fundamental changes in Britain's economic, social, and political structure. Historians have often seen the 1880s as a critical decade of transition in British history.[11] For contemporaries, the central fact of British economic history was what they called the "Great Depression." We know now that the period 1873 to 1896 was not a depression. Instead, we discuss this period as the beginning of British industrial retardation. For contemporaries, the economic problems of the period were a fundamental psychological shock that by the twentieth century had all but destroyed Victorian confidence in England as the workshop of the world and the master of a Pax Britannica.

In agriculture, however, the depression was real. Between the mid 1870s and mid 1880s rents dropped by one-fourth. The repeal of the Corn Laws in 1846 did not immediately threaten British agriculture, but after 1870, peace and prosperity in both Europe and America, new agricultural technology, cheap ocean transport, the building of the intercontinental railways, and inexpensive grains from the virgin lands of North America and Russia endangered the prosperity of English arable agriculture. Market gardening and dairying fared much better in close association with towns and cities. These forces, combined with the land question, especially in Ireland, produced considerable interest in such themes as peasant proprietors, the nature of rent, and the links between rural development and national prosperity. The problems of British arable agriculture also saw an absolute decline in the social and political position of landed society within the nation.[12]

In trade and industry there was no general depression during the period. However, lower prices, declining profits, and foreign competition caused a serious crisis of confidence. To contemporaries, the fear of foreign competition was especially severe and culminated in the fair trade movement of the early 1880s and the more vigorous tariff reform program initiated by Joseph Chamberlain in 1903. Britain, which had long been accustomed to being the major exporter of manufactured goods in the world, was now vigorously challenged at home and abroad by an industrial and imperial Germany. In iron, shipbuilding, machine tools, and even in textiles – the staple trades – Britain experienced a relative decline due to lower productivity, slower technological innovation, the survival of family management, and the failure to link education closely with industry. This retardation was also evident in the newer industries of steel, chemicals, and later electricity. There were of course bright spots in the economy, especially in the retail, food processing, home product, clothing, and pharmaceutical industries. The late nineteenth century also witnessed the growth of the size of firms and the advent of the corporation. Indeed, Britain ranked with the United States as having a few of the largest corporations in the world. In general, however, the family firm survived more widely in Britain than in the United States. By the 1890s there was a growing demand among economists that something be done in Britain to provide education for modern business. By contrast, the growth in invisible earnings was an apparent bright spot in the economy. Between 1873 and 1896, earnings from trade and financial services, investments, and insurance rose from 12% to 24% of British import costs. Thus, the stage was set for a fundamental debate between those who argued that this demonstrated the wisdom of free trade and those that argued that this constituted one of its chief follies.[13]

The last quarter of the nineteenth century saw a gradual improvement in the standard of living, because wages remained relatively stable as prices fell. Although the overall rate of population growth did not diminish significantly from its average rate of much of the century, the Malthusian specter seemed to have been laid to rest as the standard of living visibly increased for large segments of the population. Indeed, from the 1870s, a decrease in the birth rate in the middle classes became pronounced. It was hoped that this, along with middle class morality, would percolate down to the lower classes. Despite this generally optimistic picture, from the 1880s there was a marked increase in demand for the improvement of the "condition of the people," a consequence of a variety of factors. Chief among these was the severity of cyclical business crises in 1879, 1886, and 1893, which led to a greater employment insecurity than during the 1850s. Charles Booth's famous surveys of London during the 1880s demonstrated that at least thirty per cent of London's population lived in extreme poverty and that the chief cause of poverty was irregularity of employment. Labor unions had been virtually legalized in 1871. The late 1880s also saw the emergence of the "new unionism." This movement brought whole industries and some unskilled labor into the labor movement and a new militancy that had been largely absent from the craft unions of the previous decades. The question was no longer what were the costs and benefits of labor unions, but how to deal with their claim for a share of power.[14]

In politics and social theory, the 1880s were a watershed in British history. The Reform Act of 1867 did not in fact bring democracy to England, but contemporaries were not far wrong in arguing that it would have that ultimate effect. The Reform Act of 1884, as well as the secret ballot and a series of corrupt practices acts which insured a system of open and honest elections, created nearly universal male suffrage in Britain. In politics these developments saw the creation of modern political parties with constituency electoral organizations and the emergence of labor candidates. To this must be added the dilution of the aristocracy in government by ambitious members of a rapidly expanding middle class. Indeed, during the 1880s England began to acquire that characteristic twentieth century class structure in which the middle class finally achieved a significant share of power, especially in the professions and the bureaucracies.

The establishment of laissez faire in England, as we now know, was accompanied by the gradual erection of a new system of state intervention that has been traced to the 1830s. But during the 1870s and 1880s, a considerable increase in the scale of public expenditure and state regulation took place. Particularly important were the Civil Service and Education Acts of 1870, the Trade Union Act of 1875, the Employer Liability Act of 1880, the Diseases Prevention Act of 1884, the Parcel Post Act of the same year, the Land Act of 1881, and the Housing Act of 1890. These and many other pieces of legislation greatly extended the power of the state. Legislation was often preceded by far ranging Royal Commissions, on Agriculture in 1882, on the Depression in Trade in 1886, and on Labour, Poor Reform, and Currency in the 1890s. Finally, beginning in the 1870s, large English cities began to build systems of "municipal socialism" that included the ownership of utilities and transportation, the regulation of businesses, and the provision of numerous services. While economists and other social theorists debated all this as exceptions to laissez faire, these ad hoc exceptions were becoming so numerous that we can speak of the regime of state intervention.[15]

After 1870, faith in religion was rapidly being replaced by faith in science. Though, as we shall see, Christian Socialism, broadly conceived, and teleological views of history largely derived from religion had a considerable impact on the work of several of the English historical economists, among many social theorists of the period religious fervor was being replaced by an evangelical faith in various versions of the science of society. Whether Comtean, Spencerian, Marxist, Idealist, or an amalgam of these, social theories were all historicist in their formulation. Evolutionary forms of social theory had already become dominant during the 1860s, replacing a more static utilitarianism of the earlier period as the orthodox creed. At the same time, the late nineteenth century saw the professionalization, and consequent specialization, of each of the social sciences. By the early twentieth century, social sciences were becoming safely embedded in their own university departments. These intellectual and social changes had important repercussions upon the debate in economics of the period.[16]

In politics the period saw the emergence of both the theory and reality of what has been called "positive freedom." This concept held that in modern industrial society isolated individuals could achieve neither material welfare nor effective freedom. Thus, it became the function of the state to actively promote a social basis for both welfare and freedom. The negative freedoms of classical liberalism were no longer deemed sufficient to rule an empire of 8 million square miles and 265 million people, and an island nation of labor unions, corporations, democracy, growing contrasts between wealth and poverty, and serious foreign competition. The theory of the new liberalism has been especially linked to the philosophy of T. H. Green during the 1880s; it was already present, however, a generation earlier in the work of J. S. Mill. The social and political theory of the new liberalism did not easily and neatly carry over into actual politics. The 1880s saw not only the birth of a new radicalism within the Liberal Party, but also a host of socialist organizations and a new social conservative movement. Imperialism was but one of the complications, though an important one. Such historical economists as Ashley, Hewins, and Cunningham were part and parcel of a social imperialism that transcended the old political parties and dominated politics in the early twentieth century.[17] Thus, the debate within economics during the last third of the nineteenth century was not an isolated phenomenon, because many of the key issues reflected fundamental social, political, economic, and intellectual currents of the period. It is in this wider context that we must understand the crisis of the old political economy and the conflicts over its reconstruction.

The crisis of classical political economy and attempts at reconstruction, 1870–1885

The 1870s and 1880s were the formative years of English historical economics. The late 1860s and the 1870s have been called the crisis of the old English political economy. Until the publication of Marshall's *Principles* in 1890, the immensely popular economic writings of J.S. Mill remained the dominant work in economics and served to shore up the illusion that the classical postulates, deductive methodology, and policy conclusions inherited from the Ricardians remained valid into the last third of the nineteenth century. As we will see, however, Mill's methodology, theory, and policy conclusions seriously compromised the Ricardian structure. Indeed, the economic views of Mill offered a significant opening for the heretical views of several of the historical economists. The last of the classical economists, J.E. Cairnes, sought to repair what he saw as dangerous tendencies in Mill's work by returning to a more rigorous deductive method and by disassociating economic theory from its popular policy maxims. Cairnes's efforts, however, only deepened the crisis of classical economics. Finally, during these same years the brilliant work of W.S. Jevons and Alfred Marshall laid the foundations for neoclassical theory. Before 1885, however, neoclassical theory had not yet become the dominant school of economics in England.

The crisis of political economy

To celebrate the one-hundredth anniversary of the publication of the *Wealth of Nations*, the Political Economy Club, itself nearly a half century old, held a centenary dinner at the Pall Mall Restaurant on May 31, 1876. It met to discuss the question: "What are the most important results which have followed from the publication of the *Wealth of Nations* just one hundred years ago; and in what principal directions do the doctrines of that book still remain to be applied?"[1] Present at the discussion were such politicians as W.E. Gladstone, Robert Lowe, and W.E. Forster; the distinguished reforming civil servant Edwin Chadwick; the literary and political figure John Morley; the economic and political writer Walter Bagehot; and the university professors of economics Henry Fawcett, Thorold Rogers, Cliffe Leslie, and W. Stanley Jevons. Both the question and the guest list express important assumptions concerning British economics during the period. It was assumed that Adam Smith and his successors had put forth "doctrines" that were both theoretically sound and applicable to policy making and suggested that educated men could meet on common ground with economists to discuss both the principles of political economy and their application. Indeed, before the 1890s English economics had not yet become a professional subject.[2] But instead of serving as an affirmation of the prestige, unity, and the practical utility of English economics, the centenary dinner gave witness to deep-seated disagreements over issues of policy, methodology, and theory and revealed the growing gulf between politicians and academicians.

Robert Lowe, a doctrinaire liberal, opened the discussion. Though Lowe acknowledged the recent criticisms of political economy, he thought the science complete and saw no "very large or any startling development of Political Economy" in the future. Lowe pointedly noted that Adam Smith, although possessing great learning in history, law, and philosophy, had been essentially a deductive economist who had laid down "principles and rules so wide, so weighty, and so true, that they had served for the guidance of mankind from his time to the present, and, so far as we can judge, they will last as long as mankind shall seek after the truth." If Adam Smith had occasionally erred, Lowe continued, especially in such matters as the Navigation Acts, it had been because he had not had sufficient faith in his own principles. Happily, Lowe concluded, Ricardo had amplified and corrected his master's teaching. Lowe announced that Smith's principles could be reduced to the propositions that wealth was a consequence of "work and thrift," while the causes of poverty were "idleness and waste." He associated free trade with the former and mercantilism with the latter pair of characteristics. Lowe ended by expressing the hope that the workers would see the wisdom of laissez faire and the folly of trade unions, and he urged other nations to pursue the free trade example set by Britain.[3] As the finance minister in Gladstone's first administration, Lowe represented the voice of a popular economics which we can justly call dogmatic, insular, laissez faire, or, with Carlyle, "the dismal science."[4]

Popular orthodoxy was questioned so seriously during the 1870s that several speakers rose to defend its economic and political wisdom. William Newmarch, a statistical economist who had a very different view than Lowe of Adam Smith's methodology, agreed with Lowe on the vital principle of laissez faire. He warned: "There is exceeding danger in a free and vigorous country like this in the unceasing and unmitigated application of this new system of interference, supervision, inspection, repression, revision, reporting, altering, direction, and recasting, which is now being applied in the whole force of government machinery."[5]

Gladstone also spoke in favor of free trade as a moral and economic imperative. But significantly, Gladstone felt it necessary to deal directly with the criticism of English free trade associated with Friedrich List and his successors in Germany and America. Gladstone noted that "they contended that we had served our own purposes by protection, and thus having served our own purposes we then proceeded to dispense with it, as a man takes down the scaffolding by means of which he erected the building."[6]

Two foreign economists present gently reminded the audience of the limitations of English economic orthodoxy. While the French economist Leon Say spoke of the universality of Adam Smith's teaching, he also expressed disappointment at the apparent inability of organized labor to play the role economic orthodoxy had assigned to it and lamented rising protectionist sentiment abroad. M. de Laveleye, the noted Belgian specialist in the economics of land, made it clear that there were serious divisions concerning the nature, content, and purpose of political economy. After praising Adam Smith's work on production, Laveleye observed that economics was now engaged on its second great problem – the theory and practice of distribution. He declared that there were two theories of distribution: The orthodox economists held that the natural laws of economics could solve the problem of distribution through laissez faire, and the German historical school (he called them "Katheder Sozialisten") sought to employ political institutions to insure that the distribution of wealth would be in accordance with religious, moral, and historical convictions. He called upon English economists to join their continental brethren in the great task of reconciling political economy with morality, justice, law, religion, and history. Ending on a conciliatory note, he declared that Adam Smith's true immortality was to be found in the universality of his work because the orthodox and the historical school pointed to him as their master.[7]

Thorold Rogers, an English historical economist, was far less moderate in his views. He boldly declared that "Adam Smith had a clear title to be called an inductive Philosopher." Further, Rogers continued, to assert that Adam Smith had opposed combinations was a distortion of the facts because he had known nothing of trade unions. Instead, the employers had combined to lower wages and had justified such action with the erroneous doctrines of Ricardo.[8] The mention of Ricardo's name was significant. Everyone could agree on the value of Adam

Smith's contribution to economics. On the legacy of Ricardo, however, the late nineteenth century witnessed some of its most bitter argument and unrestrained rhetoric.

The centennial dinner thus revealed deep divisions concerning the proper method of economics, the interpretation of its history, the issue of state intervention, the distribution of wealth, and even the validity of free trade.[9] Commenting on the dinner, Walter Bagehot, the editor of the *Economist* and himself an important critic of the "postulates of political economy," noted that political economy "lies rather dead in the public mind."[10] William Cunningham, who was formulating his own views on historical economics, observed that, despite the great influence that political economy had enjoyed in England in the past, it was now losing its hold upon the nation: "The mercantile public are not awed by it; working class leaders notoriously disregard it, and foreign states-men do not pretend to listen to its teachings."[11] Bonamy Price, Oxford Professor of Political Economy and an exponent of "practical" econom-ics, complained that "marked feelings of dissatisfaction with the actual position of Political Economy" were a consequence of the rigidity of economic science. The result was that men no longer studied it and "the authority of economical writers was declining."[12] Disagreements within English economics were gaining so much notoriety that an attempt was made to oust the subject from the meetings of the British Association for the Advancement of Science. In 1877, Sir Francis Galton, the stat-istician and biologist, headed a committee that urged the exclusion of Section F on Economic Science and Statistics from the Association on the grounds that the papers of this section had failed to live up to acceptable scientific standards.[13] In 1885, the discussion at the Industrial Remuneration Conference further demonstrated that the debate on the relations between economics and policy had been exacerbated rather than solved during the intervening years.[14]

At the height of England's mid-Victorian prosperity, the triumph of orthodoxy had seemed complete. Nassau Senior had told a Frenchman: "It is a triumph of theory. We are governed by philosophers and political economists."[15] No such comment could be made concerning the last third of the nineteenth century. The minutes of the Political Economy Club during this period demonstrate the existence of fundamental dis-agreements in economics, especially on matters of policy. In 1865 Tho-rold Rogers questioned the policy of laissez faire and free trade. In 1866 Cliffe Leslie raised the troublesome issue of the problems of Ireland and its significance for political economy. In 1877 A.J. Mundella ques-tioned the likelihood of Britain's continued industrial preeminence. In 1880 W. Stanley Jevons called for a science of the principles of state intervention. In 1883 H.S. Foxwell asked whether the contemporary method employed in economic investigation was not different from that used by Ricardo and the two Mills. In 1889 W. Fraser Rae questioned unilateral free trade and suggested an imperial customs union for the British Empire.[16] These documents suggest that consensus was increasingly difficult to achieve on fundamental issues of economic policy by the late Victorian period. The disputes among economists themselves were equally serious.

The "half-way house" of J.S. Mill

J.S. Mill's economic writings began as an effort to solve some of the unsettled questions of English classical political economy. The chief result of this effort was his two volume *Principles of Political Economy: With Some of Their Applications to Social Philosophy*. First published in 1848, it reached its seventh edition in 1871. This hastily written treatise[17] was intended as a synthesis of the work of Adam Smith and that of Ricardo, James Mill, and the Saint-Simonians. Mill argued that the great Scotsman had understood that public issues could not be decided solely with reference to economic theory. This is why, Mill continued, Adam Smith "gives that well grounded feeling of command over the principles of the subject . . . owing to which the *Wealth of Nations*, alone among the treatises of Political Economy, has not only been popular with general readers, but has impressed itself strongly upon the minds of men of the world and of legislators."[18] Mill hoped that his work would achieve a similar success and purpose for a new generation. Thus, he wrote not only a theoretical treatise, but he also included numerous suggestions for public policy and profusely illustrated it with contemporary and historical material.

Mill's *Principles* did, indeed, achieve a remarkable public success. Upon Mill's insistence, it was made widely available in a cheap edition. It spoke to economists, government officials, businessmen, the educated elite, university students, and the aristocracy of labor. His work was also widely popularized through the issuance of many outlines of political economy based upon his work. The most famous of these catechisms was Henry Fawcett's *Manual of Political Economy*. As Cambridge Professor of Political Economy from 1863 to 1883, Fawcett offered up a simplified version of Mill that did not always do justice to the complexity of the original.[19] To this complexity must be added another dimension. As Mill's views evolved on such critical issues as labor unions, the land question, and socialism, he did not always include his new views in the later editions of the *Principles*. By 1871, as Mill himself perhaps understood, it was becoming ever more difficult to combine the divergent views on methodology, theory, and practice of Adam Smith and his successors into a coherent whole.[20]

The late 1860s and early 1870s have been called the "Jevonian Revolution" in economics and the "Decline and Fall of English classical political economy."[21] But despite the growing criticism of Jevons, Leslie, Thornton, Long, Bagehot, and others, Mill's *Principles* remained the standard authority in English economics for another generation. As a result, proponents of state intervention and of laissez faire; partisans of free trade, reciprocity, and even of protection; staunch champions of free competition and evolutionary socialists; adherents to labor, cost of production, and marginal utility theories of value; and advocates of deduction and induction all pointed to Mill as a source of recognized and respected economic authority. Indeed, Mill's prestige and authority were so pervasive as to move the heretical Jevons to "protest against deference for any man, whether John Stuart Mill, or Adam Smith, or Aristotle, being allowed to check inquiry."[22]

One of the major problems with Mill's economics was his adherence to what Schumpeter called the four theoretical postulates of classical political economy. First, every man desires to obtain the maximum of wealth with the minimum of effort. This was the assumption of the "economic man." Second, the population tends to outstrip the food supply. Third, the productivity of labor can be increased indefinitely through the application of capital to manufacturing. Fourth, when agricultural improvements remain stationary, agricultural production will experience diminishing returns.[23] The second and fourth postulates became especially untenable during the last quarter of the nineteenth century, and the existence of an 'economic man' was questioned by anthropology, economic history, and evolutionary social theory. Mill sometimes stated that these postulates not only were true in theory, but also constituted an empirical statement of reality. As Newmarch noted in 1871, however, the abstract doctrines of the population principle and of diminishing returns in agriculture could no longer be verified empirically.[24] One historian of Ricardian economics has convincingly argued that the contradictions between theory and practice had already become evident during the 1830s, and that Mill's eclectic economics saved the wobbling Ricardian structure for another generation. Mill saved the structure, primarily because of its political import, "and in the final analysis, Mill was less interested in the 'principles of political economy' than in 'their application to social philosophy.' "[25] Mill, in harmony with the majority of classical economists, sought to sanction social and economic policy with the authority of science, but in a far more complex fashion that the crude identity between theory and practice set out by Ricardo.

The basic difficulty with Mill's economic methodology was that in his purely methodological writings he emphasized the need to use a deductive method for economic science, yet in his application of that method to economics he was often much more eclectic. Depending upon one's perspective, one can call Mill's economic methodology a logical muddle or one can attempt to appreciate his wider ethical purpose. Schumpeter, in his elegant defense of Mill, argued that his economics was a "half-way" house between Ricardo and Marshall.[26] Indeed, if Ricardo's method was excessively abstract, Mill went a long way to making it more realistic, without losing the scientific rigor of economic theory that was possible only through the use of a deductive methodology. As Schumpeter asserted, Mill's method was a "Concrete Deductive Method supplemented by the Inverse Deductive or Historical Method for research into historical changes of the social set-up as a whole."[27]

Mill has told us that by 1830 he had already rejected his father's rigorous deductive method for social and political philosophy. Instead, he sought to steer a middle ground between the excessive deduction of his father and the Baconian empiricism of Macaulay.[28] While working on his *System of Logic*, he published his methodological views for economics in the *Westminster Review* of 1836. Economic science, Mill argued, was not the study of what made a nation wealthy, but was limited to the scientific study of the laws that governed economic phenomena. He divided these phenomena into those governed by the laws of the physical universe and those ruled by the moral laws of the mind. Political economy presupposed all the physical sciences which dealt especially with the physical properties of nature upon which the production of wealth depended. The laws of the mind were set forth by the moral or social sciences. Political economy also dealt with these laws, but only in so far as they were psychological laws dealing with economic phenomena. Thus, economic science considered mankind as "occupied solely in acquiring and consuming wealth"; it investigated the laws of economic activity "under the supposition that man is a being who is determined by the necessity of his nature, to prefer a greater portion of wealth to a smaller in all cases." Mill hastened to add: "No political economist was ever so absurd as to suppose that mankind are really thus constituted," but the abstraction of human motives as "flowing solely from the desire of wealth" is essential if economics is to be a science.[29]

Mill held that, in general, the physical sciences followed an "a priori" method and the moral sciences employed an "a posterior" method. Because he postulated an economic man, he advocated an a priori method for economic science that he likened to that of geometry. Economics, then, was rooted in an abstraction of humans and various fundamental laws of physical matter. Hence, the truth of economic science could be assured only "in the abstract," because in the real world the political economist would have to take into account "disturbing causes." Further, for applied economics, theoretical principles should first be verified inductively.[30] Despite Mill's careful theoretical qualifications, his use of a classical economic man – an economic man who mechanically followed Bentham's table of the springs of action rather than the more complex psychology of Mill's own modified utilitarianism, became a prime target for moral, historical, and theoretical criticism during the last third of the century.

In order to counter William Whewell's intuitionist challenge to British empiricism, Mill's *Logic* outlined a theory of induction for general social science that he claimed to have developed before reading Comte's *Cours de Philosophie Positive*.[31] It was not, however, a Baconian method of induction, for Mill held that such a "chemical" or "experimental" method was inappropriate for a science that did not allow for experimentation. At the same time, he also repudiated the deductive, or geometric, method because it could not adequately deal with the complexities of social and historical realities.[32] He had, however, already learned from Comte that social science could be conveniently divided into static and dynamic branches.[33] The first of these, dealing with social existence in a stationary state, considered the uniformities inherent in the stationary and progressive states, while the second dealt with the laws of social evolution in progressive society. Mill held that the proper method for static social science was the concrete deductive method. This method, analogous not to the method of geometry but to that of the more complex physical sciences such as astronomy, proceeded deductively: "But by the deductions from many, not from a very few, original premises; considering each effect as . . . an aggregate result of many causes, operating sometimes through the same, sometimes through different mental agencies, or laws of human nature."[34] It was a method of composition. Further, Mill warned that the conclusions of social science thus arrived at could be held confidently only if they had been verified through observation of the real world. Comte held that it was observation that made social science "scientific"; Mill maintained that it was deduction that made it such.[35] It was this concrete deductive method of composition, rather than the even more rigorous deductive prescriptions of his 1836 essay, that he generally employed in his theoretical economic writings.

For dynamic social science, or the discovery of the laws of social evolution in progressive society, Mill advocated the inverse deductive method. It "obtains its generalizations by a collation of specific experience, and verifies them by ascertaining whether they are such as would follow from known general principles." This method he ascribed to the influence of Comte.[36] Mill held that this process of induction, which became science through deductive verification, was especially suited to historical and statistical investigation. In economics, however, Mill refuted Comte's methodological suggestions, which were to have considerable influence in England during the late nineteenth century. Mill argued that by denying that political economy was a "positive science," Comte had condemned it as a mere branch of "metaphysics" and had attacked "the only systematic attempt yet made by any body of thinkers, to constitute a science, not indeed of social phenomena generally, but of one great class or division of them."[37] Mill did allow, however, that the scientific principles of economics were "relative to a given form of civilization and a given stage of social development."[38]

In his 1848 preface to the *Principles*, Mill claimed that the "design of the book is different from any treatise of Political Economy which has been produced in England since the time of Adam Smith."[39] This claim of originality was chiefly based upon his division of the subject into the laws of production and those of distribution. According to Mill, the laws of production were static: "There is nothing optional or arbitrary in them. Whatever mankind produces must be produced in the modes, and under the conditions imposed by the constitution of external things, and by the inherent properties of their own bodily and mental structures."[40] These laws, largely taken over from Ricardian economics had been derived deductively from the psychology of an economic man and the physical laws of the universe. For these laws, Mill claimed the sanction of a hypothetical science. Conversely, the laws of distribution were "unlike the laws of Production, for those of Distribution are *partly* of human institution . . . since the manner in which wealth is distributed in a given society, depends upon the statutes and usages therein containing."[41] Later in the volume, however, he held that the laws of distribution were "a matter of human institution *solely*."[42] In the manner suggested by Comte, Mill also divided his economics into static and dynamic analysis. Unfortunately, these two divisions in his *Principles* did not always fit neatly together. Although the emphasis in Mill's work was certainly upon the relativity of the laws of distribution, it also contained highly abstract and deductive laws of distribution for both the static and dynamic modes. Further, in his methodological writings and in his *Autobiography*, and even publicly in Parliament, he argued that his economic science should not be seen as a "practical guide" for specific action. In his economic writings, which bore the double burden of improving humanity and advancing economic science, he did not always emphasize this qualification.[43]

In a comment often quoted by both theoretical and historical critics, Mill asserted that the question of value was of crucial importance. "Happily," he continued, "there is nothing in the laws of value which remains for the present writer to clear up; the theory of the subject is complete."[44] As the neoclassical economists demonstrated, the fundamental problem with the classical theory of value, and of Mill's modification of that theory, was that it began its analysis from the side of production and supply, rather than from the side of demand and consumption. Mill's famous dictum that "demand for commodities is not demand for labor" was as much a political and ethical statement as a scientific principle; it condemned Mill to a theory of value largely imprisoned in an analysis of production.[45] Mill did, however, make a significant contribution to value theory that constituted, as Schumpeter argued, a half-way house between Ricardo and Marshall.[46]

The historical economists would often point to the discrepancies between Mill's classical theory of production and empirical facts. Indeed, he himself offered evidence suggesting that his version of the Malthusian population principle showed signs of empirical falsification.[47] Nonetheless, he confidently stated that the population tended to double every twenty years. He also defended the principles of population: "The evidence of them is so ample and incontestable, that they have made their way against all kinds of opposition and may now be regarded as axiomatic."[48] He had a similar faith in the law of diminishing returns in agriculture: "Were they different, nearly all the phenomena of production and distribution of wealth would be other than they are."[49]

While Mill's treatment of profit and rent made significant alterations in the received Ricardian doctrine, his theory of wages can be seen as a hardening of the classical wage theory into a categorical doctrine, the wages-fund.[50] The result of Mill's tortuous analysis was a near tautology: "Wages cannot rise, but by an increase of the aggregate fund employed in hiring labourers, or the diminution of the number of competitors for hire."[51] Although there has been much discussion concerning the theoretical significance of the entire wages-fund controversy, there seems little reason to doubt that a good deal of the popular opposition to the smal science was rooted in an antipathy to its implications.[52] Further, by the 1870s there was considerable empirical evidence that trade unions were in fact raising wages through combinations. In his famous recantation of 1869, Mill appeared to sanction the aims of the trade union movement:

The doctrine hitherto taught by all or most economists (including myself), which denied it to be possible that trades combinations can raise wages . . . is deprived of its scientific foundation and must be thrown aside. The right and wrong of the proceedings of the Trades Unions becomes a question of prudence and social duty, not one which is peremptorily decided by unbending necessities of political economy.[53]

Mill hastened, however, to hedge his position. He warned that any attempts to raise wages above their natural level through combinations would inevitably damage the interests of the nonunionized workers.[54] In the last edition of his *Principles*, he concluded that unions could not improve wages generally, for "unfortunately the effect is quite beyond attainment of such means."[55] Thus, despite Mill's recantation, the wages-fund remained a focal point of theoretical and political dissatisfaction with classical economics.

Mill's teaching on the inevitability of the stationary state further seemed to strengthen the reputation of classical economics as an obstacle to social reform for the working classes. As an economist, Mill remained wedded to a highly abstract and deductive theory of distribution which forecast a gloomy future: "The economical progress of a society constituted of landlords, capitalists, and labourers, tends to the progressive enrichment of the landlord class; while the cost of the labourer's subsistence tends on the whole to increase, and profits to fall."[56] Sidestepping the fact that there was little empirical evidence of its imminent realization, Mill declared that if the stationary state has not arrived it "is because the goal itself flies before us."[57] For Mill, and classical economics generally, the villain remained the English landlord. During the 1870s and after, however, the focus of the debate concerning distribution shifted from the wealth of the landed class to the contest between the capitalist and labor. Moreover, both the historical and neoclassical economists feared the class antagonisms inherent in the Ricardian theory of distribution.

One of the constantly reiterated themes of Mill's economic writings was his insistence that the principles of economic science were not to be interpreted as maxims of public policy. Indeed, on the occasion of Lowe's opposition to Irish land reform legislation, Mill rose in Parliament to declare what would become one of the crucial propositions of English historical economics: "No one is at all capable of determining what is the right political economy for any country unless he knows its circumstances."[58] Although most of the classical economists were not as staunchly committed to laissez faire as has sometimes been argued,[59] Mill especially applied the principle of historical relativism to a variety of economic policy issues. To be sure, Mill often argued that, as a general rule, laissez faire ought to be the presupposition upon which government should act. However, by the end of his life he had put forth so many possible exceptions that they threatened to undermine the general principle.

The complexity of Mill's position on government intervention was even evident in that mainstay of nineteenth century economic liberalism, free trade. In his 1829 essay on international trade, Mill had all but conceded the justice of List's and Carey's criticism that Britain's advocacy of universal free trade amounted to the imperialism of free trade.[60] Despite this admission, he nonetheless rejected the economic arguments of List and Carey in his *Principles*. He did, however, agree that Carey's arguments carried weight on political grounds, for a nation engaged in the same pursuit, or entirely agricultural, "cannot attain a high state of civilization."[61]

The solution, he argued, was to adopt Wakefield's scheme of systematic colonization. Further, for a young and rising nation, protective tariffs might be employed in the hope of "naturalizing a foreign industry in itself perfectly suitable to the circumstances of the country."[62] Although Mill subsequently qualified his support for the protection of infant industry, as late as 1871 he still conceded the strength of Carey's claims for protection on political grounds.[63] Indeed, Mill was never an exponent of unilateral free trade for even a mature industrial society such as England. In a passage often quoted by the historical economists, he conceded that a nation could use its legislative power to "engross to itself a larger share of the benefits of commerce, than would fall to it in the natural or spontaneous course of trade."[64] He also suggested that reciprocity should rule England's policy toward machinery exports and that under prescribed conditions revenue tariffs should not be limited without reciprocity.[65]

Mill's exceptions to laissez faire constituted a well-known catalogue of Victorian state intervention. As I will show in my discussion of Cliffe Leslie, Mill's support for the limitation of property rights and Irish land reform was a fundamental challenge to the rights of private property championed by most classical economists. He insisted that property rights were not absolute, sacred, or natural, but must be grounded solely upon utility. He quoted even Sir Henry Maine, an authority claimed by the historical economists, that property rights were relative to a particular stage of civilization.[66] Mill's economic writings also contain numerous references to the limitation of competition through monopolies sanctioned by government, which he thought pernicious, and through the role of custom. In a theme often repeated by the historical economists, he noted: that if political economists had emphasized the principle of competition in their writings, "this is partly intelligible if we consider that only through the principle of competition has political economy any pretension to the character of a science."[67] In practice, however, Mill was clearly not fond of the ideal of economic individualism. Instead, he envisioned the cooperative ownership of the means of production as a solution to his pessimistic Ricardian distribution theory. Moreover, he declared that history was in fact moving in that direction.[68] Finally, his objections to socialism were not chiefly economic, but amounted to moral and intellectual qualifications.[69]

Like the work of Adam Smith, which he had sought to emulate, Mill's economics was not elegant and pure. He sought to discuss economic theory and to deal with its application. Although Mill made important contributions to economic theory, his chief contribution was not the creation of a professional and coherent system of economic science. Rather, he was one of the great English *political* economists. His economic writings included far more applied economics and economic history than abstract economic theory. His long career was a bridge between the more static and abstract social theory of his youth and the evolutionary and historical views becoming current in his old age. His half-way house may have contributed to the crisis of political economy in the 1870s and early 1880s, but it was also an invaluable aid to attempts at its reconstruction by both the historical and theoretical economists.

Cairnes and the reassertion of classical economic theory

J.E. Cairnes, who died the year before the Adam Smith Centennial Dinner, was Mill's chief theoretical disciple. He was educated at Trinity College, Dublin. As the Professor of Political Economy at University College, London, he became the leading academic economist of his time.[70] Cairnes responded most directly to both historical and popular criticisms of classical political economy during the early 1870s. He also rejected Jevons's marginalist challenge. He especially repudiated Jevons's attack upon the "noxious" influence of Mill in economics and urged that it is "anarchy . . . rather than despotism, with which we are menaced."[71] But in attempting to restore classical economics to its former preeminence, he further aggravated its crisis through his insistence upon a narrowly deductive method and his reiteration of the pessimistic Ricardian theory of distribution.

As Cairnes himself announced, the aim of his *Character and Logical Method of Political Economy* "has been to bring back the discussion of Political Economy to the tests and standards which are formerly considered the ultimate criteria of economic doctrine, but which have been completely lost sight of in many modern publications."[72] He outlined three important corrupting influences upon economic theory. First, political economy was being debased through its identification with laissez faire. Second, the sophistry of Bastiat's harmony doctrines and the popularizations of the Manchester School threatened to make the science into an affirmation of false natural law and popular opinion. Third, the attack of Comte and the historical economists upon the nature of the discipline threatened to submerge the discipline into the morass of sociology. Cairnes's major economic work, *The Leading Principles of Political Economy, Newly Expounded*, made an important contribution to classical economic theory. The net result, however, of Cairnes's often brilliant retreat into pure theory was, as one historian judged, "to open the way for the historicism of Rogers, Leslie, and Ingram."[73]

In an important essay of 1870, "Political Economy and Laissez Faire," Cairnes denied any logical connection between the principles of economics and the policy of laissez faire. He argued that the maxim of laissez faire was based upon two fundamental principles. First, the interests of human beings were essentially identical. He agreed with this proposition. However, he disagreed with the second, that men always knew their interests. Looking at the history of laissez faire, Cairnes concluded that its theory was "a pretentious sophism, destitute of foundation in nature and fact, and rapidly becoming an obstruction and nuisance in public affairs."[74] He warned that, if political economy was to survive as a science, its neutrality toward social arrangements and its hypothetical nature must be insisted upon.[75] Moreover, the identification of political economy with such popular doctrines as free trade had identified economic science with a defense of the social and political status quo. Everyone now claimed to be a political economist; "while even those who had mastered its doctrines, in their anxiety to propitiate a popular audience, were too often led to abandon the true grounds of the science, in order to find for it in the facts and results of free trade a more popular and striking vindication."[76] The vulgarizers whom Cairnes probably had in mind were such politicians as Robert Lowe, John Bright, and Richard Cobden. But Cairnes judiciously aimed his criticism at Cobden's friend and French counterpart, Frédéric Bastiat, who taught a doctrine of social and divine harmony with a strident defense of the sacredness of private property.[77] The most extreme criticism of orthodox political economy by the historical economists was

generally reserved for, always excepting Ricardo, the "popular" economics of Bastiat and Cobden. This criticism carried the implication
that false notions of natural law were also to be found in the work of
the best economic theorists. Recognizing this danger, Cairnes sought to
end the association of popular economics with orthodox economic science. His suggestions for a science of economics, rather than a political
economy, had much merit from the perspective of science. Society,
however, was clamoring for a social science to help it deal with pressing
new social and economic problems.

Cairnes directly confronted the criticism of Comte, the historical economists, the statisticians, and the emerging mathematical economists. His
objection to Comte was especially vocal. In fact, his methodological
treatise had grown out of an attack upon the French social theorist.
Comte's challenge to economics amounted to a demand that it become
a mere inductive subdiscipline of a grand sociology. Instead, Cairnes
insisted, economics, like the pure physical sciences, ought to be an
independent and hypothetical science. Its conclusions were to be seen
as "tendencies" and, in any case, their truth was to be found only in
theory. Further, its scope should be narrowly confined to dealing with
the phenomena of wealth and begin with the true postulates of the
science such as an abstract economic man, the law of population, and
diminishing returns in agriculture. Its method should be thoroughly
deductive – a method "incomparably, when conducted under the proper
checks, the most powerful instrument of discovery ever wielded by human intelligence."[78] In short, Cairnes sought to restore the science to
the methodological prescription of Mill in 1836.

Cairnes devoted a major portion of his methodological treatise to the
growing empirical attacks upon the postulates of classical economics.
Although he accepted the mounting statistical evidence that challenged
the classical theories of population and diminishing returns in agriculture, he nonetheless denied their ability to compromise his economic
theory. The method, Cairnes declared, of comparing actual phenomena,
such as the actual food supply and the actual rate of population growth,
cannot express a truth of economic science, for they are "not deduced
from the principles of human nature and external facts, but from the
statistics of society, or from the crude generalizations of history."[79] He
shrewdly pointed out that Malthus's population principle had been deductively derived from the principles of human nature and that its extensive factual data merely gave his work the appearance of having been
formulated inductively. Cairnes was also extremely proud that in a series
of essays on the gold question, he had deductively arrived at conclusions
that had been inductively supported by the statistical work of Jevons.[80]

But Cairnes' victory was chimerical. Having relegated the role of inductive and historical evidence to verification, he forged a "model" of
economics akin to geometry, which grew increasingly less relevant to
an evolving society in which the postulates of classical economics were
being challenged by reality. At the same time, he rejected the possibility
of a mathematical approach to economics – an approach that would
have been consistent with his method.[81]

Cairnes's theory of value made significant improvements over that of
Mill. His theory of distribution, however, reiterated the deepest pes-
simism inherent in the Ricardian structure. Despite Mill's recantation
of the wages-fund doctrine, Cairnes upheld the theory. He did, however,
grant it an entirely new interpretation that allowed him to conclude that
the effort of the trade unions to raise the general level of wages was
theoretically impossible.[82] Unlike Mill, who had papered over the class
antagonism between capital and labor, Cairnes emphasized this disagreeable aspect of the dismal science.[83] Moreover, Cairnes denied that
Mill had advocated any version of socialism. He maintained that the
fundamental difficulty of socialism was strictly economic and doubted
that the cooperative movement was capable of solving the condition of
England question.[84]

Cairnes's defense of free trade doctrine was also more categorical
than that of Mill. He held that free trade was the best policy for Britain's
particular circumstances and that its theory was an unimpeachable truth
of scientific economics. Though fully aware of growing foreign competition, he predicted that investments abroad would assure the continued success of British free trade policy.[85] Such predictions, as Cairnes
himself must have realized, were not the result of a deductive science.
Cairnes's chief aim in economics had been to restore the lost authority
of classical economics by insisting upon the hypothetical nature and
deductive methodology of the science. His popular critics did not always
appreciate this effort to divorce economic science from its "social applications." Further, the historical economists repudiated the desirability
of the goal.

Jevons and Marshall: Toward neoclassical economics

The "Jevonian Revolution" of the late 1860s and early 1870s in English
economics consisted of three basic shifts of emphasis. First, Jevons proposed a marginal utility analysis as the central solution to the problem
of value. Second, he initiated a movement in economics in which the
central focus of economic analysis came to be a psychological analysis
that sought to explain how individual units maximized gain in the ex-

change of goods and services. Third, Jevons shifted the focus of economics from cost and labor – thus away from such issues as the principle of population and the wages-fund – toward an explanation of utility and demand in the central theories of value and distribution.[86] This approach allowed him to reemphasize the deductive, and even mathematical, nature of economic theory. It was upon this foundation of a rigorous scientific method and the principle of marginalism that the next generation built economic science into a professional discipline.

Jevons combined his reconstruction of classical economics with a vigorous and well-known series of attacks upon Ricardo and J.S. Mill. These attacks were at least as abrasive as those of the historical economists and became a commonplace of the historical critique of classicism. Writing in his *Theory of Political Economy*, he prophesied that his mathematical method would be vindicated despite its having been neglected by his contemporaries. He combined this claim with a rejection of the Ricardian tradition: "When at length a true system of economics comes to be established, it will be seen that that able but wrong-headed man, David Ricardo, shunted the car of economic science unto a wrong line – a line, however, on which it was further urged towards confusion by his equally able and wrong-headed admirer, John Stuart Mill."[87] In private correspondence, Jevons was even more critical of Ricardo and Mill; he believed that the latter's influence had damaged his academic career, prevented the publication of his works, and forced him to teach what he knew to be false.[88]

Despite his ultimate fame as a theorist, at the time Jevons was most widely known for his inductive writings. It was his statistically derived conclusion that Britain's industrial competitiveness was but of limited duration because it rested upon England's finite coal supplies that allowed Jevons to break through the barrier of anonymity. Ironically, it was a speech by Mill in Parliament that made this work, and its author, first widely known. Yet, his sensational and often brilliant *Coal Question* of 1865 involved very few statistics; rather, it contained a predictive law, somewhat akin to that of Malthus, that captured the public's imagination.[89] His reputation for solid inductive research rests more solidly upon his statistical work on the gold question, especially his use of index numbers and geometric averages.[90] In 1862 Jevons presented to the British Association his famous paper, "On the Study of Periodical Commercial Fluctuations," in which he attempted to find statistical patterns in the business cycle. His argument that these cycles were concurrent with sunspots has often obscured the significance of this essay. Its originality did not lie in its attempt to link commercial cycles to the seasons and the harvest, for this Jevons had learned from Tooke, Newmarch, and Rogers. To this he had simply added the causal factor of sunspots. Jevons later abandoned his sunspot theory, emphasizing instead a credit theory of economic irregularity. Its real importance, however, lay in his use of sophisticated statistical methods to discover inductively economic generalizations from the raw material of economic history. Several of the historical economists later pointed to Jevons as one who had attempted to develop economic theory from economic history.

H.S. Foxwell, a close friend of Jevons and a fellow bimetalist, regretted that Jevons had not produced a clear statement as to the general relationship between the inductive and deductive method of economics.[91] Jevons, however, had at least left some specifically methodological comments that were to be prophetic of future developments in economics. Jevons specifically opposed Leslie's and Ingram's historical criticism of economic theory. Instead, he urged the bolstering of deductive economic theory through the use of the differential calculus and a strict adherence to the principles of deduction. He conceded that such a science would be highly hypothetical and abstract, and thus could not be used for the solution of practical economic and social problems. As a consequence, he proposed that social and economic policy be grounded upon a new branch of economics, employing a statistical and historical method, which would apply economic theory to the particular conditions of a specific society. Indeed, Jevons himself made an effort to contribute to such a branch of economics. Finally, he called for a third branch of the discipline that would investigate the economic history of a nation and attempt to develop laws of social development, or at least indications of the general direction of progress, by using an inductive, historical, and statistical method. His solution to the *Methodenstreit* was to subdivide the discipline into economic theory, applied economics, and economic history, allowing each part its appropriate method.[92] This left of course, as Foxwell had observed, still the potentially difficult problem of the relations among the subdivisions and their relative priority. Although there was little doubt that for Jevons a recast economic theory would hold the central position in economics, his call for inductive and historical study in the other branches of the subject, as well as his critique of Ricardo, served his reputation well among the historical economists.

The recasting of classical into neoclassical economics in England has become synonymous with the career of Alfred Marshall. As professor of Political Economy at Cambridge from 1885 to 1908, he became the undisputed leader of the English school of economic theory and presided over its transformation into a professional and academic discipline. He also, as has often been noted, did valuable work on a number of commissions dealing with pressing practical problems and published major works in applied economics. Moreover, Marshall claimed a keen interest in economic history. It was especially during the 1870s and 1880s that Marshall sought to reconcile his conflicting interests in an effort to come to terms with the English *Methodenstreit*.

Marshall began his academic career as a student of mathematics. As a Fellow of St. John's, Cambridge, in 1868, he translated many of Ricardo's theories into mathematics. His growing interest in psychology and ethics brought him face to face with practical problems for which he turned to the study of economics.[93] In 1869 he was elected College Lecturer in Moral Science at St. John's. While he was moving toward the study of economics as his main subject by the early 1870s, he retained a keen interest in moral philosophy for the rest of his life. He infused his economics with broad social and ethical concerns.[94] He has often been criticized for these interests by later theorists, but they preserved him from embracing a narrow individualist utilitarianism. During the early 1870s, he expressed his relativist position by noting, if we are to understand the history of economic thought, "the personal element becomes as important in reading a book in Political Economy as in reading one on any other branch of Social or Political Philosophy."[95] Before leaving Cambridge for Bristol in 1877, he had already become the leader among Cambridge economists, being influential with H.S. Foxwell, Henry Sidgwick, and J.N. Keynes. As principal and professor of Political Economy at Bristol, he became more directly involved in lecturing to business leaders and trade unionists and in public controversy. His wife, Mary Paley Marshall has noted that his lectures at Bristol "were less academic than those at Cambridge; and were a mixture of hard reasoning and practical problems illuminated by interesting sidelights on all sorts of subjects."[96] Upon Arnold Toynbee's death, Marshall went to Oxford in 1883 for four terms to lecture for the Indian Civil Service Exam. Then, after Henry Fawcett's death, he was elected to the professorship at Cambridge in 1885.

One of the hallmarks of Marshall's economics was his deep respect for the work of his predecessors, particularly that of Ricardo and J.S. Mill. He praised and defended Ricardo throughout his career as a brilliant theorist in whose work could be found the principle of marginalism. His admiration for Mill, however, was of another order that was equally significant for the history of British economics. Commenting upon Jevons's address before the Manchester Statistical Society in 1875, Marshall noted:

I incline to think that the substantive difference between us is less than I once supposed. We appear to be held apart more by the divergence of our views with regard to Mill than by any other cause. As a result of many courses of lectures on Mill, I have been convinced that his work instead of being full of plausible sophistries, appears at first sight, and perhaps even more at second sight, to contain fallacies where there are only incomplete truths. I admit, however, that the theory of political economy is in its infancy; that Mill was not a constructive genius of the first order and that generally the most important benefits he has conferred on that science are due rather to his character than to his intellect.[97]

What appealed to Marshall about Mill was the latter's modified utilitarianism, full of personal ethical content, which was much closer to Marshall's own beliefs than the more Benthamite utilitarianism expounded by Jevons. Marshall was also taken with Mill's evolutionary views on the progress of individuals and society, though Marshall saw this in a more particular biological and even Darwinian framework than Mill. During these early years Marshall was also impressed by the work of the German historical economists, particularly that of Roscher, and he gradually became familiar with the theoretical work of Walras, the Austrian School, and the Americans.[98]

Marshall laid the foundation for his economic theory prior to 1885. It is, however, important for an understanding of the challenge of the historical economists that very little of this was published at this time. During these same years Marshall also gathered material in economic history and applied economics. Mary Paley Marshall later described his lectures to the women of Newnham Hall in about 1873:

Mixed up in the lectures on theory were some on the History of Economics, Hegel's Philosophy of History, and Economic History from 1350 onwards, on the lines of the Historical Appendices to the *Principles*. He would give half an hour to theory and half an hour to history. He was keenly interested in Economic History. In 1875 he compiled what he called his "Red Book." It was arranged so that if a pin were run through its many pages at any given year the pinhole would show what was happening that year in Philosophy, Art, Science, Industry, Trade, etc.[99]

His notebooks of his visit to America in 1875, as well as his notes on India and those on medieval economic history, demonstrate Marshall's relentless search for facts and statistics. Marshall's use of this data, however, especially in the *Principles*, amounted largely to illustration rather than being an essential element of his work.[100] He failed to grasp fully the nature of the rigorous documentary historical research then being pioneered in England by the historians and historical economists. His strengths in this area, especially in his later years, lay in applied economics rather than economic history.[101]

Though Marshall did not play a prominent role in the *Methodenstreit* before the late 1880s, his early writings do insist upon the essentially deductive nature of economic science and upon its hypothetical character. He argued that economics was not a science that justified free trade, laissez faire, or any other convenient public maxim of the time. Rather, it was a science "because it collects, arranges, and reasons about one particular class of facts. A science brings together a great number of similar facts and finds that they are special cases of some great uniformity which exists in nature. It describes this uniformity in a simple and definite statement or Law."[102] It does not, however, lay down a guide for life, for this is a function of an art. To emphasize the difference between science and art, he argued in *Economics of Industry* (1879) that "Political Economy" should give way to "Economic Science," or simply to "Economics." But, as his wife noted, he never liked this book "for it offended against his belief that 'every dogma that is short and simple is false.' "[103] In rare public utterances, he was brought to repeat his assertion that, as science, economics could not be a simple guide to action as so many of its popularizers claimed.[104] He specifically sought to defuse the methodological debate. He suggested that:

Science, when obtaining new Laws, is said to be inductive; when reasoning from them and finding how they are connected with one another, it is said to be Deductive; its third task, that of verification, has just been described. There has been a controversy as to whether Economics is an Inductive or a Deductive Science. It is both: Its Inductions continually suggest new Deductions; its Deductions continually suggest new Inductions.[105]

Notwithstanding these conciliatory comments, so characteristic of his career, Marshall adopted Jevons's approach, calling for an essentially deductive method for economic science and a more varied methodological approach for applied economics and economic history.[106]

Marshall served on several royal commissions. He was, however, extremely reluctant to publicly comment on issues of social policy. He did assert the common concerns for social reform of the time and even called himself a socialist. In fact, he rejected the general principles of state intervention. His support for cooperation was qualified. He was skeptical about the future of trade unions. He argued that protection would not solve England's difficulties. Instead, he urged raising the productivity of labor through capital investment, the beneficial effects of competition, and the education of the people.[107] On the land question, which became central to the origin of historical economics in England, he specifically criticized Mill and Cliffe Leslie, as well as Henry George, who was his immediate target. He argued that the system of large landed and highly capitalized estates, however unsuited perhaps to other countries, was the best agricultural system for England, for it provided the necessary labor for industry and brought the laboring poor from rural England to the higher wages and education available in its cities.[108] Marshall's ultimate goal for economics was his hope that it would aid

society in creating a sufficient material base upon which could be constructed a more noble world.[109] While his ethical views at least softened
the criticism of the dismal science as immoral, his vision of economic
science severely limited its social application, and he directed most of
his energy to developing theory and to promoting its status as a professional academic discipline.

With the publication of Marshall's *Principles* in 1890, the effort to
reconstruct classical economic theory in England had succeeded. It
would, however, take at least another decade before Marshall's vision
of economic science became fully established as a professional discipline.
The result was a solution to many of the theoretical problems of economic theory of the 1870s and 1880s. Like the classical school it replaced,
it was highly individualistic and cosmopolitan in its policy implications.
Unlike the classical tradition, however, which emphasized the problems
of growth and distribution, neoclassicism was primarily concerned with
static equilibrium analysis. Further, it claimed universality for its principles based upon its deductive and increasingly abstract methodology
and it carefully noted the hypothetical nature of economic science. Pre-
ferring to use its analytical tools to probe the behavior of consumers
and individual firms, it offered little guidance on public policy in its first
few decades. It was precisely the inability of classical economics to serve
as an appropriate guide to action in the solution of such problems as
the Irish question, the condition of the working classes, and international
competition that motivated the historical economists to challenge classical economics in England. In later years, they would attempt a similar
critique of neoclassicism, including welfare economics as developed by
Marshall's successor, A. C. Pigou.

CHAPTER 2

Foreigners, forerunners, and the Irish contribution to historical economics

From the late 1850s until his premature death in 1882, T.E. Cliffe Leslie's efforts to solve the problems of Ireland produced a critique of classical political economy that laid the chief intellectual foundation for English historical economics. Intellectually, Leslie's economics owed debts to the historical protest of Richard Jones during the 1830s, the heretical tradition of Trinity College, Dublin, the historical jurisprudence of Sir Henry Maine, and the work of J.S. Mill. Leslie's critique of orthodoxy consisted primarily of contemporary economic history and applied economics. During the 1870s, another Irish economist, J.K. Ingram, took up Leslie's banner, but, despite the contemporary popularity of his work, Ingram's writings in historical economics were to be far less intellectually influential marred as they were, by an increasing adherence to his Comtean system. Earlier in the century, H.C. Carey and Friedrich List had already challenged the universal truth and social applicability of the English classical tradition. This historical criticism was formed into the German Historical School of Economics during the second half of the nineteenth century.

Foreigners and forerunners

Many of the concerns raised by English historical economists were anticipated by the work of List and Carey. Their protest against the theory, method, and policy prescriptions of English classical economics constituted a national and historical critique which sprang from their belief that British free trade theory and practice was injurious to the economic development of the relatively underdeveloped economies of Germany and the United States. They formulated the fundamental proposition of historical economics in Germany, England, and America: Economic theory and policy ought to be relative to a particular stage of production. As national economists, they took the nation, as opposed to the individual or the firm, as their basic unit of economic discussion.

List, a civil servant, journalist, publicist and professor, published his

Das nationale System der politischen Ökonomie in 1846. The basic message of the work was, however, already available to English readers in 1827 as his *Outlines of American Political Economy*. Although his *National System of Political Economy* was not published in England until 1885, an English edition had been published in the United States in 1856.[1] List, who is perhaps best known for his advocacy of railroad construction in Germany and for his support of the formation of the German Zollverein, announced his purpose to be the formulation of a national system of political economy through the use of a historical and comparative method in opposition to the cosmopolitan system of Adam Smith. After a rapid historical survey of the rise and decline of the Italian city states, the Dutch Republic, and the Hanseatic League, he concluded that their ultimate collapse was caused by their free trade policies, which had neglected the development of domestic manufacturing industry and agriculture. On the other hand, he maintained, Great Britain had created and preserved its agricultural, commercial, financial, and manufacturing wealth through mercantilist measures.[2] But, he continued, now that Britain was the workshop of the world, it advocated, with a religious zeal based upon claims of a superior morality and cosmopolitanism, a system of free trade which was in fact designed to preserve its national paramountcy by preventing others from following in its footsteps. In an analogy that Gladstone would specifically refute at the Adam Smith Centennial Dinner, List compared Britain to a man "who kicks away the ladder by which he had climbed up, in order to deprive others of the means of climbing up after him."[3] It was an argument the Germans called imperialism and that Cunningham later developed in his analysis of Cobdenite free trade policy as "Free Trade Imperialism."

From his comparative and historical data, List constructed a stage theory of economic growth that saw a developing nation passing from free trade to protection, and in the final or mature stage it returned to free trade. He agreed that free trade was the best system for an industrial and developed nation such as Britain, but urged an industrializing nation to adopt a scheme of protection for its nascent industries.[4] List insisted that a nation's goal was the achievement of great power status. The policy of favoring commerce over manufacturing he labeled as a policy of "cheap consumption" that ignored the necessity for building up a nation's "productive power."[5] Although such a policy might enrich a few individuals, it ignored the larger issues of power and welfare that faced an underdeveloped nation, and penalized future generations for the benefit of present commercial classes. In an argument often repeated by the historical economists, List emphasized that the primary source of a nation's wealth was its home market and that its growth required the balanced growth of its agriculture and industry.[6]

List often used and extended Adam Smith's arguments for limited protection. List recognized that under universal free trade primary producing nations were at a permanent disadvantage with manufacturing nations. Indeed, Marshall admitted that the "brilliant genius and national enthusiasm of List overthrew the presumption" that the Ricardian theory of free trade, developed for a manufacturing country such as Britain could be transposed wholesale to agricultural nations.[7] List's often fiery patriotic rhetoric,[8] though it touched a responsive chord in Australia, America, and Ireland, was too strong a medicine for Britain. His message, however, that economic thought and policy ought to be relative to a particular stage of civilization was heard. When toward the end of the nineteenth century, Britain's own international position had been greatly altered from its earlier supremacy, List's teaching on the need to augment national power, his theory of "productive powers," his emphasis upon balanced economic growth, and his historical approach was reiterated and developed by English historical economists.[9]

The national economics of Henry Charles Carey, one of America's best known nineteenth century economists, was well known to both Mill and Leslie. Carey's major work, *The Principles of Social Science*, grew out of a tradition of American national economics to which List had contributed.[10] Carey developed his economics in conscious opposition to Ricardo. Outlining a methodology for what he called the "social sciences," he combined Comte's inductive method for the social sciences with an appreciation for the utility of the deductive method when the deductions proceeded from premises that themselves had been derived inductively.[11] He rejected the ability of the classical economic man to serve as a valid premise upon which to construct economic science. He urged, instead, that it be grounded upon the reality of social men, who acted not only for the sake of power, but also out of sympathy, friendship, and human happiness.[12] Within the *Principles*, Carey drew conclusions, that he claimed to have derived inductively from a range of comparative and historical data far exceeding that to be found even in Mill. Abandoning the Ricardian theory of value and denying such classical doctrines as those on population, rent, and agricultural productivity, Carey rejected Ricardian economics as the economics of conflict. Carey's proposition, that Ricardian economics aided and abetted socialism was to become an important theme of English historical economics.

Despite many differences between the work of Carey and Leslie, the former's characteristic argument on the value of the "association of labor" within a balanced national economy foreshadowed many of Leslie's arguments on the land question and general economic development, especially in Ireland. Carey specifically pointed to the employment benefits to be derived from the close association of agriculture and industry within a national economy. As an American economist, he emphasized the need for geographical proximity of these two sectors, or what has come to be called the economic development of the frontier and its colonial relationship with more developed regions. In the British context, Carey's emphasis upon the balanced growth of the home market was a criticism of the Ricardian championship of making England the workshop of the world while condemning outlying regions to remain agricultural. Carey described historically how either wholly agricultural, commercial, or industrial nations had founded their prosperity and power upon an excessively narrow base. Carey's father, Matthew Carey, had an Irish rebel background, and his son often used Ireland as an example. The latter argued that the cumulative effect of British colonial control over Ireland, first under mercantilism, and then under free trade, had reduced the Irish to "hers [sic] of wood and drawers of water for the Saxon."[13] Ireland's fundamental problem, he argued, was a lack of sufficient and varied employment. This could only be remedied through balanced national development and required the establishment of a protective tariff.[14]

He also warned that an exclusive emphasis upon commerce and industry would make Britain dependent upon other nations for an adequate supply of raw materials and agricultural products. This would make Britain extremely vulnerable in times of war, encourage ruinous commercial fluctuations, lead to the neglect of the home market, and promote an excessive division of labor, which would ultimately lead to social revolution.[15] Carey's arguments were well received in Ireland and Australia. In England, his influence was more ambiguous. Yet, combined with the writings of List, Carey's economics formed a powerful and early indictment of the method, theoretical conclusions, and policy recommendations of classical English economics.

While the links between the economics of Carey and the later American Institutionalists appear tenuous, the connections between List and the German historical school were clear and direct. The latter has been called the academic offspring of List's national economics.[16] The German historical economists sought to create a body of economics which was national, organic, historical, and state centered as an alternative to what they called the cosmopolitan, individualistic, deductive, and laissez-faire British tradition. The elder German historical economists

– primarily, William Roscher, Bruno Hildebrand, and Karl Knies –
created a German school of historical economics upon whose authority
the early English economists often leaned. The Younger German historical school, which came to prominence during the 1870s, and whose
members came to be known as *Kathedersozialisten* (academic socialists,
or socialists of the chair), clustered around the Verein für Sozialpolitik,
urged a variety of state sponsored schemes for social reform, and produced significant monographs on economic history and applied economics. Though it was the Younger school, led by Gustav Schmoller, that
engaged the Austrian marginal utility economists in the famous *Methodenstreit*, the school's impact upon English economics was largely de-
layed until the 1880s and was primarily associated with Ashley,
Cunningham, and Hewins.[17]

The writings of the older German historical economists were, like
those of List, also rooted in the German rejection of the Enlightenment's
rationalist and natural law teaching. They were, more specifically, the
economic counterpart of Savigny's repudiation of universally applicable
codes of rational law in favor of a historical, Germanic, and relativist
legal system. As we shall see, there was a parallel in English jurisprudence. The historical economists worked in an intellectual framework
that took into account historical, cultural, geographical, and national
characteristics as modifying, or even replacing, universal economic
laws.[18] William Roscher especially objected to the wholesale adoption
of "Smithianism" – a version of classical political economy devoid of
the subtleties and complexities of classical economics in England. His
1843 *Grundriss zu Vorlesungen über die Staatwirtschaftlehre, nach ge-
sichlicher methode* laid the groundwork for German academic historical
economics. During the next four decades, he published five volumes of
his largely historical and descriptive *System der Nationalökonomie*.
Roscher set forth his principles in the *Grundriss* preface, which became
widely known among English historical economists. First, political economy was not only a science, but also an art for the formulation of policy;
as such, its chief task was a descriptive and historical account of "what
nations have taught, willed, and discovered in the economic field, what
they have striven after and why they have attained it."[19] Second, because
the nation was not merely a collection of all the individuals alive, but
also an organic society with both a past and a future, a true investigation
of the national economy must explore both a nation's history and its
future prospects, as well as its contemporary circumstances. Third, because the critical problem in economics was to separate the essential
from the mass of phenomena without falsely creating laws that were
largely hypothetical, a comparative and historical method must be em-

ployed to discover realistic uniformities. Finally, the historical method would emphasize the relativity of economic thought and policy and of economic institutions to a particular stage of civilization. Diverse critics have charged that Roscher's economics was primarily a historical and descriptive illustration of orthodox English classical economics.[20] Nonetheless, the English historical economists pointed to his work as an alternative framework for economic studies.

Hildebrand and Knies launched a more radical attack upon classical political economy. Hildebrand argued that the hitherto dominant schools of economics had sought "to infer generally applicable theories from the facts of single peoples or stages of development." Further, they had attempted to create universal theories of the "relations of man to goods," forgetting that man was "always a child of civilization and a product of history." By contrast, he proclaimed that "the only sure foundations whereupon may be erected any further useful construction of economic science" could be legal and economic history, as well as statistics. Hildebrand's aim was the discovery of broad laws of economic development. Knies, the most philosophic and ethically oriented of the older German historical economists, went so far as to suggest that the historical method would ultimately produce a universal theory of economic development.[21] The German historical economists could not agree on the exact nature of their historicist enterprise. They could, however, agree that economic theory and policy must be relative to a particular stage of civilization. They further agreed that the classical economic man did not correspond to universal reality; that self-interest was not the sole, nor even the prime, mover of the economic process; that the state should be both a moral force and the promoter of national economic development; and that the market society endorsed by classical economics, which separated man from himself, his society, his labor, and his culture, was a mechanical abstraction. English historical economists, though their primary inspiration was not derived from German historical economics, were nonetheless delighted that they could point to this respectable body of academic opinion that was also at odds with the theory, method, and policy conclusions of classical English political economy.

The English historical economists did not have to look only to Germany or America in support of their views, for there was also a historical, inductive English economic tradition. This tradition, which had been overshadowed by the success of Ricardo and James Mill, was rediscovered by the later English historical economists.[22] Several speakers at the Adam Smith Centennial Dinner had urged that Adam Smith had been a historical economist. Some also saw Malthus in these terms. There was general agreement that Richard Jones (1790–1855) had been a historical economist. Edgeworth, a mathematical economist, called Jones "the founder of the English Historical School."[23] In 1897, Marshall praised Jones generously: "He said just what was needed at the time; and his influence though little heard in the outer world, largely dominated the minds of those Englishmen who came to the serious study of economics after his works had been published by Dr. Whewell in 1859."[24] Marshall's claim for Jones was surely excessive and Jones was not the father of English historical economics, as Edgeworth claimed, but he was an authentic and influential forerunner of that movement.

Richard Jones was educated at Cambridge. He became professor of Political Economy at King's College, London, and succeeded Malthus at the East India Company's Haileybury College. At King's College, he hoped to found an inductive school of economics, complete with its own periodical, but he gave up this project and instead supported the creation of Section F of the British Association and the London Statistical Society as centers for inductive economic research.[25] In his *Essay on Distribution*, Jones announced that the inductive study of the causes of a nation's wealth had convinced him that:

The deep gloom which was thought to overlay the subject was but an illusion; that no causes of inevitable decay haunt the fortunes of any class during the progressive development of the resources of the country; that the interests of no portion of society are ever permanently in opposition to those of any other; and that there is nothing either in the physical constitution of man, or in that of the earth which he inhabits, that need enfeeble the hopes of those who [labour] . . . to secure the permanent harmony and common prosperity of all classes.[26]

He based his conclusion of social harmony upon his contention that historical and contemporary facts contradicted Malthus's theory of population, Ricardo's theory of agricultural productivity, and the classical economists' pessimistic view that profits would fall to a minimum in a progressive capitalist and industrial society. Jones also emphasized the influence of custom upon wages and profits. His original scheme for the classification of rents, according to capitalist rent and various forms of customary rent,[27] was used by Mill in his treatment of agriculture in the *Principles*.

Jones directly attacked the efficacy of the deductive method in political economy. It was this method, he believed, that had been at the root of Ricardo's errors. In an often paraphrased comment, Jones argued:

He, must indeed, be a shallow reasoner, who by mere efforts of consciousness, by consulting his own views, feelings and motives, and the narrow spheres of his own personal observations, and reasoning *a priori* from these, expects that he shall be able to anticipate the conduct, progress and fortunes of large bodies of men, differing from himself in physical and moral temperament, and influenced by differences, varying in extent and variously combined, in climate, soil, religion and government.[28]

Instead Jones urged that political economy should be reconstructed upon the solid foundation of historical and comparative data, and called for realistic study of the "economical structures of nations." Using German historical jurisprudence as his model, he planned an extensive research project in economic history for the realization of this task. Jones called others to the Baconian "duty of dwelling long and humbly among things";[29] his own economic writings, however – except for his work on rents – remained fragmentary. In his "Primitive Political Economy," he did begin that slow rehabilitation of mercantilist theory and policy that was to flower later among English historical economists.[30] Jones thus anticipated many of the concerns and conclusions of English historical economics. But during his lifetime, Jones's fragmentary writings could not compete with the dominant position of orthodox political economy. This was particularly true during the early 1850s when Mill established his *Principles* as the great work in English economics and when British free trade, industrial supremacy, and laissez faire appeared triumphant. Not until two decades later, when the intellectual, social, political and economic context of England was being transformed, could a full blown historical attack upon classical economics find a receptive hearing in England. This context was most evident in Ireland, and from there the English historical protest found its first effective voice.

T.E. Cliffe Leslie, Irish social reform, and the origin of English historical economics

J.S. Mill suggested in 1870 that the great gaps between economic theory and the realities of postfamine Ireland had divided political economists not only on practical policy but also on economic theory.[31] T.E. Cliffe Leslie hoped to end this dichotomy by forging a historical economics capable of meeting the pressing economic difficulties of Ireland from the inductive and historical side of Mill's economics, the historical jurisprudence of Sir Henry Maine, and the heretical school of Irish economists rooted in Trinity College, Dublin. Schumpeter observed that "his advocacy of the historical method . . . was both judicious and effective and did not fail to impress."[32] Mill noted that he was "one of the best living writers on applied political economy."[33] Ashley added that Leslie had been among the first Englishmen to understand the work of the German historical school.[34] L.L. Price observed that Leslie's writings had "forced dissentients to examine with care the grounds of their refusal to agree and it aroused the desultory and superficial from their sluggish or ignorant acquiescence to traditional routine."[35] J.K. Ingram stated that Leslie had been "one of the ablest and most original of English economists of the present century." Ingram helped Leslie publish a new collection of his essays in 1879 and aided the now nearly disabled economist to see them through publication, as Leslie sought to gain a sympathetic hearing for Ingram's famous 1878 attack upon orthodoxy.[36] Leslie had wide European contacts; abroad, too, his contribution to economics was held in high esteem.[37]

Cliffe Leslie was the son of an Anglican rector. He was born in the county of Wexford, Ireland, in 1827. At first educated by his father, he received his formal training at King William's College on the Isle of Man and at Trinity College, Dublin. At Trinity he studied the usual classical subjects and took a particularly keen interest in both ethics and logic. He received his BA in 1847 and earned an LLB in 1851. Two years later he was elected to the part-time and meagerly paid chair of Jurisprudence and Political Economy at Queen's College, Belfast. He normally resided in London, where he was admitted to the bar at Lincoln's Inn in 1857. In order to supplement his income, he wrote dozens of economic articles for magazines and reviews and did a great deal of public examining.[38] Having lost, on a visit to France, his nearly completed manuscript of an economic history of England, Leslie never completed his planned magnum opus. Instead, he collected most of his articles in three volumes of essays.[39] Though his 1870 volume of inductive studies on the land question, *Land Systems and Industrial Economy of Ireland, England, and Continental Countries*, must be considered his major work, Leslie has been most frequently remembered for his later writings on methodology and the history of economic thought.

In 1870 Leslie published his pioneering article "The Political Economy of Adam Smith," which held that the methodological crisis of English political economy could be traced to a duality within the economics of Adam Smith. The founder of British economics had spawned two schools of political economy: the narrowly deductive school of Ricardo and his followers and the more inductive school of J.S. Mill. Leslie traced the ambivalence within Smith's economics to Smith's varied roles as natural theologian and moral philosopher and as political economist. Smith's study of Roman law and his theological belief in a beneficent and just order in the universe led him to believe that the natural order of the moral world could be imposed upon the physical world, if only people were set at perfect liberty to pursue their own interests. It was this belief, Leslie announced, that stood at the base of the deductive fallacies of political economy.[40] Leslie also recognized this doctrine of harmony as the chief element of distortion in the economics of Carey, Bastiat, and Whately.[41] Yet Smith had also been nurtured in the Scottish historical school: "The inductive method preserved the great Scotsman from grave errors into which not a few of his English followers in the mother-country of inductive philosophy have been led by the *a priori* method."[42] Leslie's interpretation of the duality within Adam Smith's economics, which was no doubt partly an effort to claim the prestige of the founder of English economics for the historical movement, has become commonplace in the history of economic thought.

In striking contrast to his fellow Irish economist J.E. Cairnes's deductive methodology, Leslie called directly for the creation of a historical economics in an 1875 article that became the classic methodological formulation of English historical economics. Leslie maintained that a person was not, as the classical economists had assumed, a being who moved society through a "desire for wealth," but instead was a complex organism ruled by "passions, appetites, affections, moral and religious sentiments, family feelings, aesthetical tastes, and intellectual wants."[43] Leslie conceded the general validity of the Ricardian theory of production; however, its simplistic view of people had permitted the formulation of a thoroughly unrealistic theory of distribution and demand. Although Mill and W.S. Jevons had understood these twin errors, Leslie believed that even they had still not recognized the complex historical causes which explained economic phenomena. Only historical economists such as William Roscher, Leslie suggested, had begun to appreciate the true complexity of economic activity.[44]

Leslie charged that orthodox political economy had also distorted economic opinions by an excessive emphasis upon the individual's role in society:

The conclusion which the study of society makes every day more irresistible is, that the germ from which the existing economy of every nation has been evolved is not the individual, still less the personification of an abstraction, but the primitive community – a community one in blood, property, thought, moral responsibility, and manner of life; and that individual interest itself, and the desires, aims, and pursuits of every man and woman in the nation have been moulded by, and received their direction and form from, the history of that community.[45]

Echoing a general revolt against individualism and the facile optimism of some nineteenth century liberals, Leslie emphasized the persistence of primitive and collective forces upon contemporary society. When Walter Bagehot attempted to limit the truth of orthodox political economy to industrial England, Leslie welcomed this as an admission that classical theory was insular and unhistorical and thus could lay no claim to universality.[46]

The shallow and dogmatic exposition of the "truths" of political economy at the Adam Smith Centennial Dinner by Robert Lowe provided Leslie with a convenient straw man for another frontal attack upon deductive economics. Indeed, Leslie told Ingram: "I am glad that Lowe is at the white heat necessary to have goaded him to write."[47] Leslie insisted that even though all the economists had repudiated Lowe as one of their number, he nonetheless represented a "reductio ad absurdum of their own system."[48] Either the economists must follow the narrow path of Lowe's economic man, or their deductive method would condemn them to "contend that they have an intuitive knowledge of all the moral, religious, political, and other motives influencing human conduct, and of all the changes they undergo in different countries and periods."[49]

Leslie reserved his most bitter condemnation for Ricardo, whose deductive method had allowed the formulation of an entire theory of distribution without any reference to real conditions, resulting in a labor theory of value, an iron law of wages, and a law of declining profits which had become the breeding ground of the socialist economics of Marx and Lassalle.[50] Happily, Ricardo's abstract system did not correspond to actual conditions. One of the chapters of Leslie's economic history had been designed to prove inductively that contrary to Ricardian theory, profits did not actually decline in advanced industrial communities.[51] He charged that what Ricardo had labeled friction was in fact the real world. Leslie recognized that Cairnes had insisted only upon the hypothetical truth of the Ricardian model. But, Leslie asked rhetorically, what would be the worth of a treatise "deducing the economy of Germany from the assumption that every man is occupied solely in the acquisition of wealth?"[52] Instead, Leslie demanded an economics that would have more practical value to the statesman.

Such an economics he might have found in the work of Malthus; indeed, as we shall see, in his inductive studies on the land question, Leslie had already implicitly rejected, like Malthus, the distinction between productive and unproductive consumption. Leslie now explicitly questioned this important theoretical and political proposition of classical economics: "Unproductive expenditures and consumption . . . do not necessarily tend to diminish wealth. They are the ultimate incentives to all production, and without habits of considerable superfluous expenditure . . . a nation would be reduced to destitution."[53] Leslie's historical method had finally led him back to Malthus, but, having rejected

Ricardo, he shrank back from embracing Malthus. Instead, Leslie turned to the impeccable authority of J.S. Mill.

Just as Leslie had been able to forgive Adam Smith for his lapses into deductive economics, so too could he pardon Mill's reversions into error. In Mill Leslie recognized a kindred and generous spirit who had first brought him to the attention of English economists and who had freely accepted criticism while attempting to steer economics into a more historical direction. William Roscher had said of Mill that despite the numerous exceptions which Mill noted to his theoretical framework in his *Principles*, he was unable to challenge the very principles themselves for "his is not an historical mind."[54] Leslie disagreed. Mill had indeed possessed a historical mind, but it had been stifled by the education imparted to him by John Austin, Jeremy Bentham, and his father.[55] Mill, Leslie continued, "had been brought up in the straitest sort of the economists," and "since his method was formed before his mind was matured," he had been prevented from breaking decisively with the past.[56] Leslie himself had been reared in a very different tradition.

Leslie's often bitter attacks upon orthodox political economy during the 1870s were rooted especially in the distinctive needs of Ireland. The history of Ireland during the nineteenth century can be described as that of an agrarian and pastoral colony of England. Despite the consolidation of many small landholdings, massive emigration, and the growth of a moderately successful export-based livestock industry after the famine, the majority of Ireland's population remained mired in a subsistence economy characterized by small plots, short leases, cash and rack rents, and little or no compensation for tenant-made improvements. Faced with British competition under free trade, lacking an effective internal demand, and having few entrepreneurial skills, Irish industry consisted primarily of export-oriented brewing and ship building industries centered in Dublin and Ulster.[57] The eruption of violence in 1867 again brought the plight of Ireland to the attention of the British Parliament. Combining earlier demands for political reform with a program for the fundamental alteration of the land system, the Fenians pressed for security of tenure, long leases, and compensation for tenant-made improvements. The granting of the essence of these demands, in the Irish Land Bills of 1870 and 1881, was accompanied by a lively economic debate which questioned several basic assumptions as well as the very method of classical economics.

Between 1815 and 1870 the solution offered by most English economists to the problems of Ireland was to impose the English agricultural system upon Ireland through the consolidation of landholdings and by the application of capital to the land.[58] Robert Lowe repeated the orthodox position in its most dogmatic form. Expressing the confident universalism characteristic of the popular liberalism of the period, Lowe told Parliament: "It is ridiculous to inveigh against a law which is the same in Ireland as in England; and whatever may be the difference between the two countries, it is impossible that there can be any fundamental injustice in a law which works with entire satisfaction in a country like this."[59] For Lowe, the solution to the Irish problem lay not in new legislation; it was to be found in capital, confidence, and free trade in land in accordance with the principles of political economy which stood as an "oasis in the desert of politics upon which we may safely rest."[60]

Rising in Parliament to respond to Lowe's attack upon Irish land legislation, Mill demonstrated the inductive side of his economics. He declared that "no one is at all capable of determining what is the right political economy for any country until he knows its circumstances."[61] Mill's comparative and inductive work on European land tenure led him to conclude that England's much admired system of large farms had in fact proved inferior to the continental system of peasant proprietorship. The reestablishment of a class of peasant proprietors in Ireland, Mill suggested, would not only increase agricultural productivity and repopulate the countryside, but also promote political stability, moral improvement, and prevent revolution. To this end, Mill supported legislation designed to provide fixity of tenure, fair rents, compensation for tenant-made improvements, and a scheme of "home colonization" on waste lands. To the objection that land legislation might endanger the sacred right to private property, Mill responded that property rights in land were wholly different from property rights in capital; its "appropriation is wholly a question of moral expedience."[62]

It was especially on the land question that Leslie became Mill's disciple. His views competed directly with Mill's orthodox disciple, J.E. Cairnes, who was noticeably less dogmatic on Irish issues than in his general approach to economics. Indeed, he even admitted that free trade which had destroyed English demand for Ireland's cereal products.[63] Nonetheless, he insisted that the ultimate solution to Ireland's economic difficulties lay in the export of her surplus population and the investment of capital in large-scale grazing.[64] As we will show, Leslie's views on Ireland differed fundamentally from those of Cairnes. In addition, Leslie, like Jevons, complained bitterly about the authority possessed by the orthodox school and was particularly unhappy about Cairnes's neglect of his writings.[65] In a critique of his views in the *Westminster Review*, Leslie maintained that he, and not Cairnes, represented the wave of the future in economics:

Mr. Cairnes was careful throughout his economic career to draw no attention to my views, and never to name them; but I believe I was, and am, the exponent of the ideas and tendencies of a new generation of economists already numerous on the Continent, whom no silence on the part of the followers of Ricardo can prevent getting the ear of the public.[66]

Leslie's hostility to Cairnes also owed much to his distress at Cairnes's close relationship with Mill. Moreover, Leslie resented that he held a provincial chair at Belfast and Cairnes was a professor at University College, London. Finally, having difficulty publishing his work in the serious reviews, Leslie frequently complained to Mill that publishers hung on every word of Cairnes.[67]

From 1861 until his death in 1873, Mill encouraged Leslie's inductive work in economics. Unfortunately, their correspondence does not reveal much discussion of methodology, but they did discuss such economic questions as the income tax and the impact of the recent gold discoveries upon prices, the abandonment of the wages-fund doctrine and such political issues as electoral reform and women's rights.[68] Mill attempted to further Leslie's career by recommending his work to the editors of the *Edinburgh Review* and the *Westminster Review*.[69] When Cairnes fell ill in 1867, Mill suggested Leslie as his replacement at University college, London, telling Cairnes that: "Leslie is, next to you, by far the fittest person I know to fill the place, among those that would take it."[70] More serious health problems forced Cairnes to resign his London professorship in 1872. Mill again recommended Leslie, and told Cairnes that "of all the candidates Leslie seems to me to have much the strongest claims."[71] When the time to relinquish his London professorship came, Cairnes supported Mill's friend and biographer Leonard Courtney for the post, and Leslie remained at Belfast.[72]

Lacking an influential academic position, independent means, or social prestige, Leslie had great difficulty in creating a school of historical economics in England. His correspondence, however, leaves no doubt that this was his aim. He complained about the constant labor of examining and book reviewing: "It is exceedingly tiresome going over old ground, and yet I can't shred all my thoughts into fugitive articles. I should be glad now to stop reviewing, at least until after my new book is out. Yet, I am afraid to refuse the work lest some champion of the old method should cut in and give a triumph to its followers."[73] He saw his opposition as the London and Cambridge establishment in economics. He had an especially low opinion of economics at Cambridge. He wrote of Fawcett that "finding that he could not be a king himself over political economy, he resolved to be a king-maker and crowned Cairnes."[74] He also had a low regard for the young Cambridge lecturers, despite the fact that they asked him to reprint his essays for their students. Both Arnold Toynbee and H.S. Foxwell wrote to him expressing interest in his work. Although Leslie thought highly of Toynbee, he did not value Foxwell, and noted that "Marshall seems to be his real demigod."[75] He was, however, greatly pleased when J.S. Nicholson was awarded the Edinburgh Chair and told Ingram that "Nicholson is on my side."[76] Leslie assiduously watched the reviews for the progress of his cause. Hoping to secure a sympathetic hearing for his 1879 collection of essays, he told the historical economist J.E. Thorold Rogers, "as you are one of the few economists in this country interested in the inductive and historical treatment of Political Economy . . . you might review my volume . . . as soon as it comes out."[77] He was extremely pleased when he was offered a chair in political economy in the United States, with a handsome salary, and observed that "my writings meet with attention in Germany."[78] But, even in England, he noted that, despite the opposition of the orthodox school, his examining, reviewing, and letters of support from several younger economists indicated "that my ill repute among the orthodox for heresy & schism has not had all the results that might have been expected, considering how strong the old political economy has been among the official classes, and at the universities where Cairnes for a short term was almost supreme."[79] As he noted in a more optimistic tone, "I have had a very uphill battle to fight these last twenty years, with small encouragement until lately from anyone save Mill."[80]

There were influences other than Mill's in shaping Leslie's outlook; first of all, there was the Irish tradition in economics. Though not partisans of a historical economics, several Trinity College, Dublin, economists had already warned of the danger inherent in excessive abstraction in economics.[81] In contrast to Leslie's purpose, the Trinity economists were attempting to construct a system of economic theory to oppose that of the dominant Ricardians. Longfield and Whately created a utility theory of value, which approached economic analysis from the side of demand, and others questioned the Malthusian theory of population and the Ricardian theory of rent.[82] Trinity's Isaac Butt, the first British academic economist to advocate protection, argued that the protection of native industry was the only viable solution to Ireland's economic problems.[83]

Second, Leslie was indebted to the historical jurisprudence of Sir Henry Maine. Commentators have often seen Leslie as a follower of the older German historical school of economics. Leslie himself rejected this thesis. Writing to a reviewer, Leslie insisted that "my line was taken ten years before I ever saw a German book on economics. So far as my method is taken from anyone, it is taken from Sir Henry Maine."[84] He often mentioned Maine's support for his views and bracketed himself with Maine as the leaders of the new political economy in England.[85] Indeed, Leslie claimed that he had first learned the historical method as a student of Maine at the Middle Temple in 1857. In 1879 Leslie attributed differences between himself and Mill to the fact "that whereas Mr. Mill in his youth attended the lectures of Mr. Austin, the author had the good fortune to attend those of Sir Henry Maine."[86] Further reflection had convinced him that the English economist should be trained both in the schools of Maine and Stubbs, as well as in the tradition of Mill.[87]

In his *Ancient Law* of 1861, Maine set forth his view that law was not the product of a rational lawgiver, as Bentham and Austin had argued, but had its origin in primitive status society. Only when society moved from status to contract could a rational and universal system of law become possible. Even here, Maine continued, law should not be judged only by universal standards; it should also be evaluated in the light of the historical evolution of a particular nation. In his influential 1871 study, *Village Communities*, based upon both continental scholarship and his Indian experience, Maine concluded that private property in land was not a universal system, as many English utilitarians appeared to argue. Property had been held collectively in village communities, and only in modern times, and then only in particular places did private property in land develop. A vocal Conservative, antiutilitarian, and proponent of a dogmatic laissez faire, Maine rejected all radical implications that his argument on the relativity of private property had for the land question in Britain. He did, however, support protection.[88]

After Leslie had popularized Maine's method in economics, Maine himself set forth the implications of his historical jurisprudence for political economy. Maine declared that the orthodox theories of rent, wages, and prices were generally inapplicable to the past. In order to arrive at more realistic economic conclusions, Maine urged that political economy begin a comparative and historical study of land systems.[89] Moreover, because survival of ancient customs into the present often made nonsense of conclusions based upon a model of contract society, orthodox economic categories were of limited value even for the present. In an argument similar to that of Bagehot,[90] Maine admitted, however, that orthodox political economy would become ever more viable as society moved from status to contract.[91] Cliffe Leslie denied the validity of orthodox political economy even for a modern and industrial England.

Ingram's famous Comtean indictment of English orthodox economics in 1878, which Leslie assiduously sought to disseminate,[92] led Leslie to be viewed as a follower of Comte. Leslie himself told a reviewer, "Whoever told you that I simply followed Comte, only showed that he knew neither Comte's work nor mine. On some points I am opposed to him, in some cases I agree with him; but the greater part of my work related to points he never touched at all."[93] There were, indeed, some important issues on which Leslie found himself in agreement with Comte. Leslie agreed that the assumption of an economic man resulted in the formulation of shallow laws of production. With Comte, Leslie pointed to Adam Smith as the last true English political economist. However, Leslie rejected Comte's all-embracing claim for a universal sociology, which would have relegated economics to a mere inductive branch of that larger science of society. Indeed, when Ingram suggested that Leslie's *Essays in . . . Philosophy* be entitled *Essays in . . . Science*, he rejected the latter term on the grounds that his work was not "definite enough to be best termed science."[94] He also had little regard for the contemporary Positivist critic of economic orthodoxy, Frederic Harrison.[95] Above all, he was especially critical of Comte's notions of collective humanity, the religion of humanity, and the belief that the improvement of mankind was inevitable. Leslie wrote to Ingram that "the idea of Collective Humanity seems to me an unreality – a mere abstraction." Further, he continued, if any collective judgment were to be made about humanity, people "seem to me more malevolent than benevolent."[96]

Leslie first employed the historical method in his writings on moral philosophy and political theory during the late 1850s and early 1860s. He rejected both orthodox utilitarian moral philosophy and the prevailing Cobdenite hopes for international peace. Citing historical examples, Leslie argued that the latter hopes were rooted in a false psychology, for "the desire of wealth is not the one ruling thought which moulds the currents of the national will."[97] Anticipating an argument of the later historical economists, Leslie's espousal of social reform was partly rooted in his belief in the necessity of breeding an imperial race.[98] Already in 1863, Leslie observed that Adam Smith's conception of harmony had been tempered by the realization that the "acquisitive and selfish propensities of mankind . . . are in their very nature principles of aggression and injury instead of mutual benefit."[99] Leslie's essays on moral philosophy reveal a mind that questioned utilitarian and harmony visions of society, for these were marred by an unverifiable faith in the goodness of humanity driven by an enlightened self-interest or a benign Providence. He rejected all absolute systems of the good, for Maine had shown him that "no complete and final philosophy of life and human aims has been constructed . . . and man's ideal of virtue is both historical and progressive."[100]

Leslie's early inductive studies of wages and prices convinced him of the gaping discrepancies between economic theory and the conditions of the real world. He warned that the recent gold discoveries could not be assumed to have had effects similar to those of the sixteenth century. He supported William Newmarch's contention that the recent price increases were not so much the product of a larger gold supply as a consequence of a growing international demand for gold.[101] These inductive studies led Leslie to a growing skepticism of all economic generalizations. He rejected the quantity theory of money on the grounds that it had neglected important variables. He questioned the value of statistical studies conducted with crude averages, and urged as early as 1865 that a system of moving averages be devised. Though not denying the utility of all carefully stated economic generalizations, he concluded that "the lesson . . . which investigation of fact impressed more and more on one's mind is distrust of economic generalizations."[102]

His economic criticism was especially directed at the wages-fund doctrine and what he held to be the classical contention that competition would equalize wages, as well as prices, throughout the economy. In an 1851 pamphlet, Leslie had taken Mill to task for supporting labor combinations and had spoken of the wages-fund doctrine in approving terms. Two years later, Leslie had already made the reversal which led him to an early rejection of the doctrine.[103] Longfield had employed a theory of noncompeting groups to explain differential wage rates analytically. Leslie, however, attacked the problem historically. He insisted that the phrase "the average rate of wages" had little relevance, for wages were largely established by a host of institutional factors such as custom, habit, and local conditions.[104] Further, equal rates of wages were not necessarily determined by competition.[105] Even in competitive industries, Leslie argued, wages were chiefly determined by productivity and trade unions. Concerned especially with the condition of agricultural laborers, Leslie charged that the classical teaching on wages had needlessly alienated the workers from political economy by justifying the payment of low customary wages with the principles of an erroneous science. Moreover, it had inhibited those very inductive studies of wages and the incidence of taxation that were essential for the improvement of the condition of the working classes.[106]

Thus, before Leslie turned his attention to the Irish question, he had already become a critic of classical economics.[107] However, Leslie's passionate interest in agrarian social reform during the 1870s in both England and Ireland provided his later work with a thorough critique of economic orthodoxy that had been absent from his earlier writing. Beginning with Leslie's writings on Ireland in 1867, his debt to Mill also became increasingly apparent. Leslie asked why Ulster enjoyed peace and prosperity while violence and poverty ruled the rest of Ireland. Reviving the arguments of List and Carey,[108] Leslie claimed that eighteenth-century English mercantilist legislation had destroyed the manufacturing potential of Ireland. Moreover, England's attempt to impose its own land system upon Ireland had contributed to the same result. He attributed Ulster's industry and prosperity to the security of tenure enjoyed by its tenants and to their ability to transfer land freely. Thus, he urged that Ulster's tenant right – security of tenure, fair rents, and compensation for tenant made improvements – should be extended to all of Ireland and that the free transfer of land ought to be enhanced through the removal of such legal restrictions as entail and primogeniture.[109]

Following Mill, Leslie argued that because land was a special category of wealth, with justification based upon its social utility, its limitation would transgress neither the laws of political economy nor any universal maxim of social policy. Leslie explained that historically land had been held in either military or civil tenure under the Crown, and that such tenure had carried with it the social obligation of public service. After military tenure had been abolished, land was held on long leases with the provision that improvements had to be made to the land. Subsequently, landlords had used their monopoly position as occupiers of the soil to evict tenants at their will, to remove capital from the land, and to hinder the formation of capital on the part of the tenant. This had prevented the rise of industry in Ireland and had retarded her agricultural progress. The result was that the landlords, in conspiracy with the state and with the blessings of the political economists, had "forced the great mass of the population to become competitors for the occupation of the land as a means of subsistence."[110]

Free transferability of land and security of tenure appeared to be Leslie's panacea for economic development. In a series of comparative studies of the land systems of Great Britain and Europe, which were also indebted to the ideas of the Belgian economists Leonce de Lavergne and Emile de Laveleye,[111] he extolled the benefits to be derived from peasant agriculture. He especially praised the success of the peasant proprietor agriculture of Flanders and its role in the balanced economic development of Belgium. He had given peasant agriculture as one of the causes of Ulster's industrial progress, and he had even argued that this had partly accounted for the success of German industrialization in the Rhineland.[112] In fact, Leslie provided a more sophisticated program for Irish economic development from the side of demand and he approvingly cited Adam Smith to argue: "Towns, manufactures, and brisk and flourishing home trade are the natural consequences of rural prosperity, because agriculture, after providing for the first wants of existence, creates both a demand for higher things, and the materials and subsistence of those who supply it."[113] Leslie maintained that if agricultural profits were diffused among the peasants – rather than being appropriated by a few landlords who, in Ireland, even spent their profits abroad – a considerable increase in the effective demand for the products of Irish industry and commerce would follow.[114] This theme was carried forward in his analysis of Irish emigration as well. Instead of viewing Irish emigration as a sign of the revival of Ireland's economy, as Cairnes and other orthodox English economists had done, he saw emigration as further proof that Ireland was a plundered and neglected English colony, that was little more than a "sheep farm for England."[115] Leslie concluded that the development of Ireland's population, natural, and capital resources through the extension of effective demand, a peasant agriculture, and a vigorous home market would provide employment for all of Ireland's labor.

For Leslie, peasant proprietors were also a source of political stability. He warned that imperial policy in France and industrialization in Germany were now driving the peasants from the soil, removing the only social class capable of averting the coming clash between capital and labor.[116] The consequences of such policies were even more evident in England, where large farms and industrialization had turned agricultural laborers into restless and unemployed urban dwellers and had overturned the old social certainties. Much of Leslie's rhetoric on the problems of the cities was traditional antiurban sentiment, but also implicit was an agrarian critique of industrialization akin to that of Malthus and E.G. Wakefield.[117] Recognizing that the cities contained unemployed labor and capital, he suggested that if the unnatural restrictions upon the land could be removed, "the population and capital in our straitened cities would forthwith find an outlet and a relief, and much capital which leaves our shores would find new and profitable employment upon English ground."[118] Leslie's program of freeing the land from its ancient encumbrances and of reestablishing a class of peasant proprietors in Britain amounted to a scheme for home colonization designed to raise effective aggregate demand and balance national economic growth. Further, such a program would prevent social revolution in both England

and Ireland. Finally, Leslie warned, Britain's survival as a great power in future competition with Europe and America could be assured only if it first revitalized its countryside.[119]

Unlike some Irish national economists and subsequent English historical economists, Leslie remained true to the dominant free trade convictions. For Ireland, however, the success of his program appears to have demanded tariff protection. He could have found theoretical support for Irish tariffs in the writings of Butt, in Maine, and even in Mill. Though Leslie was not an Irish national economist, his criticism of English economic policy in Ireland, his distrust of full industrialization, his rejection of Irish emigration, his faith in the ability of a balanced economy of agriculture and industry to employ Ireland's surplus labor, his support of peasant proprietorship, and his bitter attacks upon orthodox English political economy bore a striking resemblance to the characteristics of later Irish national economics.[120] Leslie feared, however, that Irish independence would lead to a "furious war of religions and races."[121] Instead, he urged that Fenianism could be defeated and the Empire maintained only through the vigorous pursuit of his more moderate program.[122]

As an Irish economist and an outsider, one of Leslie's important services to English historical economics was his praise of foreign, especially German, historical economists. Ashley suggested that Leslie's 1870 essay on Adam Smith had brought German economic ideas to England. Schumpeter noted that Leslie's methodological essays "read much like a reformulation of the Schmollerian program."[123] Although Leslie encouraged the spread of German economics in England by mentioning the economists' work and finding outlets for their writings in English journals,[124] he had little sympathy for their system of state intervention. He told Ingram that "the German Katheder Socialists made donkeys of themselves by rushing at practical doctrine on the subject, when they really had nothing to say beyond the negative proposition that individual interest was not the only thing to look to."[125] Not having found a universally valid system of economic theory or policy in England, he also failed to discover such a system in Germany, France, or the United States. Indeed, he denied the possibility of such a system. As an advocate of Irish and English social and economic reform, he responded most vehemently to those who opposed his suggestions with arguments that claimed the authority of classical economics:

Political writers and speakers of this school have long enjoyed the double satisfaction of beholding in themselves the masters of a difficult study, and of pleasing the powers that be, by lending the sanction of "science" to all established institutions and customs, unless, indeed, customs of the poor. Instead of a science of wealth, they have given us a science *for* wealth.[126]

Instead, Leslie sought an inductive economics, relative to a particular time and place, that was both sympathetic and useful to social reform.

Cliffe Leslie laid the intellectual foundation of historical economics in England. As a true historical critic, and however naively, Leslie never suggested, other than in rhetorical moments, that a historical method could be employed to build a valid and universal system of economic analysis. Unduly critical of all economic theory, he believed that patient inductive, comparative, and historical research was the only path to molding an applied economics capable of solving specific social problems. Although he never succeeded in integrating his descriptive economics into a coherent economic history as he had hoped, its example, combined with his history of economic thought and his methodological writings, provided a powerful stimulus for later English historical economics that would go beyond Ireland and agriculture to challenge the theory and suitability of free trade and free competition for an industrial Britain.

J.K. Ingram and the claims of positivism

John Kells Ingram was the second prominent Irishman during the 1870s and 1880s to call for the creation of a historical economics in Britain. His contribution was both less extensive and less original, though his history of economic thought was wider in scope, than that of Leslie. The chief source of Ingram's inspiration and the characteristic feature of all his work was Comtean Positivism. His enthusiasm for Comte extended even to an unflinching support of the religion of humanity and diminished his influence among soberer minds. His goal was to seek a solution to contemporary social difficulties by forging a new science of society that would be historical in method and infused with ethical concerns. Economics would be subordinated to a larger Comtean sociology.

Ingram's main contribution to the development of English historical economics lay in the dissemination of the historical critique of deductive economics. His pioneering and successful *History of Political Economy*, which was designed to demonstrate the relativity of economic thought to general economic and intellectual history, was for a time the only general history of economic thought published in Britain. The wide popularity it gained for him beyond academic economic circles exceeded knowledge of Leslie's work.[127] Schumpeter observed that Ingram failed to develop any analytical or theoretical tools for economic analysis. But to dismiss Ingram as one whose "knowledge of economics and whose interest in it did not go beyond general 'philosophies' that were inspired by generous enthusiam for the great slogans of the day but never came to grips with real problems" is to miss his significance.[128] Ashley had no illusions about Ingram's originality and analytical abilities in economics. Nonetheless, in 1888 Ashley told Hewins, "Don't despair about Economics in England. Ingram's book cannot fail to put people on what we think the right line; and time is with us." Shortly thereafter, Ashley told Seligman at Columbia that he was well aware of Ingram's shortcomings, but "the appearance of his book in England was epoch making" and one could not afford to "neglect the foremost representative in Great Britain of the antiorthodox movement." Moreover, the Positivist critique of orthodoxy in general was an important contribution to the demise of classical economics.[129]

Ingram was born in Ireland in 1823 and was, like Leslie, the son of an Anglican rector. In 1837 he went to Trinity College, where he studied law, literature, philosophy, and political economy. At first he served as a professor of Oratory and English Literature at Trinity and in 1866 was awarded its professorship in Greek. Ingram published work on Greek and Latin etymology, the weak endings of Shakespeare, and ancient philosophy, as well as on political economy. He was a leading voice in the Dublin Statistical Society and the Irish Academy. He helped found and directed the National Library of Ireland, served on a committee to publish the Brehon Laws, and played an important role in the editing of Trinity's journal, *Hermathena*. In 1891 he was awarded an honorary membership in the American Economic Association, but never joined its English counterpart. Ingram retired in 1900 and died seven years later.[130]

In 1847, a distinguished group of Irish economists founded an Irish Statistical Society, which announced its aim as the application of the principles of political economy to the condition of Ireland after the famine. Ingram and Nielson Hancock moved the society from a narrow statistical path to a greater social awareness signified by the addition of "Social Inquiry" to the name of the Society in 1861.[131] Speaking before the Society in 1863, Ingram held that "our business is to discover and demonstrate, by the application of scientific principles, the legislative action appropriate to each phase of society and each group of economic conditions."[132] Cliffe Leslie was also a frequent participant in the society's affairs and vigorously pursued Liberal causes. Ingram, however, warned that the Irish Statistical Society should remain above partisan politics.[133]

As a youthful advocate of the Young Ireland Movement of the 1840s,

Ingram published an anonymous poem, "Who Fears to Speak of Ninety-Eight." The poem, glorifying the Irish rising of 1798, became a rallying cry for Irish nationalism during the second half of the nineteenth century. It exhibited Ingram's organic view of society that was common to both the Young Ireland Movement and Positivism's emphasis upon the continuity between past, present, and future generations. This view was in marked contrast to the individualism of orthodox Liberalism of the period. In 1882, when the poem was first set to music, Ingram's name became linked with the poem, even though he did not publicly acknowledge his authorship until 1900. Even then he felt compelled to defend his youthful literary outburst: "Their political projects were, as I soon saw, chimerical; but their action, though violent and precipitate, was not sordid or demoralizing." Although, he believed that a free and independent Ireland was inevitable, for the present, he warned, violence would be counterproductive.[134]

Despite his enthusiasm for Irish nationalism, he confined himself to the promotion of Irish cultural and educational institutions and to inductive inquiries into the conditions of society. He urged the reform of the Irish Poor Law to bring it into conformity with England's more liberal practice of outdoor relief, promoted security of tenure for the development of Irish agriculture, and investigated the education of pauper children. Unlike Leslie, Ingram supported a system of large scale agriculture as a basis for the reconstruction of the Irish economy and suggested emigration as a solution to poverty.[135] Compared to Leslie, Ingram's inductive economic research into the conditions of Ireland does not appear to have played as large a role in fostering his opposition to orthodox political economy. Nonetheless, his general appreciation of the Irish problem and his organic view of society, rooted in Comtean Positivism, was a hospitable climate from which to launch his attack upon orthodox British economics.

As joint president of the Statistical and Social Inquiry Society of Ireland in 1878, and of Section F on Statistics and Economics of the British Association, Ingram delivered a dramatic address, that became a focal point of economic discussion during the late 1870s and early 1880s. This address, "The Present Position and Future Prospects of Political Economy," which Leslie tirelessly disseminated in England, was delivered a mere year after Galton's attempt to evict economics from the British Association and two years after the public argument over the proper method of political economy at the Adam Smith Centennial Dinner.[136] The dramatic impact of the address was due to its prestigious setting and was further enhanced by its unusal frankness. The ill repute of British economics, Ingram proclaimed, was in great part due to the "vicious methods followed by its teachers" and to its blatant opposition to social reform.[137]

His objections to deductive economics were fourfold. First, economic phenomenon could not be studied in isolation from other aspects of society, but must be "subsumed under and absorbed into sociology."[138] Second, the conceptions of economists were necessarily abstract and did not correspond to real conditions. The most dangerous of these abstractions was what he assumed to be the Ricardian premise, that "the sole human passion or motive which has economic affects is the desire for wealth."[139] Third, and closely related to the second, he objected to orthodoxy's logical structure. Noting that Mill himself had conceded that deduction could be used only as verification for inductively derived conclusions, Ingram maintained that "social phenomena are ... too complex, and depend upon too manifold conditions" to be capable of a priori treatment.[140] Finally, the excessive abstractions of the dominant economics had made its conclusions unnecessarily insular: "In most enunciations of economic theorems by the English School, the practice is tacitly to presuppose the state of social development, and the general history of social conditions to be similar to that of modern England."[141] For Ingram, neither England nor any other society of a particular time could serve as a model of universal economic conclusions. He did agree that the purpose of political economy was to aid in the discovery of useful laws of social development. But these laws could never be drawn from an economics which assumed an economic man and pursued a metaphysical method. Instead, Ingram demanded a positive economics that would employ an inductive and historical method because "the nature of any social fact of any degree of complexity cannot be understood apart from its history."[142]

While Ingram's 1878 address clearly revealed his submission to Comte's suggestions for the proper role and method of economics, it was not until his retirement in 1900 that he admitted publicly his firm adherence to the religion of humanity. He declared, in the first of his numerous writings on Comtean Positivism, that he had first been drawn to Comte through Mill's *Logic*, but "when the philosophical doctrine rose into the Religion of Humanity, I became fully convinced that it was what mankind wanted in the spiritual sphere."[143] His poems on such traditional Positivist subjects as the transformation of Christian symbols into those of Positivist ritual also reflected this conviction. His efforts to popularize Comtean Positivism were designed to promote the intellectual and spiritual regeneration of humanity as a prelude to the actual establishment of the Positivist conception of society. At the center of this regeneration stood the necessity of forging a harmony between the egotistical and altruistic forces within people and between the organic and the inorganic matter of the universe. It was perhaps Ingram's abhorrence of modern human alienation from the social and physical environment – which he believed to be encouraged by classical economics and perpetuated by its public policy suggestions – that was the fundamental cause of his rejection of deductive economics.[144]

In an 1880 address before a workers' association, he set out his Positivist vision of society. The socialists, he observed, had seen correctly that the atomization of society and the alienation of people from their labor were the fundamental problems of Western industrial civilization. But, neither the old economists, who had unconsciously given birth to modern socialist theory, nor the socialists themselves had an adequate solution to these problems. For his part, he offered a vision of society consisting of well-fed workers and "captains of industry," both infused with a sense of social and moral responsibility, that would end the alienation and industrial conflict of modern society. Likewise, the old antagonism between government and the people, and between government and government, would dissolve in a world transformed into a host of small republics knit together by the bonds of good will and commerce. Ingram remained a firm adherent to a cosmopolitan world order based in this instance not upon Cobden, but upon Comte. When Chamberlain announced his scheme for imperial preference in 1903, Ingram, alone among living historical economists, defended the free trade conclusions of orthodox political economy. Ingram had little understanding of the neoclassical economic defense of free trade. Despite his concession that orthodoxy had made many mistakes in the past, its adherence to internationalism, which it shared with Comtean Positivism, was for Ingram its redeeming feature.[145]

The chief message of his best-selling *History of Political Economy*, as well as his articles on leading economists,[146] was that the past had not yet produced a true system of economics, for all systems of economic thought were relative to the political, social, and intellectual conditions of a particular time and place. He confidently announced that the history of economic thought could be divided into the three Positivist stages of intellectual development: the theological, the metaphysical, and the positivist. Though he was able to find anticipations of modern economic views from the thirteenth century onwards, he classified pre-Enlightenment economics as "theological." Nonetheless, his work contained a sympathetic view of mercantilism. In addition to a liquidity explanation of bullionism, he also offered a cameralist interpretation of mercantilism as a whole. He recognized its progressive and beneficial elements in encouraging the development of national industries. He noted that its policy and theory had been appropriate to its particular stage of civilization but was no longer appropriate to the needs of developed societies. Mercantilism's lasting contribution, he argued, was its recognition that economics ought to be a practical science.[147] By contrast, he saw the economists of the metaphysical period as primarily theorists who were no longer addressing themselves to actual conditions. He did not deny that the Physiocrats had performed valuable service; on the contrary, they had cleared the way for the growth of a "positive" political economy by their sweeping theoretical and political assault on a decaying mercantilism.[148] Among the later mercantilist writers, such as James Steuart, David Hume, the inductive side of Adam Smith, and the Scottish Historical School, Ingram located the birth of an inductive economics. Yet, these precursors of a "positive" economics were stifled by the emphasis upon deduction in Smith's economics. Ingram's analysis of the duality within Smith's economics owed a great deal to the work of Leslie, but Ingram's criticism of Smith was far more categorical. He warned that a return to Adam Smith would be a fruitless endeavor, for ultimately his work was a product of "the negative philosophy of the eighteenth century, resting largely in its ultimate foundation on a metaphysical basis."[149]

The core of Ingram's history of economic thought was an attack on English classical economics. Unlike the other historical economists, who often saw Malthus as an ally, Ingram was extremely critical of him. According to Ingram, Malthus's view of human nature threatened hopes for human regeneration. Moreover, he condemned Malthus's apparent historical method as a mere afterthought to his preconceived conclusions.[150] But, along with other historical economists, he reserved his most damning criticism for Ricardo. "Through the influence of Ricardo, economic method was perverted, the science was led into a mistaken course of turning its back on observation, and seeking to evolve the laws of phenomena out of a few hasty generalizations by a play of logic."[151] The fatal flaw of Ricardo was his assumption of an economic man who acted purely out of his self-interest. All of Ricardo's subsequent deductions compounded the error. Ingram's attack upon Ricardo was unusually vehement. He labeled his influence as "vicious." Ricardo's economic theory had contributed to the atomization of society, encouraged the spread of revolutionary socialism, and alienated people from their labor. Further, his system's very intellectual elegance had encouraged people to endow its slogans with the aura of scientific truth, even though in fact these slogans were little more than expressions of class interests. Ingram did recognize the tensions within Mill's economics, but he nevertheless classified him with Cairnes as a follower of

Ricardo and judged him as the last of the metaphysical economists who had prepared the way for the emergence of a positive economics.[152]

Ingram's rigid Comtean Positivist framework for the history of economic thought diminished his influence within serious economic circles. Further, his criticism of classicism's adherence to a strict deductive method was often exaggerated. Finally, his rhetoric was often immoderate. Indeed, his assaults upon orthodoxy were more appropriate to popular versions of classical economics than to the complexities inherent in the works of its great theorists. In calmer moments, Ingram admitted that deduction had a valid role in economics. But when in 1907, Edgeworth claimed that Marshall had answered Ingram's challenge by criticizing Ricardo and by limiting deduction in his *Principles*, Edgeworth was merely attempting to soothe fundamental disagreements in an obituary. When Ingram defended deduction, he did so in Comtean terms as a mere complementary tool and not as the basic scientific method in economics.[153]

Ingram's reputation as a historical economist did not reside in the originality of his economic writing. Although Ingram disagreed with Leslie on numerous issues, especially in his treatment of Mill, Ingram freely adopted many of Cliffe Leslie's arguments. Ingram did not create an academic tradition of historical economics in Ireland, for he did not hold an academic position in economics and spent relatively little time on the subject. Instead, Ingram's reputation as a historical economist rested upon the popularity of his *History of Political Economy*. Ingram helped to bring the work of foreign historical economists to a wide English audience and magnified the role of English historical economics. He provided a popular plea for the relativity of economic thought and policy to particular stages of civilization and challenged the popular slogans of classical economics that were still widely held by the public but that had been largely jettisoned by the professional economists. Both Cliffe Leslie and Ingram had urged that a historical economics could be constructed through research in economic history and inductive studies of contemporary social and economic problems, and they had championed the statistical method as one of the prime tools of the historical economists. It was the growing statistical societies that first provided an organized framework for the promotion of inductive work in economics.

CHAPTER 3

Statistics, historical economics, and economic history

The nineteenth century saw the flowering of the statistical movement in England. The first statistical societies were formed during the 1830s. The growing appetite of the state for more reliable information led to the development of statistical departments within the government. Early in the century the word statistics was still closely tied to its German origin, "*Staatenkunde*," which meant the knowledge of the political arrangement of states. Subsequently, statistics came to acquire its modern connotation of a quantitative representation of facts. Such a science was assumed to be objective if it concentrated on simply collecting and arranging facts and left others to interpret their political or moral significance.[1] This claim of objectivity was also insisted upon by those working in economic statistics, such as G.R. Porter, Thomas Tooke, William Newmarch, Robert Giffen, Leone Levi, Charles Booth, and J.E.T. Rogers. Moreover, they held that the collection, arrangement, and interpretation of economic statistics would produce more useful economic knowledge than the deductive method. Nonetheless, they freely used their statistics to defend their particular political, social, or moral persuasions. Such verification or refutation of economic doctrine with the actual facts of a particular time and place, as Cairnes had warned,[2] seriously weakened the perceived universal validity of orthodox economic theory.

Ricardian economics, as has been noted,[3] was particularly susceptible to empirical falsification. H.S. Foxwell observed in 1887 that this was one of the prime causes of its ill repute. However, he continued, this problem was now at last being remedied by the introduction of statistical methods into economics by Giffen and others.[4] Foxwell noted that, although most of the statistical economists held rather orthodox views on matters of economic policy and theory, they often presented evidence that seriously impugned the validity of key aspects of orthodox economics. Charles Booth, for example, seriously weakened faith in laissez faire through his massive research on the condition of the people of London. Thorold Rogers added a statistical dimension to the developing discipline of economic history. Indeed, in this regard, Rogers was one of the great pioneers. He firmly believed that the economic expert ought to be a practical reformer and employed his economic history to serve liberal causes. Before the universities became the leading centers for economic study during the late nineteenth century, reluctant support for statistical economics came from the statistical societies and Section F of the British Association.

The statistical societies and their troublesome economists

During the 1830s, a host of statistical societies sprang up in Britain and in part addressed themselves to the application and testing of the teachings of classical economics. Although they were on the whole reluctant to depart from the safe womb of facts to the stormy world of economic criticism and the public controversies associated with applied economics, their activities greatly encouraged an inductive approach to economics. At the second annual meeting of the British Association for the Advancement of Science, held at Oxford in 1832, Charles Babbage, the father of the computer, suggested that the Association add a section on statistics. No action was taken on the proposal until the next meeting in 1833, when William Whewell invited the Belgian astronomer and statistician L.A.J. Quetelet to a discussion on the Poor Laws with Jones and Malthus, among others. Section F, "Statistics," of the British Association was founded at these Cambridge meetings in 1833. The phrase "and Economics" was not added until 1856.

The decision to form Section F was made without the consent of the Association. Whewell, the president of the Association, attempted to exclude the new section on the grounds that it would taint the fledgling Association with public controversy: "Who would propose . . . an ambulatory body, composed partly of men of reputation and partly of a miscellaneous crowd, to go around year by year from town to town and at each place discuss the most inflammatory and agitating questions of the day."[5] When the Association recognized the new group, it added the warning that the section could live in harmony with its parent body only if it dealt with "matters of fact, with mere abstractions and with numerical results." It might deal with the "raw material of political economy," but since its subject "touched the mainspring of passion and feeling," it must not deal with larger political and economic generalizations or the section would be "dissevered from the objects of the Association."[6]

Until 1885, very few economists became president of Section F. The post was generally held by a civil servant. Nassau Senior did hold the post in 1860 and used the occasion to call for a redirection of the section's focus toward economic science, but little came of this. In 1870 Jevons was elected president. The participation of economists did increase after Galton's attempt of 1877 to oust the section from the Association. As we have seen, Ingram was president in 1878 and used the occasion for his call for the submergence of economics into a grand science of sociology. Sidgwick's presidency in 1885 signaled a dramatic increase in the involvement of economists in the section. In addition to Giffen and Booth, who both served as president, virtually every economist of the period presented papers to the section in subsequent years. However, the diversified nature of the Association, its *Proceedings*, and the link with statistics became increasingly cumbersome for those economists who were attempting to make their discipline into a profession. To better suit their needs, the British Economic Association was formed in 1890. Though the British Association remained a significant forum for economic debate for many years thereafter, the main focus of the economists shifted to their own society and its *Economic Journal*.[7]

As early as 1833, the proponents of statistics had already become dissatisfied with the limited opportunities that the British Association offered them. Babbage took the initiative that led to the creation of the London Statistical Society in the following year. Financially tied to the support of "honourable gentlemen" and careful to separate itself from party politics, the Society's prospectus announced its aim as the collection and classification of social "facts calculated to illustrate the Condition and Prospects of Society . . . and . . . to exclude carefully all Opinions from its transactions and publications."[8] In 1837 the Society began publication of its *Journal*, which provided at least a limited outlet for inductive economic research. For seventy years it treated virtually every controversial policy issue of the day from early factory legislation to tariff reform.

The Society's motto – *allis exterendum*: "to be thrashed out by others" – came under repeated attack. The Society's claim that statistical material "must constitute the raw material of all true systems of economy and legislation," while at the same time it sought to exclude generalizations, led Lord Overstone to charge the Society with an excessive fascination with facts. After a heated quarrel, the motto barring controversial opinions was struck from the journal. But this did not settle the conflict. In 1868 a member proposed that, since the Political Economy club was the only institution in London devoted to economic discussion, the Statistical Society ought to form a separate section for the treatment of political economy. The motion was narrowly defeated, and subsequently a similar motion was tabled indefinitely. In 1885, however, a motion was carried that called upon the Society to encourage economic discussion. But in the following year, when H.D. Macleod offered a paper, "On the Definition of Wealth," he was told that the essay could not be accepted unless it treated its subject statistically and had first been submitted to a panel of referees. In 1890 a final effort was made within the Society to expand its economic discussions. The attempt was again defeated. Instead, the Statistical Society rented its back room to the new British Economic Association. When most of the economists had left the Society, the statisticians believed that they had finally turned their backs upon the more controversial aspects of political economy. The Society even refused a handsome offer of prize money for economic papers in 1896. It could not, however, completely divest itself from economic controversy. During the 1890s, Charles Booth reminded the statisticians that Giffen's optimistic conclusions on the condition of the working classes were not in accordance with the facts, and during the first decade of the next century, the Society was plagued by the statistics of tariff reform.[9]

The London Society, though the most prominent, was not the only statistical society in Britain. Similar societies could be found in virtually every major city in the country. The most successful of the provincial societies was that of Manchester. It concentrated on social and economic investigation and counted Jevons, Levi, and Bonamy Price among its members. In Ireland, the Dublin Statistical Society (later the Irish Statistical Society) was founded in 1847 for the specific purpose of finding solutions to Ireland's social and economic ills. Less cautious than its English counterparts, it became a forum for the heretical opinions of such economists as Isaac Butt, Neilson Hancock, J.K. Ingram, and Cliffe Leslie.[10] During most of the nineteenth century, the statistical societies and Section F constituted a major framework for the airing of economic views supported by an inductive rather than a deductive method.

Thorold Rogers, Statistics, and Economic History in the Service of Social Reform

Before the publication of Thorold Rogers's monumental work on the history of wages and prices, important research in this area had already been done by G.R. Porter, Thomas Tooke, and William Newmarch. All three were strident supporters of free trade and laissez faire and were generally orthodox in their views on economic theory. They did, however, offer some cautious comments on the utility of an inductive method in economics. Porter's *Progress of the Nation*, published in 1836 and 1843, was much less quantitative than the work of Tooke and Newmarch. He sought to chronicle the rise of British material and moral progress during its period of industrialization. His comments on the bullionist controversy illustrated his methodological aims:

Our "practical men" have erred because they reasoned from partial and insufficient premises, and sought for the solution of a general question in the particular circumstances that passed under their limited observation; while the theorists . . . have erred because they have made little or no allowance for disturbing influences, the operation of which has been palpable to every man actually engaged in commercial pursuits.[11]

He hoped to correct these errors with "well authenticated facts," supporting them with "principles, the truth of which has been recognized by common assent."[12] Porter's method was to verify the best principles of economics through inductive research.

The massive *History of Prices and the State of the Circulation* by Tooke and Newmarch served as the model for Rogers's even more ambitious history of English prices and wages.[13] Tooke, an adherent to the Banking School of English monetary theory, set out to prove through a study of prices from 1793 to 1857 that prices were not primarily dependent upon the amount of currency in circulation, but were largely determined by such noneconomic factors as war and the seasons. His history was primarily a year-by-year catalogue of prices combined with illustrations of disputed business practices, but when Newmarch joined the enterprise, the work took on a more historical cast. The latter provided the project with a systematic treatment of the effects of free trade and the impact of the new gold discoveries of the 1850s. His use of an index number also greatly increased the usefulness of the study. Although the authors argued that the inflation of the 1850s was a consequence of a greater demand for gold and labor, instead of a result of increased gold discoveries, they failed to generalize to a wider criticism of orthodox economics' neglect of demand analysis. In an 1871 address, Newmarch did broaden his cautious call for an inductive economics contained in the *History of Prices*. He argued that English political economy had long been conducted according to a "metaphysical" method in which the premises of the science had been "sought in the ingenuity and fancy of the writers," and discovering the true facts of economic existence had been left to the painstaking labor of the statistical economists. He declared that political economy must again become a "science of observation, experience, fact, and induction." Now that the method of Bacon had been used by Tooke for prices, by Jones for rent, and by Edwin Chadwick for social legislation, Newmarch continued, he was certain that political economy was now returning to the inductive legacy of Adam Smith.[14]

The career of James Edwin Thorold Rogers illustrates better than most the failure of the historical economists to constitute themselves into a coherent school with a leader, a band of followers, and a common research program. Despite Rogers's claim that he was a historical economist, he did not emphasize the relativity of economic theory to a particular time and place. His prime interest was in the development of economic history. Ashley judged Rogers's work fairly in a searching 1889 review. He argued that Rogers was essentially an orthodox economist who saw history "as the handmaid of economic theory, as furnishing illustration and confirmation of 'laws' arrived at without her aid."[15] He went on to demonstrate severe weaknesses in Rogers's work and to insist that it should not be viewed as a model for the development of historical economics. His claim to heterodoxy, Ashley argued, rested largely upon Rogers's own loud insistence that he was an economic heretic and upon the example of his immense inductive labor. Similar views on Rogers were voiced by Hewins, Cunningham, and Price. In the end, however, Ashley recognized that Rogers's name "was a tower of strength to rebellious economists" and that his massive application of a statistical historical method pointed to economic history as the main area of labor for the historical economist.[16] Ashley might have added two further points. First, Rogers's difficult personality limited his influence in an Oxford that was otherwise receptive to historical economics. Second, Rogers, with Ashley, saw economic history as a practical discipline. Rogers, however, used its results to promote laissez faire, free trade, and an extreme individualism.

Rogers, born in Hampshire in 1823, obtained a BA and an MA from Oxford in the 1840s. Ordained an Anglican priest, he served as a curate at St. Paul's, Oxford, but after 1860 he lost sympathy with the Tractarians and abandoned clerical work. Originally interested in classical scholarship, he increasingly turned to economic subjects. In 1859 he was elected as the Tooke Professor of Statistics and Economic Science at King's College, London. Three years later he was elected to the Drummond Chair of Political Economy at Oxford, but he failed to win re-election in 1868. Worcester College, however, provided Rogers with a lectureship until in 1888 he was restored to his Oxford chair upon the death of his old rival Bonamy Price.

Throughout his career, his blunt talk involved him in endless difficulties. As an undergraduate, he was described as a "loud, dominating, rapid talker." At a discussion on economic history with the equally blunt historian Edward R. Freeman, the latter had ventured the opinion that "Political Economy seems to be so much garbage." "Garbage is it?" Rogers replied. "The very thing then for a hog like you."[17] He also engaged in public controversy, such as his attack on the tutorial, examination, and college system. He even supported the admission of women to the University.[18] He told his students in 1888 that his failure to retain the Professorship twenty years earlier had been due to his having traced "certain social mischiefs to their origin."[19] However, in 1868 his economic research had not yet produced significant heretical conclusions. Rather, his sharp tongue and his political Radicalism had made him controversial. Rogers seems to have had little direct influence upon the young historical economists at Oxford during the 1870s and 1880s. He did found the Oxford University Political Economy Club, but as L.L. Price noted, "he went far to kill his child by his loudly assertive copious talk, spiced as it was, I fear, so often with suspiciously 'broad' stories."[20]

In politics, Rogers was a Cobdenite. Related to Cobden by marriage, he became a close friend and supporter and was called upon to deliver the oration at his funeral. With John Bright, he edited several volumes of Cobden's speeches and later performed the same service for those of Bright.[21] From 1880 to 1885, Rogers served as the Liberal M.P. from Southwark. During his maiden speech, in support of Bradlaugh's famous refusal to take the religious oath, he was reprimanded by the Speaker for his sharp language.[22] A friend of the worker, Rogers lent his parliamentary support to the extension of employer liability, the protection of friendly societies, civil liberties, and certain artisan measures. Like Cobden, Rogers's most characteristic politics were his attacks upon the aristocracy. In support of the extension of the franchise to agricultural laborers in 1884, he told the Commons that the House of Lords had been a power in England's Parliament for 250 years, and he "challenged anybody to find that during that time they had ever done a single just act or expressed a single generous sentiment."[23] Rogers viewed history as the contest between the forces of good and evil and he left little doubt that the Liberal Party of Cobden, Bright, Gladstone, and himself represented the forces of light struggling against those of darkness.[24] A supporter of Irish land reform in 1881 (on the grounds of laissez faire), he lost his Parliamentary seat in 1885 when he followed Gladstone's lead on Irish Home Rule.[25] Rogers believed that his often vehement political and moral views were justified by his inductive research in economics.

Rogers's 1868 *Manual of Political Economy* was only selectively opposed to economic orthodoxy, although he boldly announced in the preface that the volume expressed opinions widely divergent from accepted views.[26] The arrangement of the book was modeled upon Mill's *Principles*, but it bore a much closer resemblance to Fawcett's catechism of Mill than to Mill's more complex work. Rogers defended trade unions while warning of their detrimental effects upon nonunionized workers. He employed an unsophisticated labor theory of value and provided an implicit defense of the wages-fund doctrine. The ultimate solution to the condition of England question, he argued, could be achieved only if the workers practiced thrift and trusted in the process of the free market. Speaking of Mill's argument for the protection of infant industry, Rogers charged that "few statements made by any writer have . . . been more extensively, though unintentionally, mischievous than this admission of Mr. Mill."[27]

His claim to dissent in his *Manual* rested more solidly upon his criticism of the Ricardian theories of rent and population. Instead of limiting the Ricardian theory of rent in its application and supplementing it with Jones's historical classification of rent, as Mill had done, Rogers offered his own universal theory, which was to become a constant leitmotif of his writings. He declared that rent was a consequence of greater agricultural productivity derived from the skills of England's farmers. On population, he argued that it tends to grow as a consequence of agricultural productivity and increased only to the customary level of welfare rather than to the margin of subsistence.[28] His *Manual* also hinted at his methodological position. He warned that the book should be supplemented with historical illustrations, for he who "disdains the inductions of history is sure to utter fallacies." Further, the study of contemporary economic institutions demanded a realization that the hand of the past bore heavily upon the present.[29] In 1869 – the year before Cliffe Leslie's famous article on Adam Smith – Rogers produced an edition of *Wealth of Nations* in which he claimed Adam Smith as an inductive economist, for "among economists, Smith possessed the inductive mind to the highest degree."[30]

Rogers's scholarly reputation rested primarily upon his six volume *History of Agriculture and Prices in England*, published between 1866 and 1892. A seventh, posthumous volume of 1902 was prepared by his son. As the new Tooke Professor of Statistics and Economic Science, Rogers attended an 1860 international statistical conference in Brussels and first developed an interest in the history of prices and wages.[31] The example of Tooke and Newmarch seems to have captured Rogers's imagination, for he modeled his work upon theirs and ended his at the date that theirs had begun. As early as 1862, Newmarch, who had lectured at King's under Tooke and hoped to continue under Rogers, told him that Rogers's research was changing the "face of medieval economics."[32] Rogers's volumes were essentially a compendium of wages and prices between 1259 and 1793. Building upon the Victorian fascination with statistics and the new interest in historical documents then being imported into England from Germany – though without the more sophisticated techniques of either – he compiled his statistics from the records of colleges, the Public Record Office, and manorial rolls. He listed these as average annual prices, year by year, locality by locality, without the aid of research assistants, calculators, or even available statistical tools such as moving averages or the index number. Despite Rogers's prodigious labor of nearly a quarter century, he was nonetheless unable to push his original research beyond the early seventeenth century.

The popular appeal of Rogers's economic writings was not due to the endless columns of figures in his *History of Prices*. Rather, it was a result of his literary digest *Six Centuries of Work and Wages*, published in 1884, and the two courses of lectures that appeared in 1888 and 1892. The first work in particular, along with Arnold Toynbee's *Lectures on of the Industrial Revolution* of the same year, enjoyed a generation popularity as a text for friendly societies, labor unions, and even socialist-sponsored educational activities.[33] The acceptance of Rogers's books within these circles was due to his bitter attack upon classical economics, his defense of the rights of labor, and his virulent criticism of the ruling establishments, positions taken despite Rogers's often repeated opposition to socialism, whether evolutionary or revolutionary.

In the preface to the first volume of his *History of Prices*, Rogers suggested that his painstaking statistical research might ultimately lead to a scientific theory of history. Expressing some skepticism toward such a grand scheme, he noted that it could not be constructed from traditional political and constitutional historical scholarship: "Yet if there be, as some writers have perhaps over-hastily asserted, a science of history, that is a method of analyzing facts by which the future of a nation may be predicted, this will certainly be found most fully in that portion of its annals which is economical."[34] Such a history, he later argued, must be written by laboriously examining classes of materials that had been little studied, such as farming accounts, construction reports, economic legislation, manorial court records, pipe rolls, and the Domesday Book.[35] Ultimately, however, Rogers became increasingly disenchanted with the possibilities of a scientific theory of history and, indeed, of theory in general. In 1888 he told his students: "I am almost weary of the philosophy of history. It has become as unreal to me as alchemy and astrology or metaphysics."[36] Instead, Rogers devoted his energy to the field of economic history, for this he saw as the "true history of the race."[37] Such a history was not to be a mere addition to knowledge for its own sake. On the contrary, Rogers believed that economic history had a political and moral purpose: "The historian of social life . . . is therefore engaged in seeking out past causes for present distresses."[38]

If for Rogers the historian had an important moral and political duty to help solve the contemporary problems of society, this responsibility was even more true of the economist. The role of the economist, he insisted, was "to suggest remedies for the evils under which society is labouring."[39] Thus Rogers saw little utility in a hypothetical science of economics. Rogers went so far as to suggest that the economist "is, as I have often alleged, only removed in a slight degree from the practical politician."[40] Moreover, the conclusions of economics should be "the basis of Parliamentary and Administrative Action."[41]

In 1866, Rogers could still be content with illustrating economic theory with facts, although he hastily added that "these facts form the basis of economical inductions."[42] Encouraged by his own research, naturally controversial in temperament and opinion, and buttressed by the historical criticism of Leslie and Ingram, he became increasingly vocal during the 1870s in his call for an inductive and socially applicable economics. In 1879, Rogers specifically aligned himself with the historical economists.[43] He chided economists for their lack of interest in facts, especially historical facts: "It cannot be doubted that much of the discredit that attaches to political economy in the present time is due to the dogmatism of writers on the subject, and to their habitual disregard for facts." They have used, he concluded, a "metaphysical method."[44] One way in which economics could recapture its former popularity and social utility was to trace contemporary problems to their roots through the study of economic history. He also insisted that historical and statistical research could lead to the correction of economic theory, especially on such issues as rent and population. Although he often felt isolated and unappreciated by both historians and economists, he confidently predicted in 1882: "I do not doubt that at no remote period, all history which has neglected the study of the people, and all political economy which has disdained the correction of its conclusions by the evidence which facts supply, will be cast aside as incomplete and even valueless."[45] It was this hope that inspired his labor.

The most characteristic theme of Rogers's economic writings was his historical explanation of the poverty of the people, especially of the miserable conditions then current among the agricultural laborers during a period of agricultural depression. Others had argued that the poverty among English workers was a result of the iron law of wages, or the Black Death, or the price revolution of the sixteenth century, or the Industrial Revolution, but Rogers saw all such impersonal explanations as products of a false method of inquiry, that the historical economist was called upon to correct.[46] He concluded that the wages and the welfare of the people at the end of the eighteenth century were little better than during the thirteenth century. He saw the fifteenth and early sixteenth centuries as a golden age for the English worker; after the Black Death, they had been able to acquire land, raise their wages, and achieve fixity of tenure.[47] But from the reign of Henry VIII to the nineteenth century, and especially during the reign of Elizabeth, the English aristocracy had used the law to degrade the laborer. He expressed it in a liberal theology of personal morality: "I contend that from 1563 to 1824, a conspiracy concocted by the law and carried out by parties interested in its success, was entered into to cheat the English workman of his wages, to tie him to the soil, to deprive him of hope, and to degrade him into irremediable poverty."[48] Whereas Cunningham would uphold the Elizabethan labor code as an example of a wise and just social policy, Rogers viewed the Statute of Apprentices as a device for lowering wages, a tool for the theft of land, and the means by which labor was prevented from organizing its own defense.[49] In short, for Rogers the poverty of the people was caused by unwise state intervention in the market. At the same time, his conclusions bore the mantle of scientific truth because he presented them as the result of thousands of pages of wages and prices.

Rogers's solution to the condition of England question consisted of laissez faire, free trade, the legal recognition of the trade unions, and the improvement of English agriculture. This belief in the beneficent effects of laissez faire underlay his *History of Prices*. He announced in its first volume that it was "to no real purpose to learn the lesson by which wealth is produced, unless we are also ready to leave to their natural freedom those agencies by which wealth is distributed."[50] Later in life, when the principle of laissez faire had been roundly attacked from many quarters, he became more ambivalent about the role of the state. He now claimed that its proper function was "to arbitrate between contending interests"; he still insisted, however, that the folly of modernity was the state's "equitable settlement of their relations, and even their contracts."[51]

While Rogers often criticized Mill for the latter's backhanded support of the labor movement, his own defense of labor was laced with arguments that Mill had popularized. Rogers maintained that labor could not be stored up for future use and a worker had only his labor to sell. By contrast, the capitalist could both store up capital and accumulate it in ever larger amounts. Thus, the equalization of bargaining positions between capital and labor demanded the formation of strong labor unions which classical political economy had condemned. He specifically repudiated his own adherence to the wages-fund doctrine. In truth, however, he did not understand the theory behind this rejection, for the doctrine was to be found implicitly even in his latest writings.[52]

Rogers believed that his most substantial doctrinal disagreement with classical economists was to be found in his analysis of agriculture. He argued that his historical research had demonstrated that neither the theory of diminishing returns in agriculture, nor the Malthusian law of population, could stand up to empirical verification. Indeed, having questioned the twin props of Ricardian rent theory, he even believed that this theory could be disproven inductively, for while the value of corn had risen eight times since the thirteenth century, rent had increased some eighty times during the same period. Perhaps recognizing that he had failed to account for changes in the value of money during the period, Rogers noted that Ricardo's theory of rent – which he labeled "partly a truism" and "partly a fallacy" – could also not explain why rent on arable land had risen far more than rent for pasture. Moreover, he insisted that Ricardo's theory of rent was also a positive hindrance to finding a satisfactory solution to England's current agricultural crisis.[53]

His own explanation of rent consisted of the argument that rent was the result of agricultural productivity, which was in turn dependent upon the skill of the tenant and upon tenant made improvements. He conceded that this theory of rent was valid only for modern competitive rents. It could be used to analyze neither rents before the seventeenth century nor the contemporary "famine" rents in Ireland. Although admitting that even in contemporary England some rents were survivals of earlier customs and habits, he insisted that modern English agricultural rents were largely a consequence of profit from skill and improvements that were derived from demand for agricultural products. Thus Rogers concluded, in contemporary England neither enlightened landlords nor high rents were opposed to the essential harmony of society.[54]

His belief that high contemporary rents under the regime of free competition were compatible with harmonious class relations and were of crucial importance both to his faith in the beneficent harmony of the universe and for his solution to the contemporary depression in agriculture. As a committed free trader, Rogers repudiated the argument that foreign competition may have been responsible for the problems within English agriculture. Instead, he saw the difficulty as one of insufficient investment in land improvements, low productivity of agricultural labor due to low wages, insecurity of tenure among some tenants, and the confiscation of tenant-made improvements by some landlords. His solution was the acceptance of Cobden's program of free trade in land: the removal of such legal encumbrances from the soil as entail, primogeniture, and strict settlements. This position was not an attack upon laissez faire, he argued, but to the contrary, an effort to restore laissez faire through the removal of a "barbarous law" that had severely compromised freedom of contract in agriculture.[55]

When Rogers carried his analysis beyond agriculture, he exhibited the same strong physiocratic tendencies of which he had accused Adam Smith.[56] He attacked the classical distinction between productive and unproductive labor. Although agreeing that demand for luxuries was not as conducive to economic growth as demand for capital goods, he nonetheless insisted that the demands of the rich, including the landlords, constituted a legitimate demand for labor.[57] He also emphasized the importance of the home trade, arguing that "a pound of home trade is more significant in manufacturing industry than thirty shillings or two pounds of foreign."[58] Further, a nation's prosperity was built first and foremost upon its agriculture. In order to revitalize the home trade, he suggested a program that would redirect English foreign investment to English agriculture and raise agricultural labor productivity through unionization, higher wages, peasant proprietorship, and the reduction of urban unemployment through home colonization upon vacant land. Such a scheme would revitalize English agriculture, restore prosperity to its industry, decrease Britain's dependency upon foreign food supplies, and promote the economic and political stability of the nation. In short, he was an advocate of a balanced economy.[59]

The success of Rogers's program seems to have called for a measure of state intervention beyond free trade in land. Nonetheless, he claimed to be an advocate of laissez faire. He was certainly a vigorous opponent of socialism and of those theories of economics that he believed had contributed to its popularity. He pointed to Ricardo's theory of rent as the origin of the socialist theory of Henry George and warned that George's scheme of expropriating the "unearned increment" would not stop at land.[60] He also believed that Ricardian theory was the intellectual root of German socialist economics. Because he viewed both the Ricardians and the socialists as theorists of class conflict, for him neither could be true political economists: The "true function of the political economist" was the exposition of "the harmony of interests."[61] For Rogers, it was Ricardo – the "parasite of opulence" – and his school who had spawned the theory of socialism by their adherence to a false deductive economics, but Adam Smith's inductive method had demonstrated the true harmony of interests.[62] Rogers often quoted Adam Smith to support his own views, but his arguments on rent, population, value, and social harmony were more akin to those of Carey and Bastiat than to those of Smith. Although Rogers had dimly perceived the possibility of a general glut arising from insufficient effective demand, he remained wedded to his optimistic faith that prosperity and social harmony could be restored to England by the reversion to laissez faire.

Rogers also hinted that England's agricultural depression was in part due to increased foreign competition. He nonetheless remained true to his free trade path. He roundly criticized Adam Smith for his defense of the Navigation Act. He also assured his readers that Mill's arguments for protection were the product of "metaphysical speculation" and thus had "no foundation whatever in economic history."[63] In his historical writing, he attacked List's view that the decline of the Dutch Republic proved the ineffectiveness of free trade in maintaining a nation's prosperity. Instead, he argued that the Republic's decline was a result of its reversion to mercantilism under the aristocratic influence of the House of Orange and its affiliation with Hanover. He held that likewise in England the aristocracy had devised a mistaken protectionist policy designed to promote its own interests rather than those of the nation.[64] Despite such confident statements in his own economic history, he reluctantly admitted that British mercantilism of the eighteenth century had provided the opportunity for the creation of its industrial preeminence: "Though, in the judgment of all those whose judgment is worth anything, the policy which has created the opportunity is an erroneous one, and was certain to bring its own nemesis with it, it is the duty of the historical economist, to take measure of facts which have had their effects on the destiny of nations."[65] He conceded that it had been protection and the old colonial system that had provided Britain with both a ready market for its industrial products and a source for its raw materials. Further, protection had granted England the stability and confidence that had allowed for a rapid rate of capital accumulation. Nonetheless, he concluded, Britain's rate of economic growth had been greater under free trade than under protection; thus, the essential soundness of free trade remained indisputable.[66] In a thoroughly Cobdenite manner, Rogers argued not only that free trade would diminish the likelihood of war, decrease the price of foodstuffs, and curtail monopolies, but also explained that the purpose of the repeal of the corn laws had been the perpetuation of England's industrial preeminence through the exchange of manufactured goods for primary products.[67]

When protectionist sentiment again revived in Britain during the 1880s, Rogers mounted the platform to denounce this ancient heresy. He held that the growing earnings from such invisibles as financial and commercial services more than offset the increasing deficits in Britain's international commodity account. But in his last years even Rogers became increasingly concerned over the growing gap in the balance of payments. Furthermore, his emphasis upon the home market was difficult to square with his apparent readiness to accept for England a rentier status under free trade.[68] Following Cobden's lead, Rogers relentlessly attacked the nineteenth century British Empire as excessively costly, leading toward the dissipation of British power, and involving it in endless foreign entanglements. But Rogers, like Cobden, was no anti-imperialist. While calling for the creation of a partnership of independent English-speaking states, as Adam Smith had done, he also suggested that any surplus British capital, labor, and goods might as readily be exported to other parts of the globe as to the formal empire – an argument Cunningham would call "the imperialism of free trade." Finally, with Cobden, he also supported the retention of the Indian Empire.[69]

Subsequent English historical economists applauded Rogers's criticism of the deductive method, his belief that classical economics had promoted theories of class antagonism, and his conviction that both the historian and the economist must ultimately justify their labor by its social applicability. However, they did not share his Cobdenite liberal politics and found his rhetoric too strident. In 1889, Ashley argued that Rogers had failed to use his inductive research as the basis of historical laws in the German manner.[70] Cunningham noted in 1894 that Rogers had not produced a national economic history of England, but had merely dealt with the bargains of individuals in the past.[71] Rogers had learned his economic history from Tooke and Newmarch, but his statistical sophistication did not advance much beyond Tooke. He had learned from his Oxford colleague William Stubbs a reverence for historical documents, but he had failed to learn the lesson taught by the new historical scholarship that these documents should be treated critically. Moreover, Rogers never explicitly stated that economic policy and theory were relative to a particular stage of production. His moral and political views, which permeated all his work, were not relative. They were dogmatic, absolute, and represented a Cobdenite liberalism with little appeal for the twentieth century.

Rogers often complained bitterly of his isolation and lack of influence. Nonetheless, he noted in 1882, "I have the satisfaction of knowing that my work is not unappreciated abroad, especially in Germany, the *magna mater viru.*"[72] Ironically, Rogers knew little of German historical economics. Such sentiments were common among the historical economists. Indeed, they are often a consequence of pioneering work. In the case of Rogers, however, his difficult personality and archaic liberal views added powerfully to their truth. Despite its many flaws, Rogers's great contribution to English historical economics was his monumental *History of Prices*. Building upon a half century of work by the statistical societies,

Rogers provided a quantitative dimension to economic history that suggested its future required professional attention. In later years this contribution was recognized by the younger historical economists. In 1919, Cunningham attributed the creation of the discipline of economic history to the example of Rogers: "From his time it has been regarded not merely as an aspect of history . . . but as a department of economic study."[73]

Toward a statistical analysis of free trade and welfare: Levi, Giffen, Bowley, and Booth

Although Rogers freely commented on contemporary industrial society, which he distrusted deeply, his economic research was largely confined to the medieval period. The other statistical economists of the late nineteenth century, however, primarily investigated Britain's contemporary commercial, industrial, and social situation. Leone Levi, Robert Giffen, and A.L. Bowley were optimists who chronicled the progress of the English working classes and remained confident that free trade would continue to ensure Britain's prosperity. They insisted that the truth inherent in orthodox economic conclusions lay not in its deductive but in its inductive formulation. By contrast, Charles Booth dissented vigorously from these optimistic conclusions and argued that free competition left a large percentage of people in poverty. The research of all four lent a statistical dimension to applied economics and to modern economic history.

Levi and Giffen, in particular, attempted to demonstrate the benefits derived from laissez-faire capitalism and an improved standard of living. Leone Levi (1821–1889), who was closely associated with the London and Manchester statistical societies, was the Bastiat of statistical economics. Born of foreign parents, he traveled widely in Europe and represented Britain at various international statistical conferences. In 1861 he was awarded a doctorate in economic and political science from the University of Tübingen; but despite his German connections, there were few traces of the German Historical School in his work. In 1852 he was appointed to the newly created Chair of Commerce at King's College, London. He was a friend and admirer of Cobden and became known for his work on international law reform and legal statistics. He believed in the existence of a universal harmony between divine, natural, and human law – a harmony which he felt was often frustrated by human law. His considerable statistical and historical research in comparative law was designed to restore this harmony through the promotion of uniformity in commercial law, the establishment of chambers of commerce throughout the world, and the expansion of international trade.[74]

At the meetings of statistical societies from the 1850s until the late 1880s, Levi presented numerous studies that outlined the progress of the British people under free trade. He also wrote a *History of British Commerce*, which treated the period 1763–1878. As Levi himself stated this book was not a mere history of prices and wages, but a "historical account of the principal events by which commerce has been affected, and of the influence which commerce has in turn exercised on the economic conditions of the country."[75] Levi's economic history concentrated on the history of legislation and was designed to prove inductively that Britain's rapid rate of economic growth was a result of free trade and laissez faire. He confidently urged other nations to follow England's example, for "economic laws were not limited to their operation in time and place."[76] Although he admitted that the Paris Exhibition of 1867 had shown that Britain had forever lost its industrial preeminence, he saw the economic problems of the 1870s as transitory and confidently looked forward to Britain's continued prosperity as long as it adhered to the principles that had brought its earlier success.[77] Levi rarely criticized classical economic theory. Nonetheless, he insisted that inductive research made economics a science: "It is by the use of statistics that political economy has acquired the character of a fixed science; and by it that it has ceased to be tentative, and has become to a large extent an inductive or experimental science."[78]

Robert Giffen (1837–1910) was the best known statistical economist of the period. He served as Bagehot's assistant at the *Economist* from 1868 to 1876. From the latter year until 1897, he was the chief statistician at the Board of Trade. In later years he became the first head of the newly created Labour Department. A sometime president of the London Statistical Society, he edited its journal from 1876 until 1891. When the *Economic Journal* was created, Giffen wrote its financial section. In politics he was a Liberal who joined the Unionist cause in 1900. More so than even Rogers, who praised his work, Giffen designed his historical research to illustrate the truth of the orthodox conclusions of political economy.[79] Giffen argued that the abstract and hypothetical truths of political economy were of little practical utility, for "in the real world quantities must be dealt with; and in the measurement of tendencies or forces, statistics are absolutely essential."[80] Only a statistical and historical method, he insisted, would produce an economic science capable of solving contemporary problems. In old age, he even went so far as to promise the construction of an inductive science for the application of the principles of economics, as Jevons had suggested. He never accomplished this task, but his statistical studies of foreign trade, wages of labor, and the rate of capital formation served as a model for such a science; and, as he himself recognized, they were also an important contribution to the development of the discipline of economic history in England.[81]

In an 1883 presidential address before the London Statistical Society, in which he dealt with the condition of the working classes since Porter's earlier study of 1833, Giffen laid the foundation of the optimistic assessment of the impact of the Industrial Revolution upon the standard of living of the people. He sought to prove that the workers had in fact received their share of England's remarkable economic growth in opposition to those who demanded the "whole produce of labour."[82] Using index numbers, he argued that the real wages of the working classes had risen from 50 to 100 percent during this period. In opposition to those who held that Britain's economic gains had gone into the coffers of the capitalists, he replied that the period had also seen a great expansion of moderate incomes; and, indeed, "almost the whole of the great material improvement of the last fifty years had gone to the masses."[83] Giffen's findings spawned considerable public debate – especially at the Industrial Remuneration Conference in 1885. The next year he returned to answer his critics. He charged that most ideas, such as those of Rogers, on the welfare of the people were of little value, for they had failed to consider the changing value of money, the altered composition of the population, and the different social and economic organization of the country. He declared confidently that, if sound statistical methods were followed, research would support his contention that the condition of the people had improved from century to century.[84]

Giffen's methods were a considerable improvement over those of Rogers, but what they made up for in statistical sophistication, they lost in historical understanding. He failed to recognize the importance of such matters as unemployment, underemployment, and the strains resulting from the disruption of a traditional society. It was such issues that Arnold Toynbee and the Hammonds would emphasize in their interpretations of the social effects of industrialization in England.[85] By refusing to deal with the period before 1800, Giffen had also partly sidestepped the central issue raised by Toynbee: whether the condition of the workers, both qualitatively and quantitatively, had become better or worse than before the coming of industry. When Giffen argued that the general standard of living had risen considerably between 1833 and 1883, almost everyone agreed. Observers disagreed, however, on the distribution of this new wealth. Nonetheless, Giffen confidently concluded that the poor were now far less numerous.[86]

Another issue that occasioned considerable statistical debate around the turn of the century was the vexatious matter of tariff reform. Giffen's pioneering studies of the rate of capital formation produced results as optimistic as his views on the standard of living. Addressing himself to the economic difficulties of the 1880s, he denied that Britain's rate of economic growth was declining relative to that of other countries. He conceded that the British textile, iron and steel, and shipbuilding industries were facing a relative decline, but he noted this decline was to be expected as other nations became industrialized. Giffen advised that Britain should maintain its free trade system, raise productivity, and switch its emphasis to those industries in which it enjoyed a comparative advantage.[87] In fact, his optimistic predictions were not based upon statistical studies of the success of specific British industries, but upon the general rate of capital accumulation. Further, his claims on comparative rates of growth were extremely tenuous because his work made but scant reference to the experience of the United States and Germany. Nonetheless, he concluded confidently that for Britain "there must have been improvement all round."[88] He did provide a negative argument against protection. In 1882 he argued that merely to demonstrate a deficit in Britain's balance of trade was an insufficient argument for protection, for earnings from invisibles easily filled this gap in the balance of payments. Moreover, mere statistics could never prove the "cardinal question between free trade and protection, *viz.* which *regime* favours most the general prosperity of most of the people."[89] Any such argument, he insisted, would have to take into account the moral and political situation of a people.

Despite this cautious and negative argument against protection, he could also be dogmatic on the issue. In an 1898 essay, which sought to refute Mill's argument for the protection of infant industries with inductive material, he prophesied that within a generation or two protectionist politicians would vanish from the earth: "The breed, I am confident, is very nearly extinct, because the modern atmosphere and conditions, not theory, are making the policy next to impossible."[90] Five years later, when the protectionist issue had again erupted openly in British politics, he repeated his negative argument against protection. Despite his assurances that the system of free trade was "complete both theoretically and experimentally," he came to support Imperial Preference in 1903 on political rather than economic grounds.[91] Several years later, he was to complain that both sides in the fiscal debate were using statistics "in an entirely illogical manner."[92] Ironically, Giffen's own plea for an inductive method had opened a Pandora's box that helped undermine the categorical faith in the correctness of British free trade theory and policy.

A.L. Bowley, Giffen's successor as the leading economic statistician in Britain, produced a defense of free trade that offered much ammunition for the tariff reformers. His important *England's Foreign Trade in the Nineteenth Century* proclaimed that free trade theory had not yet been successfully controverted. His book was squarely based upon the doctrine that free trade would deepen the world's division of labor. Bowley argued that the mineral resources, which were becoming ever more important in balancing Britain's international payments, could not be expected to last much longer than another generation. At the same time, he also admitted to a relative decline in the nation's staple industries. Yet, he concluded, Britain's earnings from invisibles could be expected to keep its international payments in balance for the foreseeable future.[93] Bowley's statistics for the years 1898 to 1902 demonstrated that Britain's bill for imported food was by itself equal to its earnings from invisibles. Moreover, his prediction for further declines in staple industries, the coal trade, and the entrepôt trade failed to offer a solution to the problem of how England was to pay for its raw material imports in the future.[94] In any case, his faith in the ability of invisible earnings to expand sufficiently to cover even larger trade deficits was of little consolation to either the owners or the workers in the staple industries. Bowley himself admitted that invisibles were of slight value in providing employment for England's workers; but in the finest cosmopolitan tradition, he argued that to increase the wealth of the world as a whole, "one country will be sacrificed for the economic benefit of the world."[95] Such a prospect for England, he argued, was still far in the future. He nonetheless accepted this possibility fatalistically:

If it is found that in England few industries can find a place that are not undertaken better elsewhere, it will mean that the Englishman will gradually forsake his home country, that English enterprise will be successful in some other quarter of the globe, and that England will still be the home and mother of successful and multitudinous offspring.[96]

Others, perhaps more nationalistic, perhaps more personally involved in its declining industrial system, and perhaps more deeply impressed with the social necessity of finding labor for its workers, could not accept with equanimity Bowley's sacrifice of Britain's industrial, military, and political power.

The sociologists have laid claim to Charles Booth as one of the founders of modern empirical sociological research. Most of his contemporaries, however, saw him as a statistical economist.[97] Booth, a

Liverpool businessman of substantial means, exhibited an interest in the welfare of the workers and the responsibilities of capital that made him a model of Comte's captain of industry. A Unitarian and liberal, he campaigned for various liberal causes, participated in Liverpool's municipal politics, and joined Joseph Chamberlain's Birmingham Education League. While engaged in these political activities, he became acutely conscious of the widespread poverty that plagued Britain's major cities. Like so many other late Victorians, he rejected the thesis that this poverty was either divinely ordained or a necessity of economic growth under capitalism; and after a crisis of faith, he became closely associated with contemporary positivist circles and believed that the first prerequisite for the eradication of poverty was the scientific investigation of its extent and causes.[98]

Associated with Octavia Hill, the Charity Organization Society, and the London settlement houses of Toynbee and Oxford Hall, Booth challenged H.M. Hyndman's conclusion, published by the Social Democratic Federation in 1886, that at least one-fourth of London's people existed on a level below minimal subsistence.[99] In 1887 Booth told the London Statistical Society that his own preliminary research demonstrated that Hyndman's estimate had been too low, for perhaps one-third of the London population lived at the level of abject poverty. This conclusion, which Levi promptly criticized, Booth emphasized was not the product of mere economic deductions, but the result of patient, if preliminary, inductive research. Although Booth did tell the statisticians that the failure of a priori political economy was due to its false assumptions and its disregard for facts, and although he did occasionally engage Beatrice Webb (then still Potter) in discussion on the proper method of political economy, he generally felt uncomfortable in stating the implications of his work for economic theory. Instead, he concentrated on presenting the economic facts that he had accumulated.[100] With the help of a personal staff, volunteers from Toynbee Hall, Beatrice Webb, Clare Collett, and W.A.S. Hewins, he undertook a monumental survey of London poverty, industry, and the various efforts of the churches to rectify social and economic abuses. The conclusions of his seventeen-volume *The Life and Labour of the People of London* confirmed his 1887 report that at least one-third of the city's people lived in poverty. This study, along with the work of Seebohm Rowntree and the Royal Commission on the Poor Laws, brought the nation face to face with a statistically documented scale of poverty that had previously only been guessed. Booth's conclusions, in particular, were not easily faulted, for Booth had meticulously surveyed London, street by street; had carefully worked out classifications of income and expenditure; and had published his findings in both statistical and literary formats.[101] Booth remained, however, firmly committed to capitalism. It was, he argued, an excessively naked and brutal version of individual competition that was responsible for the misery of a third of London's people. In his study of London industry, he went further, noting that "it cannot but be admitted that the industrial conditions under which we live lead to poverty."[102] The chief problem with modern industry, Booth argued, was its irregularity: "Of all the causes of poverty and misery, irregular work, coupled as it must be, with irregular lives, is by far the greatest."[103] This theme of irregularity, which had already been popularized by Toynbee and constituted an important contribution of Foxwell, became a characteristic theme of English historical economics.

A student of Booth has concluded that Booth's solution to the problem was a "limited state socialism" for the poorest third of society. Even though Booth argued that "the entire removal of this class out of the daily struggle for existence I believe to be the only solution to the problem of poverty," his specific proposals for social reform were far from amounting to even a limited socialism.[104] In the early 1890s, he suggested the adoption of a system of old age pensions. Later, believing that tariffs would provide both fuller and more regular employment than free trade, he also took part in Chamberlain's tariff reform campaign.[105] But, as Booth himself stated, he was reluctant to suggest specific remedies and preferred to let his research promote a proper awareness of the problem. He never claimed originality as an economist, but he was willing to allow that his work hastened the "undiscriminating advocacy of *laissez faire* from the field" and "even shaken seriously the stability and hold of political opinion of orthodox economic opinion."[106]

By providing economics with a more solid factual foundation, the statistical economists ultimately strengthened the position of both orthodox and historical economics. During the late nineteenth century, however, their justification of both theory and policy through inductive research challenged the very universality of the theories and policies that they had sought to defend. Rogers had gone further by rejecting orthodox economic theory – though he remained faithful to a Cobdenite version of laissez faire policy. In terms of political impact, Booth's research was most important, for he had shown deductively that free competition was the root cause of widespread poverty in modern society. To be sure, the statistical economists had neither sought nor succeeded in replacing deductive economics with a historical economics; they had, however, added to the scientific and popular prestige of an inductive applied economics and had provided economic history with a statistical dimension. By the turn of the century, the troublesome economists increasingly left the statistical societies for their own society. Within the universities, Edgeworth and Bowley laid the foundation of a mathematical economics that in time would become a professional subject.[107]

CHAPTER 4

Historical economics at Oxford

Between about 1885 and 1920, British economics grew into a professional, primarily academic, discipline. With the revitalization of Oxford and Cambridge during the 1880s and the establishment of new universities in major industrial and urban centers during the next two decades, historical economists vied with theoretical economists for a still limited number of academic positions in economics. While Cunningham and Foxwell struggled to advance the claims of historical economics at a Cambridge increasingly dominated by Marshall, neoclassical economic theory failed to find an effective leader in F.Y. Edgeworth at Oxford.[1] However, historical economics flourished at Oxford during the 1880s. This was largely due to the remarkable influence of Arnold Toynbee, T.H. Green, and the vigorous tradition of historical research then current in Oxford among such students as W.J. Ashley, L.L. Price, and W.A.S. Hewins. Among the major figures, only Price remained at Oxford to promote a cautious version of historical economics and economic history. Ashley, after an illustrious career across the Atlantic, returned to England in 1900 as the first head of the Birmingham Faculty of Commerce. Hewins became the first director of the London School of Economics and Political Science in 1895.[2]

The work of Leslie and Rogers primarily treated agricultural topics and criticized society for having failed to maintain a balanced economy. This theme found a powerful echo in the work of the later historical economists and indeed constituted one of the constant themes within this tradition. However, the emphasis of the later group was on Britain's industrial and commercial circumstances as they sought to confront the problems of a mature industrial economy faced with growing international economic and political competition. In addition, new and alarming manifestations of social unrest appeared during the 1880s. These developments led to a frontal attack upon the theory and practice, and even upon the ideal, of a free market. While neoclassical economics defended the free market, the historical economists questioned both its existence and desirability. Instead, they supported the regulation of the domestic economy, the protection of industry, and the consolidation of the empire. The young Oxford economists' suggestions for state intervention were especially derived from their concern with the fragile nature of modern capitalist society. They charged that many aspects of classical economics, and of nineteenth century liberalism as a whole, had fostered insecurity through naked competition; had retarded, and continued to inhibit, social amelioration; and had thus provided both the social conditions and the intellectual underpinning of modern revolutionary social movements.

Arnold Toynbee and the consequences of the industrial revolution

Arnold Toynbee's short but influential career at Oxford was spent in the study of modern industrial society and classical economic theory and in the diffusion of his views both within and outside the university. His aims were frankly counterrevolutionary. Toynbee inspired young Oxford economists to believe that economic history, applied economics, and the advocacy of political and social activism by the economic expert could peacefully move society toward a more stable order. Social stability was central to Toynbee's vision of a social democratic society in which free men would form corporate institutions and would be regulated by a paternal state and guided by leaders who placed Christian ethics above materialism.

Toynbee entered Pembroke College, Oxford, in 1873, but soon transferred to Benjamin Jowett's Balliol. Upon obtaining a degree in history in 1878, he was immediately appointed tutor and served in this capacity until his youthful death in 1883. His literary work consisted almost entirely of his posthumously published *Lectures on the Industrial Revolution of the Eighteenth Century in England*, which, together with popular addresses and some fragmentary writings, were pieced together from Toynbee's literary remains, newspaper accounts, and the lecture notes of his students William Ashley and Bolton King. His popular, if slender, *Lectures* became a powerful stimulus for the historical economists and exerted a considerable influence upon the interpretation of the Industrial Revolution well beyond this circle.

Toynbee combined his academic career with service as a Poor Law guardian, efforts to educate the artisans through the university extension movement, and the encouragement of Friendly Societies. His career summed up the Oxford tradition of religious, intellectual, and social idealism articulated by T.H. Green. This tradition derived from the mid-Victorian protest of Carlyle and Ruskin against utilitarian rationalism and the economics of the Manchester School. Green amalgamated this protest with the religious enthusiasm of evangelicalism, the theology of the Tractarians, the heady metaphysics of German Idealism, and the spirit of English liberalism into a philosophy of public service. Green's ideals were designed to satisfy the religious soul's quest for personal salvation during the crisis of conscience characteristic of late Victorian England. In religion, he supported the broad church movement, which attempted to make the Anglican Church responsive to the social needs of the nation. In politics, Green was one of the important architects of a new and more advanced Liberal creed, that not only promoted the freedom of the individual, but also attempted to use corporate institutions and the state to promote a social and positive freedom.[3] Such freedom would be attained by providing the working classes with a minimum level of material well-being, designed to remove the debilitating uncertainty of body and spirit that he believed was a consequence of modern industrial society. The middle classes, whose sons were entering Oxford in larger numbers, would achieve freedom by devoting themselves to a life of social and political service to the nation.[4]

Contemporary descriptions of Toynbee were extremely eulogistic in tone. Alfred Milner described him as a noble youth, who, weak of body but strong in spirit, had learned the lesson of "Evangelical Christianity" and provided the best example of the combination of intellectual achievement and public service that Green had attempted to instill in his students. Milner granted Toynbee a "prophetic power – the kind of influence exercised in all ages by men of religious and moral inspiration."[5] Price spoke of him as a man of "noble ideals and aspirations" and credited him with having exerted a "magnetic influence" upon his contemporaries. Marshall called him the "ideal representative of the medieval saint." Ashley described him as a "sensitive and overwrought scholar who lived a saintly life."[6] Such references to Toynbee as "saintly" were partly due to his brief life, unsoiled by the compromises of maturity, and his religious interests. Toynbee was an active supporter of a social Christianity within the context of a broad state church. Spiritually and emotionally, he emphasized the need to restore the unity between God and man and the harmony within society, which he believed had been neglected in modern philosophy and religion alike and imperiled by the rise of modern industry.[7] His religious and emotional ideals were the mainspring of Toynbee's rejection of utilitarianism and classical political economy.

Ashley observed that Toynbee was also the "initiator of a new and fertile development in English political economy," for, at a time when English political economy was held in low popular esteem, Toynbee had created a new interest in it by wedding it to a program of social and economic reform. Further, Toynbee was the first English academic economist who had recognized elements of truth in modern socialism. Ashley boldly concluded that Toynbee rightly deserved to be compared to the German *Kathedersozialisten*.[8] Toynbee, however, knew little of German historical economics. Instead, he based himself upon the work of Leslie, Maine, and Stubbs, and the spirit that infused his work was not that of Hegel, but the "positive liberalism" of Green and the moral tone of Ruskin. Moreover, Toynbee emphasized voluntary rather than state regulation. This corporate vision led to the christening of one of Oxford's settlement houses in London as Toynbee Hall.[9]

Toynbee's fragmented writings reveal three central purposes: to provide an economic history of Britain during the period of industrialization, to explain and criticize classical political economy historically, and to suggest a program of social reform. As an economic historian, Toynbee provided a deeply pessimistic interpretation of the social consequences of the Industrial Revolution. Indeed, Toynbee brought the term "Industrial Revolution" into the English language. The distinguishing feature of Toynbee's work for modern audiences has been his eloquent description of the plight of the agricultural workers and artisans faced with the coming of machinery and competitive capitalism. He sympathetically described what the Hammonds would call the "moral economy" of the eighteenth century and forcefully condemned its destruction by the power of naked competition wielded by capitalist landlords and industrialists.[10] Like Marx, Toynbee was an inspired historian of alienation.

As an economist, his chief aim was his historical argument that classical political economy had worsened the lot of English workers and had subsequently stood in the way of improving their condition. Nonetheless, he argued, Leslie had been too sweeping in his rejection of deductive economic theory. Toynbee insisted that deductive political economy was capable of producing economic generalizations, if deduction proceeded with the proper checks and was carefully limited to the theoretical sphere. Thus, there was no fundamental opposition between deductive and inductive economics. Nonetheless, he demonstrated little enthusiasm for such an abstract, hypothetical, and scientific economics. Rather, his prime interest in economics lay in its utility as a guide to moral political action.

Much of Toynbee's economic criticism was aimed at the rigidity and abstractness of popular versions of applied orthodox economics. He argued that popular economic orthodoxy had employed Ricardian economics as slogans to oppose social reform regardless of altered circumstances. For Toynbee, practical economics had to be historical. Its aim was to categorize the stages of economic development and to trace the influence of institutions on social and economic arrangements. This emphasis led him to a pervasive relativism in applied economics. He noted prophetically, for example, that the policy of free trade was not a universal principle, but a practice relative to a particular time and place: "No English economist . . . has dared say this . . . but it is an unjustifiable prejudgment of the question to lay down that this policy must be wise at all times and places."[11] In order to appreciate the relativity of economic doctrines, Toynbee urged his students to investigate the social and economic history of England. He conceded that Maine's historical method had led to profoundly conservative conclusions. Toynbee, however, rejected such determinist arguments in both religion and historical studies: Although "the modern historical school of economists appear to be only exploiting the monuments of the past, they are really shaking the foundations of many of the institutions of the present."[12]

Toynbee believed that the history of economic thought would also undermine orthodox political economy's opposition to social reform. He began with a critique of Adam Smith akin to that of Leslie. Even though Adam Smith had often relied heavily on a historical method, his insistence on the value of competition and the principle of self-interest had been taken over from the natural law teaching of the physiocrats, Toynbee argued. The essential significance of Adam Smith's economics, and of the Industrial Revolution, was the destruction of the medieval and mercantilist regulatory systems. These systems had been replaced by a regime of natural liberty that neglected the interests of the consumer in favor of those of the producer and had made unequal the relations between employer and employed. The fruits of free competition were higher prices, monopolies, periodic overproduction, a "great increase in wealth" for some and increased pauperism for segments of the common people. The final result was a dangerous "alienation of classes."[13]

According to Toynbee, these disastrous consequences of the Industrial Revolution, originally supported by the ideas of Adam Smith, were perceived as inevitable by Ricardian economics. Although he was willing to admit that not all of Ricardo's conclusions were mistaken, Toynbee did insist that they were relative to particular circumstances. He rejected such assumptions as the mobility of labor and the tendency of wages toward geographical equality within a trade. He also attacked the theory of rent and the wages-fund, not on the basis of careful comparative, historical, and statistical research, but primarily out of a moral repugnance for the very idea of a market economy. Toynbee believed that the root of Ricardo's errors was that his abstract system was based upon an economic man that never was:

a world of gold-seeking animals, stripped of every human affection, for ever digging, weaving, spinning, watching with keen undeceived eyes each other's movements, passing incessantly and easily from place to place in search of gain, all alert, crafty, mobile – that world less real than the island of Lilliput, which never has had and never can have any existence.[14]

But why, Toynbee asked, should Ricardo's abstract system, devoid of social sympathy, have exerted such a powerful influence on the English? The solution, he answered, lay not only in the intellectual appeal of this abstract system to a generation fascinated by natural law, though this was a factor. Rather, its popularity resulted from its justification of the political and economic program of a middle class primarily concerned with its own wealth and power. Further, the longevity of Ricardian economics was partly due to the use that modern socialists such as Karl Marx and Henry George had made of the system.[15]

Toynbee held up Malthus and J.S. Mill as counterweights to Ricardo. Although he sharply criticized Malthus's teachings on population, he also praised him for having studied the problem inductively. He pointed to Mill as the originator of a new movement in economics and praised him for insisting upon a relativistic theory of distribution. Furthermore, Mill's ethical argument that competition required regulation had infused the science with a new moral purpose.[16] Toynbee believed that the very meaning of civilization revolved around the effort to bring self-discipline and social control to the brute struggle of individual competition.[17] Competition was neither all beneficent, as the Ricardians held, nor all evil, as the socialists maintained. Instead, it was a neutral principle demanding social direction that must be combined with the sentiment of benevolence.

In order to prevent violent social upheaval, he set out to repair the prestige and practicality of political economy by proclaiming an ethical and historical economics dedicated to social reform. His economics was especially designed to appeal to that aristocracy of labor that had been granted political democracy. He formed a society at Oxford to discuss economic questions with the workers and became a pioneer of the university extension movement. He told his artisan audiences that people no longer needed to "crouch and shiver . . . under the shadow of an inexorable law" because human nature was pliable and human will could freely alter industrial conditions for good or ill.[18] In short, they had been delivered from the necessitarian assumptions of classical political economy. Toynbee's program of state intervention was limited to urging the adoption of old age pensions, providing housing for the artisans, and regulating working conditions. The heart of his program was voluntary corporate action. He encouraged the development of friendly societies, cooperative societies, charitable organizations, and, to a lesser extent, trade unions. These voluntary bodies would promote social cohesion, encourage industrial peace, and act as a buffer between the solitary individual and the full force of society.[19] His "radical socialism" was a paternalistic and Tory version of Green's positive liberalism.

Of all the members and works of the English historical economists, Toynbee and his *Lectures* are today probably most widely known. Intellectually, Toynbee's historical economics was much less significant than that of Cliffe Leslie. Toynbee's combination of economic history and the history of economic thought, his criticism of the economic man, and his attack upon Ricardo were squarely in the mold laid down by Leslie. His catastrophic interpretation of the social consequences of the Industrial Revolution, however, was an original contribution that laid the groundwork for an historiographical tradition in economic history, the impact of which is still felt. His infusion of ethical, social, and religious ideals into economics made his work influential with Cunningham, Foxwell, the Webbs, and the Hammonds; but his magnetic personal inspiration was especially evident among the young Oxford economists of the 1880s.

An opportunity lost: economic study at Oxford

After Rogers's failure to retain his tenure, the Oxford chair of Political Economy was held by Bonamy Price from 1868 to 1888. He appears to have had little influence upon the views of the younger Oxford economists. Indeed, they rarely mentioned him in their writings, and then only parenthetically in this period of the ascendancy of college lecturers and tutors. In political economy in particular, because the examinations were optional subjects, an Oxford professor's prestige did not come naturally with his position within the university. He did little teaching and had few institutional levers by which to control college fellows, lecturers, and tutors. Further, Bonamy Price was, like Rogers, an old style liberal. Moreover, he exhibited little enthusiasm for contemporary social questions and adhered to a natural law view of social harmony. His published writings were few and amounted to little more than a manual of "practical economics" for businessmen and legislators that emphasized banking and currency, only L.L. Price among the younger economists showed much interest in this area and he cited Bagehot and Jevons rather than the Oxford professor. Broadly considered, however, Bonamy Price was part and parcel of that Oxford tradition that criticized theory and called for a practical economics. He distinguished "Practical Political Economy" from "Scientific Political Economy": "It is intended to indicate a mode of treatment which not only does not claim to be scientific but which supposes the strictly scientific method to be a mistake."[20] He also singled out Ricardo and the wages-fund for criticism. He hailed Adam Smith as the supreme practical political economist and urged a return to his mode of treatment of the subject. Finally, although he was a staunch defender of free trade, he defended it strictly on practical grounds.[21]

Oxford of the 1880s was a difficult place to launch a career in economics,[22] if one had to earn a living. Few positions were available for tutors, lecturers, or fellows in economics. Political economy was taught as a supplemental subject in classics or in the Honour School of Modern History, and virtually anyone with the vaguest familiarity with the subject felt competent to expound upon the subject. Toynbee's magnetic influence had briefly increased its popularity, but even he had to be content with a position as lecturer for the Indian Civil Service Examinatio· Upon Toynbee's death, Marshall brought real competence and enthusiasm for the subject to Oxford; however, after four terms – during which he had a considerable influence upon his student L.L. Price – he left to take up a professorship at Cambridge. Ashley had won a College fellowship at Oxford in 1885. Faced with the need to provide for his own income, he accepted a professorship at Toronto in 1888. Thus, another opportunity for a strong leader in Oxford economics was lost. A few years later, Hewins also left to become Director of the London School of Economics and Political Science.

One source of opportunity at Oxford was its university extension movement. Toynbee had given lectures at the local cooperative society, and after his death a trust was organized in his memory. With the aid of the co-operative movement the trust sought to establish centers of economic study in the provinces by dispatching resident lecturers from Oxford to conduct economic research and to teach. The scheme was designed both to promote economic knowledge among the workers and to enrich the university, "to which they would return strengthened by that experience, and touch with actual life, the actual flesh and blood of economics, which could be gained nowhere else so well as in the industrial centres."[23] The trust approached the university extension scheme for a combined effort. The latter was being prodded into action to provide greater opportunities for economic study and teaching by H.E. Sadler. In 1886, L.L. Price became the first to be appointed to a position in the new scheme. An extension summer school was founded in 1888 and Hewins became Secretary. Ashley also briefly lectured in the extension movement.

The scheme summarized some important aspects of the Oxford tradition in economics. It emphasized the practical nature of economics by its close relation to contemporary social and economic problems; it afforded an opportunity for the teaching of economic history; and it sought to increase the economic literacy of a wider population. The plan did little, however, to increase stable and long term employment for economists, because it entailed an itinerant life at low pay and recruited its lecturers from those who themselves were but a few years away from their degrees.

Another expression of the Oxford spirit in economics was the founding of the *Economic Review* in 1890. In both England and America, the 1880s saw the creation of a number of professional journals in history and the social sciences. In 1888, a group of Cambridge economists, led by Marshall, began discussions that led to the formation of a professional society for economists in England and the publication of a journal. But before the *Economic Journal* was founded, and with prior knowledge of the project, as Cunningham at Cambridge was deeply involved in the Oxford project, the *Economic Review* was launched at Oxford.[24] In 1889, Canon Scott Holland, a High Church Tory, formed the Oxford Branch of the Church Social Union as a center for the discussion of social and economic subjects. The *Lux Mundi* group, to which Ashley had links, dominated the Union and urged a fairly radical program of state sponsored social reform. This group founded the new journal. Edited by the Rev. L.R. Phelps, the *Review* called for the addition of an ethical dimension to economics and urged it to become a practical science again. The *Review* declared that it would not serve as "the organ of those who lean to historical methods" but would be open to all schools.[25] It was clear, however, that the journal was sympathetic to historical economics. Its first few issues contained articles by Cunningham, Hewins, Ashley, Laveleye, and R.T. Ely. Some of the most vehement attacks upon Marshall and his school appeared in these early issues. Conspicuous by their absence were articles by the theorists tied to Marshall. Despite the hope of some that the Oxford periodical would become the organ of historical economics in England, the impartiality and prestige of the *Economic Journal*, combined with the increasingly religious tone and the decline in quality of the *Review*, assured that the latter would not become the voice of academic historical economics.[26]

After the death of Bonamy Price, Rogers was reelected to the Oxford Chair in Political Economy. The other candidates included J.N. Keynes, Cunningham, Foxwell, Edgeworth, Inglis Palgrave, L.R. Phelps, and L.L. Price. This list gives some indication of the paucity of academic positions in England because it was widely felt, especially by the outside electors, that the place rightly belonged to Rogers. Marshall believed

that Price was the best qualified for the position.[27] Two years later
Rogers died. This time, it was felt within Oxford that L.R. Phelps, who
had done some research on the poor but little else in economics, should
be appointed. Ashley also entered the race from Toronto, but he was
never seriously considered. The election was won by Edgeworth, the
editor of the *Economic Journal*. The deciding factor in the choice of
Edgeworth appears to have been the Balliol connection. Edgeworth was
a Balliol man, as were two of the electors, and he was supported by
Jowett, Green, and Marshall.

The election of Edgeworth was unfortunate for Oxford economics,
although Ashley noted that Edgeworth was at least "a man of power
and distinction" whereas Phelps was an "evident mediocrity."[28] He was
completely out of sympathy with the prevailing historical and ethical
direction of economic studies at Oxford. Even though Price presented
a warm portrait of Edgeworth as a person, he was extremely critical of
his inability to promote economic study at Oxford. Price described economics at Oxford under Edgeworth as "slumbering quietly." He attracted few students to his "recondite education" and, as an *ex officio*
member, did not regularly attend meetings of the board of the Faculty
of Modern History.[29] Edgeworth's tenure prevented the flowering of
promising developments in historical economics at Oxford. Moreover,
his unassertive personality, his work in obscure mathematical economics, and his deference to Marshall also prevented the creation of a
theoretical school of economics at Oxford. First under Bonamy Price,
then under Rogers, and finally under Edgeworth, economics at Oxford
floundered without the direction of a strong leader such as contemporary
Cambridge enjoyed under Marshall.

L.L. Price and the study of economic history

Of the young men who studied at Oxford during the 1880s and who
became professional economists, only L.L. Price remained to promote
historical economics and economic history at the University.[30] Price was
born in London in 1862. He won a scholarship to Trinity College, earned
a first in Honours Moderations in 1882, and then won a first in Literare
Humaniores. He was trained by Marshall during his four terms at Balliol.
Marshall, who was a trustee of the Toynbee Trust, helped Price win the
trust's first lectureship. Price, well regarded by Marshall, had the honor
of reading Marshall's *Principles* prior to its publication. Early in his
career Price defended Marshall's views, but from the mid-1890s he took
a more independent line. After breaking with Marshall over tariff reform
in 1903, Price gradually aligned himself with the historical economists.

Before the First World War, Price was an active member of the new economics profession in England. He served as an external examiner at numerous universities, including Cambridge; as the Newmarch Lecturer on Statistics at University College, London, in 1895–96; as a member of the International Statistical Institute; and as a regular contributor to the Royal Statistical Society's *Journal*. He served on the original council of directors of the *Economic Journal* and was an honorary secretary of the Royal Economic Society. At Oxford, he was elected treasurer and a fellow of Oriel College in 1888 and resigned the former in 1918 and the latter in 1923. In 1907, he became the University's first lecturer in economic history and served as reader of the new discipline from 1909 until 1921. Despite his long and significant career at Oxford, he retired and moved to Brighton in 1923, never to return to Oxford prior to his death in 1950.[31]

Throughout his professional career at Oxford he worked to promote economic studies at a university that seemed determined to do little for the subject. For a quarter of a century he served as the secretary of the Oxford University Political Economy Club, originally founded by Thorold Rogers, and he attempted to keep the group alive despite Edgeworth's deadening influence on the organization. In 1902, Price wrote an open letter to the Chancellor to suggest the formation of a postgraduate school of economics at Oxford. He deplored the unsatisfactory position of economic studies in Oxford's Honours Schools. Noting the fuller development of economic studies at the newer universities, the LSE, and Cambridge (which is "continually producing young economists of capacity and attainment"), he appealed to Oxford's ideal of liberal education: "Those, indeed, who are interested in avoiding the dangers which threatens 'commercial education' if it becomes excessively technical, will welcome the liberating infusion of the study of Economics; and it has certainly as good a title as any branch of knowledge yet systematized to the prerogatives of a 'science of business.' " Further, if economics was to be one of the tools for improving the condition of the masses and of maintaining the economic well-being of the empire, then England would also have to train far more economic experts for both government and business, as was already being done in the United States and on the Continent. Ironically, just a year before the tariff controversy that rekindled the English *Methodenstreit*, he suggested that the acrimonious debates in economics characteristic of the last generation had passed, for the discipline had now attained "a considerable amount of general agreement on essential points." Finally, he appealed to the Oxford tradition of economics, "which is full of human interest, and has shaken itself free of the dry and barren legomachies which once hindered its advance."[32] In 1903, the University created a Diploma in Economics and a Committee for Economics. Price was Secretary of the latter from 1904 to 1922. The Oxford Diploma, to which Political Science was added in 1909, was a far cry from the Honour School Price had envisioned, though it did increase the demand for teaching economics. The program leaned heavily toward practical, historical, and inductive work. Only in the 1920s was an Honour School of Philosophy, Politics, and Economics created at Oxford.[33]

During the early part of his career, Price defended Marshall against the criticism of Cunningham and Ashley, though he was careful not to offend the historical economists. He did, however, question Marshall's view of the scientific economist as a neutral observer and noted in 1895 that economists have generally, and rightfully so, been advocates of social reform. Moreover, he insisted that the "professor has claim to take part in the guidance of economic affairs, which is derived from his scientific study."[34] For Price, economics was "essentially an applied science." He hastened to explain that economics did not merely furnish precepts immediately applicable to practice, but also supplied a body of systematic knowledge, the possession of which was crucial to the direction of practical affairs. In 1909, he returned to this subject. This time he pointed to the tariff controversy as an illustration of his argument and criticized those who applauded the divorce between theory and practice as leading to a more scientific economics. He, for one, was willing to give up some of the exactness of theory in order to attain a more general utility for the subject.[35] Nonetheless, he was not opposed to all neoclassical economic theory within its proper sphere. He, too, reminded his readers in 1892 that Adam Smith had practiced both deductive and inductive economics, but had used them for different purposes. Price concluded: "It is hard to draw a rigid line between deduction and induction, and to say where the province of the other begins."[36] This comment was characteristic, for he had little taste for controversy and was not primarily interested in the discussion of method. Rather, he sought to maintain a middle ground by allowing each component of the discipline to use its appropriate method.

In 1892, when Marshall was being assailed by Cunningham and Ashley, Price defended his former teacher in a review of Marshall's *Principles*. He noted that economics was leaving behind "a period of bitter, and sometimes idle, controversy" for a regime of conciliation in which "economists of different schools will pursue their own lines of study, and yet recognize that other methods may lead to useful results."[37] Moreover, Cliffe Leslie's charge concerning the insularity of English economics had been laid to rest, since Marshall had freely drawn upon the work of the Germans, the Austrians, the Americans, and the French. In addition, the special genius of Marshall's work was that he had restored the unity of economics by extending Jevons's pioneering marginal utility theory of value from the side of demand to that of production. Price also took great pains to demonstrate the influence of the historical economists upon Marshall's work. Marshall viewed Cliffe Leslie's revolt as a much needed corrective to the "dogmatic conclusions of some irresponsible disciples of the great masters." Price concluded that the historical movement emphasized the importance of facts, drew attention to the relation of economic phenomena to the whole of social and political life, and taught that economic theory had developed "under the influence of the particular environment of the time and place."[38] Thus, he insisted that Marshall had demonstrated the continuity of the economic tradition in England, and therefore, no revolution in methodology was needed. Instead, a methodological corrective had been required. The historical movement had supplied it and Marshall had accepted it.

Price did not share in the general criticism of Ricardo that was characteristic of historical economics. When Ashley criticized Marshall's defense of Ricardo, Price came to Marshall's defense. In 1888 he spoke out in favor of some aspects of the Ricardian theory of wages. A few years later, he observed that Ricardo's theory of rent ultimately amounted to the argument that rent was a payment for differential advantages and was thus consistent with modern theory. In addition, its applicability to such contemporary issues as the land question and the socialism of Henry George was a classic illustration of a false effort to apply the particulars of a theory of rent developed under one set of circumstances to an altered contemporary reality.[39] In later years, Price commented with some satisfaction that the Ricardian theory of rent, which "had been decreed a specimen of extremely abstract speculation" had been corroborated by his experience as Treasurer of Oriel College.[40]

When Cunningham attacked Marshall's comments on economic history in the *Principles* as mere theory, Price defended the utility of economic theory in the study of economic history. Here he was extremely cautious to argue that economic history ought not to be conjectural, for it must largely rely upon painstaking inductive research. Nonetheless, he claimed that without some theory intelligible economic history would be impossible.[41] In a review of J.S. Nicholson's *Principles* of 1893, he praised Nicholson's debt to historical economics as he criticized his value theory and his failure to use economic theory to enlighten his economic history.[42]

From the mid-1890s, at a time when Price was no longer a young economics graduate and had made a name for himself in both Oxford and the profession at large, he became increasingly independent from Marshall. He was especially critical of the use of mathematics in economics and feared that economics would thereby lose its popular audience in return for a dubious exactitude devoid of social application. To be sure, this fear was shared by Marshall, though Marshall used mathematics and Price did not. Some of the younger Cambridge students, such as A.C. Pigou, did delight in mathematical economics. Meanwhile, Edgeworth's example constantly reminded Price of this problem. In 1931 he told Cannan that he despaired over the future of English economic theory as it became increasingly abstract.[43]

Despite Price's skepticism concerning developments in mathematical economics, he remained convinced of the essential continuity and scientific value of English classical and neoclassical theory. Yet, ultimately, his views were closer to those of historical economics than the views of Marshall's school. First, Price constantly reiterated the theme that inductive research and economic history were essential limiting and corrective forces to economic theory. Second, he rapidly lost whatever interest he had had in the study of economic theory; from 1903 until his retirement, he devoted almost his entire career to the promotion of economic history and applied economics. Third, he saw little value in the study of economics as science and focused primarily upon its practical application. In this he followed Toynbee rather than Cairnes. His support for the study of economic history was equally utilitarian. He believed that, if men were to guide the future, they must first determine the direction of social evolution through the study of economic history. Fourth, his support of tariff reform created differences between him and Marshall that were never resolved. Price noted that in 1904 "Marshall chide me like an irate dominie flogging a naughty schoolboy, for my support of Tariff Reform."[44] Subsequently, Price became increasingly critical of Marshall's authority over the economic profession. Finally, and most importantly, Price asserted the cardinal principle of historical economics that economic theory was relative to a particular time and place. He held that it might in the future be possible, through supreme effort and persistent labor, to arrive at some kernel of universal economic theory, but the task was more difficult than had hitherto been imagined.[45]

Price devoted a good deal of attention to applied topics in economics such as industrial conciliation, the cooperative and trade union movements, money and prices, and tariffs. With so many other commentators of the time, he praised England's genius for "moderate and gradual social reform, based upon past experience of fact," rather than on theory.[46] As the first lecturer for the Toynbee Trust, he conducted a study of industrial relations in the Newcastle-upon-Tyne shipping industry that established the pattern of much of his subsequent work. He compared society to a biological entity, in which gradual and minute changes predominated. This discovery of the process of gradual social evolution, he argued, was carried over into social investigation by the historical economists and constituted one of their chief contributions.[47]

When Ashley praised Price's *Industrial Peace* as a work that, unaided by modern theory, demonstrated the merit of applying common sense to statistical and historical data, Edwin Cannan replied that the book's lack of theory was precisely its weakness.[48] Price responded that he had in fact used economic theory in his study, but that theory alone could not possibly prescribe the exact basis of the pacific settlement of wages. Although he agreed with Cliffe Leslie and Ingram that the role of custom and habit severely limited the mobility of labor, and called upon the theory of noncompeting groups, he insisted that their rejection of competition as a useful hypothesis was too extreme.[49] Price's careful inductive studies, aided by modern value theory, concluded that voluntary industrial conciliation schemes were preferable to both authoritative arbitration and the naked competition of unions and management. He especially advocated that wages be tied to a sliding scale of prices, as in Newcastle, but he was careful to note that different industries had different requirements and that no universal set of maxims could be asserted for the maintenance of industrial peace. Finally, he concluded that competitive forces were strong enough in most areas of the economy to maintain a theoretic minimum and maximum for the settlement of wages, to which any system had to adhere.[50] After about 1900, his view of trade unions as socially neutral gave way to a more positive view.

Beginning in the early 1890s, Price wrote a series of articles on co-operation that were synthesized in his 1914 study, *Co-operation and Co-partnership*.[51] He argued that the movement labored under a false theory. He began with an attack upon Karl Marx's theory of surplus value. Acknowledging Marx's contribution to a historical view of society, he repudiated his economic theory as too abstract and his forecast of the future as too cataclysmic.[52] He felt no need to dismiss Ricardo or Marx with abundant rhetoric, as other historical economists sometimes did. Instead, he counseled historical understanding: "We should approach the dead or dying notions of the past from the sympathetic standpoint of historical esteem."[53] Only in this fashion, he argued, would it be possible to appreciate how ideas themselves influence subsequent history, even if the ideas are no longer appropriate to subsequent circumstances.

After a balanced review of the social consequences of the Industrial

Revolution, he proceeded to an analysis of the nature and social context of the theory that came to be known as the doctrine of the wage-fund. For Price, it was Mill who was chiefly responsible for the erroneous theory of cooperation because Mill had prophesied a discouraging future for the working class and only through cooperation did he see a means of escape from this future for the workers. In short, Price noted, Mill's support of cooperation constituted "a half-way house" toward socialism. Finally, because Mill's authority over economic ideas was "monarchal," his view had become orthodoxy.[54] Price explained that Mill had worked with defective theories of population and capital that were better suited to the reality of the early nineteenth century than to the later period. Recently, Price continued, statistical evidence demonstrated that the standard of living of the workers had improved immensely under capitalism. Moreover, modern capital theory was able to take account of recent historical developments and thus prominently featured the role of the corporation and the wages of superintendence in its analysis. Price argued that, unlike classical economics or its socialist derivatives, modern theory did not predict disaster for the worker under capitalism. Instead, "the wage earner becomes an independent bargainer, using the strength which he possesses to improve his condition and increase his wealth."[55] Price's historical study thus broadly supported competition as the determinant of wages, but he did not argue for individual competition. Rather with Ashley he supported the collective bargaining of organized business and labor, aided by various state supported and voluntary schemes of conciliation, as the best hope for industrial peace.

Price also had a considerable interest in the problems of money, prices, and banking. In these areas he acknowledged the influence of Jevons and especially of Bagehot.[56] In *Money and Its Relation to Prices*, he argued that the impact of the new gold discoveries and the end of the monetization of silver in 1878 constituted a convenient empirical test of the effect of chance and government action upon prices. He concluded that, although in the long term the discovery of new bullion sources had influenced prices, the specific extent was impossible to measure by any general theory because a host of other factors had also been responsible for changes in the general price level. Though he saw perfect price stability as unattainable, he preferred a moderate increase in prices as more conducive to economic well-being than an equal decline.[57] In 1895, he judged bimetallism as superior to a sole reliance upon the gold standard; after World War I, he supported Irving Fischer's scheme of a variable currency tied to an index number and convertible to gold.[58] His moderate support of monetary reform was similar to the stronger views of Foxwell and Ashley. Its purpose was one means of smoothing out the irregularity of modern capitalism.

On the tariff issue, Price aligned himself with the historical economists in support of Imperial Preference. Starting out as a Liberal, he broke with the party over Home Rule. Speaking of the Oxford University Political Economy Club during the 1880s, he later wrote that the "majority of us would probably have been labeled as nursing a broad Conservatism, or, alternatively, as clinging to a moderate Liberalism."[59] In the early 1890s Price was still a free trader. He argued that Adam Smith's view of mercantilism had been perhaps too critical and conceded the cogency of List's National System and Mill's argument on the protection of infant industry, but remained convinced that free trade was the best policy for Britain. He based his arguments upon the value of freedom in general and upon the cosmopolitan benefits of an international division of labor in particular.[60] By 1900, however, he had become much more enthusiastic about the success of English mercantilism and lauded it as a national system that had laid the foundation of England's later industrial preeminence.[61]

For Price, as for so many others, the turning point appears to have been the Boer War, which so dramatically exposed Britain's increasingly precarious international position, demonstrated its domestic social needs, and heightened its imperial sentiments. In 1900, he wrote an important article on "Some Economic Consequences of the South African War." It was ostensibly a discussion of the impact of the war upon money and prices, but in reality it was a prophetic call for a debate on the need for an Imperial Zollverein as a component of Imperial Federation. He noted that it could not be denied that "the tendency of later economic reasoning had been to weaken some of the arguments urged for Free Trade." He went on to caution that protection carried with it both the political cost of corruption and the possibility of some immediate economic loss. Nonetheless, Imperial Preference also held out the hope of political gain through a strengthened empire. Further, a temporary economic sacrifice could lead to economic gains in the future.[62]

In 1902 Price reminded readers of the *Economic Journal* that the man in the street had been converted to the repeal of the Corn Laws by the logic of events in Ireland and the reality of British industrial preeminence. A half century later, however, the facts had been drastically altered, thus he continued, defense of free trade ought to be carefully reexamined.[63] He admitted the benefits to be derived from cosmopolitanism, but placed greater emphasis on the nationalist component within mercantilism that had been recognized by List, Carey, and the economic historians. He also used the argument, later popularized by Ashley, that the realities of trusts, labor unions, and monopolies suggested that some revisions might be required "of that assumption of competition between individuals, on which, Free Trade, together with the scheme of economic theory, with which it is linked, is, in the last analysis based."[64]

Before the details of Joseph Chamberlain's scheme for Imperial Preference had been provided, the leading British theoretical economists had publicly condemned his general proposal in a professors' manifesto in the *Times* of August 15, 1903. This hasty letter, signed by fourteen academic economists, among them Marshall, Edgeworth, Pigou, Bowley, and Cannan, and including their university affiliation, was truculent in tone and dogmatically denounced all arguments for an alteration in Britain's free trade system. The professors not only declared that free trade was the best system for Britain's particular circumstances, but also insisted that free trade theory was unassailable. Within the next few weeks, the historical economists Ashley, Cunningham, Hewins, Foxwell, and Price publicly declared that the manifesto had not taken account of their views and thus did not represent all "expert" academic opinion. Further, they noted that their historical and relativistic view of economic theory and policy barred them from categorically opposing all changes in Britain's fiscal policy without first conducting a careful inductive investigation of both the theory and Britain's circumstances. Finally, they complained bitterly that, despite the many recent voices of moderation in the *Methodenstreit*, which claimed that everyone now agreed on the hypothetical nature of deductive theory, modern theorists had ignored the message of the last few decades. Indeed, their support of free trade policy and theory was as dogmatic as classical theory had been.[65] Price's letter of protest to the *Times* appeared immediately following the manifesto he had refused to sign. He argued that the likely effect of the manifesto would be to stifle professional debate on the subject and push the debate in the direction "where the economist will be heeded solely for his value as a partisan and not invited to assist as an impartial expert."[66] In a rare public comment, Marshall reluctantly defended the professors' manifesto in response to his former student's criticism. Price committed himself to tariff reform in 1903 and became the president of the Oxford University Tariff Reform League.

Price argued that Imperial Preference offered real economic as well as political gains. He cited trade statistics to show Britain's declining exports outside the empire, a projected decline in the coal trade that was already evident, and the serious competition in the domestic economy offered by foreign manufactured goods. By contrast, he pointed to the recent growth in Britain's trade with the empire and offered the hope that tariff reform might allow Britain to offset losses in foreign trade with gains in the empire. To be sure, his scheme was not very far sighted, for he frankly envisaged an Imperial Zollverein in which Britain would export manufactured goods while the colonies – he included the Dominions in this phrase – exported food and raw materials with little realization of their own needs for industrial development.[67]

Price laced his arguments on the tariff issue with critical comments on the professors' manifesto and the harm it had done to the recent methodological reconciliation in British economics. The issue, he pointed out, demonstrated the importance of the economic historian to the discussion of public policy: "They would be more likely than those whose interests had not drawn them to the close scrutiny of recorded facts, to appreciate the need for the qualification of theory, and the adaptation of a policy, when circumstances to which their original acceptance had been due were altered or transformed."[68] Price went on to note that he despaired of the future of economic theory in England. Indeed, after 1903, which coincided with his public efforts to improve economic teaching at Oxford, he devoted the rest of his career at the University to teaching economic history and the history of economic thought. Having openly quarreled with Marshall in 1903, in 1904 Price also became embroiled in a controversy with Pigou. He severely criticized Pigou's inability to understand both the political issues and economic theory in favor of tariffs. Even though Pigou's defense of free trade was far bolder than Marshall's, Price could not resist noting that Pigou had an "almost filial" respect for the "utterances of Professor Marshall."[69]

Price never lost his respect for economic theory. He did, however, become increasingly critical of mathematical economics and abstract theory that claimed universality. Instead, he insisted that economics should remain a practical science relative to a particular time and place. Yet, Price never called himself a historical economist. His interest in economic history, his work in applied economics and the history of economic thought, and his increasing despair over the direction of economic theory under Marshall's successors had, however, finally brought him into a reluctant alliance with the historical economists. Price preferred to think of himself as an economist devoted to economic history. Ashley, his early colleague at Oxford, had no such reluctance and freely characterized himself as a historical economist.

CHAPTER 5

W.J. Ashley: the English socialist of the chair and the evolution of capitalism

Inspired by Toynbee and guided by the scholarship of the German Historical School of Economics, William James Ashley was the most promising and brilliant English historical economist. As a young Oxford economist, his politics were liberal. His opposition to Irish Home Rule, his experience in North America between 1888 and 1900, and his belief that capitalism's contradictions were bringing the liberal phase of history to a close made him an active supporter of imperialism and social reform. When still at Oxford, Ashley hoped that a historically derived economic theory would replace deductive theory as the core of English economics. Just prior to his departure for North America, he had already modified this historicist vision to a historist critique of deductive theory. During the 1890s he focused his attention on the development of economic history as a separate academic discipline. After 1900 he also devoted his talents to applied economics and the creation of a business curriculum at Birmingham. As a historical economist, he insisted that the relativity of economic theory could be demonstrated through economic history and the history of economic thought and that the purpose of economic scholarship was to help guide the nation peacefully toward a more orderly and just "socialized capitalism."

The Legacy of Toynbee, the Germans, and America

Ashley was born in 1860. He was the son of a sometimes unemployed London hatter and was brought up in the religious and political tradition of dissent. Educated in dissenting schools, he later carried his interest in a social Christianity into the established church, and became a supporter of the Church Social Union. After extensive coaching from the historians T.F. Tout and S.R. Gardiner, he won a Brackenbury historical scholarship to Balliol, Oxford, in 1878. He studied constitutional history under Stubbs and political economy in association with Toynbee. He earned a first in Modern History in 1881, won the Shakespeare and Lothian prizes, and obtained his MA in 1885. After gaining his degree, he earned a fellowship to Lincoln College. He found supporting himself difficult as a tutor and fellow at Oxford, and in 1888 he became professor of Constitutional History and Political Economy at the University of Toronto. Four years later, he moved to Harvard to become the first professor of Economic History in the English speaking world. He remained at this post until 1901, and then returned to England as professor of Commerce and director of the newly created Faculty of Commerce at the University of Birmingham. He died in 1927 as the first President of the Economic History Society.[1]

Ashley has been compared to Gustav Schmoller, the leader of the German *Kathedersozialisten*. Of all the English economists, Ashley was in closest sympathy with the Younger German Historical School.[2] In 1872, Schmoller led a group of younger German historical economists in the creation of the Verein für Sozialpolitik. The Verein combined the historical program of the older German Historical School with an active program of social reform designed to expand the role of the state in social and economic affairs. These *Kathedersozialisten* were not socialists; they advocated instead a program of state initiative and directed social reform in order to curb the instability and danger of class conflict, which they believed to be inherent in modern industrial capitalism and perpetuated by deductive social theory.

By 1879 the Verein had broken into warring factions. Adolf Wagner, whom Marshall cited as evidence that he had taken the criticism of German historical economics seriously,[3] led those who held that the historical criticism of economic orthodoxy was now complete. Thus, the time was ripe for the building of a new and historical economic theory derived from economic history. Schmoller headed a rival group that held that the time for such generalizations was not yet near and called instead for a vast research program in economic history. Schmoller championed the historical method against the deductive Austrian School in the famous *Methodenstreit* and gathered around him an extensive school of economic historians. Like the Marxists, Schmoller recognized the danger of class conflict in modern capitalism, but he rejected their solution of violent revolution. Instead, he argued that history exhibited a gradual evolution of the stages of economic, political, and ethical development that would ultimately contain the social problem with the aid of the growing ethical and administrative power of the state. The Verein was also politically divided. Schmoller defended Bismarck's opportunistic and protectionist policies, while the more liberal Lujo Brentano opposed the Chancellor's protection of industry and agriculture.[4]

In 1900, Ashley dedicated a volume of essays to Schmoller. He noted that although there were many matters on which he could not agree with the professor at Berlin, "I feel that for a dozen years I have received more stimulus and encouragement from your writings than from those of any others."[5] This encouragement Ashley defined as Schmoller's promotion of economic concerns in history, and of historical concerns in economics. From Oxford, Toronto, Harvard, and Birmingham, Ashley did more than anyone else to keep English readers abreast of German historical economic scholarship. He was extremely pleased when the University of Berlin awarded him an honorary doctorate in 1910.[6] Ashley, however, was not merely an imitator of German historical economics. The early influence of Oxford remained visible throughout his life, and his experience in North America also had a considerable impact on his ideas.

During the Oxford period of Ashley's career, his knowledge of German scholarship was limited. In 1880 he spent a month at Göttingen, where he was greatly impressed with the serious scholarship carried out in German universities. In 1883 and 1884 he spent two more brief holidays in Germany. There is no evidence that he had direct contact with leading members of the German Historical School during these visits. Further, he apparently did not yet read German comfortably. In later years he met Roscher, and just prior to the outbreak of World War I, he delivered a lecture course at the Hamburg School of Commerce. During the 1880s, however, his knowledge of German scholarship was derived from his reading of Cliffe Leslie and the enthusiasm for the scientific study of history that had been brought to Oxford by Stubbs.[7] Ashley himself acknowledged that his views were formed under the triple influence of Stubbs, Toynbee, and Schmoller.[8]

As part of his duties as a history tutor at Oxford, Ashley was required to lecture on political economy. Because he knew little of the subject, he went to Toynbee for instruction; but Toynbee refused to take him as a student and instead suggested that they jointly work out a historical treatment of the economic theories of wages. In 1890, Ashley told Brentano that he came to the serious study of economics through Toynbee, "whom I regard more than any other man as the source of whatever inspiration has come to me in the investigation and teaching of the subject."[9] While studying with Toynbee, he took up the work of Cliffe Leslie; only after having studied Leslie's praise of German economics did he turn directly to the Germans for further guidance.

Ashley's political views were much closer to those of Toynbee than to Schmoller's. Although assigning a larger role to the state than most English Liberals or contemporary Conservatives, he did not glorify the state as the embodiment of the ethical ideals of the nation. For Ashley, the state was a regulatory body that promoted industrial stability and national welfare through its mediation between the corporate interests of large combinations in both industry and labor. Further, such groups would serve as a buffer between the individual and society and create order out of the anarchy of individual competition. If Ashley's political views must be compared to those of a German economist, they ought to be likened to those of Lujo Brentano. Indeed, in 1887, Ashley praised Germany as the country from which a "more fruitful development of Economics" had been derived but he also criticized it for its narrow range, for "German writers seldom realize the atmosphere of individual initiative in which English and American thought moves."[10]

Ashley's lifelong interest in the connection between religion and social reform also owed its chief inspiration to Oxford. He credited Green with having substituted the "freedom from restraint" of the utilitarians with a new and more positive freedom that allowed "men to make the best of themselves,"[11] and Jowett had financed one of Ashley's trips to Germany. Though never a religious enthusiast, Ashley did participate in the Church Social Union in America. In England he supported various movements to provide Anglicanism with a social Christianity. Ashley contributed many articles and reviews to the *Economic Review* and continued to do so after many other economists no longer wrote for its pages.[12]

In 1886, a group of about twenty graduate students, teachers, and senior undergraduates formed the Oxford Economic Society. Ashley, its first Secretary, described the group as meeting twice a term to discuss original research in economic history and contemporary economic issues, and once a term to discuss economic theory. In 1887 he complained to E.R.A. Seligman at Columbia: "We work under great disadvantages – for those of us who teach for the Honour School of Modern History have still to struggle for the due recognition of Economic History and most of the rest of us are still expected by general opinion to teach Fawcett & Mill in a cut and dried fashion easy to be 'got up.' " On the same day, he wrote to Richard T. Ely, an early leader of the American Economic Association, to ask for a copy of its journal and program, so that the Oxford group might learn from the AEA's historical approach to economics.[13] From this Oxford group were drawn many of the early founders of Oxford's *Economic Review*.

In 1888 Ashley accepted an offer to become the first professor of Constitutional History and Political Economy at the University of Toronto. Ashley told Seligman that he left Oxford because the university burdened him with tutorial duties, leaving few opportunities for historical economic scholarship.[14] In 1890 Ashley presented himself as a successor to Rogers for the chair of Political Economy at Oxford. Ashley admitted that he had little chance of winning the post. Nonetheless, he was "convinced that the one chance for Pol. Econ. at Oxford is to bring it into sympathy & contact with the strong historical studies of the place."[15] Ashley collected testimonials from many prominent English and foreign academics, but he had little support within Oxford. He asked Seligman to recommend him as a historical economist, but without giving offense. He predicted that "they will elect Edgeworth: & Oxford will be doomed, for its sins, to unlimited psycho-mathematical economics."[16] In 1905 Ashley applied for one more position at Oxford, the Beit Chair of Colonial History. By now he had become bitter about his exclusion from Oxford. He told Bonar Law that he would probably be passed over because of his connections to the tariff reform movement: "That is dear old Oxford all over: the odium economicum taking the place of the odium theologicum."[17]

Ashley has been credited with laying the foundations of the Toronto Historical School of Economic History. He offered courses on such subjects as the elements of political economy, the history and criticism of economic theory, the history of economic development, and modern economic questions. He also organized a wide ranging voluntary seminar and was a popular and inspiring teacher. His tenure in Canada also had an impact upon his own development. He became increasingly troubled by the disintegrating forces within the empire. Conversely, he was impressed with the economic possibilities of trusts and government subsidies to the railways.[18] In 1890 he was offered the History chair at Sydney, Australia, but despite its handsome salary, he refused the post in order to continue his work in economics.

In 1892, when Ashley had become dissatisfied with the substantial burden of both lecturing and directing research on constitutional history that his post at Toronto required, he accepted President Eliot's invitation to become professor of Economic History at Harvard. At Harvard he played the role of a conciliator between the rival historical and theoretical views in economics. He developed courses in economic history and applied economics within a hitherto all theoretical department. It was Ashley who first developed the professional study of economic history at Harvard.[19]

As an associate editor and frequent contributor to the *Quarterly Review of Economics*, he sought to influence economic opinion in England. He asked Brentano, for example, to contribute a critical review of English economics and suggested that this article might note the neglected work of the English historical economists.[20] Throughout his career he kept the views of English historical economics before the readers of the learned journals, university students, and even the general public. He often achieved this aim by invoking the prestige of German and American historical economics to strengthen his case.[21] It had been Toynbee's Oxford, however, that had originally provided Ashley with his economic, social, and ethical inspiration.

Historical economics and economic history

While still at Oxford, Ashley stated his economic faith to his fiancee in the form of a critique of the theories of modern socialism. He argued that both the Marxist theory of surplus value and its doctrine of the inevitability of class war were based on an erroneous deterministic view of history and a too narrow Ricardian theoretical framework. He did agree, however, that such conclusions of socialist theory as the concentration of capital, the elimination of many small firms, and the pauperization of a large segment of the working class appeared to have been verified by economic history. The solution to the poverty problem, in particular, might lie with higher wages and the intervention of the state in the economy. Unfortunately, he continued, much contemporary economic theory seemed irrelevant to these problems.

Ashley saw the role of the economist as a social scientist geared to action. He told his future wife; "We can leave to the Cambridge people hair splitting analysis of abstract doctrine." Instead, after a historical inquiry into the direction of social evolution, the political economist must prod society in its natural direction. He told his fiancee, "That the principal branches of production and exchange will ultimately be organized socially, is as certain as the rising of tomorrow's sun." Indeed, the coming of socialism was not to be regretted; it was inevitable and "therefore it must be good, and therefore I must help it."[22] He expressed a similar faith in his inaugural lecture at Toronto.[23] In an essay toward the end of his life, in which he used the American term "evolutionary economics," he refused to speculate whether the process of evolution necessarily brought improvement. He was still insisting that the future called for an even larger role for the state in the economy; but by now he had moderated his enthusiasm for socialism and suggested that the desire for personal property was probably too deeply rooted in Western society to be completely eradicated.[24]

Ashley was also convinced that the evolution of society required the replacement of deductive economics with a historical approach to the subject. Nonetheless, his earliest comments on the *Methodenstreit* were moderate and conciliatory. After unfavorably comparing the prestige and study of economics in England with its position in Germany and America in 1887, he praised the historical work of Leslie, Ingram, and Toynbee. He argued that historical criticism had convinced the abstract economists that the main Ricardian theories are "only hypothetically true" and only under certain assumptions. Even if the historical economists believe that these assumptions can never be fully realized in reality, "to continue fighting this ground is to slay the slain."[25] The real divergence, Ashley argued, lay in how deduction would be used. Orthodox theorists insisted on beginning with abstract principles, introducing actual social conditions, and then determining how the principles were verified by facts. The historical economists, however, begin with a historical and statistical study of the circumstances of a particular country, trade, or industry. They then compare their results to those of deductive theory and suggest the need for alterations in theories derived from a different time or place. To the historical economist the discussion of economic theory must remain subordinate to the task of a broad historical understanding of society's evolution. But, he continued, the deductive economists will argue that the historical method will never produce truth in the form of economic laws. It is here, he argued, that the hold of Ricardian theory was pervasive, for by truth was "here meant, unconsciously perhaps, a number of neat abstract propositions, professing to explain large bodies of phenomena." He agreed that the historical method was unlikely to discover this kind of truth: "But if by 'truth' is meant such generalizations about the condition of things now and the direction in which they are going, as one of practical value to the politician or philanthropist, then historical inquiry has discovered truth, and will discover yet more."[26]

A year later in 1888, when Ashley presided over his own program at Toronto, he was more aggressive in his criticism of orthodox economic theory. In the preface to the first edition of his *Introduction to English Economic History and Theory*, he declared that all economists could now agree that evolution occurred in economic thought as well as in economic development. Thus, modern economic theories "are not universally true, they are true neither for the past . . . nor for the future." However, he continued, the controversy over the proper method of the subject remained to plague economics. Whatever the outcome of the *Methodenstreit*, he insisted, it was now clear that there was little utility in deductively deriving laws of the economic relations between individuals, such as those of wages, prices, rents, and profits. There was, however, great value in the use of the historical method in an "attempt to discover . . . the laws of social development – that is to say, generalizations as to the stages through which the economic life of society has actually moved."[27] This required not the mastering of a "modicum of abstract theory – no difficult task," but the tackling of contemporary problems through "direct observation and generalization from facts,

whether past or present: a method you can call 'inductive' if you wish
to be polite, or 'empirical' if you wish to indicate scorn."[28] Thus, what
Ashley had in mind when he spoke of the theory to be gathered from
historical economics was akin to modern stage theory of economic development, rather than the static theory of equilibrium taught by Marshall and his school.[29]

In 1888, Ashley sought to claim Price's work in applied economics as
the product of historical economics. He noted that Marshall had kept
the "old deductive Political Economy" alive in England not by proclaiming "dogma," but by forging "an engine for the discovery of concrete truth, an organon of universal application" for work too difficult
"to be done well by unaided common sense." But, Ashley argued,
Price's work precisely demonstrated the usefulness of the application of
common sense to historical and statistical material and it exhibited little
evidence that Price's knowledge of orthodox theory had significantly
aided him in this study.[30] Moreover, Price's advice on arbitration
stemmed from his knowledge of the empirical and historical circumstances. Thus the book's very character demonstrated its debt to historical economics rather than its adherence to Marshall's conception of
the discipline. Edwin Cannan, a young Oxford economist whose relations with Ashley were stormy, replied by defending economic theory,
though he did so as a relativist and not as a supporter of Marshall.
Cannan argued that the prime defect of Price's work was its neglect of
available economic theory. Further, the "new Political Economy,"
which Ashley heralded, had as yet produced few generalizations and
was nothing more than economic history.[31]

The relative merit of Ricardian theory was a constant source of disagreement between Marshall and his critics. Ashley was willing to praise
Ricardian theory as a brilliant formulation for a particular time and
place. He rejected, however, its universal applicability. In 1890 Marshall
entered a spirited defense of Ricardo in his *Principles*. Although his
defense was primarily aimed at Jevons's attack upon Ricardo, it was
also a response to the vigorous criticism that the historical economists
had aimed at the classical economic tradition – the continuity of which
Marshall, as the leader of deductive economics, staunchly defended.
Marshall insisted that Ricardo could not have fathered modern socialist
theory, because he had not advocated a labor theory of value; further,
he saw Ricardo's theory of agricultural productivity as a brilliant anticipation of marginal theory.[32] Marshall also charged that the historical
economists were poor theorists. Ashley retorted that, although Marshall
was perhaps England's finest theorist, he was a poor historian. A careful
reading of Ricardo, rather than a biased exegesis of the text, he insisted,

would show that Ricardo had indeed held a labor theory of value that furnished socialist theorists "with a text wherewith to disprove the justice of the modern system of distribution."[33] Throughout his career, Ashley rarely missed an opportunity to announce that Ricardian economics had finally been banished from England as a useful theory. In the controversy between Marshall and Cunningham over the nature and purpose of economic history, Ashley also supported the latter over the former.[34] In spite of these exchanges, relations between Marshall and Ashley remained cordial during the 1890s, although they had very little contact. Speaking of Cunningham in 1895, Ashley told Seligman: "I am very fond of him – & not without liking, of more recent origin, for Marshall – & like you, I have heard both sides – my professions being with C."[35]

In 1892 Ashley was again preaching conciliation between the two camps. This was partly due to intellectual conviction, to his new position at Harvard which forced him to work closely with economic theorists, and to his dislike for the shriller rhetoric which accompanied the Cunningham-Marshall exchange. With gratification, he observed that adherents of both induction and deduction had assigned a larger recognition to each other's methods in economic study. He also admitted that the historical economists had not realized Leslie's and Ingram's ambition of a complete transformation of economics into a historical discipline, for the aim had been too sweeping. Three years earlier he had told Seligman: "I only feel myself happy in the lowest depths of the 'historical school.' "[36] In 1893 he specifically repudiated the goal of replacing all deductive theory with a historical economics. Instead, as the professor of Economic History, he called for the establishment of economic history as a separate and respected academic discipline that provided conclusions as to the "character and sequence of the stages of economic development."[37] Historical economics had already achieved a subtle success by demonstrating "that economic conclusions are *relative* to given conditions, and that they possess only *hypothetical* validity." He also publicly deplored the acrimonious nature of both the "English and German *Methodenstreit*; "if only a band of fit scholars could be attracted to a field ønomic history] that cries out for labourers, we might call a truce to controversy as to economic method."[38] In 1899, still safely installed in his chair at Harvard but feeling increasingly drawn back toward England, he was also confident of the ultimate academic recognition of economic history and of its social utility. He proclaimed: "We who study economic history have with us the current of the world's thought."[39]

As a historical economist, Ashley insisted that the study of economic history must have a practical purpose. In 1899, Joseph Chamberlain helped to create the University of Birmingham out of an amalgam of existing institutions. He also urged the establishment of a Faculty of Commerce at the new university to provide practical economic guidance to the industry of the Midland city. With a recommendation from both Marshall and Cunningham, and his reputation as a distinguished historical economist, he was invited to leave his successful chair of Economic History at Harvard to head the new Faculty of Commerce at Birmingham and to become its first professor of Commerce. He told Seligman in 1901: "My feelings are naturally mixed. We are entirely glad to get 'home'; and I think I can do something for the old country."[40]

At Harvard, Ashley had been much impressed by the close connection between modern industry and American higher education. He had seen at first hand how the younger economists, who had learned in Germany that a "historical and statistical and inductive" method was essential for the study of concrete economic phenomenon, had created a number of business schools, including the famous Harvard Graduate School of Business Administration.[41] He warned that the coming competition between Britain and the United States would find Britain falling even further behind unless it was able to combine the spirit of enterprise and innovation, characteristic of America, with the rigorous professional training for business and government, that was taking place in Germany, France, and the United States. Marshall also often expressed such sentiments; making closer the relationship between business and education was one of his key arguments for the revitalization of British industry. It was Ashley, however, who worked to make the vision a reality.

Ashley believed that the best hope for professional education in business and engineering lay with the newer universities: "As an Oxford man, I say it with sorrow – the alienation of the business classes in England from the older Universities has gone so far that it is practically hopeless to expect to bring them now within their embrace."[42] He recognized that businessmen were reluctant to send their sons to the older universities, as after their return from college they were often unsuited to head the family firm or take their place among the new generation of corporate managers. This was a result, he argued, not only of the social atmosphere of the older universities but also of the lack of practicality offered by economic training at those institutions. At Birmingham, however, the university was "following the practical example of America."[43] He designed a broad business curriculum consisting of modern languages, accounting, applied science, business management, as well as commerce and economic history.

Conspicuous by its absence at Birmingham was a course in economic theory. He held that the role of the academic teacher was "not to elaborate some *a priori* theory, but to gather, arrange, and present the lessons of practical experience."[44] A student would learn an applied political economy not only of an individual firm, but also the underlying rationale of various commercial policies and the application of an inductive method to contemporary public and business problems. By the end of his career, Ashley was proud to have created a faculty of commerce in which economics followed a "concrete, descriptive, statistical, historical" method. He noted with some satisfaction that even Marshall had belatedly recognized the need for such a method, and added that Marshall's *Industry and Trade* was in fact the best book on applied economics that had thus far appeared in England.[45] Ashley's increasing involvement in public controversy on such matters as tariff reform and labor questions, as well as his government work, must be seen in the context of his new employment at Birmingham.

When in 1907 Ashley again reviewed the condition of political economy in England, he launched a strong protest against the marginal utility school. He charged that this thoroughly deductive new economic orthodoxy was "not much more than a verbal description of the superficial facts at a particular point in time."[46] He could still, however, be conciliatory; he noted that the deductive and inductive methods ought properly to be reserved for different purposes, and the word "analysis" might be broad enough to comprehend both methods. But such occasional peaceful overtures did little to enhance his position with the theorists. When Marshall retired in 1908, Ashley applied for the Cambridge chair. Marshall used his considerable influence to secure it for the much younger economic theorist, A.C. Pigou.[47]

The Cambridge chair was the last for which Ashley applied. His role in the tariff controversy also apparently excluded him from ever becoming president of the Royal Economic Society. Foxwell later referred to this as the "Ashley Scandal."[48] Seeing himself as an outsider in an economic profession that in England had become dominated by the followers of Marshall, he was both surprised and pleased when he was asked to be president of Section F of the British Association in 1907. He told Milner that his status as an outsider was a result of his pleas for historical economics and Imperial Preference. As a student at Oxford, his humble background had made him a social outsider.[49]

The economic historians paid tribute to Ashley by electing him the first president of the Economic History Society in 1926. In his presidential address, he expressed disappointment that, though the historical movement in economics had succeeded in gaining academic recognition for economic history as a separate field of study, it had failed to create a "doctrine of the economic development of nations" as Roscher had hoped.[50] He warned that the division of economics into its constituent branches threatened to undermine even the limited success that historical criticism in economics had achieved. Noting that the history of economic thought was now to be housed within departments of economics, rather than being located with the economic historians, he warned that this would leave the theorists without the continual reminder of the hypothetical nature of their conclusions, which had been provided by the economic historians; at the same time, the economic historians would be divorced from economic theory. Thus, by the end of Ashley's life, the *Methodenstreit* had resulted in a truce based upon the division of economics into its various branches that allowed each its appropriate method. Ashley, however, was never able to wholeheartedly accept the solution of cultivating "a little garden plot of our own."[51]

The lessons of economic history and applied economics

J.H. Clapham recognized Ashley as one of the founders of economic history as a separate academic discipline.[52] Even when Ashley treated constitutional questions, he did so in social and economic terms. His aim was "to try to discover the meaning of institutions, their growth and decay, their relation to one another, and to generalize from his comparative data."[53] He cited Karl Lamprecht, a well-known German social historian, to argue that the dynastic and political emphasis in most history had resulted in the neglect of crucial social and economic factors, the conditions that primarily determined the history of a nation. Similarly, he warned that economic history could not be a mere history of wages and prices, but that it must adopt a largely "institutional" framework. Stubbs had taught him at Oxford to emphasize the study of primary sources, but his twelve years in America made original research in unpublished sources difficult. As a result, his history was primarily a synthesis of the work of others, especially of German scholarship. He defended it as an attempt to provide a typology of the stages of production accounting for the economic theory and political organization within each stage.[54]

In his medieval economic history he was especially critical of the use of modern economic theory to understand the past. He held that the medieval economy had no competition, cost of production, profit, or mobility of labor, as modern economic theory understood these terms.[55] He was also critical of the "mark" theory which had been popularized by Maine and the German historians. He maintained that the theory's argument that serfdom in England had been imposed upon a free village community – an argument that had been used by Henry George for the nationalization of land and by Maine as a justification of conservatism – was, like so many other theories, contrary to the facts.[56] Instead, he patiently chronicled the rise of a natural manorial economy and plotted its transition to the limited market economy of the craft and merchant guilds. Though he much admired the regulated economy of the medieval town, he insisted, in opposition to Rogers, that the nationalization of the craft guilds and the Elizabethan system of social legislation had indeed improved the condition of the people; moreover, the concern for using the state to promote social well being "conveys a perpetual lesson to modern economists."[57] Unlike Cunningham, who saw the Tudor period primarily as the birth of English nationalism, Ashley's interest in social reform led him to emphasize the social aspects of Tudor legislation.

Ashley was much impressed with the political, social, and economic benefits of a landowning peasantry. He offered a "rise of the gentry" explanation for their demise. Further, during the nineteenth century, the classical economists had sanctioned the self-interest of the Tory landlords in large-scale agriculture, and the "social gulf between the farmer and the laborer was left bridgeless."[58] In addition, the gap between owners and workers had been widened by the Industrial Revolution, which had both seriously eroded living standards before 1840 and more recently increased economic insecurity. Replying to criticism of his pessimistic interpretation of the social consequences of nineteenth century economic history, he declared: "I do not see how it can be denied that the most grievous features in the condition of the people were in the main a result of the unbridled competition of the previous century."[59]

In the tradition of Leslie and Toynbee, Ashley saw the history of economic thought as an integral part of economic history. In his history of medieval economic thought, which comprised half of his work on medieval economic history, he protested against a view of the subject "as a museum of intellectual odds and ends, where every opinion is labeled as either a surprising anticipation of the correct modern theory or an instance of the extraordinary folly of the dark ages."[60] Instead, he held that economic thought was a continuous stream, dependent upon its past and moving towards its future, that reflected the economic conditions of a period. Even in his important study of Canonist economic thought, he could not refrain from the observation that the medieval conception of economics as a practical and useful art was better suited to the needs of its time than were modern hypothetical and abstract doctrines suited to the needs of the present.[61] He also undertook a substantial study of mercantilist writers of the period 1673–1713, with emphasis on the empirical method of their economic writings and their practical solutions to contemporary problems.[62]

Ashley planned a systematic study of nineteenth century economic thought, but he never completed this task. Of all the classical English economists, Ashley was most drawn to J.S. Mill, whose work he edited for a student edition. Though he often criticized many aspects of Mill's work, he praised his efforts at social application and observed that "even Mill had been breathed upon by the historical spirit."[63] If modern economics had made advances in theory, Ashley concluded, it was not "the result of an acuter analysis of unchanged facts, but the reflex of thought in phenomena newly emerging, from time to time in the external world."[64]

By the late 1890s Ashley was increasingly dealing with contemporary history. In 1903 he described his frustration at being characterized as a medieval and early modern economic historian, at a time when his developing interests were contemporary: "I never wanted to be a medievalist for medievalism's sake."[65] At Harvard, however, Taussig developed theory and Cummings worked in applied economics. Ashley's place was the promotion of economic history, especially English economic history. As an outsider, he found it difficult to apply his scholarship to contemporary issues. His chair at Birmingham, however, provided him with the perfect opportunity to turn his attention to the inductive study of modern labor, industry, fiscal policy and agriculture. In 1908, he suggested that historical economists had perhaps devoted too much time to the study of economic history; though economic history was essential in suggesting the future of society, it could not be assumed that the "history of earlier centuries would of itself indicate the meaning and tendency of modern conditions."[66]

In his applied economics, which included large doses of economic history, Ashley described the relations between the employer and employed under laissez faire as industrial warfare. His aim was to prevent that warfare from breaking out into open and violent class conflict. Instead of free competition, he sought to foster the growth of corporate institutions to act as a buffer between individuals and society. His chief hope for establishing industrial peace in modern society was "through the combination, alike of workpeople and employers."[67] Going beyond Toynbee, he also confidently embraced the regulating power of the state. He no longer believed, as he had at Oxford, that the social consequences of nineteenth century capitalism would inevitably lead to socialism. Instead, he now held that through trusts, labor unions, and government regulation "the evils attending capitalism can be vastly lessened without abolishing the existing system in toto."[68] In short, he hoped to "social-ize" capitalism.

His admiration of trusts flowed naturally from his Toynbean rejection of the ideal of individual competition and was greatly strengthened by his experience in America. Writing in support of the Canadian Sugar Trust in 1889, he held that, despite the teaching of orthodox economic theory, there was nothing sacred about the principle of competition. The sugar combine, for example, had ended competition. Yet, it had provided the industry's workers with regular employment, as at the same time it had reduced risks for the owners. By contrast, unbridled indi-vidual competition had provided England with cheap manufactured goods, but it had also brought irregularity of employment that threat-ened the nation with "social revolution."[69] As Booth was beginning his investigations into London living standards, Ashley pointed to the un-healthy conditions in London's sweated trades as powerful inductive proof of the consequences of unlimited individual competition.

In 1899 Ashley declared that trusts were not merely the incidental results of protection, commercial crisis, or temporary overproduction, as many theorists held, but the natural and inevitable outgrowth of free competition. In fact, trusts represented the next stage of business or-ganization.[70] Even in England, where trusts were less prevalent than in America, he argued that they were technologically necessary, encour-aged efficient production, and fostered industrial peace. Further, they also contributed to the welfare of the people: "I am convinced that in future generations the era of unrestricted competition, with its recurring crisis will seem like a malady of childhood . . . I regard the regularization of production as the best hope for the labouring classes, for whom steadiness of remuneration is far more important than the amount of remuneration.[71] His subsequent support of tariff reform was to be partly based upon this demand for regular employment, which he believed was encouraged by modern large scale industry.

Ashley was also a lifelong supporter of the trade union movement. Even in Canada he urged the acceptance of trade unions.[72] Likewise in the United States, he worked on their behalf.[73] He believed, however, that there was more hope of advancing the cause of labor in England than in America. He was often critical of such solutions to the labor problem as the cooperative movement or profit-sharing. He deemed such schemes impractical, for they failed to take account of the fun-damental differences between capital and labor in modern industrial society. Lasting social peace and industrial stability, he insisted, could be secured only through the collective bargaining of organized labor and organized capital. To aid collective bargaining, he urged the establishment of boards of conciliation for key industries. Such boards, consisting of industry and union representatives, as well as a nonvoting public member, would meet periodically to adjust wages before actual industrial strife erupted. In private correspondence, as a member of the Unionist Social Reform Committee, and as a participant in various government commissions, as well as in his writings, he continually urged the business and government establishments to accept the trade union movement as an indispensable aid to the creation of industrial peace.[74] He also attempted to devise measures for the pegging of wages to changing prices and exhibited sympathy toward a bimetallist monetary solution to industrial fluctuations.[75]

Ashley presented an original analysis of tariff reform that was heavily indebted to his argument on trusts and his interest in social reform. It began with the conviction that a nation should aim for a balanced and diversified economy. The Ricardian dream of world specialization, based on the assumptions of the perfect mobility of labor, free competition, and the international adherence to free trade, he believed to be demonstrably inconsistent with historical reality. He was especially alarmed at the decline of Britain's staple industries. With an eye on the relatively small and inefficient industries of Birmingham, he declared that the British home market was not sufficiently large to derive the economies of scale inherent in modern large scale heavy industry, or that such economies were at least not attainable to the same extent as in the large protected American home market. An imperial market, however, might offer similar advantages to Britain. Even without such an imperial solution, he warned, the problem of trusts would demand some form of protection for England, since foreign trusts periodically dumped their surplus goods upon the English market at a price below both the domestic and international cost of production. Further, because large scale production was capital intensive and demanded a continuous production process that could not be periodically interrupted to make room for dumped goods, it would erode Britain's productive capacity.[76]

He also rejected Giffen's contention that England could survive on its earnings from invisibles, for he perceived that the shipping trade was already declining and forecast that the entrepot trade would also vanish from British soil. Finally, a reliance upon the earnings from invisibles would neither provide employment nor maintain Britain's productive capacity. Both were essential to its economic and political survival. Under free trade, Britain's future would present the spectacle of a London dominated by sweated industry and the rest of England like a new Holland, surviving as an "agreeable place of residence for *rentiers*" and becoming dependent upon a flourishing tourist industry.[77] To prevent such disagreeable prospects, he suggested the implementation of a carefully constructed program of protective tariffs and imperial preferences, designed to protect England's staple industries until such time as a growing Imperial market, combined with the rationalization of British industry, could reap the increasing productivity derived from large scale production that was already evident in Germany and America.

Ashley agreed with other historical economists that free trade neglected British industry in favor of British finance. He invoked the writings of List to argue that the orthodox economists championed cheap and immediate consumption over the more important interests of long term productive capacity, political power, regular employment, and industrial security.[78] He frankly acknowledged that his program would indeed increase the price of food. He also pointed out, however, that the incidence of this taxation was not yet known and was certainly not predictable without a careful inductive investigation. In a study of Germany under protection, he lauded its effects upon both German industry and the standard of living of its workers. He also praised Bismarck's scheme of social welfare legislation and observed that the Social Democratic Party's abandonment of its revolutionary program and its acceptance of revisionism had clearly proven that the combination of protection and social reform had successfully blunted the revolutionary potential of capitalism in Germany.[79] Protection, Ashley argued by analogy, might also foster social peace in Britain.

Ashley insisted that his views were a consequence of his social imperialism. In 1913 he told Brentano that, although he had been brought up a strong Liberal, from the time he had come under the influence of Toynbee, he had developed a serious interest in social reform and had begun to move away from the Liberal Party, because the "party has never . . . been fundamentally the party of social reform."[80] During his last few years in America, while working on a study of "The Tory Origin of Free Trade," the physiocrats, and contemporary economic problems, he became increasingly concerned about the direction of English Liberalism. In 1897, he told Graham Wallas that he had joined the Imperial Federation League. In Canada, however, imperial federation had appeared hopeless, for the younger generation had little contact with England and looked toward integrating the Canadian economy with that of the United States. More recently, he continued, the Canadian tariff had made him more hopeful that some imperial scheme might yet be designed and "my residence in the U.S. has worked up the John Bull within me so that I feel a keener desire for British unity." He concluded this argument with the observation that his "Socialist Imperialism" was also rooted in his belief that the very large scale industry made possible by a secure imperial market would give Britain the opportunity of "socializing our industries."[81]

When Joseph Chamberlain announced his tariff reform campaign in 1903, Ashley became one of the most articulate academic supporters for the program. John Morley charged in Parliament that Ashley's *Tariff Problem* had been written at Chamberlain's request and that Chamberlain had even suggested its content. Ashley replied both publicly and privately: "My book was written entirely of my own notion, and without the slightest inspiration or direction." He added that his position at Birmingham had been a mere accident and that if he had been at Manchester, the professors' manifesto would nonetheless have produced a similar response from him.[82] Indeed, while still in America Ashley had begun to collect material for a study of English trade policy. The new political situation, to be sure, did hasten the study and gave it a specific focus. Moreover, Ashley, who often defended Chamberlain publicly, freely criticized him privately for his economic ignorance.[83]

In 1904, Ashley contacted Bonar Law for facts and figures on current trade statistics for an article in the *Economic Journal*. He apologized to Law for his intrusion on such an academic matter, "but it is of the utmost importance that we should know what the facts are: and I do not despair of breaking down the unfortunate resistance of most of my Economic colleagues to new ideas if facts can be produced on which the reasonable man can agree."[84] He also supplied Law with information on the opinions of British, American, and German economists in favor of tariff reform – arguments later used by Law in his speeches. It was not until 1906 that Ashley formally joined the Unionist Party. He became a member of F.E. Smith's Unionist Social Reform Committee and helped formulate an unauthorized social program, that urged the establishment of boards of conciliation, a minimum wage, provisions for the casual and dead-end laborer, and an agency for the collection of adequate statistics as a basis for further social reform.[85]

One of the constant themes of Ashley's advice to politicians was that they should associate tariff reform with social reform; further, they certainly ought not to oppose social reform on the grounds of individualism. He suggested, for example, that the Fabians were not necessarily opposed to tariff reform. Shaw, for example, was a protectionist and Sidney Webb was not unsympathetic. Ashley went on to note that they are not very enthusiastic about "merely protective" measures, and they have been very much disgusted about the way the "Liberal Party has fallen back into its *Individualism*"; but if tariff reform was combined with social reform – a social imperialism – they might be much more favorably disposed to Chamberlain.[86] Ashley was also linked, but less closely, with Stanley Baldwin. In addition, he served on a Unionist agricultural committee in 1913, a 1915 Committee on Trade Relations after the war, a wartime Royal Society Food Committee, a committee on the effect of reparations upon trade and industry (for which he produced a joint memorandum with J.M. Keynes), a Safeguarding Committee of 1921, and an Agricultural Tribunal of 1923. In all these varied activities Ashley advocated an imperial approach to tariff protection and did not neglect to push for policies that he believed in the general interest of social reform. He told Law in 1913: "I am perfectly ready the State should regulate everything it *can* regulate. I believe that is the essential Tory principle."[87] But during the 1920s, Ashley and Hewins learned, much to their regret, that the Conservative Party generally placed its narrow protectionist interests before those of imperial preference and social reform.[88] Instead, Ashley focused on the dominions and argued for a "Democratic Imperialism."[89]

Despite his frequent involvement in the public discussion of social and economic policy, Ashley remained a "socialist of the chair." He reminded his audience that the continued adherence to principles of laissez faire was not based upon the principles of science, but upon a "mental attitude, an outlook, a philosophy of society." If only economists had listened more attentively to the historical economics of Cliffe Leslie, Ingram, and Toynbee, he continued, economic policies might already have been adopted in England that were more appropriate to its stage of production.[90]

At Oxford, Ashley had become convinced that orthodox political economy would be unable to solve, and would even intensify, the contradictions that he believed inherent in nineteenth century capitalism. He had set out to build a historical economics capable of peacefully guiding England toward the collectivist society that history had taught him to be inevitable. Such an economics, as Ashley believed Toynbee, Cliffe Leslie, and the German historical economists had taught, might be constructed from inductive economic research and would ultimately replace deductive economic theory as the central concern of economic study. Chiefly engaged in the establishment of economic history as a recognized component of economic study while in America, he came to realize, as had Schmoller, that his earlier goals had been too sweeping. Upon his return to England, he became increasingly skeptical of the specific social utility of economic history. He did, however, see it as critical to understanding the direction of social evolution and for distinguishing stages of production and as a reminder of the relativism and hypothetical nature of economic theory. At Birmingham, he was a pioneer in providing a professional education for business and simultaneously lent his economic expertise to politicians and government in an effort to foster his social imperialist ideals. Meanwhile, the claims of historical economics were advanced at Marshall's Cambridge by Cunningham and Foxwell.

Historical economics at Marshall's Cambridge: H.S. Foxwell and the irregularity of capitalism

While Alfred Marshall labored to provide a solid foundation for neo-classical economics at Cambridge, H.S. Foxwell and William Cunningham advanced the claims of historical economics at the University. Foxwell especially sought to limit the uncertainties characteristic of industrial capitalism. During his long career at Cambridge, he became increasingly hostile to Marshall's vision of economic thought. Unlike Cunningham, however, Foxwell cannot simply be catalogued as an inductive economist as Marshall is taken to represent the deductive tradition.[1] Nonetheless, as A.L. Bowley suggested, "Foxwell's bent was historical."[2] His emphasis was on historical and inductive work in applied political economy and the history of economic thought. Marshall's interests, on the other hand, were primarily theoretical, especially during the period of his Cambridge professorship from 1885 to 1908.[3] In addition to divergent methodological emphasis, Foxwell and Marshall also disagreed over the direction of economic studies at Cambridge and on such policy issues as tariffs, bimetallism, and the advantages to be derived from free competition. Finally, they promoted nearly opposite interpretations of the history of British economic thought, particularly on the value of Ricardo's contribution. Although both Marshall's and Foxwell's positions on many of these issues were considerably more ambiguous than those of Marshall's student and successor at Cambridge, A.C. Pigou, or the more vehement historical positions of Cunningham, Marshall championed the utility of deductive theory both for creating a science of economics and for promoting Britain's welfare, and Foxwell placed his faith in inductive economics as the best guide to policy.

Foxwell's emphasis on the irregularity of capitalism was heightened by his personal and academic experience. Born in 1849, he was the son of a merchant who had lost a large part of his capital in the financial crisis of 1866. The cost of his own extensive collecting of rare economic books and pamphlets brought him often to the edge of bankruptcy. His religious views also strengthened his dislike of the insecurity of laissez faire capitalism. He quoted with approval the maxim: "The two great controlling and transforming elements of society are religious ideas and economic forces." A devout Wesleyan Methodist, who in his youth exhibited a more than ordinary interest in sermons, he was sympathetic to the moral earnestness and corporate idealism characteristic of the Oxford of Green and Toynbee and shunned the more individualistic, logical, mathematical, and scientific tradition prevalent at late nineteenth century Cambridge.[4]

Foxwell's academic career was as precarious as his financial position. He matriculated into the University of London in 1866 and received his BA in 1868. In the same year he entered St. John's College, Cambridge. After being placed senior in the Moral Science Tripos in 1870, he won the Whewell Scholarship in International Law in 1872. He was elected a fellow of the college in 1874. Under the old statutes he was forced to vacate his fellowship when he married in 1898, but he was able to resume it in 1905 and retained it until his death in 1936. From 1875 until 1905, he served as college lecturer. At first he taught the whole area of the Moral Sciences, but while Marshall was at Bristol and Oxford from 1877 to 1885, Foxwell taught honors courses in Economics. Appointed as a university extension lecturer in 1874, he taught widely in the north of England. From 1874 he also served as an examiner for the Moral Science Tripos in association with Jevons. In 1876 he became a lecturer at University College, London, and succeeded Jevons as its professor of Political Economy in 1881.[5]

Foxwell was recommended to the London post by Cliffe Leslie, Sidgwick, and Marshall. Significantly, Marshall commented that Foxwell's chief interest lay in the history of economic thought, a subject that also fascinated Marshall early in his career but that he later found of less consequence.[6] From his deathbed, Leslie wrote that despite the numerous differences between himself and Foxwell, "of all the probable candidates for the Chair . . . you are the one to whom I should look with the greatest hopefulness to keep the teaching of Political Economy in the chief College of London on a level with the movement of modern thought, historical research, and scientific method."[7] As if to counter Leslie's hope for the propagation of historical economics at University College, Sidgwick noted that, although Foxwell exhibited historical tendencies, he was in no danger of disparaging abstract and theoretical work, for he will "always seek and find a safe middle course between these opposite dangers."[8]

Despite his frequent travels to London, Foxwell remained firmly committed to Cambridge life. He lived a few doors from J.N. Keynes in Harvey Road and was well-known in Cambridge economic circles. When Marshall returned to Cambridge in 1885, he quickly overshadowed Foxwell. Marshall's efforts to embody his conception of economics in the

Cambridge curriculum left little room for historical economics and economic history.[9] Forced to compete with the personal and intellectual influence of Marshall and his successors, Foxwell failed during his sixty-year career at Cambridge to achieve an academic post above that of college lecturer and, from 1905 to 1936, director of Economic Studies at St. John's College.

Foxwell's chief inspiration in economics was derived from two critics of Ricardo: Toynbee and Jevons. From Jevons, Foxwell derived his interest in statistics, credit cycles, bimetallism, and book collecting. He was also an enthusiastic supporter of Jevons's effort to construct a mathematical economics and especially of his attempt to construct such a theory inductively from the statistics yielded by economic history. Toynbee, who used Foxwell's library to document his attack on Ricardo, had taught Foxwell the importance of economic history and a catastrophic interpretation of the Industrial Revolution.

In 1887 Foxwell wrote an important account of the crisis of English political economy during the 1860s and 1870s.[10] His study was both a criticism of English classical economics and the best contemporary account of the origin of English historical economics. He located the latter's roots in the trade depression of the last quarter of the century, in the loss of Britain's industrial leadership, and in the growing awareness of the immorality of an economic science that promoted excessive individual competition. Nonetheless, he generously praised Marshall's economics. Speaking of his *Economics of Industry*, he applauded Marshall's repudiation of the classical theory of value, "while in the handling of practical questions, it showed that a theorist need not be a materialist or a doctrinaire"; moreover, "the work gained for economics the forfeited respect of the abler artisans."[11]

Ten years later Marshall wrote a similar account of British economics, in which he made major concessions to the historical position. Marshall's chief thesis was that the old political economy had been too confident and dogmatic. Since the older generation had not been sufficiently aware of the evolutionary nature of society, he argued, it had employed its own world as a model from which to construct a universal science.[12] Although Foxwell agreed that the theories of classical economics needed to be qualified as to time and place, he also declared that classical economics was fundamentally unethical:

In its spirit, it was strongly materialistic, sacrificing national welfare to the accumulation of individual wealth. . . . Worst of all, it was distinctly unmoral (a more serious defect than immorality, which provokes a reaction) in as much that it claimed that economic action was subject to a mechanical system of law, of a positive character, independent of and superior to any laws of the moral world.[13]

In 1884 he told an artisan audience that the old political economy was also false, for it consisted of superficial laws of industry and trade, "Imperfectly based on history, and uncorrected by statistics," upon which had been founded a "dismal and ungenerous dogmatism" of laissez faire.[14] Despite Marshall's frequent moralizing, he argued that vigorous individual competition was the critical assumption that made economic science possible; furthermore, competition constituted an essential element of human freedom and provided the fundamental explanation of England's industrial wealth.[15] Foxwell, to the contrary, criticized orthodox economic theory precisely because it championed the benevolent consequences of individual competition. This encouragement violated his moral framework, which was perhaps ultimately rooted in his religious sympathies. Instead, he held that laissez-faire capitalism fostered social instability and even social revolution.

Foxwell argued this theme in his lectures, in a pioneering article of 1888 on the benefits of monopoly, and in his remarkable statistical and historical study, *Irregularity of Employment and the Fluctuations of Prices*, published in 1886. This much neglected book reemphasized the arguments of some early nineteenth century economists that irregularity of employment, rather than the level of wages per se, was the chief cause of distress to the working classes. Because the classical economists had viewed capitalist society as a mere mechanism, characterized by perfect competition and a complete mobility of labor and capital, Foxwell argued, they had greatly underestimated the social impact of structural alterations in the economy on the weaker elements of society.[16] Foxwell also directly challenged Robert Giffen's optimistic assessment of the condition of the working class. He insisted that statistics demonstrating the higher wages of workers failed to consider the precariousness of such wages in the irregular employment characteristic of a cyclical laissez-faire economy.[17]

Foxwell, and English historical economics as a whole, had considerable sympathy for the stability and corporate existence of the Middle Ages. He saw its social stability as having been shattered by the growth of capitalism. Moreover, the Industrial Revolution of 1760 to 1850 "marks the reign of industrial anarchy" and the birth of that "half starved misery" known as the proletariat. The proletariat in particular was the result of the "uncertainties of the labor market."[18] He conceded that most of the unfortunate social consequences of the Industrial Revolution had now been alleviated by the growth of state interference, although laws had often been passed in opposition to the doctrines of classical economics. Nonetheless, he warned, the recent wave of worldwide industrial protest continued to attest to the chronic instability of modern industrial society, which placed the value of individual profit above that of corporate responsibility.[19]

Foxwell's program of social reform exhibited his essentially Toynbean ideal. "The new political economy," he noted as early as 1884, "does not dogmatize as to the best social policy. But few will study it long without forming some general views as to the direction of future progress."[20] He advocated such measures as increased government regulation of major industries, support for profit sharing and cooperative schemes, the encouragement of trade unions, an expanded role for the state in providing housing, health, and education, the promotion of friendly societies and other voluntary associations, a wider diffusion of economic information, and efforts to smooth the operation of the financial and commodities markets. Thus far, his program was orthodox, though progressive. In a highly suggestive line of analysis, however, he broke new ground by suggesting that an increase in government employment would enhance industrial stability through the creation of a large and constantly employed civil service; furthermore, he noted that large-scale improvements in public works should be reserved for years of sluggish industrial and commercial activity.[21] His ideal solution to industrial instability was, as was Toynbee's, a conservative one. He promoted a corporatist scheme based upon a vertical organization of society inspired by the medieval guild structure.[22]

Foxwell's explanation of the benefits of monopoly was a natural outgrowth of this attack on unregulated competition. He asked whether competition was a benevolent force that promoted welfare, as Adam Smith had maintained, or whether it was detrimental to many, as Thomas Carlyle and Robert Owen had suggested. He noted that for most English economists the answer was the former; furthermore, this very assumption made deductive economics possible. He agreed that there were desirable forms of competition, but he found most competition to be largely destructive; most competitors had not aimed at efficiency, but at destroying the productive power of other firms or nations. Thus, instead of perfect competition leading to efficiency and the multiplication of firms, as the classical model predicted, he saw competition as a process for the selection of the fittest that created unregulated monopolies.[23]

To those who saw society as becoming ever more permeated by competition, he replied: "It is competition which is transitional; and monopoly presents itself, not as something accidental, a stage through which we pass in a backward age, but as something more permanent, more fundamental, than competition itself."[24] Properly controlled monopolies, he suggested, would increase productivity and lower prices by curbing unnecessary duplication and by reducing such costs as advertising. Foxwell also noted that the development of trusts would encourage trade unions and make possible orderly collective bargaining between government regulated trade unions and large firms. His plea for an orderly capitalist society was also a constant theme in his writings on money. During and after World War I, Foxwell returned to this theme of the 1880s and called for the creation of a "national economy" of regulated monopolies to deal with the near military competition offered by Germany. Indeed, he went so far as to cite Friedrich Naumann's social-imperialist scheme as a better model for English economic organization than the "old line of haphazard, untrained, individual enterprise." By contrast, Marshall argued that only free competition would allow Britain to survive in the troubled years after the Great War.[25]

Foxwell's program of social reform envisaged a growing role for the state, but despite his occasional rhetoric on the inevitability of socialism during his youth, his purpose was not to bring socialism to England in either its revolutionary or evolutionary form. Indeed, one of the leitmotifs of his writings was his fear that socialism could be prevented only if the age of laissez faire could be brought to a close. He believed that: "If the State does not become a social reformer, it inevitably will become socialist."[26] Toward the end of his life, his Toynbean democratic idealism of the 1880s had turned to a yearning for a strong leader to end what he saw as the anarchy of the second labor government.[27]

Foxwell's technical writings dealt chiefly with the monetary and fiscal affairs of the City. Jevons had convinced him that monetary and fiscal policy lay at the heart of economic instability. He ascribed the deflation and sluggish economic growth of the late nineteenth century to an international liquidity crisis that had been caused by the widespread demonetization of silver coupled with decreased gold production. To alleviate this crisis, he promoted an international bimetallist standard at a fixed ratio, insisting that his solution was based not only upon the facts of history, but also upon the opinions of the best economists. Marshall, to the contrary, opposed bimetallism and suggested instead his own complex scheme.[28] Advancing an argument later made famous by J.M. Keynes, Foxwell asserted that inflation of a moderate amount, which his bimetallist solution would probably cause, was far more conducive to full employment and an expanding industrial production than deflation; inflation also produced preferable social effects. He hoped to alleviate the detrimental impact of inflation on wages and pensions through their periodic adjustments.[29]

Foxwell's interests in the affairs of the City were not primarily a result of his concern with the structure and operation of the financial community per se; rather, his interest derived from the City's broader impact upon economic security. He suggested that support for bimetallism emanated largely from manufacturers who pointed to a dear currency as endangering Britain's exports and reducing domestic employment. The City financiers, on the other hand, were wary of bimetallism and argued that it would damage London's worldwide financial and investment position. His investigations taught him to distrust all automatic mechanisms, whether of the domestic or international market, but he especially located the origin of industrial instability in the supply and demand of the monetary metal itself.[30] During the 1920s, Foxwell stood, with J.M. Keynes, against orthodox economic opinion by opposing the return to the gold standard. In specific opposition to Marshall in 1922, he urged the creation of a managed international system of exchange that allowed a gradual rise in prices in order to stimulate production.[31]

Both Jevons and Toynbee had taught Foxwell to distrust the Ricardian tradition. It was Foxwell's strident attack on Ricardo that especially alienated him intellectually from Marshall, who, as is well known, saw his own work as a synthesis of Ricardo's and that of later economists and who consistently defended both the method and content of the classical tradition. Marshall told Price that economic thought "is the product of the age" and not the work of an individual mind. However, he added, "perhaps an exception should be made for Ricardo."[32] Foxwell's interpretation of the history of British economic thought can be summarized with his pithy comments on Ricardo and Malthus. On the inside front cover of Ricardo's *Principles*, he noted that it was "the first edition of this disastrous book, which gave us Marxian Socialism and the Class War. Deductive Playthings of this type, completely divorced from realities, make very generous literature for the half educated. It is like giving a child a razor to play with." By contrast, he noted on the flyleaf of the second edition of Malthus's *Essay on Population*: "This is a fine example of the historical method, the only possible method for the tolerable treatment of questions of practical economics."[33] Malthus's methodology, as modern historians of economic thought have shown, was not simply inductive, but Foxwell's distaste for Ricardo led him to be rather uncritical of his famous protagonist.

In Foxwell's nearly book-length study of the Ricardian socialists – a volume that has remained an important work on the subject and that expressed the original impetus behind his book collecting – he presented a full exposition of his view that the deductive economics of Ricardo was the intellectual ancestor of modern socialist theory. Thanking Foxwell for a copy of the book, Marshall commented: "I expect to read the Introduction with interest & – except perhaps in relation to Ricardo – with profit."[34] Although Foxwell agreed with Anton Menger that the root idea of socialism was to be found in the ancient demand for the "whole produce of labour," he traced the modern, and specifically Marxist, version to the English Ricardian socialists. Fostered by the trauma of the Industrial Revolution under the reign of laissez faire, they had employed Ricardo's deductive method and his labor theory of value in their attack upon capitalism. Foxwell maintained that, regardless of the subtleties that had existed in Ricardo's mind, the vast majority of his readers believed that he had held a labor theory of value. This theory, in the hands of the Ricardian socialists and later in the hands of Marx and Lassalle, constituted a "scientific" justification for the ancient demand for the "whole produce of labour."[35] Thus, Ricardian economics had encouraged the dissemination of these modern errors: first, because it was saddled by erroneous doctrines reached by a deductive method; second because, as the political economy of the middle classes, it had provided the social context for revolutionary action through its prevention of social reform; and, finally, as science it had diverted English political economy from its true course charted by Adam Smith and Malthus.

Anticipating J.M. Keynes, Foxwell suggested that Malthus had also steadfastly fixed his attention upon demand rather than production.[36] Unfortunately, Foxwell lamented, the historical method of Adam Smith and Malthus had been overshadowed by the seductive appeal of Ricardo's abstract reasoning. He blamed the late acceptance of the historical method in England on the pervasive influence of J.S. Mill. Despite Mill's generous sympathy for the labor movement, Foxwell concluded that Mill had not been able to escape from his father's training, and thus he merely "put old wine into new bottles."[37]

Foxwell was a political conservative who saw Ricardian economics, and its successor, as the prime examples of that liberal utilitarianism that appeared to value freedom above order and social cohesion. He told an American correspondent that Conservatives stood for "cautious and business-like reform," that "the great social measures were almost all carried by Conservatives," and that Liberalism "means revolutionary sentiment."[38] In 1909, he blamed Lloyd George's famous budget on Ricardo as well as on the Ricardian reformer, Henry George: "It is the rational result of Ricardo's teaching. It was Ricardo who degraded political economy into part of the electoral machinery of Radical governments; the character seems indelibly stamped on Popular English Political Economy."[39] As these comments demonstrate, Foxwell's views on Ricardo lacked balance. This lack of moderation was one of Marshall's chief criticisms of Foxwell.

Foxwell, however, was not opposed to all economic theory. He believed that the mathematical economists, particularly Jevons, were the natural heirs of classical economic theory. In a partly unpublished review of the Duke of Argyll's attack upon economic theory, Foxwell hailed the work of Jevons as successfully reemphasizing Malthus's demand analysis. He noted, further, that Jevons's mathematical treatment of economic theory extended its scope, clearly defined the limits of its principles, and prevented confusion between theory and practice. In conclusion, he generously praised Jevons: "It may be doubted whether any other influence, even the very valuable and better known criticism of the historical school, has so largely contributed to call attention to neglected elements in economics, or to broaden or recast the whole exposition of the science."[40] Foxwell did not publish these laudatory comments on Jevons's mathematical treatment of economic theory in the final version of his review. Even if he had, these comments would not have contradicted his historical sympathies, for Foxwell had adopted Jevons's solution to the *Methodenstreit*. Although willing to champion economic theory as long as it was relegated to a system of abstract analysis, and especially Jevons's rather than Marshall's theory, Foxwell was primarily interested in practical economics and the history of economic thought.

Foxwell's colleague, correspondent, and neighbor, J.N. Keynes, laid down the orthodox position on methodology in his influential *The Scope and Method of Political Economy* of 1890. Notably less dogmatic on the proper methodology for economic science than Cairnes's similarly entitled work of the previous generation,[41] still this book left no doubt that deductive economic theory was the central core of economic studies. J.N. Keynes, who was especially indebted to Marshall and Sidgwick, argued that most of the vexing controversies in economics were chiefly due to two errors: the confusion between the real and the ideal and the claim of "exclusiveness." The latter he explained as follows: "A single aspect or department of economic study is alone kept in view, and the method appropriate thereto is aggrandized, while other methods, of equal importance in their proper sphere, are neglected or even explicitly rejected."[42] His solution was to subdivide the discipline according to aims, allowing each its appropriate method. The first, and primary, component was "positive economic science," or economic theory, which alone gave economics a claim to being a science. Its goal was to derive uniformities, or laws, that were hypothetical and universal. If any general theories on such subjects as value, interest, wages, rent, and capital were to be derived, "recourse must needs to be had to a method, in which deduction from elementary principles of human nature occupies a position of central, though not exclusive, importance." [43] For the more concrete branches of the subject, however, he allowed a more historical, statistical, and inductive method. He listed economic ethics, or what ought to be, as the second component of economic study. Even though he stressed its importance he had little to offer the subject, and insisted that it was wholly separate from the first and not part of economic science *qua* science. [44]

The third branch was applied, or practical, economics. Its purpose was to attempt to achieve the ideals of economic ethics in reality. Aided by the organizing principles of deductive theory, it would deal with the particular and the local by employing an inductive and comparative method. It was the art of political economy. [45] Economic history J.N. Keynes described as a branch of concrete economics that studied economic phenomena in the past. He had little sympathy for the argument of the historical economists that it was fundamental to a realistic applied economics. Further, he was emphatic in his judgment that "economic history never provides premises for the economist or forms the basis of his doctrines." [46] Despite his occasional praise of economic history – as a discipline that illuminates the past, offers guidance to the study of economic development, reminds theorists of the hypothetical nature of their doctrines, and emphasizes the relativity of policy conclusions to a particular time and place – he clearly did not judge it to be equal in stature to economic theory. As for historical economics, his book was largely a polite criticism of the movement: "Much that is said by the historical school consists of mere negative criticism; and on the positive side, there is often wanting an adequate discrimination between what really belongs to economic science and what is no more than economic history pure and simple." [47] Thus, J.N. Keynes' important methodological statement, which was often praised as a work of conciliation, was ultimately a plea for a deductive method in economic theory – the core of the subject – while other, less central, parts of the discipline were allowed a more inductive approach.

In 1887, in a correspondence concerning J.N. Keynes's work on methodology, Foxwell told Marshall that Keynes's position was midway between that of Marshall and his own. Marshall replied that he and Foxwell were not as far apart as the latter imagined, since he himself had urged Keynes to move further toward the position of Ashley and Gustav

Schmoller. Marshall conceded, however, that there was still some room for disagreement.[48] Ultimately, the methodological differences between Marshall and Foxwell involved divergent emphasis rather than total disagreement. Despite Marshall's reputation as a moderate in the English *Methodenstreit*, his frequent criticism of pure theory, and his insistence that economic theory must be relative to a time and place and should only be applied to policy issues with great caution, his first emphasis was on his theoretical neoclassical analysis, and was what made his reputation. Indeed, Marshall even hoped to unite theory and practice so that his theory of welfare could be employed as a scientific guide to policy.[49] Foxwell, in contrast, wished to relegate pure theory to the realm of logic and historical economics for guiding economic policy. And, for Foxwell, application, rather than science, was the most important concern in economics.

Foxwell and Marshall also expressed their opinions very differently. As Marshall himself noted, they differed a great deal in temperament. Marshall sought to play the role of conciliator between the rival camps and Foxwell developed a reputation of quarrelsomeness and for stating his opinions strongly. J.M. Keynes said of him: "His open willfulness was an essential part of him, but it stood in his way in the attainment of his ends in English academic circles which hates a row."[50] Differences between Foxwell and Marshall were further widened by disputes over Foxwell's teaching, the development of the Economics Tripos at Cambridge, and tariff reform. Marshall's criticism of Foxwell's teaching led during the 1890s to a series of disputes over hours, topics, and the content of Foxwell's lectures. Foxwell told J.N. Keynes in 1900: "We have had a good many differences on these matters; culminating in his having engaged Pigou to deliver an elementary course – a man, of all I have heard, least qualified to deal with a general class as he is such a prig."[51] At the turn of the century Marshall felt keenly the competition offered by such institutions as Birmingham and the LSE. He complained to J.N. Keynes in 1902 that economics was "drifting under the control of people like Sydney Webb and Arthur Chamberlain."[52] Marshall's solution was the Cambridge Economics Tripos of 1903 which was heavily theoretical and paid but slight attention to the claims of economic history and the history of economic thought. In spite of Marshall's efforts to gain Foxwell's support for the project, Foxwell continued to press for a greater role for the historical subjects. In the end, Foxwell supported Cunningham's opposition to the new Tripos.

Frustrated by Marshall's dominance at Cambridge, Foxwell nonetheless expended considerable energy, as his correspondence attests, to the encouragement of inductive work in economics both at Cambridge and in London. But even in London, his academic career was endangered when the reorganization of economic study at that University ended the primacy of University College in London economics.[53] From 1895 he lectured at the London School of Economics and Political Science and in 1907 he was named professor of Political Economy at the University of London. In his unsuccessful application to the Birmingham Chair of Commerce, for which Marshall endorsed him in 1901, Foxwell reiterated his economic approach. He informed the Birmingham electors that he was well suited for the post because his connection with business had always been close. Further, in economics all practical questions should be studied inductively "and not by the summary references to maxims or dogmas supposed to be of universal application."[54] It was just such a dogmatic attitude, however, that he believed was exhibited by the professors' manifesto on tree trade in 1903.

Foxwell declared in the *Times* that the refusal of the historical economists to sign the free trade manifesto "goes far to justify the position they hold as to the importance of the historical study of economics."[55] Privately, he complained that the attitude of Marshall's school had again hopelessly discredited British economics and that it had "fallen back in public opinion to the position it held back about the 70's." Despite the more realistic work of the last generation, English political economists had failed to achieve the influence that German economists wielded in public affairs. He was especially critical of Pigou's "smart fencing with abstract principles" in the defense of free trade. He went on to note that he could easily show "the weak places and faulty assumptions of the Classical argument for Free Trade; and this I have done in lectures ever since 1882 and even earlier." However, he conceded, this would be only academic work. His active campaign for bimetallism had dampened his enthusiasm for public controversy, and he refrained from further public argument concerning fiscal policy. He did provide private economic advice to Arthur James Balfour, however, and declared that if he must choose, he would reluctantly follow Chamberlain.[56] Although Foxwell shared many of Ashley's views on the need for industrial stability, as well as Cunningham's interpretation of the history of free trade, he lacked enthusiasm for their public crusading on behalf of social imperialism and imperial federation.[57]

Differences in personality, economic policy, academic politics at Cambridge, and the history of economic thought made Foxwell unacceptable as Marshall's successor. When Marshall retired from his professorship in 1908, he supported the successful candidacy of Pigou. For his part, Foxwell was certain that his stand on tariff reform had finally turned Marshall against him.[58] When Henry Higgs suggested the creation of a second professorship specifically for Foxwell, Marshall suggested J.H. Clapham for such a position. Of Foxwell, he observed: "I have a fear of his judgments. On finance in particular, one of the subjects proposed for him, I think his judgment is extraordinarily bad. He seems never to see more than one side of any complex question."[59] Foxwell never forgave Marshall for having passed over him, and as late as 1927 he still refused to support Pigou as president of the Royal Economic Society.[60]

Disappointed in his academic career, Foxwell turned more exclusively to acquiring rare economic literature and assembled two magnificent collections.[61] The demise of the *Methodenstreit* and his advancing years allowed him to be elected president of the Royal Economic Society in 1930. In poor health, willing to bask in the honor that was at last awarded him for sixty years of economic work, and not wishing to offend those who had so belatedly recognized his merits, Foxwell told a correspondent that in order "not to give unavoidable offense" in expressing his well-known and strong views, he would not offer his planned critique of Ricardo as his presidential address.[62]

Foxwell's career coincided with the birth of the modern research university in Britain with its close ties to the professions, including the profession of an academic.[63] He did not share Marshall's faith in the professionalization of economics on the basis of deductive theory. He did not wholly commit himself to the development of the emerging discipline of economic history. Interested in the practical utility of economic study, he did not make public advocacy a career on the scale of Ashley, Hewins, or Cunningham. In the end he was not wholly acceptable, as his obituary stated, to either neoclassicism or to the other historical economists.[64] Foxwell left behind no great systematic work or coherent school, but he did bequeath a concern for economic regularity, several libraries of rare economic literature, and some original work in the history of economic thought and applied economics. Moreover, as J.M. Keynes suggested, "for half a century and more in discussion and conversation, though seldom in print, Foxwell propounded the view that economics is not a branch of logic or mathematics, but belongs to the art of managing public affairs by the application of sound reasoning to the whole *corpus* of experience."[65] It was Foxwell's colleague, William Cunningham, who most effectively advanced the claims of economic history at Marshall's Cambridge.

CHAPTER 7

Economic history and neomercantilism: William Cunningham and J.S. Nicholson

Both critics and supporters of William Cunningham agreed that the archdeacon's volumes on English economic history laid the foundation of the discipline in England as an academic field of study. J.H. Clapham, a student of Marshall who represented the next generation in the study of economic history, dedicated his work on English economic history to both Cunningham and Marshall.[1] Cunningham achieved his success in spite of his often bitter academic and personal disputes with Marshall. Indeed, it is difficult to imagine two more dissimilar academics than Cunningham and Marshall who shared the broadly similar goal of expanding economic studies at Cambridge. Cunningham delighted in controversy and Marshall shunned it. Cunningham derided the usefulness of economic theory and Marshall made it his life's work. Cunningham worked for the recognition of economic history as an independent subject and Marshall saw it as a handmaiden of economic theory. Cunningham was a vigorous nationalist and imperialist and Marshall's framework was more cosmopolitan.

The very qualities of stridency that gave Cunningham an independent voice at Marshall's Cambridge were not the attributes necessary to mold the often different views and interests of the historical economists into a coherent school. Other historical economists were generous in their praise of Cunningham, but they also criticized his work. Ashley noted that Cunningham's greatest fault was his failure to stress the evolutionary nature of institutions. Hewins shrewdly noted that Cunningham's view of history was governed by the abstraction of national power.[2] Foxwell described William Cunningham as a "great National Economist, the modern representative of an old English tradition, unfortunately interrupted by the atomism and premature cosmpolitanism of the *laissez faire* age," whose true ancestors were the Elizabethans and such mercantilist economists as William Petty and Thomas Mun.[3] Cunningham would have been pleased with this description of himself. He was indeed a national economist whose economic history and political efforts were placed at the service of the empire, the Church of England, and the Unionist campaign for tariff reform. J.S. Nicholson shared Cunningham's neomercantilist aims and was also sympathetic to the historical method, but he maintained an independent and classical critique of neoclassicism at Edinburgh.

Cunningham: religion, philosophy, and politics

Cunningham believed that the essential problem of modern life was the anarchism of the assertion of the individual will. He held that the restoration of an organic society would end the alienation of modern people from God, nation, and society. In discussing his contribution in historical economics, remembering that he was a clergyman is essential. He was born in Edinburgh in 1849. His father, a political Liberal, had broken with the Presbyterian Church and founded a free church, of which his son briefly became a member in 1866. He was educated at home by an English tutor and, after attending the Edinburgh Academy and Institution, he took the arts course at the University of Edinburgh from 1865 to 1869 and read history with Professor Tait. He had hoped to become ordained in the Presbyterian Church, but an attack upon a clergyman he much admired by the Glasgow Presbytery set him against a Church controlled by the elders. He had been much impressed, however, with the Anglican service while on a visit to London. During the summer of 1868, which he spent at the University of Tübingen with the family of Alfred Milner, two American friends reacquainted him with the Book of Common Prayer. Buffeted by rival religious and philosophical allegiances, he told Professor Tait that in choosing his philosophical approach, "Be it Hegelian or Comtist . . . I feel drawn on into a whirl of theory and speculation, on all sides, with nothing to rest on but faith in God."[4]

In 1869, he entered Caius College, Cambridge, where he matriculated in the Moral Science Tripos in 1872. Disenchanted with the severe Calvinist faith of his forefathers, he came under the influence of F.D. Maurice, who rejected the reality of eternal damnation and taught instead a religion of love, in which Christians would subordinate their wills to the will of God, as expressed in the personal example of Jesus and as taught by the Church of England. In addition, Maurice also preached a social Christianity that exerted a powerful influence upon Cunningham, who resolved his religious doubts, took orders in the Church of England, and for the rest of his life pursued his religious duties with vigor and enthusiasm. He served as vicar of Great St. Mary's at Cambridge from 1887 until 1908. From 1908 until his death in 1919, he was the archdeacon of Ely.

Cunningham's interpretation of the religious and social consequences of Calvinism in Scotland and Holland illustrates his youthful rejection of the Calvinist faith. He argued that the anarchic organization of Dissent had split British religion into such warring and powerless factions that they had been unable to carry out their religious and moral vocations. Devoid of guidance from a corporate and authoritarian church, the dissenting churches had fostered an individualist interpretation of the Bible, which had brought spiritual confusion; furthermore, they had emphasized the Old Testament and neglected the teaching of love and reconciliation of the New. Drawing upon the early work of R.H. Tawney and Ernst Troeltsch, he observed that, despite firm intentions, Calvin's theocracy at Geneva had quickly lost its vigilance and allowed free play to individual economic interests. Likewise in Scotland, early capitalism's attempt to develop the resources of the nation saw the Presbyterian Church grant "religious sanction to those forces of progress, without considering the incidental suffering that might arise in the onward march of progress."[5] Calvinism, he declared, had become a religion that sanctioned the pursuit of individual gain and of personal salvation and neglected the duties of charity, national organization, and communal salvation.

Despite his break with Calvinism, he nonetheless agreed with St. Paul that human nature was weak and frail; thus, the human will must be subordinated to the will of God. Cunningham's religion, like that of Maurice, was Christ centered. The archdeacon, however, insisted that men required discipline and direction. He felt that the Medieval Church had been too restrictive and the Reformation models were too anarchic and he praised the national Elizabethan Church of England as offering the ideal combination of authority and freedom.[6] Its modern version, he insisted, provided both religious ideals and corporate direction for salvation, and its balance between authority and freedom served as a model for the self discipline essential to the functioning of a modern democratic state. He participated in the efforts of the Church Social Union to provide the established church with a social conscience and freely employed his faith, even from the pulpit, to sanction his neomercantilist schemes.[7]

At Edinburgh, at Cambridge, and at Tübingen, Cunningham had studied Hegelian and Cartesian philosophy. Unable to choose between the rival systems and increasingly preoccupied with economics, he laid his philosophic studies aside and uncritically combined elements of both systems. He declared himself sympathetic to the Oxford currents in politics and social thought, stating that T.H. Green was "my master in all that I care about in philosophy."[8] His debt to Green was especially apparent in his emphasis upon the duties of democratic citizenship and his adulation of the role of the national state, particularly as the enforcer of morality, may have owed something to Hegel. His philosophical views can be broadly described as antiutilitarian. He announced that utilitarianism could never serve as a justification for government's authority, because science could neither establish ideals nor serve as the basis for social cohesion. All ultimate ideals and authority were derived from God, as expressed in the people and guarded by the Church of England. And if science per se was unable to fulfill this role, then an individualistic and atomistic utilitarianism was certainly incapable of serving as a guide to an organic and corporate society.[9]

Likewise in politics, Cunningham's ideal was not the welfare of separate individuals, but the national consciousness and patriotism of the nation, moderated by a Christian concern for the welfare of citizens and nations. The Christian Socialist flirtations of his youth gradually gave way to a social conservatism. In spite of his Liberal upbringing and occasional Liberal views at Edinburgh, his sympathies were already with Carlyle and Kingsley. Further, influenced by Maurice's imperialism at Cambridge, he became increasingly conservative during the 1880s.[10] In later years he became active in such Unionist and Conservative causes as tariff reform, the opposition to Irish Home Rule, Lord Roberts's National Service Campaign, the criticism of pacifism, and the formation of an imperialist labour movement.[11] His political activities, which greatly increased after 1903, were especially focused upon his opposition to free trade, which he saw as the last manifestation of that policy of laissez faire, cosmopolitanism, individualism, and materialism abhorred by his religion, philosophy, politics, and economics.

Cunningham's early writing in English economic history

Upon his matriculation in the Moral Science Tripos in 1872, he attempted to win a fellowship in Moral Philosophy. His failure to win the fellowship, though he did receive a scholarship to Trinity, closed off one avenue to a career in philosophy. Instead, he turned increasingly to lecturing on social issues in the university extension movement, in which he had already taught occasionally since 1870. After attending Marshall's lectures, he lectured on economics in Bradford, Leeds, and Liverpool, where he was stationed for some time, and married. During his extension teaching, he claimed to be an enthusiastic supporter of the cooperative and trade union movements, but his support of union liability for strike-caused damages quickly made him distrusted within the movement.[12]

The pattern for Cunningham's criticism of economic theory was laid in his discussion of the crisis of political economy. In 1878, he argued that the popular disdain for political economy, as well as its misuse by socialists for revolutionary purposes, was due to the excessive abstraction that had been introduced into the subject by Ricardo and Mill. Political economy, he argued, was rooted in a faulty psychology of economic self-interest that ignored the forces of custom, habit, and community. Jevons, however, had rightly recognized that economics must emphasize the satisfaction of human wants, but the effort to describe wants as uniform in a highly abstract utilitarian theory of political economy made a mockery of the complexity of human motives that were both quantitative and qualitative. This approach would intensify the reputation of economics as a science of mere "egoism," give it an "immoral guise," limit its scope, and thus would make it unable to explain the historical development of economic activities. Finally, orthodox theories of rent, wages, population, and profits had little practical value even for the present.[13] He admitted that a more descriptive approach to economics might perhaps mean a less exact science, but this loss of exactitude would be more than counterbalanced by a gain in practical and moral usefulness. In 1878, he believed that a universal economic theory might be realized, but he demonstrated little interest in its construction. Beginning in the 1880s he suggested a more modest approach to economic theory, which he preferred to call a "pure theory of exchange."[14]

Cunningham's appointment as an examiner for the Historical Tripos in 1878, combined with his experience in the extension movement, led him to the realization that a textbook on English economic history was much needed. In 1919, he told a correspondent: "It was rather accidentally that I came to devote myself to economic history. It had a place in the History Course at Cambridge from the first (1878), and as there was no teacher for the subject, I was asked by the History Board to do my best with it. I had some knowledge of Political Economy and did my best to get up the History."[15] *The Growth of English Industry and Commerce* was first published in 1882. Later known as "little Cunningham," the work grew to three volumes and passed through six editions. It was both Cunningham's magnum opus and the most substantial literary product of English historical economics.

The first edition demonstrated the debt his work owed to Toynbee. In the preface he thanked Toynbee for his help and counsel and noted that Toynbee had taught a generation of students that a study of the past could serve the practical purpose of guiding present action. Even in 1919, when Toynbean themes had become all but submerged in a primarily imperialist and nationalist document, he still paid homage to Toynbee's inspiration.[16] His method of integrating the history of economic thought with economic history was a faithful reflection of Toynbee's model. Though the 1882 edition was far less critical of classical economics than Toynbee had been, Cunningham was deeply disturbed by the social conflicts of an industrial and capitalist society under the regime of laissez faire, which, he believed, had been sanctioned by its individualistic social and economic theories. The social theories of Sir Henry Maine were another important influence evident in the first edition. Cunningham, who had traveled to India, agreed with Maine that contemporary remnants of ancient European institutions might be compared profitably to the contemporary social arrangements of the East.[17]

Cunningham agreed with Rogers's contention that the economic side of a nation's history had been too much neglected. He also found much to disagree with in the Rogers's writings. First, in addition to the college and manorial records Rogers used, he employed physical evidence and living relics of past practices. Second, he argued that Rogers, like the classical economists, had assumed that human motivations had remained constant throughout the past and falsely isolated economic phenomena from their social context and produced a mere history of prices that focused upon the exchange relationships between individuals. This led, for example, to Rogers's faulty interpretation of Tudor social legislation and to his explanation of poverty among the English working classes.[18]

Cunningham insisted economic theory was relative to particular circumstances; thus, "the principles of Political Economy, which describe the commercial tendencies of the present day, will not help us to understand the actual facts of the distant past." Pressured by time and not yet fully disillusioned with the applicability of all economic theory to economic history, he did not systematically continue his first edition beyond Adam Smith and instead left economic theory to explain developments in the nineteenth century. Echoing Maine's argument, he held that the history of the last century could be treated as an increasingly complete and practical exemplification of the principles of abstract political economy, so that "what 'tended' to happen, did on the whole happen as a matter of fact." Thus, despite his critique of orthodoxy, in 1882 he was still anchored to the rhetoric of an individualist economics and maintained that the growth of English industry and commerce had been the consequence of forethought, self-reliance, and individual initiative.[19]

One of the hallmarks of Cunningham's economic history was his praise for the Tudor epoch. Though he occasionally defended the earlier medieval regulatory system, he saw the period as a dark age of anarchy and decay brightened only by the protonationalist and protomercantilist policies of such prophetic English monarchs as Henry II and Edward I, during whose reigns the beginnings of national sentiment and national regulation first began to bridge the abyss of medieval particularism.[20] During Tudor times the monarchy, aided by a national church, forged a "National Consciousness" that laid the foundation for the nation's power through the consolidation of political and religious authority, the fostering of national industry, the building of sea power, and the regulation of trade and labor.[21]

The eighteenth century he interpreted as the "Refutation of Mercantilism." He sympathetically described the replacement of a crude bullionist mercantilism with a sophisticated balance-of-trade mercantilism. At the same time, he bemoaned a policy that pursued wealth and power through war – a policy that produced self-destructive and competing interests, damaged England's relations with its colonies, and stifled individual initiative. However, he stopped short, of categorically condemning mercantilism. Happily, he concluded, since its primary aims of power and plenty had been achieved, mercantilism could now safely give way to the new policy of free trade as "a better means of circumventing foreign competition in all markets."[22] He praised the economics of Adam Smith for replacing the "partisan" doctrines of mercantilism. Under this system of natural liberty, "individual energy had been allowed free play in striving lawfully for private gain, and the extraordinary increase of inventions and discoveries indirectly testifies to its power."[23]

Following Toynbee, he quickly added that laissez faire had also brought unfortunate consequences. Chief among these was a result of unrestricted competition, the decline in the standard of living among large segments of the working classes. Such competition between individuals was for Cunningham no more acceptable in economics than it was in religion; side by side with its beneficial effects, unrestricted competition had destroyed the older system of domestic industry, crowded people into unhealthy slums, and encouraged the alienation of workers from their labor and the organic bonds of society. He also insisted that under free trade the English home market had been ignored in favor of international trade. Repeating the argument of List and Carey, he proposed that under perfect free trade the manufacturing nations would exercise an "imperialism of free trade" and relegate less developed areas to food and raw material production. As for England, hostile tariffs, foreign wars, and other international uncertainties had limited its economic sovereignty under free trade. Although his later objections to British free trade policy appear to have been largely a response to fears of Britain's political decline, in 1882 he already suggested the economic argument that the inherent instability of British capitalism could be diminished by increasing the effective demand of its workers.[24] He believed that the regime of natural liberty had reached its pinnacle in Britain by 1830. Subsequently, the growth of industrial monopolies and the organization of labor gradually led toward the end of laissez faire and the reinstitution of a policy of "National Husbandry."[25] Although Cunningham was not specifically converted to tariff reform until 1902–1903, the basis of this conversion had already been laid in 1882.

The claims of historical economics: Cunningham versus Marshall

The publication of Cunningham's book brought him only modest academic success. In 1884 he was appointed university lecturer in Economic History at Cambridge. Under Fawcett, Cunningham was free to devote his full attention to economic history for the Historical Tripos. When Marshall became professor of Political Economy in 1885, he directed Cunningham to devote two terms to economic theory and left only one term to economic history. Greatly resentful of Marshall's authority, Cunningham resigned his university lectureship in 1888 as soon as a post became available at Trinity College. He was never again the recipient of a university appointment at Cambridge.[26] From 1891 to 1897, he filled the part-time position of Tooke Professor of Economic Science and Statistics at King's College, London. He also taught at the LSE from its foundation in 1895, and in 1899 he lectured for Ashley at Harvard. In 1906 he resigned his post at Trinity College and became archdeacon of Ely two years later. He still, however, continued to give occasional lectures at both Cambridge and the LSE.

Foxwell observed that Cunningham was an opponent of all economic theory. Although Cunningham had criticized economic theory since 1878, this comment was not quite accurate before 1903. In 1889, Cunningham acknowledged that "each of the modes of treatment which opponents advocate has a real place in the thorough investigation of economic phenomena."[27] He outlined a tripartite division of economic studies, similar to that of Jevons in form if not in substance, consisting of pure theory, applied economics, and economic history. After J.N. Keynes and Marshall identified Cunningham with Schmoller as an historicist, he responded in 1892 with "Plea for Pure Theory."

He insisted that the economic historians could not be charged with having neglected all theory. They had employed theories as hypotheses, and further, like Schmoller, they were attempting to draw valid generalizations from their inductive research. Moreover, he suggested that the Historical School – as contemporaries freely called it – would be extremely grateful, if only the theorists would devise a universally applicable typology of exchange for the use of economic historians. But despite his insistence that he too valued economic theory, Cunningham was in fact demanding only the formulation of a scheme of classification and not a science of economic theory as Marshall and his school understood the term.[28]

Cunningham's pure economic theory was designed to serve as a system of logic for the historical economist. He applauded the fact that contemporary economists, bowing to popular pressure, had left the arena of the abstract and hypothetical for the concrete and the real. Nonetheless, many of them still pretended that their subject was a science that could isolate causes of real economic phenomena just as a scientist did in a controlled experiment.[29] Believing that society and men were forever changing (though he argued elsewhere that the one constant was the pursuit of national power), he announced that the attempt to discover universal economic laws of real societies, or the effort to build economic laws upon the psychology of real and specific men, would be an inevitable failure.[30] Thus, he concluded that a deductive method could be used to construct a pure economic theory of exchange; but such a theory would of necessity be hypothetical, abstract, and unable to guide the activities of real people with any scientific authority. Moreover, because he held that the economic theory of Marshall claimed both to be scientific and to deal with real economic phenomena, and thus also claimed to be a science of causation, it could neither be a pure theory nor be socially useful. A thorough believer in the relativity of economic theory, Cunningham sought to have it both ways. While he maintained that he was in fact a supporter of pure economic theory, at the same time he rejected all Marshallian economic theory.

To dispel any remaining doubts concerning his attitude to economic theory, Cunningham became a constant critic of neo-classical economics. He granted that the mathematical theory of Jevons might have served as the foundation for a pure and hypothetical science of exchange.[31] However, the apparent virtues of universality and mathematical expression had in fact made this new version of economic theory even more dangerous than its classical predecessor. The old theory had at least founded its analysis upon the psychology of an identifiable human type – the Manchester man of self-interest and greed – so that its limited applicability was easily recognized. The modern version of economic theory, however, had lost all connection with real phenomena , and its exclusive emphasis upon psychological factors had barred the verification of its conclusions by inductive research. Yet, its mathematical formulation had given it an appearance of scientific truth. He concluded that marginal utility theory was universal in "*form*," but not "*appro-*

priate" for the study of applied economics and economic history.[32] In later years he became even more strident in his criticism of neo-classicism. He especially attacked Pigou's writings on welfare economics.[33]

Cunningham's writings on pure economic theory and his methodological criticism were tortuous and often confused and did not impress even the other English historical economists. They saw him largely as an economic historian. To counter what Cunningham believed to be socially sterile theories of contemporary economic theory, he urged students to begin their economic studies not with the principles of the subject but with a research program in economic history and applied economics. He acknowledged that such a program would not rank political economy with the modern natural sciences or with mathematics but with "botany and natural history in pre-Darwinian days as an empirical science in its classificatory stages," which would be content to "*observe* and *classify* and *describe* and *name*."[34] This program would place political economy in harmony both with the inductive methods of other sciences and in the best tradition of Adam Smith and Malthus.[35]

Despite his repeated and strenuous insistence that a new version of pure economic theory might eventually produce significant results, Cunningham believed that economics must primarily be a practical art.[36] He held that the classical writers had recognized that political economy was essentially a practical art. Although he criticized Marshall's school, he was unusually complimentary to J.S. Nicholson's attempt to restate the classical tradition.[37]

After Cunningham freed himself from Marshall's authority by resigning his university lectureship in 1888, differences between the two were reflected in a variety of professional activities. Discussions leading to the formation of the British Economic Association were held at the meeting of Section F at Newcastle in 1889. Cunningham, who had delivered a strong protest against orthodox economics at the meeting, participated in the founding of the rival *Economic Review* at Oxford. Spurred on by the planning of this publication, Marshall took the initiative by circulating a letter that resulted in the organization of the British economics profession under his leadership in 1890. During the organizational meeting at University College, London, Marshall referred to the *Economic Review* as having been "started for the purpose of dealing with problems in which ethical and religious questions took the first place, but which had a certain kernel of economic difficulty in the background."[38] Marshall did grant that there was room for both groups. Although he did not wish to offend and did not state explicitly that the *Economic Journal* would be more scientific, he left no doubt that he expected the *Journal* to become the main organ for publication of the British economics profession's scientific writings. He quickly added that every effort would be made to include "all schools and parties."[39]

When Marshall's *Principles* appeared in 1890, it contained a wide ranging survey of world economic history. Even though Marshall had spent a considerable amount of energy collecting material on economic history,[40] Cunningham bristled at the invasion of his territory. He charged Marshall with the "perversion of economic history." Economic history had become such a fashionable subject that even

the ordinary economist . . . professes himself extremely interested in History, and like a French King . . . expresses a wish to do anything he can for it. To this polite desire it is surely not discourteous to reply, *laissez faire, laissez aller*. Economists do not leave it alone; they do not pursue it seriously, but try to incorporate some of its results into that curious amalgam, the main body of economic tradition; and the result is the perversion of economic history.[41]

Cunningham was especially incensed that reviewers, including L.L. Price, had seized upon Marshall's history as an authoritative account, even though it had been drawn from "two or three badly chosen books," by one who would nevertheless sketch "you the history of the world with easy confidence."[42] The root of Marshall's errors, Cunningham concluded, was that he had assumed that similar motives for economic development had been operative in all historic epochs and implied that universally applicable laws of economics could be constructed.

Cunningham knew Marshall's interests well and was particularly critical of his historical application of the Ricardian theory of rent both to Tudor England and to contemporary India. Such misapplication, he continued, was one of the chief causes of the neglect of inductive economic studies in England. He regretted the necessity for having to attack Marshall publicly, but he believed that the very credibility of historical economics was at stake:

When critics speak of this book as authoritative on points of history, or tell us that the historical school of economists made useful protest but implicitly deny that they have necessary work to do in supplying a basis for positive economic doctrine, one cannot but feel that there is a time not only for silence, but for speech; lest silence be mistaken for acquiescence.[43]

Cunningham's criticism was also aimed directly at J.N. Keynes, who had specifically attacked the ability of economic history to supply a basis for "positive economic doctrine."[44]

Marshall rarely responded publicly to adverse criticism, and he much regretted the part he later played in the controversy.[45] However, Cunningham's repeated and sharp attacks since 1889 challenged Marshall's plans for economic study at Cambridge, and Marshall wished to disassociate Cunningham from his other historical critics, and thus Marshall was convinced to reply publicly.[46] After pointedly thanking Wagner and Ashley for their private criticism of his work, he chided Cunningham for his open assault. Marshall observed that, although he had always felt a keen need for the investigation of contemporary economic issues, he had never attacked those who had devoted their lives to economic history and who had done so "without condemning the good work that had already been done in scientific analysis."[47] Further, his economic history had not been the result of digesting the contents of "a few badly chosen books," as he had collected material on economic history for many years. Nonetheless, he did not wish to claim any definitive authority for his chapters in economic history because they had served only as an introduction to his theoretical book. He concluded that Cunningham had apparently repudiated the value of all economic theory and regretted that there thus remained little common ground between them for productive argument.

Marshall did, however, take the opportunity to defend Ricardo's theory of rent.[48] When Cunningham attempted to continue the controversy in the *Economic Journal*, Edgeworth refused him additional space. Not deterred by this rebuke, Cunningham replied in the even more public media of the *Academy* and the *Pall Mall Gazette*. The controversy, however celebrated, had ceased to be productive. Each had accused the other of misrepresentation. Each had defended his own academic territory. The controversy did, however, succeed in embittering further the relations between Marshall and Cunningham and also left Cunningham more of an outsider even among historical economists. Ashley, Foxwell, and Price all agreed that Cunningham had been unnecessarily difficult in the controversy. This isolation was somewhat reduced after 1903, when the tariff issue again inflamed methodological arguments. As late as 1919, Cunningham was still warning his economic history students that Marshall's account of the growth of free enterprise was not to be trusted.[49]

Despite Cunningham's overstatement of his case and his partial misrepresentation of Marshall's teaching, the controversy raised potentially important issues on the nature of economic history that have often been missed in the general rally to Marshall's defense in the subsequent literature. Aside from the personal and academic territory dispute – which, to be sure, was central – the skirmish raised critical issues on the nature of economic history, particularly concerning the role of theory in its study. Cunningham's economic history has often been criticized for its selectivity of topics, its emphasis upon the role of the state, the inadequacy of its original sources, and, of course, its neglect of available economic theory. At its time, however, it was a work of immense scholarship that was based upon abundant sources and constituted a skeleton of English economic history that has been fleshed out by later scholars. Conversely, Marshall's history, as outlined in his *Principles*, was little more than historical theory. It amounted to an assertion that the forces of supply and demand had operated in some undefined fashion in all known economies. His comments on medieval and early modern history, in particular, were unsupported generalizations in a field in which Cunningham had labored for more than a decade. Indeed, Marshall's *Principles* was the worst possible place to air his views on economic history, as the work was designed as the first of several volumes and contained a largely static theory of economics. His volume on economic history was never completed. His later works, especially *Industry and Trade*, were brilliant treatments of applied economics, as Ashley acknowledged. They embodied his conception of the evolution of society, employed a biological metaphor, and demonstrated his commitment to empirical investigation. They also suggested that sound applied economics and contemporary economic history ought to employ economic theory as the organizing principle of such studies. However, they were not published until a generation later and were silent on developments prior to the nineteenth century. Further, little attention was given to primary sources. Rather, their aim was to demonstrate the applicability and exceptions to the economic theory enshrined in his earlier work. A student has noted that "Marshall seems to have regarded history as mainly a tool for maintaining perspective with reference to current economic problems."[50]

Thus, Cunningham failed to fathom Marshall's aims and the brilliance of his economic theory and Marshall failed to appreciate Cunningham's pioneering work in economic history. One can also put the dispute in another light. Cunningham's economic history was stridently conservative and emphasized the growth of the state and the role of custom and the particular, and Marshall's excursions into economic history were those of a rational liberal who searched for the universal, the rise of free enterprise, and the role of competition even in traditional societies.

Cunningham keenly resented Marshall's authority in Cambridge economics and worked to frustrate his plans for the subject. He complained bitterly of the dominance of Marshall's school and claimed that dissenters found it difficult to pursue their studies and guide students and were faced by editors and publishers who viewed their "writings with misgivings."[51] In attempting to explain "why Roscher had so little influence in England," he began with a criticism of Mill's inhibiting influence upon inductive economics and then quickly proceeded to his real target. Marshall, who employing the insight of Jevons, "recast the greater part of political economy, by relating the principles contained in his Economics of Industry according to the new lights," and Marshall's school ensured "that the teaching and examining in many parts of England should be rapidly remodeled on the lines he adopted."[52]

When the Historical Tripos was created at Cambridge in 1873, it was both factual and theoretical, including papers on political economy, political science, and philosophy, as well as history. The younger men, such as George Prothero, Mandell Creighton, F.W. Maitland, and Cunningham, brought the new tradition of original research in history to Cambridge, while the professor, J. Seeley, continued an older and more general approach. At the very time when Marshall became professor of Political Economy, these younger men sought to reform the Historical Tripos by emphasizing original historical research and making social theory subjects optional. During the 1880s, all the historians achieved was to separate Political Economy from the rest. The result was to give Marshall greater control over the subject. Unfortunately for Cunningham, Political Economy also included economic history.[53] During the 1890s, the reformers succeeded in dividing the Historical Tripos so that a student could concentrate on history without doing any formal work in economics.[54]

In 1894, Cunningham edited a Report for Section F on economic teaching in Britain. With the committee controlled by Cunningham, Foxwell, Price, and Henry Higgs, the report noted that in countries where economics was studied inductively it enjoyed greater academic and popular repute. The report suggested that a larger emphasis in British economic teaching be given to inductive studies that afforded greater practical application than theory, and added that such reforms could be offered within the existing degree structure.[55] During the late 1890s, Marshall sought to block the teaching of economic history without theory under the heading of economics. He told Foxwell:

Now I do not want to attack Cunningham in any way direct or indirect. But to state that those people who are studying economic history as a mere series of facts without any scientific analysis are students of economics, would I believe be a falsehood. It would I think be misinterpreted by Schmoller's students just as much as Edgeworth's. I have stated the facts, the whole facts and nothing but the facts. I have counted Cunningham among those who [sic] teaching on the economic side because I believe his teaching is useful to those Hist. Tripos (& other men) who are also students of economics. . . . But I will not say that men who read "economic history," and avoid the economics papers in the Historical Tripos are students of economic history without qualification.[56]

However, Marshall, was unable to convince Foxwell, who increasingly moved to support Cunningham. For his part Cunningham pleaded for the separate recognition of economic history under his own direction.[57]

In 1901, when Marshall's project for the Economics Tripos was well under way, Cunningham returned to the subject. The sources of economic history, he argued, were sufficiently different from those of both general history and economics to justify its independence.[58] Further, the best students of economics at Cambridge hardly studied economic history at all; although it formed a part of the Historical Tripos, it was not even a required subject in that department. He did allow that some modern economists had begun to treat economic matters in their historical perspective. He even conceded that economists were developing a "scientific terminology which is directly applicable to bygone times."[59]

When the Economics Syndicate reported in early 1903 on the need for an Economics Tripos, he dissented from its majority support of Marshall's scheme. In a fly sheet to the senate, he objected to the specialized study of economic theory as unsuitable for a liberal education and noted that "the study itself does not appear to us to supply a good mental discipline."[60] Marshall replied by stating that his proposal was an ideal curriculum that concentrated a student's interests on a "center of intense intellectual activity," and thus "a considerable breadth may be obtained in the very process of developing thoroughness."[61] When Marshall at last succeeded in establishing his treasured Economics Tripos at Cambridge, he reserved half of the first two years and all of the final year for theory and left only one year for applied economics, economic history, and political science. Even the economic history to be taught was to be primarily that of the nineteenth century. Thus, those who wished to study economic history as their major field were to be relegated to a hiatus between history and economics.[62] The result of Marshall's reform of economic study signified the triumph of economic theory as a professional discipline at Cambridge. Maitland, a supporter of Cunningham, expressed the relief of the historians, for the economists could no longer "plague and pester us" in the Historical Tripos.[63] Cunningham, however, saw himself as both an economist and a historian.

Having failed to frustrate Marshall's plans, Cunningham now hoped for the future independence of economic history and the creation of a professorship in his subject. However, Marshall's victory was complete. In 1905 the Economics Board posted a notice advising students that Dr. Cunningham, Director of Economics at Trinity College, "has publicly declared himself to be out of sympathy with the study of economics as it is pursued under the direction of this Board"; thus, students preparing for the Economics Tripos were advised to seek counsel elsewhere.[64] The following year Cunningham retired from regular teaching at Cambridge. Upon Marshall's retirement in 1908, there was talk at Cambridge of creating a second professorship for Foxwell in applied economics and economic history. But Marshall suggested J.H. Clapham for such a post. Moreover, Cunningham would have been difficult to pass over and the project was dropped. It was not until 1928 that the university created a chair in economic history. The post went to Clapham.[65]

Cunningham's economic history as a practical art

Cunningham observed that there were two ways of treating economic history. The first was to trace the economic life of a people within the context of their own society. The second was to view economic history from a contemporary perspective by choosing incidents from the past "for the illustration of modern economic theory."[66] He accused Marshall's school of following the latter path. It can be argued, however, that Cunningham's economic history, especially beginning with the second edition published in 1890–2, was an illustration of his theory of the rise of the state. His earlier claim, that "our industrial life has been directly and permanently affected by political affairs, and politics are more important than economics in English history,"[67] was developed into a full scale articulation of this theme. In fact, though he did not rename the work, his emphasis in the second and subsequent editions was no longer upon the growth of England's industry and commerce but upon its rise to national power. His method was to define a period politically, describe its political aims, and discuss the economic policies and theories developed to achieve these goals. In a review of the second edition, Hewins concluded that Cunningham had considered "man solely as a being who pursues national power," and made an "entire abstraction of every other human passion."[68]

While Cunningham's emphasis on the rise of the state was evident in his expanded treatment of the protomercantilism of the medieval period, it was especially striking in his praise for the national economic policies of the Tudor monarchs. He saw the advance of laissez faire attitudes during the eighteenth century as a mere tactical change of policy that left the basic strategy of mercantilism unaltered. Despite much subsequent criticism of mercantilism, he concluded that from the Tudors until Adam Smith the system had provided England with political power, raised the standard of living of its workers, and made it the "workshop of the world."[69] The second edition also contained a more vigorous critique of the laissez faire policies of the first half of the nineteenth century. He insisted that the condition-of-England question was not simply a result of the coming of modern industry, but had been exacerbated by the lapse of mercantilism's regulation of labor and the growth of dangerous class conflict. Moreover, these alarming social developments had been justified as an intellectual rationalization of Parliament's refusal to seriously consider social reform during the period.[70] Despite his critique of laissez faire, he did not yet specifically advocate tariff reform in the 1890–2 edition.

His growing imperialist sentiment became more pronounced in his writings of the late 1890s. In a wide ranging history of Western civilization, first published in 1898, he offered a comparative view of the decline and fall of empires. He concluded that the Phoenician Empire had fallen from an excessive specialization in trade that had left it vulnerable to uncontrollable foreign decisions; the Roman Empire had failed due to a lack of imperial federation, an insufficiently patriotic citizenry, and inadequate domestic investment; the decline of the Spanish Empire was attributed to a narrow bullionism that had neglected the development of both domestic and colonial resources; the Dutch Empire had disintegrated because its cosmopolitan burghers had not achieved the purpose borne of a true national will; and the French Empire had been rendered impotent by the excessively minute regulations of Colbert and the autocratic policies of its monarchs. Why then, if all the others had failed, had the British Empire succeeded? Its success he attributed to its balance between freedom and authority: the individual motivation for the accumulation of wealth had been combined with a truly national will and direction. Cunningham saw this balance threatened by the selfish and unbridled pursuit of individual gain of the laissez-faire age.[71]

While lecturing in America in 1899, he told an American audience that of all the world's imperialisms, only that of Britain was cosmopolitan. He observed that the increasing exclusion of British goods from foreign markets by hostile tariffs during the closing years of the century marked the triumph of List over Cobden. Although he had still not embraced tariff reform in 1899, he did suggest that, because other nations had not lived up to Cobden's expectations by adopting free trade, Britain was justified in rejecting Cobden's anticolonialism. By expanding its own empire, Britain could unilaterally expand the reign of free trade within the world through an exercise of power. This expansion is what he termed a "cosmopolitan imperialism." Such a policy would not only promote trade, but also encourage international peace and protect native peoples from excessive exploitation by others so that they might ultimately chart their own development.[72] But his rejection of Cobden's opposition to formal empire, while at the same time he clung to a version of Cobden's dream of free trade, was a curiously contradictory melange. He solved this problem in 1903 by advocating imperial federation and tariff reform.[73] Nonetheless, he continued to insist that Cobden's cosmopolitan ideals were also his aims; their achievement, however, was to be postponed to the next world, because in this world Cobden's ideals could only be approximated by frankly recognizing the force of nationalism.[74]

Cunningham reiterated the lessons he taught in his economic history in his frequent popular writings, public speeches, university lectures, and even his sermons on the wisdom of tariff reform and the folly of free trade. Despite his vigorous support of tariff reform, he was only in slight demand as an economic adviser to its political leaders. For such responsibilities, Ashley's and Hewins's wider knowledge of contemporary economic issues was much better suited. He especially delighted in attacking the theorists who had signed the Free Trade Manifesto of 1903 and suggested that their concepts were mere ideologies of an economic policy and theory of cheap consumption that were no longer appropriate for the maintenance of Britain's industrial and political power. His brief for tariff reform, though primarily political, did contain the economic argument, rooted in his economic history and the work of Nicholson and Ashley, that England's reliance upon earnings from foreign investments and commercial services to balance its international payments failed to preserve its productive capacity and the employment of its workers.[75]

His special contribution to the tariff reform debate was his historical treatment of the origin and nature of free trade. As the Merchants' Petition of 1820 demonstrated, the motivating factor behind free trade had been simply a policy to promote the self-interest of the manufacturers. Because Britain was the only industrialized nation during the period, and as it looked forward to an apparently unlimited conquest of the market for manufactured goods, the merchants had demanded an end to the restrictive policy of the corn laws that had limited the purchasing power of foreign nations. Free trade had had the effect of lowering the cost of raw materials for industry and of food for the working classes, but its real aim had been "to crush rival industries in every part of the world."[76] List and Hamilton had recognized this motivation. Thus, the policy of free trade had brought its own nemesis. The "Manchester men, with all their professions of peace" had fostered the economic nationalism of Germany and America, which had made free trade not a universal model, but a mere stage in a nation's economic development.[77] Stripped of its moral cant, Victorian free trade had been nothing more than the "Imperialism of Free Trade."

Cunningham also agreed with List that free trade remained the best policy for the maximization of the world's wealth; however, because the world was organized into nations, and because nationalism remained, and was likely to remain, a potent force in the world, nations had been forced to devise national economic policies for the development of their domestic resources. As a consequence, Britain's dream of universal free trade had become merely insular free trade. The decline of Britain's staple industries, the mounting deficits in its balance of trade, the dwindling of its coal supplies, and its international dependence upon food and raw materials all offered ample evidence that free trade was no longer appropriate to Britain's contemporary state of production. Free trade had made Britain not a sovereign nation but a mere territory relegated to "pursue the occupations that its neighbours assign it."[78]

Chiefly interested in demonstrating the historical inadequacies of laissez faire, Cunningham's prescriptions for a proper national economic policy were extremely vague. In general, he supported the formation of an Imperial Zollverein molded chiefly by preferences for imperial corn and British manufactured goods. Such an imperial structure would regard Britain as merely the most important component of a great federated empire, which would allow for the development of each part "along the lines which are marked out by its physical resources."[79] For Britain, protection would allow it to maintain its industrial base by allowing it to adopt retaliatory tariffs. His reference to Wakefield as the English master of an Imperial scheme further strengthens our suspicion of who was to be the chief benefactor of this imperial economic policy for what he sometimes called, as befitting a student of Seeley, a "Greater Britain."[80]

In addition to providing specific economic and political gains, Cunningham's imperialism also constituted a powerful emotive ideal that he freely sanctioned with the cloak of morality and religion. Turning Cobden's argument upside down, he argued that imperialism was a true system of internationalism, under which the great empires would secure peace and order in the world.[81] And, ultimately the archdeacon suggested that Christianity was the real justification for British imperialism. When a group of Anglican clerics, following the lead of the professors, drew up their own manifesto denouncing protection as immoral, he assailed the sins of Cobdenism from the pulpits of Great St. Mary's and Ely Cathedral. He identified Calvinism and Cobdenism as the heresy of laissez faire that promoted the individual pursuit of wealth and resulted in the neglect of social welfare at home and the encouragement of "Free Trade Imperialism" abroad.[82]

There was, indeed, also a social side to his neomercantilism. In 1879 he argued that the coming of socialism to England was inevitable. Instead of Liberalism's blind opposition to its arrival, which would bring only violent revolution, he urged that England should "bring it about as gently as our forefathers passed from feudalism to the modern era, as unconsciously as we ourselves have seen it begun."[83] He defined socialism, as was common at the time, as the closing of the epoch of individual competition and the dawning of a corporate age characterized by the rise of organized business, trade unions, some municipal ownership of essential services, and the national regulation of production for the common welfare. In 1895, and much like Ashley, he declared that his earlier opinion on the inevitability of socialism had been mistaken. By this time, however, he defined socialism as the common ownership of the means of production. He labeled such a system utopian. More conservative than Ashley, he also opposed all schemes for direct progressive taxation and demanded instead a system of incentive taxation designed to encourage the domestic investment of capital in labor intensive industries and agriculture at the expense of foreign investments, rentier incomes and pasture agriculture.[84] With the other historical economists, he blamed the economics of Ricardo as the intellectual underpinning of revolutionary Marxist theory. According to Cunningham, the path to social harmony, as well as to salvation, lay in "calling forth and directing private interests so that they may co-operate for the public good."[85]

In 1912, the archdeacon wrote a draft report for the Lower House of Convocation on the labor unrest that was then rocking England. Rejected by the Upper House for unexplained reasons, Cunningham was undaunted by this hierarchal rebuff and published it independently. He argued that the causes of contemporary labor unrest were inflation, the failure of recent social legislation to provide adequate employment, the stubborn persistence of widespread poverty, the altered demand for labor caused by Britain's evolving industrial structure, the rising expectations of the workers in the face of the conspicuous consumption of the rich, the irresponsible rhetoric of some schemes for social reform, and the realization on the part of the workers that the Liberal dream of individual achievement was for them a myth.[86] His solution was to combine his imperial scheme with one of conservative social reform. He praised the ability of both trusts and labor unions to bring harmonious relations between capital and labor. His attitude toward labor unions, however, was always more cautious than that of Ashley. When in 1906, for example, the Liberals sought to undo the effects of the Taff-Vale decision, an effort that Ashley supported, Cunningham listed the effort as one of the causes of contemporary labor unrest.[87] The social side of his imperialism essentially amounted to a constant reiteration of his argument that the benefits of an imperial home market would work to the ultimate advantage of the working classes through the creation of stability and full employment. It was, as he often said himself, a modern version of Tudor mercantilism.

Cunningham's revolt against orthodox economics was a result of his religious and political ideals, his efforts to establish economic history as a respected academic discipline, and his belief that it could serve to make economic study once again a practical science. His disenchantment with economic orthodoxy was hardened into total opposition by his personal subordination to Marshall at Cambridge, by his love of combat, and by the Free Trade Manifesto of 1903. His call for the creation of an ethical, practical, and inductive economics expressed itself in his vision of economic history. In 1910, he observed that in the time of Seeley economic history appeared capable of producing maxims for public policy. Now, however, he warned against using it "as a storehouse for argument in favor or against some particular course of pressing interest." Instead, as Bacon had argued, economic history could only "cultivate a faculty of political wisdom."[88] But surely, Cunningham's economic history had provided him with material to illustrate his religious and political maxims. Nonetheless, as both contemporaries and subsequent economic historians testified, Cunningham's pioneering volumes laid the foundation for the academic treatment of English economic history.[89]

J.S. Nicholson: critique of neoclassicims and Adam Smith's project of empire

Although Cunningham hardly ever neglected an opportunity to criticize Marshall's economic theory, he was unusually complimentary to that of J.S. Nicholson.[90] Cunningham's insistence that English economics return to the empirical and inductive method of both the mercantilists and Adam Smith, his emphasis upon the necessity of safeguarding Britain's industrial capacity, and his history of free trade owed more to the economics of Nicholson than even Cunningham acknowledged. Although Nicholson did not claim to be a historical economist, his economic writings can be viewed as within the tradition of historical economics.

Born in Lincolnshire in 1850, Nicholson was educated at King's College, London, Edinburgh University, and Trinity College, Cambridge. Cunningham had known Nicholson at Edinburgh and worked with him at Cambridge, where Nicholson lectured and served as a tutor from 1876 to 1880. Like Cunningham, he also studied in Germany. From 1880 until 1927, he served as professor of Political Economy at Edinburgh, where he was the pioneer in the development of economic history as an independent discipline.[91] His economic views constituted an independent criticism of Marshall, somewhat analogous to that of Cannan at the LSE, which emphasized the continuity of the classical tradition, with special praise going to Adam Smith's contribution. Nicholson was also a fervent imperialist. He was not, however, a supporter of Chamberlain. When the latter publicly suggested that Nicholson's economics provided support for his tariff reform proposals, he repudiated Chamberlain's program. Although he was a signatory of the Free Trade Manifesto of 1903, he rejected its claim that economic theory demonstrated the futility of all tariff reform. Instead, he maintained that historical studies demonstrated that, although the aims of the tariff proposals were indeed desirable, there were nonetheless important negative reasons for opposing Chamberlain's specific suggestions.[92]

Nicholson, who had once been a student of Marshall, saw himself as the successor to Adam Smith and J.S. Mill. He was also indebted to the criticism of Cliffe Leslie and the German Historical School. He sought to follow J.S. Mill's example by writing a general treatise in the tradition of Adam Smith in which he attempted to reconcile the historical, mathematical, and statistical approaches to economics. His three volume *Principles of Political Economy*, which appeared between 1893 and 1901, was the last great effort of synthesis that the classical tradition produced. Reserving mathematical treatment for pure theory, he advocated the use of an inductive and statistical methodology for applied economics and economic history. Nicholson was never close to Marshall, but he was fond of J.N. Keynes, with whom he often stayed while examining in Cambridge. In a correspondence concerning criticism of proofs for Keynes's methodological treatise, he applauded Keynes for understanding that different methods had to be reserved for different purposes. He was, however, critical of Keynes's underevaluation of J.S. Mill and his relative neglect of Adam Smith's varied contribution. He also urged Keynes to be more sympathetic to both German and English historical economics.[93]

After the publication of Marshall's *Principles*, Nicholson told Keynes that he had let off Marshall too lightly in his recent review: "His history is vague, old fashioned and excessively weak; his examples are mainly of the old a priori kind or at best curious rather than important; the repetition is so great that his plan must be faulty; and if he is to cover the whole ground of what I understand to be P.E. he will at this same rate [need] 6 volumes."[94] He went on to argue that Marshall's "pure theory is extremely good and deserves the highest praise," but that the work would never do as a general textbook in economics and could be recommended only to some honor students. Since so much had been left out of Marshall's long awaited treatise, Nicholson announced his intention to gather his notes and to write a "proportioned textbook of about the size of Mill in the extreme." Moreover, he would "fill it with real historical examples of importance." In later years, he drew closer to Marshall's historical critics and to Edwin Cannan and relations between Nicholson and Marshall became strained. Though Cannan and Nicholson disagreed on many issues, they could agree on the importance of historical studies to economics, their view of the relativity of economic theory, and, especially, their common criticism of Marshall's school of economics. Nicholson told Cannan in 1918 that political economy had lost its popular influence because "the Marshallians and the Pigouese and *id genus omne*" have attempted to make the study mathematical – a temptation resisted by Cannan, himself, and a few others.[95]

Nicholson was involved in numerous projects during his long career, including several literary works, various bimetallist schemes, vigorous opposition to socialism, a history of the corn laws, a study of the effects of machinery upon wages, and various financial, banking, and currency questions. His importance for our purposes, however, was his restatement of the classical tradition, his opposition to neoclassical economics, and a reinterpretation of Adam Smith, which had begun with Cliffe Leslie and which sought to claim Smith as a source of historical and national economics.[96]

Following the classical tradition, Nicholson opened his *Principles* with a treatment of production. He observed that neoclassicism's identification of production with the satisfaction derived from utilities was a reversion to a fictitious abstract economic man. Instead, he emphasized the role of custom and habit in the economic mechanism of the past and the present. Rejecting marginal utility theory's dependence upon psychological motivation as unmeasurable, he suggested that economics should return to the solid and measurable ground of exchange value; further, he criticized modern theory's effort at forging a common theory of production and demand and preferred Mill's scheme of treating them as essentially dissimilar. Price saw this discontinuity between production and distribution as the main defect of Nicholson's otherwise admirably concrete and comprehensive work.[97]

His economic treatise was composed of large blocks of historical, descriptive, and statistical material from which he attempted to draw his principles. He emphasized that these principles were relative to a particular stage of production, and their application to specific circumstances was first of all dependent upon prior inductive verification. In his effort to outline the classical scheme of distribution historically, he relied almost exclusively upon German and English historical economic scholarship. His *Principles* can be described as a sustained effort, comparable to Roscher's earlier effort in Germany, to illustrate and limit classical economic theory.[98]

In Nicholson's reinterpretation of the classical tradition, he especially returned to Adam Smith; he had combined a truly historical method with a judicious use of deduction. In Nicholson's edition of the *Wealth of Nations*, as well as in his *Project of Empire*, he declared that Adam Smith had not been the advocate of a cosmopolitan economics, but a British patriot and even an imperialist. Smith's advocacy of free trade had not been designed to promote the economic development of all people; rather, it had been put forth as a means of developing the British Empire through imperial free trade. Nicholson held that Smith had insisted that the first requirement for the wealth of a nation was the full employment of its capital, labor, and domestic production. In fact, Smith's objections to mercantilism had been precisely its fostering of foreign trade at the expense of the home trade. Thus, he argued, List's and Carey's defenses of the home trade as the primary source of a nation's wealth ought to have been made in support of, rather than in opposition to, Adam Smith's teaching. Although Adam Smith had certainly been a free trader, he had allowed numerous exceptions to the system, including his famous dictum that defense was of more importance than opulence, his argument for the protection of infant industry, his support for revenue tariffs, his approval of retaliatory tariffs against foreign bounties and taxes, and, finally, his suggestion that protection for some home manufacturing could raise the domestic rate of profit so that English capital could find ample domestic investment opportunities. Nonetheless, Adam Smith had ultimately rejected all such arguments, except those for national defense, on the grounds that mercantilism would lead to the creation of monopolies, the encouragement of corruption, and the fostering of administrative chaos. Nicholson himself adhered to such a negative argument against tariffs.

Nicholson explained that Smith had hoped to transform the late eighteenth century "Project of Empire" into an actual empire. He had proposed the creation of a great federated empire for the purpose of common defense and joint political power, through imperial taxation combined with imperial representation. Nicholson argued that Smith's suggestions on imperial federation, combined with his arguments on the greater importance of industrial production over merely cheap consumption, could be employed for the strengthening of the contemporary empire. A modern British Empire was not to be a self-sufficient empire that exploited the colonies in a mercantilist fashion, but rather an Imperial Zollverein of internal free trade ringed with a common external tariff barrier. In this fashion, England would not have to export its surplus capital and labor to enhance the wealth and power of foreign nations, but could provide productive employment for these resources within a vastly expanded home market. England would also benefit from such a scheme with a more stable source of raw materials and the increasing returns to scale of modern enterprise. The colonies and federated nations could expand the market for their own products and be assured of an adequate supply of labor and capital. Finally, the empire as a whole would benefit from the aggregation of political and military power on the model of the new continental empires that would dominate the world in the twentieth century. This program, of course, would require the adoption of tariffs in England and their reformulation within the empire. In contemporary circumstances, Nicholson argued, such questions could not be dealt with theoretically, but had to be carefully weighed through empirical investigation. Further, the political benefits of greater power outweighed the dangers of possible political corruption.[99]

Nicholson's interpretation of Adam Smith as an imperialist and historical economist was solidly rooted in the tradition of English historical economics. He also specifically praised the work of List as a precursor of historical economics.[100] Although Nicholson often used the historical research of Cunningham and the applied economics of Ashley in his work and was a frequent opponent of neo-classical economics, he never specifically counted himself as a historical economist. Like the historical economists, however, he also greatly encouraged the development of the discipline of economic history in Britain. Newly creating a historical economics in England was not necessary, he argued, for one could find a proper balance between deductive theory and inductive work in the classical work of Adam Smith and J.S. Mill. He insisted that it was not the historical economists who had sought to revolutionize British economics, but the neoclassical economists who had struck out in a new and unfortunate direction by developing the abstractions of Ricardo. Nicholson's voice was thus added to a considerable, though often diverse, body of primarily historical criticism of Marshall's authority in British economics. At Cambridge, Marshall's vision of the discipline triumphed despite the often vigorous, but ultimately ineffective, opposition of Foxwell and Cunningham. Indeed, the sometimes bitter disputes at Cambridge retarded the formal recognition of economic history as an independent discipline in that university for at least a generation. At the LSE, however, economic history and applied economics found fertile ground from the school's very inception.

CHAPTER 8

W. A. S. Hewins and the Webbs: applied economics, economic history, and the LSE

In an 1894 lecture on the state of economic teaching in England, W. A. S. Hewins characterized it as "one-sided, and badly organized." Further, it was "too elementary and theoretical, and probably leaves scarcely any permanent impression on the minds of the students."[1] Economic teaching at Oxford he judged to be particularly barren. At Cambridge, he found it more "systematic, thorough, and continuous." Only at his own newly founded London School of Economics and Political Science did he consider it able to stand up to the superior status that the subject enjoyed in the United States and on the Continent. Despite the obvious bias in Hewins's views, the founding of the LSE in 1895 did provide a considerable stimulus to the academic study of economics in Britain. Under the leadership of Hewins and the patronage of the Webbs, the LSE became a "dissenters alternative" to Marshall's Cambridge.[2] It provided a fertile environment for the study of economic history, applied economics, and heterodox economic theory. The school played a central role in Hewins's career. Its early curriculum reflected his historical economic views, and it provided a platform from which he launched his neomercantilist political career. The school also expressed the social and economic views of the Webbs, who have often been categorized as socialists but can also be viewed as within the tradition of historical economics.

Hewins: in search of a career as a historical economist

The distinguishing feature of Hewins's career was his often reiterated belief that careful statistical and historical investigation of imperial and social problems was the true province of the historical economist. As an Oxford University extension lecturer, as director of the LSE, as secretary of the Tariff Commission, as member of Parliament, and in all his political activities, he believed that he embodied the spirit of a new professional type: the economic expert of the twentieth century who combines the technical skills of a recognized profession with the advocacy of public policy.

160

Hewins had impeccable credentials as an historical economist. Born in 1865, he was the son of a Midlands metal merchant. He reported that at school he had little interest in political economy, admitting only to having read Mrs. Fawcett. While traveling with his father on business during the late 1870s and early 1880s, he was much impressed by the depression in trade and its social consequences. This experience led him to begin reading economics books. He reported that he failed to perceive their importance at the time: "I disliked their theoretical outlook, their materialism leavened with sentiment and their remoteness from real events as I saw them in South Staffordshire."[3] In 1884 he entered Pembroke College, Oxford, and matriculated with a second in Mathematics from Lincoln College in 1887. Turning increasingly to social questions, he became deeply indebted to the ideas of Kingsley, Carlyle, and Ruskin. In 1885 he joined the St. Matthew Guild but judged their thought too ecclesiastical and their economics too vague. In 1886 he founded the Social Science Club, the aim of which was to find solutions to contemporary social problems through inductive investigation. He befriended the Rev. John Carter and was later associated with him in the founding of the Oxford *Economic Review* which shared some of the same purposes as Hewins's Social Science Club. As a member of the Oxford Economic Society, he associated with such other young economic critics as Cannan, Ashley, Price, and H.L. Smith.

Hewins reported that when he finally decided to devote himself to economics, he sought advice from Rogers. Rogers discouraged him, and argued that economic orthodoxy was so strong that it would wreck his chances of a productive career. Reluctantly, Hewins undertook to study history under Sir Charles Firth, whose advice he continued to value for many years thereafter. Rogers did, however, prompt him to write a history of the national debt, and Hewins devoted his historical research to economic topics. He later explained his purpose:

I set before myself as my object to substitute for, or at any rate, to supplement, the theoretical system based upon an analysis of motives and the philosophy underlying orthodox economics, a political economy based upon the study of society and pursued in accordance with the modern historical and scientific method.[4]

Failing to win a fellowship at Oxford, Hewins eked out an uncertain livelihood for the next seven years through his writing and by teaching in the university extension scheme.

His later interest in administration was already evident during his period as an extension lecturer from 1888 to 1894. He served as the organizing secretary of the Oxford University Extension Summer School from 1888 to 1890. This was an attempt to bring some of the better extension students to Oxford for more serious study than was possible in the provinces on a part-time basis.[5] In 1894 Hewins told his mother that, much to his surprise, he had become a popular extension lecturer. Two years later he admitted his gradual disillusionment with the extension scheme. He characterized it as too popular, too elementary, and unsuitable for developing research talents among the better students. The last he viewed as its greatest fault, because few of its students had gone on to pursue serious work at the university.[6]

While an extension lecturer, he wrote nearly 100 articles for Palgrave's *Dictionary of Political Economy*, as well as numerous articles for the *Dictionary of National Biography* and the *Encyclopedia Britannica*. In 1892 he published a textbook, *English Free Trade and Finance, Chiefly in the Seventeenth Century*. Despite his growing scholarly reputation, he was still unable to procure a suitable academic position. In 1891 he applied for the Tooke Professorship at King's College, London. He later claimed that his detailed plan for the reorganization of economic studies at King's was a prototype for the LSE.[7] Cunningham, however, won the professorship. During the early 1890s, Hewins also gave occasional lectures at Pembroke College, but his prospects there were discouraging. His lectures on economic history met with little success, and in the end he was reduced to lecturing to "one student and a chaperone." In 1893 Tout invited him to come to Manchester, but the proposed salary was insufficient and he still hoped for advancement at Oxford. He was associated with the settlement house Toynbee Hall, which for a brief time he attempted to transform into a center for economic study. He also worked for Charles Booth in his survey of the life and labor of London's poor. In 1895 his career took an unexpected turn when he was named the director of the LSE. During the late 1890s, he still occasionally lectured and examined at Oxford. Although he continued to despair for the future of economics under Edgeworth at Oxford, he was gratified to be recognized by an institution where his early "work was treated with studied neglect and contempt."[8]

Early in his career, Hewins was formally allied to the Liberal Party. In 1882 he reported in his diary that during the last two years, he had gradually moved from a Conservative to a Liberal sympathizer. This he ascribed to his interest in social issues.[9] In 1885 he followed Gladstone on the Irish question. His support of Irish Home Rule, however, did not mean that he was a Little Englander. Rather, it implied a faith in home rule as a sounder basis for what he saw as a Liberal imperialism.[10] He claimed that his Liberal sympathies of the 1880s and 1890s were not of the old individualist variety, but consisted of a social liberalism.[11] In 1895 he told his mother that he was questioning his Liberal Party affiliation. He argued that the only way to reform liberalism was through the complete annihilation of the Liberal Party and the creation of a new and bolder political structure.[12] It was not until 1903 that Hewins formally abandoned the Liberal Party for the Unionist Party. The root of Hewins's imperialism, however, was not political or economic. It was profoundly conservative and rooted in family, race, religion, and even soil. In his autobiography he claimed that his enthusiasm for the British Empire was born in 1888 on a visit to the Vale of Evesham and the North Cotswolds. From here members of his family had gone to all parts of the empire. He was especially taken with the ruins of the great Benedictine abbeys and saw them as an inspiration for the creation of a unified empire.[13]

In economics, Hewins's sympathies were from the outset with a practical and historical approach. In his autobiography he characterized the subject as the "scientific examination" of society's economic organization, structure, history, customs, laws, and institutions. His goal was to improve social conditions within both the nation and the empire.[14] His syllabi for his extension courses reveal that his main interests before the late 1890s were in social questions and economic history. They exhibit an eclectic use of both abstract and inductive methods in economics, with the emphasis upon the latter. He especially recommended to his students the work of Ashley, Cunningham, Price, Foxwell, Rogers, Toynbee, and Brentano. His lectures on capital were rather orthodox and even cited Fawcett. Most, however, were on such applied topics as factory legislation, trade unions, cooperatives, and the social conditions of working women.[15]

His critique of the social conditions of industrial society were far less romantic and agrarian than those of Toynbee. In an 1893 lecture, "The Industrial Employment of Women," he deplored the terrible conditions that existed in the sweated trades, but he also reminded his readers that "the advantages of the factory over the domestic system are incalculable." He argued that the suffering brought by the new technology of the factories had been an inevitable consequence of industrial change that had been compounded by bad harvests, the heavy burden of wartime taxation, and anachronistic protective tariffs. These additional factors had blinded men to the salutary effects of industrialization and modern competition.[16] Commenting on Beatrice Webb's treatment of industrialization, he noted that "this root and branch treatment of the Industrial Revolution was all very well years ago when a great deal of sympathy passed for social investigation." Although not minimizing the suffering of those who experienced the trauma of industrialization and writing movingly about those who were still caught up in the old system of the sweated trades, Hewins's inductive studies provided an optimistic critique of laissez faire capitalism. Rapid industrialization had brought into sharper relief the evils of the old system, laid the basis for factory legislation, prompted state-sponsored social reform, and, most importantly, provided the workers with the opportunity to effect their own improvement through the trade union movement.[17]

In spite of Hewins's flirtations with Christian Socialism, trade unions, and cooperatives, his ultimate goal was not to bring a democratic socialism to Britain. He remained firmly committed to capitalism. His suggestions for state intervention were designed to prevent its violent overthrow and to preserve the empire. During the late 1890s his imperial theme became predominant. Prior to this, he still believed in the possibility of educating the workers to accept their role as partners in an enlightened capitalism. This education required that they be taught a historical economics that was free of dangerous socialist theory and the useless abstractions of economic orthodoxy.[18] This goal lay behind much of his intellectual justification of the extension movement and other schemes for worker education. At the same time, he urged the middle and upper classes to abandon their individualist economics of laissez faire and assume their rightful social responsibilies.

With the other historical economists, Hewins was especially critical of the influence of Ricardo upon the subject. He argued, for example, that Ricardo's work was too much influenced by the mobility of capital on the stock exchange, and that Mill's lapses into abstraction owed something to having been "born under the shadow of the Bank of England."[19] There was a certain amount of anti-City and antiestablishment sentiment in his Midlands view of orthodox economic theory and its advocates. Hewins concluded that the chief problem was that principles derived from observation of a particular time and place had been falsely universalized. He quoted Marx to demonstrate that conditions between buyers and sellers were never completely free and thus made a mockery of a science based upon the assumption of perfect competition. He also frequently cited the experiences of agricultural laborers to attack the doctrine of the mobility of labor. Likewise, he criticized the universalist assumptions inherent in Malthus's principles of population. Nevertheless, he continued, there was no need to condemn all of orthodox economics. Rather, "one's attitude to the economists of the old school should be one of patient separating and sifting truth from falsehood."[20] He believed that with Cairnes classical economics had taken a more hopeful direction, for he had at last recognized that an abstract economics cannot be a guide to policy.

Hewins had been trained as a mathematician, but he did not believe that mathematics could be a useful tool in economic analysis. Indeed, he argued that economics would "unfit the mind for grappling with complex problems."[21] Moreover, although he advocated the statistical analysis of economic data, he had an unsophisticated view of its possibilities. Unlike Cunningham, as Price admitted, Hewins was reasonably familiar with contemporary economic theory.[22] His close ties to Midland society, however, had taught him that orthodoxy's picture of a society of the rational, individual economic man was a fiction. Instead, he subscribed to an organic view that emphasized the ties of family, race, religion, patriotism, and industrial structure as its key elements. "Society," he argued, "determines the individual."[23] Though not a Comtist, he held with Comte that economics was part of a larger social science that ultimately had a practical purpose. And thus, he concluded: "We are inevitably led to the conclusion that the historical method is the only possible one for social science."[24]

Hewins held that economic history had a particularly valuable role to play in demonstrating the relativity of economic ideas. Like Ashley, during the late 1880s he insisted that economic history "promises to yield really satisfactory data for determining the laws of production, distribution and consumption of wealth."[25] But Hewins also quickly abandoned his historicist hopes. He condemned German historicism as without scientific foundation. Their approach, he argued, amounted to a justification of "whatever is, is right" and would "banish economic history to the planet of Saturn to keep company with the old political economy."[26] Instead, he emphasized that there were no iron laws of social evolution and thus the purpose of economic study was to provide the opportunity for moral choice in the organization of society.[27] One could not, however, simply apply past solutions to contemporary problems. Careful inductive research was needed for each specific problem. Economic history was especially useful for developing such a mental habit. His early work in economic history showed considerable promise that he might develop into a first rate modern economic historian. He was wary of unsupported generalizations and scrupulous in citing diverse sources.

This professional attitude toward economic history comes out well in two reviews published in 1892. Although praising the immense labor that Rogers had brought to his task, he was critical of many of Rogers's sweeping generalizations, particularly those on trade unions and guilds.[28] Despite Tout's advice not to pour "vinegar in the wounds made by the theoretical school,"[29] as a struggling young scholar, he also boldly attacked Cunningham and characterized his "pure theory" argument as "worthless." Happily, Hewins continued, Cunningham himself had ignored this approach in the body of his economic history. He also faulted Cunningham for having neglected available source material and for employing broad generalizations where tentative conclusions might have served better. He concluded that Cunningham's synthesis was premature, because the necessary scholarship for such a vast undertaking was just being assembled.[30]

In his autobiography, Hewins maintained that his research for Palgrave's *Dictionary* "destroyed in my mind the illusion that Adam Smith and his successors represented the only English economic tradition."[31] The bulk of his writings for this and other reference works was on sixteenth- and seventeenth-century topics and demonstrated familiarity with German as well as English scholarship. His writings exhibit the characteristic approach of the historical economists to the history of economic thought, which they sought to integrate with the economic and political history of the period. His published work prior to 1896 also showed that Hewins was still nominally a free trader during this period. At the same time, and especially in his unpublished notes, he became gradually more sympathetic to neomercantilist notions. In an early lecture on the history of the corn laws, he argued that the protection of agriculture had not been a policy of principle but had arisen out of expediency directed towards promoting the wealth of a class and the national security of a still agricultural nation. Their repeal, although appropriate within the context of the period, had involved a real cost that he argued, had often been overlooked in the general chorus of support for free trade. The repeal had made the country dependent upon foreign grain without appreciably lowering its cost and it was "necessarily accompanied by the depopulation of the rural districts, the sacrifice of generations of improvement, the destruction of agricultural capital, and the loss of an immense number of subsidiary industries."[32] His analysis was reminiscent of Cliffe Leslie's agrarian critique of industrialization under free trade.

His 1892 study, *English Trade and Finance, Chiefly in the Seventeenth Century*, of which Ashley thought highly, was a judicious treatment of mercantilism. He defended bullionist and balance of trade theories of mercantilism as reasonable explanations of the time but saw little value in them as prescriptions for the future. He dealt extensively with the history of the great trading companies, but did not advocate them as models to be imitated. He noted that state efforts under mercantilism to relieve the misery of the workers were largely designed for the interests of a particular class, person, or group and were inappropriate for modern industrial and democratic society.[33] At the same time, he warned that the laissez faire critique of mercantilism was largely specious, for it transferred nineteenth century assumptions to a very different social, economic, and political context.

A few years later, he became less circumspect in drawing lessons from his economic history. In an 1894 account of English economic history from the late medieval period to the eighteenth century, he argued that neomercantilist writers had understood that the "unrestricted operation of the motive of self-interest led to disorders in the state." In order to create an "efficient system of industrial and trade organization," they set out to foster the "public good," by which they meant the balancing of various interests consistent with "economic efficiency" and the "self-sufficiency of the nation."[34] In 1896 he converted what he had once categorized as the practical and specific writings of the mercantilists into a general statement of policy that constituted the framework of his own political goals for the next twenty years: "The object of the mercantile system was the creation of an industrial and commercial state in which, by encouragement or restraint imposed by the sovereign authority, private and sectional interests should be made to promote national strength and independence."[35] He now even went so far as to suggest that in England the concept of imperial federation might require the return to some of these mercantile principles.

Before 1895, Hewins was a young economist in search of a secure academic post. Although his inductive research on particular industries, his experience as a lecturer in industrial areas of England, and his studies in the history of economic thought made him increasingly critical of orthodox economic theory and policy, his views were still restrained by his need for employment. After being named director of the LSE in 1895, the promising and careful young economic historian rapidly became the more confident academic and bold publicist who advocated protection and imperial federation.

Hewins and the LSE

When Professor Hayek reviewed the history of the LSE in 1946, he noted that Hewins had been, like the Webbs, in revolt against orthodox economics. Hayek characterized him as an imperialist, protectionist, and a historical economist who had been greatly influenced by the German Historical School of Economics.[36] By the time Hewins resigned his directorship in 1903 to become head of the Tariff Commission, this characterization was a reasonable description of him. In 1895, however, his views were more moderate. Indeed, Hewins developed his strong imperialist and protectionist views at the LSE. That Sidney Webb picked Hewins as the organizer and first head of a school that has a reputation of having a socialist origin is not as surprising as it might first appear. First, Hewins's imperial views were not yet stridently put forth before 1895. In any case, the Webbs were not opposed to British imperialism. Hewins still called himself a Liberal and, like the Webbs, he was extremely critical of the narrow individualism that he associated with the party. Third, the state socialism of the Webbs in 1895 amounted to a modest program of social reform and was not wholly incompatible with Hewins's views. Fourth, both Hewins and the Webbs were in revolt against aspects of orthodox economics. Fifth, they shared the conviction that a new generation of economic experts was required to tackle the nation's ills with the aid of an inductive social science and they despaired of being able to reform the examination systems of the older universities. Finally, Hewins had scholarly credentials, he had experience as a lecturer and as an organizer, and he was available. Dissatisfied with his extension teaching, he saw few prospects for his career at Oxford. Help came from an unexpected quarter. Not yet thirty, Hewins was approached by Sidney Webb with his scheme of founding a school of economics and political science in London.

The local government reforms of 1888 established an elected London County Council. Sidney Webb, a member of the LCC, hoped to improve technical education with the help of the Council. Moreover, the Webbs believed that providing higher education to the broad middle classes was both an essential requirement of social reform and a step that would prevent the possibility of violent social revolution. Sidney Webb's main efforts at the LCC were directed toward the Technical Education Board, which sought to improve commercial education in the London area. In addition, he also participated in various schemes to reorganize the University of London with a view toward improving economic education. The Tooke Professorship at King's College was part-time and seemed to offer little scope for the expansion of economics teaching. Moreover, its professor from 1891 was Cunningham, who devoted almost all his energies to Cambridge and to his writing. Under Foxwell at University College, the position of economics seemed somewhat more hopeful. In 1890 a political economy club was formed there that, in addition to Foxwell, included Henry Higgs, Charles Booth, Beatrice Potter, Sidney Webb, and James Bonar. Cunningham also joined at a later date, and even Marshall attended on one occasion.[37] In terms of official recognition for economics, however, the situation looked less promising. Economics was only part of a pass degree at University College and did not figure in the London University examinations. Discussions concerning the reform of the university during the 1890s resulted in the work of two royal commissions. The second, the Cowper Report of 1894, recommended that a single university be created in London with both internal and external students and examinations. Sidney Webb promoted a university reorganization bill with Haldane – who was much impressed with the quality of German scientific and technical education – but the scheme was defeated in the Lords in 1897. The university was finally restructured in 1898.[38] During 1894–5, the London Chamber of Commerce also encouraged technical education in London on the German model. Under its auspices, Cunningham gave a series of lectures on the history of European finance.[39] The Chamber of Commerce scheme was supported by the TEB and Sidney Webb played a crucial role in its inception.

In 1894 a powerful argument for improving the quality of economic teaching in England was offered by a report on economic education for Section F of the British Association. Edited by Cunningham, it was almost entirely the work of those opposed to Marshall.[40] During the same year, Henry Hutchinson left a substantial sum to the Fabian Society for the promotion of its ideals. Sidney Webb, the chairman of the trust, seized the opportunity to devise a plan for using a large portion of the funds to found a school of economics in London.[41] Graham Wallas later reported that the idea for the LSE was born in August of 1894 at Borough Farm in a discussion between G.B. Shaw and the Webbs. It was to be modeled on the Ecole Libres des Sciences Politiques in Paris. The central aim was the diffusion of the Fabian gospel. This was to be carried out in part through the foundation of a country-wide Fabian extension lecturing scheme. The Webbs believed that before such a project was possible, an opportunity had to be provided for the training of capable lecturers and for the employment of their professors. Beatrice Webb reported that they became convinced that the immediate need was "hard thinking": "Above all we want the ordinary citizen to feel that the reforming of society is no light matter, and must be undertaken by experts especially trained for that purpose."[42] The Webbs were confident in their belief that, if contemporary social and economic issues were studied dispassionately, society would ultimately choose socialism. This faith in the victory of their cause allowed them to demand the creation of a center of objective research. This emphasis on objectivity also made possible the support of the TEB and the Chamber of Commerce. In late 1895, Beatrice Webb put the matter succinctly: "We have turned our hopes from propaganda to education, from the working-class to the middle class."[43] A further reason for their interest in education for the middle classes was their fear of the growing power of the ILP, its radicalism, and its exclusiveness.

The Webbs first met Hewins at the Bodleian Library in 1893. Although they did not remember him, Hewins recalled their meeting. The Webbs had, in fact, given several papers at the Social Science Club. Subsequent to their formal meeting, they had read Hewins's economic history with appreciation. They consulted him, as someone with experience as a summer school organizer and extension lecturer, about the proposed school in 1894. They first offered the directorship to Graham Wallas. On March 24, 1895, Sidney Webb told Hewins that the project did not look very hopeful, because Graham Wallas would not take the job. Five days later, Webb offered the position to Hewins and noted that, "Unless you can undertake the Directorship and carry out the scheme, it will probably have to be abandoned." Hewins accepted the post the next day.[44]

Beatrice Webb later sought to separate herself politically from Hewins. She wrote in her autobiography that their political views were dissimilar: "His views sprang from an instinctive sympathy with medievalism which led him spiritually, in the course of a a few years, to join the Roman Catholic Church, and politically into a life-long advocacy of a scientific tariff."[45] Her comment on Hewins's fascination with medievalism was curious, for his analysis of medieval society was hardheaded and unromantic. As for Hewins's later fascination with the authoritarian social teaching of Catholicism, it had perhaps not a dissimilar psychological root than her own uncritical attitude toward Soviet Communism. Hewins was not far wrong when he observed: "Married to anyone else, Mrs. Webb might have followed an Imperialist line."[46] Beatrice Webb also listed areas of agreement with Hewins:

First, our common dislike of the so-called Manchester School, of its unverified inductive reasoning and abstract generalizations, of its apotheosis of the "economic man," exclusively inspired by the motive of pecuniary self-interest and of the passionate defense of the rights of property as against the need of humanity. And, secondly, our common faith in the practicability and urgent necessity of a concrete science of society implemented through historical research, personal observation and statistical verification.[47]

Finally, in 1895 she also saw him as a socialist.[48] For his part, Hewins later sought to downplay the school's links with socialism. Instead, he emphasized its ties to business and claimed that for eight years "we worked in complete harmony."[49]

On being charged with organizing the school, Hewins set out to rally support for his project, especially from those opposed to orthodox political economy. Cunningham replied quickly, telling Hewins that he was delighted with the scheme, "though I am a little sorry that the mainstream of economic history at Oxford is to be removed." He also offered to give some public lectures and, in a conspiratorial note, asked Hewins for help in publishing a primer on political economy that Cambridge had refused "because I am not orthodox."[50] W. Smart wrote from Glasgow that "it realizes what I have mapped out for my own place here."[51] Foxwell, who felt his position at University College threatened by the project, nonetheless offered his cooperation.[52] From Southwest Harbor, Maine, Ashley sent a warm personal letter of support, promised to support the school in America, and offered to lecture while on sabbatical in the future.[53] Encouragement also came from Germany. W. Bauer commented that the school represented "a great triumph for University Extension and Economic History." The school was of course not so much a triumph for the university extension movement, out of which it partly grew, but signaled its transformation into a center for the professional study of economics and other social sciences aimed especially at a middle class clientele. Bauer's comment about a triumph for economic history was closer to the mark because the school's emphasis upon economic history and applied economics, especially distinguished the school from Cambridge. Significantly, Bauer added: "While the doors of the Universities are closed to dissenters in economics, they will give fresh life to your young institution."[54] Marshall, who was at first reticent in commenting on the school, but suspicious of its purposes, became increasingly critical of the institution. When Hewins prepared a critique of English economic teaching for Sadler's Blue Book, Marshall told Hewins pointedly that he ought not to advertise the London School by criticizing Cambridge. The success of the LSE and the creation of the Birmingham Faculty of Commerce under Ashley finally convinced Marshall that, for his vision of the discipline to triumph, the recasting of economic education at Cambridge was an urgent necessity.[55]

The school was not shy of its historical direction. Hewins's prospectus for the school declared: "The special aim of the School will be, from the first, the study and investigation of the concrete facts of industrial life and the actual working of economic and political relations as they exist, or have existed, in the United Kingdom and in foreign countries."[56] Hewins recruited a faculty of dissenters for the LSE. In addition to Cunningham, Foxwell, and Hewins, early lecturers included J.E.C. Munro from Manchester on law and economics, Halford J. Mackinder on geography and commerce, W.M. Acworth on railway economics, A.L. Bowley on statistics, and Edwin Cannan on taxation and finance. Cannan's subject during the first few years was significant, for it was an inductive and applied one. It was not until two years later that Cannan began to lecture on economic theory.[57] Occasional lecturers at the school during the 1890s also included such dissenters as J.A. Hobson, H.L. Smith, and Ashley. There were also some orthodox lecturers on the staff during these years, such as Edgeworth, E.C.K. Gonner, R.H.

Palgrave, and Robert Giffen, but despite this sprinkling of Marshall's allies, the early years of the school were dominated by dissenters, and especially by historical dissenters.

When the Webbs recruited Graham Wallas to lecture on political science, Beatrice Webb commented, after reviewing many unsatisfactory candidates, that one even wished "to construct a 'Political Man' from whose imaginary qualities all things might be deduced."[58] Neither the Webbs nor Hewins wished to build an institution in which deductive theory in politics, sociology, or economics predominated. They sought to build a school dominated by an inductive spirit that could produce scholarship geared to solving practical problems and teach students who would enter the civil service, politics, and the professions. Such subjects prevailed at the school during this period. The three year course in economics paid little attention to economic theory. Instead, it emphasized economic history, the history of economic thought, applied economics, and, in the final year, supervised research in an applied area with a stress on the proper method of investigation. Symbolically, it was the LSE that in 1902 appointed Lilian Knowles as the first full-time lecturer in economic history in Britain.[59]

Hewins claimed that the divergence between his aims and those of the Webbs became apparent during their trip to America in 1898. First, he discovered that their influence with the LCC was much overrated. The occasion was an attack, led by Ramsay MacDonald, on the TEB's subsidy for the school and focused on the LSE's failure to provide commercial education. The storm was weathered, but the issue was crucial. The school had now largely divorced itself from educating the aristocracy of the working class, and even the clerks of the lower middle class, and was establishing itself squarely as a university-level teaching and research body. There was also a second significance. The Fabian connection with the school, which had been deemphasized at the outset, was further circumscribed through the creation of an independent board of trustees for the school and its incorporation as the Faculty of Economics in London University. Hewins, in any case, had no use for Fabian socialism: "I have always regarded Fabianism with contempt and have attached no practical importance to it."[60] Hewins's objections to Fabianism were the familiar ones of the historical economists. He was opposed to socialism in principle and saw Fabian economics as a derivative of Ricardian economics.[61] Instead of looking for support from among Fabian and labor sympathizers on the LCC, Hewins argued that the school should turn for help to the business world. The key issue between Hewins and the Webbs, however, became Hewins's rejection of their

Liberal imperialism and his wholehearted embrace of what he called his "natural conservatism and imperialism."[62]

Hewins claimed that his movement toward imperialism and tariff reform took place gradually while he was lecturing at the LSE on economic diplomacy between 1895 and 1900. He especially credited the influence of his German students, who suggested that a return to England's traditional mercantilism best suited its threatened position in the world. Hewins's actual adoption of a neomercantilist program took place in 1899.[63] His imperialist enthusiasm, however, was apparent in his letters to the Webbs in the previous year. He told them that he had been much moved by Gladstone's lying in state, but that the old liberalism he represented was an anachronism. There had been some talk of endowing the school in his memory, but he counseled against this: "It would be fatal to identify the School with official Liberalism." He envisaged a great economic and political struggle between nations and the school "ought to be able to do great work in supplying the groundwork for constructive statesmanship and the consolidation of the national forces." He went on to note that, despite the success of the school in reorganizing economic studies in England, there were still few career opportunities for professional economists. However, he continued, "Years hence, when we are all dead, the School may become a place for training economic students. But it has first to inspire public policy, not by drafting programs, but by presenting ideas clothed in the living garment of reality." Despite his call for objectivity, there was increasingly little doubt about his own imperial interests. He told the Webbs: "If I had the means, nothing would please me better than to enter Parliament and appear unmasked as the advocate of the policy I wish to see carried into effect."[64] Two years later, when the LSE had become part of the reorganized University of London, he told his mother: "I mean to do my best to make the University an 'instrument of Empire,' to weld together the different parts of the English race, to infuse a new spirit into British administration."[65] By 1903 the Webbs commitment to "knowledge and science and truth" was considerably less partisan than Hewins's embrace of Joseph Chamberlain's Unionist crusade.[66]

During 1903 Hewins valiantly attempted to convince the Webbs to join the tariff reform cause. Sidney Webb warned Hewins that his tariff reform articles for the *Times* might compromise the school. Despite Hewins's argument that tariff reform was a social as well as an imperial project, Webb advised caution because: "You and I are already 'suspect' on the subject." He also predicted a Liberal victory because "Chamberlain, as usual, is going to spoil a good idea by rash and reckless adoption of an impossible device for carrying it out just as he did about Old Age Pensions."[67] In November of 1903, Hewins informed the Webbs that he had decided to leave the school for a full-time position as secretary to the Tariff Commission.[68] Despite Hewins's efforts to alter the position of the Webbs, they remained "agnostic" on the tariff question. Hewins had turned from the study of economic history to its administration and to politics. The Webbs had become increasingly scholarly in their own pursuits.

As the LSE matured and Hewins entered politics, the school became less of a dissenting institution. It did not, however, lose its historical sympathies quickly and played a key role in the development of economic history as an academic discipline. When the LSE became part of London University, Beatrice Webb declared that their efforts at the school had resulted in an economics degree whose program of studies was in harmony with the inductive methods of the physical sciences.[69] The second director of the school was Halford John Mackinder. He was, like Hewins, an Oxford product and a fervent imperialist. The creator of "historical geography," he also became a supporter of Chamberlain and resigned his position at the school in 1908 in order to devote more of his efforts to tariff reform and imperial federation.[70] In 1908 Ashley was considered as director of the LSE; fearing that the selection of yet another tariff reformer would identify the school too closely with the cause, and as no otherwise suitable economist was available, the Webbs turned to the free trade imperialist, W. Pember Reeves.[71] From 1919 to 1937, William Beveridge was the director of the LSE. Beveridge also had little interest in economic theory, but he was not a historical economist. He hoped to make economics more statistical and to wed it to the natural sciences.[72] During his tenure, Lionel Robbins and F.A. Hayek joined the school and made it the bastion of orthodoxy in English economics. They, rather than the dissenters headed by J.M. Keynes at Cambridge, championed the role of economists as detached scientists and reasserted the ideals of nineteenth century liberalism.[73] Under Hewins and Mackinder, however, the LSE played the key role in opposing the Ricardian and Marshallian tradition in English economics. And, it was largely, though not exclusively, the historical economists who stamped the early character of the school with an emphasis on applied economics and economic history.

Hewins: historical economics and politics

While at the LSE, Hewins became impressed with the critical role of the German economists in the formulation of policy. He told the Webbs that they were much esteemed by Professor von Halle, of whom he had lately seen a great deal, and that among the Germans Marshall's "book is not considered intrinsically important." He reported that Schmoller was very keen on the London School and "we seem be getting a firm hold on the younger men. I think the transference of the 'centre of force' in economics from Germany to London is by no means impossible."[74] But educating a cadre of experts who might eventually change national economic policy was a slow and laborious process. Reporting on several attacks upon the school in 1903, he told S. Webb: "it will be exhilarating and provide a pleasant relief from the intolerable burden of lecturing every day in the week."[75] Although he continued to give occasional lectures at the school, he devoted the bulk of his career after 1903 to the politics of imperialism and tariff reform.

Hewins's public advocacy of tariff reform was quickened by the experience of the Boer War and by the adoption of a preferential tariff scheme by Canada in 1898. In 1900 Schmoller invited Hewins to contribute an article on British trade policy for his famous *Jahrbuch*. Hewins consulted Chamberlain, who replied that he favored a preferential tariff for the British Empire but thought it politically impossible for the moment. Ominously, Chamberlain also suggested that the adoption of an imperial policy did not necessarily have to include the state regulation of labor and educational reform advocated by Hewins.[76] Hewins's contribution to Schmoller's *Jahrbuch* appeared in 1901 and was based on a series of lectures he had given several years earlier at the Society of Arts. He distinguished between three kinds of imperialists. First, the Liberal imperialists hoped to hold the empire together through laissez faire and self-interest. This he believed an utter illusion manifestly contradicted by recent developments. Second, the political imperialists sought to consolidate the empire through various forms of imperial federation. He judged them more effective, though their continued advocacy of an outdated system of free trade left them without an adequate economic policy. Third, the constructive imperialists saw the empire, rather than the nation, as the arena of public policy. They advocated a program designed to postpone the immediate interests of the consumer in cheap consumption for the long-term interest of developing the productive capacity of the empire. This program required not only a scheme of imperial preference, but also the reform of imperial governance, public finance, education, and labor policy. In short, he advocated "neo-mercantilism" – a term coined by the Germans in reference to Hewins and other advocates of this policy in England.[77] Hewins suggested that substituting "empire" for "national" in his 1895 definition of mercantilism would express the essential aim of his policy: Each nation within the empire would, "by encouragement or restraint imposed by the sovereign authority," mold "private and national interests" into imperial "strength and efficiency."[78] Hewins's economic history had now become a guide to public policy.

When Chamberlain announced his scheme for tariff reform in 1903, he was widely attacked for his erroneous economics. Chamberlain told Hewins: "I do not pretend to be an economic expert. I once read Mill and tried to read Marshall. You must supply the economic arguments."[79] Hewins became Chamberlain's chief economic adviser and orchestrated the counterattack on the orthodox economists in the press.[80] Ashley quickly cautioned Hewins that, if Chamberlain wins the campaign, "it will be with the aid of the fund of crudest and most selfish and stupid Protectionism."[81] Hewins's devotion to the crusade of imperial integration did not make him a good party man and limited his political success. He had admitted Chamberlain's shortcomings in 1903, and by 1906 he was roundly criticizing his economic ignorance and his false use of statistics.[82] In 1904 Balfour reminded Hewins of his academic career: "I heartily wish you were back at the School of Economics; doing there work of unequalled usefulness instead of cursing with bell, book, and candle the besotted followers of Pitt, Peel, and Cobden."[83] Hewins, however, did not turn back. Instead, he provided Balfour with economic advice during the latter's tortuous wandering through the labyrinth of the tariff issue. He also offered his services to Bonar Law, apparently with little success. He was somewhat closer to Stanley Baldwin and was still providing him with technical information on the tariff issue in 1929.[84] After several unsuccessful attempts, Hewins was elected to Parliament, where he served from 1912 to 1919. In 1917–1918, he was the Under Secretary for the Colonies. Despite several efforts, he never regained his seat in Parliament. Ironically, on the day of his death in 1931, the national government introduced emergency tariff legislation in its attempt to deal with the world economic crisis.

From 1903 to 1917, Hewins was employed as secretary of the Tariff Commission. He typified the role of the economic expert of the twentieth century who headed a private lobbying group tied to a political program and party and who claimed to use the principles of scientific research to promote his program. He insisted that the commission was "purely scientific and not propagandist" and that "it was in direct line with the objects for which the London School of Economics had been founded."[85] The memorandum establishing the commission stated that " all members of the Committee should be favorable to Mr. Chamberlain's views." This, Hewins explained, meant that everyone should support a general imperialist policy, but did not have to be wedded to a particular version of it.[86] Despite the obvious bias, the commission's method of operation appears to have been thorough, and it was an impressive inductive enterprise with the purpose of drawing up specific proposals for tariffs and imperial preference. Charles Booth lent his experience as a social investigator to the commission, and its mode of operation was essentially his. When it was suggested to subsume the commission under the overtly political Tariff Reform League, Hewins resisted on the grounds that the commission was a scientific body while the league was propagandist.[87] In a 1916 dispute with Asquith over tariffs, Hewins defended his role as that of a scientific investigator.[88] Despite its nominal independence and Hewins's academic illusions, the Tariff Commission owed its existence to the Unionist Party. During the war, the commission did research for the Unionist Business Committee and the Balfour of Burleigh Committee on Trade and Industry. Hewins resigned from the commission in 1917. When he returned to it in 1921, he found its affairs in a shambles. It was at first amalgamated with the Tariff Reform League and then became the short-lived Empire Development Union. This in turn became the Empire Industries Association, which was later transformed by L.S. Amery to the Empire Economic Union.[89]

Although Hewins concentrated his rhetoric after 1903 on imperial integration and economic development, he continued to insist on the need for social reform. He made little headway, however, on this issue with the Conservative Party. He always claimed that he had come to imperialism and tariff reform through his concern for social reform and noted that this was also true of many others: "They were Social Reformers first, and became Tariff Reformers."[90] Despite his connection with trade unions, the cooperative movement, and Christian socialism during his extension days, by the late 1890s Hewins's approach to the social question had become authoritarian and state-centered. In 1899 he had argued that the modern relief of poverty must be carried out by a vast scientific effort of the state, for "the modern State is the Christian Church in its workaday clothes."[91] In 1901 he advocated the state regulation of wages as a superior system to free collective bargaining.[92] During a debate in Parliament on a minimum-wage bill for miners in 1912, he lectured Parliament on the history of trade unions – a lecture that the next speaker described as "a kind of academic discussion." He reminded the House that he had defended the labor movement for twenty-five years, but that for the sake of the national interest, he wished to regulate it severely.[93] Hewins's warnings on the dangers of socialist revolution were a constant theme of his career. During the 1890s he had dismissed socialism as an erroneous policy of a few middle-class intellectuals which enjoyed little support from the working classes. But in 1913, as labor unrest became threatening, he warned that syndicalism had transformed parliamentary and evolutionary socialism into a revolutionary force.[94] During the war, he welcomed the curbing of the trade unions and the state regulation of wages and hailed the moves as a model for the future. After the war, his fear of revolution became increasingly shrill, and he urged Lloyd George to adopt a corporatist program as advocated by the Catholic teaching of Pope Leo XIII and the German Center Party. During the 1920s, Hewins became increasingly interested in corporatism. He admitted some connection between his Catholicism and his "searching up of ancient economic Gods."[95] In the end, his most consistent social policy was his counter revolutionary argument that imperialism "should bring back the great body of working men to their natural home."[96] Hewins's writings and lectures on imperial policy after 1903 reiterated many of the arguments from his early writings on economic history. This time, however, they were more vigorous and absolute.[97] His career as scholar, teacher, academic administrator, publicist, and political figure was the most activist version of the historical economists' conception of the role of the social scientist in society.

The Webbs as historical economists

Beatrice and Sidney Webb, who have often been viewed as historians and sociologists, can also be seen as historical economists. Their politics, which is still often popularly called socialist, as has been shown for many years now, can also be characterized as social-imperialist. They hoped, through the process of permeation to convince both Liberal and Tory imperialists of the necessity of combining social reform with their imperial schemes.[98] If the term had not taken on a more sinister meaning in the twentieth century, their views might be labeled as national socialism. During the South African War, the Webbs associated the pro-Boer position with an individualist and laissez-faire Gladstonian Liberalism that they vigorously opposed, and they suggested that Lord Rosebery, a Liberal imperialist, had forged a more palatable and progressive liberalism by combinng imperialism with social reform.[99] Beatrice Webb believed Chamberlain's tariff program to be "politically impractical," but "absurd notions that the 'natural' channels of trade are necessarily the best" ought to be abandoned. Thus, although the Webbs remained "agnostics" on the tariff issue, Beatrice nonetheless suggested that she would set the "Fabian Society at work to prepare the ground for some intermediate plan for combining imperialism with sound national economy."[100]

The joint historical and economic work of the Webbs, and especially that of the 1890s, bore such trademarks of historical economics as a vigorous opposition to the method and many of the conclusions of orthodox economics, a pessimistic interpretation of the social effects of the Industrial Revolution, an embrace of a state-regulated economy of trusts and labor unions, an appeal for a measure of national social reform that they termed evolutionary socialism, and a healthy respect for a British imperial mission. Their social, administrative, and economic history had primarily a practical purpose. In 1923, they observed that their scholarly efforts had been devoted to tracing "the rise and growth of the industrial and social institutions which, we believe, should and will gradually supersede the reign of capitalism."[101] What they meant by capitalism was not its twentieth century variants but the laissez-faire capitalism of the century of the Industrial Revolution. Their research program had been Toynbean. They claimed to have used their historical research to determine the direction of social evolution; having determined its path through the history of trade unionism, the cooperative movement, the Poor Laws, and local government, they hoped to guide society peacefully along its natural path of evolution.

Before her marriage to Sidney Webb, Beatrice Potter especially demonstrated her sympathy with the method of historical economics. In her revealing autobiography, Beatrice Potter, the daughter of an upper-middle class businessman, suggested that, as Toynbee had taught, the middle classes could atone for their sins by reconstructing society on a more egalitarian and stable foundation.[102] She was made personally aware of the uncertainties and poverty of industrial society through her visits to working class relatives. Also inspired by the Religion of Humanity, she called for the creation of a science of society able to implement her social ideals. To this end, she began in 1886 a study of political economy. Finding the subject a "most hateful drudgery," she nonetheless persevered so that she might discover "its necessary assumptions" and the "data upon which political economy is based."[103] Her essays of 1886, "The Rise and Growth of English Economics" and "The Economic Theory of Karl Marx," demonstrated a historical dissatisfaction with the method of orthodox economics.

She began her study with the commonplace historical argument that the mercantilists ought not to be roundly condemned, for they offered practical suggestions for policy suited to their own time and place. Adam Smith, she argued, was one of the greatest of all economists because he was "no pedant in the use of method; he used the Historical, Inductive, and Deductive methods, as they respectively suited the nature of his subject."[104] She insisted that Smith could not be properly appreciated if one only mined his work for abstract generalizations, for he was also a committed social reformer. As such, he suggested numerous areas for state intervention, including the use of state power on behalf of the workers. She did find fault with Smith's labor theory of value and especially criticized its universalization by Ricardo and the German socialists into a faulty doctrine of scientific socialism.[105] Despite this and other criticism of his work, she found his economics superior to that of his followers; for in "dealing with the origin of economic facts he used the historical method," and "the generalizations upon which he based his reasoning were wider and were drawn more from abstract observation than from an a priori idea of man."[106] Her characterization of Ricardo's place in the history of English economics might have been written by almost any of the historical economists. Ricardo had introduced an exclusive deductive method into English economics; his work provided the basis for the dangerous socialism of Marx and Henry George. With Ricardo, she concluded, the science of economics ceased to concern itself with people, and became, as Bagehot called it, the "science of business," or, as she called it, "The Employer's Gospel."[107]

She especially credited Carlyle with initiating the revolt against laissez faire economics and policy. Marx was another great critic of economic orthodoxy, but unfortunately his system was deduced from an abstract and erroneous value theory and thus could offer no escape from the old political economy.[108] Fortunately, however, the old political economy had been largely abandoned by contemporary economists, if not yet by the public at large. She credited a long line of thinkers from Malthus to Cliffe Leslie and Arnold Toynbee with having rejected the deductive method and having substituted an inductive and historical one. But even among the straight line of the orthodox, she continued, Ricardo's teaching has been restricted and refuted.[109] Here she especially pointed to Jevons, Sidgwick, and Marshall.

Indeed, Marshall was the hero of her essay and the "savior" of economics. However, it was her own version of Marshall that she praised. She was especially impressed with his psychological and historical metaphors and with his insistence on the need for more inductive methods.[110] She demonstrated little interest in or understanding of his theoretical work. By 1890 she found Marshall "disappointing" and called for a "reorganization of Economics if it is to continue as a science."[111] In 1897 she stayed with Marshall in Cambridge and reported on his penchant for making "an astounding observation with no basis in fact" whenever he sought to refute some popular notion. By this time, she believed that they had forced him to be an "intellectual reactionary," for his socialism was nothing more than a vague faith in the cooperative movement.[112]

Beatrice Webb advocated what she called "the economic organism of research," which began with certain "indisputable facts of human nature," such as that demand for material goods must be assumed to operate in all people to the same extent in all times. However, the goal of the economist as economist was to measure these ends in particular situations by using an inductive and biological method as "opposed to the mechanical and metaphysical method of Economics."[113] She did not explain how such a method would operate in practice. Although the influence of Comte was clearly present in her work, and her ultimate aim was a science of society rather than a science of political economy, she did not see this as wholly incompatible with Marshall's methodology.

Her diaries demonstrate that she invested considerable psychological capital in her essays on the history and method of economics. She alternated between believing that she was writing a path breaking essay and the view that it was merely an object of study for her larger goals. After completing her manuscript, she sent it to Mary and Charles Booth for review. They both replied severely and suggested it needed "maturing." She also sent it to Herbert Spencer, who replied that her criticisms of economic orthodoxy "are a good deal of the kind that have of late years been made, and, as I think, not rightly made."[114] Despite her dejection at these criticisms, she revised the work and continued her study of political economy. But, instead of writing and publishing work on the history of economic thought and methodology, she turned to more concrete historical studies of contemporary social problems. In truth, her brief study of the history of economic thought was not equal to the task she had set herself, and her study of economics cannot be judged as professional. As she herself, perhaps too readily, admitted, it had carried her "out of my depth as a reasoner."[115] In social and economic history she found that larger science of society that served her hopes for social reform.

Her initiation into social research came as a participant in Charles Booth's survey of London poverty. This survey convinced her that the proper method for social research was the "historical method."[116] Her analysis of the London sweated trades concluded that the difficult social conditions prevalent in these trades were not caused simply by the greed of evil men, as she had originally supposed; rather, they were the natural outgrowth of the system of individual competition. It was the ideal of free competition itself that she repudiated, as well as the efforts of private charities to provide adequate social amelioration. Instead, she embraced a Toynbean model of corporate organization and state regulation. Although she had not yet conducted any historical research into the period of the Industrial Revolution, she nonetheless confidently reiterated Toynbee's pessimistic conclusions on the condition of the working classes during industrialization under laissez faire. Some thirty years later, the Webbs asserted that their historical inquiries had confirmed the correctness of this interpretation; moreover, they now added, in tones characteristic of historical economics, that "the horrors of the unregulated factory, the mine and the slum – made abstract in what was called the 'natural rate of wages' – were defended by Ricardo and Nassau Senior . . . Rev. Thomas Malthus and Archbishop Whately."[117]

Beatrice Webb was originally an enthusiastic supporter of the cooperative movement. By the time she wrote a historical treatment of the movement, however, she concluded that the rationale for cooperative production was based on a labor theory of value that was false and therefore the movement could be of little utility in solving the social problems of capitalism. Nevertheless, she did retain her faith in the consumer cooperative venture. A better solution than cooperative production, she argued, was to equalize the bargaining power of capital and labor through the full recognition of the trade union movement. Further, to improve the lot of the old, the young, and the infirm, she suggested that the state maintain them at a "National Minimum" standard of life. Prior to her marriage to Sidney Webb, her socialist ideal remained suspicious of too large a role for the state. She described it as:

a vision of a gradually emerging new social order, to be based on the deliberate adjustment of economic faculty and economic desire, and to be embodied in an interlocking dual organization of democracies of consumers and democracies of producers – voluntary as well as obligatory, and international as well as national – that seemed to me to afford a practicable framework for the future co-operative commonwealth.[118]

If Beatrice Webb's ideal society was socialist, it was the socialism of the young historical economists of the time.

With their marriage, the Webbs commenced a partnership of historical research that criticized the ideal of free competition and chronicled the rise of alternative models of social organization so that their proposals for social reform seemed to flow naturally from the process of historical evolution itself. Sidney Webb, a civil servant and a Fabian, brought to their partnership both a healthy respect for the state's role in society and a greater appreciation for deductive economics. Indeed, his views on economic theory owed much to neoclassicism and were not those of the historical economists. In a series of lectures, chiefly at the Workingman's College in London during the 1880s, he addressed himself on several occasions to the crisis of political economy and its proper method. He argued that the chief problem of contemporary economics was its inability to understand the dichotomy between the universal principles of economics as science, which were true for all times and places, and the prescriptions of economic policy, which were to be suited to a particular time and place. He saw no need for an endless argument on the nature of economic method. The economist should employ all methods when appropriate: "Observation, Experiment, Induction, Deduction, and Verification will all lend their aid, and if the bewildering German metaphysicians bring to light some new organon for scientific investigation, it may be safely asserted that the Economist will not, any more than the geologist, refuse its help."[119]

Despite such catholic statements, he allowed himself some methodological judgments. He believed that Cliffe Leslie had done little more than offer some useful criticism of the concrete deductive method of Mill. His premature death had "deprived the world of any more systematic work," but he doubted that even Cliffe Leslie would have been successful in raising the empirical to a scientific method.[120] Indeed, the work of the historical economists, he concluded, belonged to the discipline of history rather than to economic science. He was equally critical of what he called the "abstract intuitive" method of Marx and the socialists. Marx, Webb argued, had made a mere abstraction of human beings and had universalized motives unnecessarily. He did find praise for the socialists as practitioners of ethics and of "the art of living." "As economists," however, "they had produced nothing, corrected nothing, discovered nothing, and the only useful method of Political Economy remains the much abused but still triumphant Concrete Deductive Method of Ricardo, Mill, and Cairnes."[121] Despite caustic comments – such as "attentive students still sit at the feet of such 'antiquated' teachers as Professor Marshall and burn midnight oil over 'hidebound pedants' like Professor Sidgwick" – Sidney Webb believed that contemporary economic theory had been saved from irrelevance by J.S. Mill. He argued that Mill had introduced a new spirit into English economics, as Comte had done on the continent. These writers, Webb continued, had understood the fallacies of the individualist bias of the classical economists and the sophistry of the popularizers.[122] In 1888, Sidney Webb offered his own thoroughly deductive economic theory of "economic interest" rooted in Ricardian and marginal utility theory.[123] Although Fabianism attempted to erect a social democratic economics on the neoclassical tradition, Sidney Webb, like his spouse, did not pursue his work in economic theory. Instead, they turned their long and productive partnership to historical research and applied economics.

At a time when sociology was also emerging as an independent academic discipline, there were as yet no sharp distinctions between historical sociology, social history, and economic history. Indeed, all three were components of historical economics. In 1884, Sidney Webb gave a course of lectures on English economic history from the origin of the village community to the present. The virtue of history, he argued, was that it demonstrated the universality of change and would thus free men from the force of habit. Such history must especially be social and economic history. It would not simply be a chronicle of the evils of the past, however useful this might be in reforming the present, but would constitute a "sociology of the past."[124] During the 1890s, the Webbs believed that their research was a contribution to economics, history, and sociology. Moreover, they perceived as their special contribution the combination of these into a historical science of society. Such a science of society was both an intellectual endeavor and a guide to reforming society. They held, for example, that their 1894 *History of Trade Unionism* was an economic study, the purpose of which was to present a history and origin of the functions of the movement, an analysis of its relationship to profit-making enterprise, its links to the consumer cooperative movement, its ties to the rise of political democracy, and an economic defense of the trade unions against the charges leveled against them by some of the orthodox economists.

The Webbs wrote of their 1897 study, *Industrial Democracy*, that "we alternate between thinking that the work will be so great in its effect on political and economic thought, as Adam Smith's *Wealth of Nations*, to wondering whether the whole of it is not an elaborate figment of our imaginations."[125] A combination of applied economics and economic history, the work was an analysis of modern industrial society which bore a close resemblance to the ideas of Ashley. One of Ashley's most persistent arguments was that domestic social peace required a strong and fully legal role for organized labor. It was the Webbs, however, who provided a full defense of the movement. Through an elaborate analysis of the wages fund doctrine, the Webbs concluded that, if economic theory had been properly understood, it could not have been used to oppose the rise of labor. This hostility to labor, they continued, was rooted in a vulgar popular tradition of economics.

The Webbs did not reject the truth inherent in economic theory per se. Like Ashley, however, they found it of little utility in dealing with real economic phenomena. They concluded: "We are loathe to pin our faith in any manipulation of economic abstractions, with or without the aid of mathematics. . . . We are inclined to attach more weight to a consideration of the processes of industrial life as they actually exist."[126] Further, like Ashley, the Webbs even hoped to use their own history as the foundation for a new theory of competition. They declared that the old theory of competition had been made obsolete by the rise of the all-pervasive monopolies – monopolies, both legal and natural, and of both producers and consumers. In such a world, the essential justification of trade unions was that they provided a bulwark for the maintenance of a "Standard of Life," first, against the fundamentally unequal bargaining position between capital and labor, and second, as a defense against the barriers erected by other organized groups in society. Although praising the unions for being "positively conducive to national efficiency and national wealth," the Webbs also argued that they were a valuable model for the democratic organization of society.[127]

Their study of the labor movement also provided the Webbs with the concept of the "National Minimum," which they popularized in their efforts to reform the Poor Laws. But in this project, they placed less reliance on their model of the "co-operative commonwealth," and demanded, instead, that the state entirely remove the poorest groups in society from the marketplace. The Webbs envisaged a role for the state in the economy, that by 1918 went considerably beyond the proposals of Ashley, Hewins, and Cunningham. Further, instead of pointing to medieval and mercantilist precedents, the Webbs based their advocacy of state intervention on their mammoth study of local government from 1688 to 1934, in which they traced its evolution from voluntary associations, designed to deal with local and temporary problems, to compulsory bodies committed to solving the nation's difficulties.[128]

The Webbs' 1932 description of inductive research noted that their methodological writings could offer no guidance on whether a pure science of political economy was attainable. They emphasized that their aim had been to combine all the social sciences into a grand science of society.[129] Despite their gravitation toward sociology, much of their work, especially that of the 1890s, can be viewed as a contribution to historical economics. It was designed to indicate the direction of social evolution and to urge society peacefully in that direction. It bore a close affinity in spirit, method, and content to the path sketched out by Toynbee and traversed by the historical economists. This similarity, added to the fact that they were also social-imperialists, makes the connection between Hewins, the Webbs, and the early days of the LSE far less surprising. The Webbs, despite Sidney Webb's adherence to the value of a deductive method for economic theory and his continued faith in its Ricardian and neoclassical framework, ultimately agreed with Hewins that the most important part of economics should be its practical branches of applied economics and economic history, for it provided a realistic and wide framework for the making of policy. It was this view that Hewins and the Webbs incorporated into the early LSE, and it was this view that for the Webbs and the historical economists was the chief justification for being social scientists.

CHAPTER 9

Conclusion and epilogue

Fifty years after the Adam Smith Centennial Dinner, Ashley, the first president of the Economic History Society, warned the economic historians: "The theoretical economists are ready to keep us quiet by giving us a little garden plot of our own; and we humble historians are so thankful for a little undisputed territory that we are inclined to leave the economists to their own devices."[1] Ashley's comment was the swan song of English historical economics. Ashley himself would be dead within a year. Cunningham had already passed away in 1919. Although several of the historical economists continued to be heard after the First World War, by 1926 Cliffe Leslie's program of the 1870s had been dissolved in the professional study of economic history and applied economics.

Historical economics and the history of economic thought

Most accounts of the history of British economic thought pay but little attention to the contribution of the historical economists, although recent scholarship on the subject holds hope for the future. Modern work in the sociology of science offers many explanations for the relative neglect of historical economics. Ashley, however, had already grasped the central issue. The historical economists protested against a Whig version of the history of economic thought in which pride of place went to those who anticipated developments in modern theory and neglected the work of dissenters. Paradoxically, as Ashley understood, the success of the historical economists in creating a discipline of economic history removed them from being considered economists. Instead of revolutionizing all of economic study, the historical economists subdivided the subject. The critic of economic theory who fails to offer a satisfactory alternative theory is soon forgotten in the history of the subject. Those who subdivide a field are honored as founders by the adherents of the subdivision, but are often relegated to obscurity within the core of the subject. The core of economic study remained economic theory. If, however, we seek to understand the history of economic thought in a

187

wider and more realistic historical perspective and to gain a broader perspective on the direction, scope, and purpose of economic study, the contribution of the English historical economists, as well as that of other dissenters, must be given a more prominent place in the history of economic thought.

Between about 1870 and 1926, the English historical economists challenged the theory, policy recommendations, and academic dominance of classical and neoclassical economics in Britain. They established economic history as a separate and academically recognized field of study, encouraged the study of applied economics, promoted the study of public and business administration, produced valuable work in the history of economic thought, and limited the claims of universality and social utility of deductive economics. English historical economics failed to constitute itself into a "school of economics" with an acknowledged leader, a central text, and a common research program. If the historical economists were a "school" at all, they became the first academic school of English economic history. As historical economists, they offered a primarily "historist" critique of economic orthodoxy rather than an "historicist" research program designed to discover inductively the laws of economics. At Cambridge, Marshall assured the dominance of economic theory in the new economics curriculum, but at the LSE, Birmingham, Oxford, and other institutions, the efforts and influence of the historical economists resulted in economics programs during the first few decades of the twentieth century that included large doses of economic history and applied economics.

The origin and growth of English historical economics was rooted in the social, economic, political, and intellectual controversies of late Victorian Britain. Their work was a response to the arrival of political democracy, the rise of the labor movement, the alteration of Britain's agricultural and industrial structure, the growing political and economic competition of the United States and Germany, the evolutionary and historical framework of late-nineteenth-century social thought, and the theoretical crisis of English political economy during the 1870s. They condemned orthodox economics as a barrier to social reform, as unresponsive to Britain's increasingly precarious international position, and as unnecessarily impractical and metaphysical. Instead, they called for the creation of a new social and economic vision that, although it became increasingly conservative and neomercantilist, nonetheless had the virtue of focusing on macroeconomic issues rather than the microeconomic emphasis of neoclassical theory. They insisted that their views were more ethical and in greater harmony with the evolutionary view of society than the economic selfishness of the deductive orthodoxy. As committed social and political reformers, they championed the role of the economist as both an academic and an advocate of public policy.

During the 1870s and 1890s, the revolt of English historical economics often appeared to be a protest against the popular economics of the Manchester School. Invoking the legacy of Adam Smith, David Ricardo, and J.S. Mill, popular commentators and politicians wielded simplified classical economic theories as weapons in their advocacy of a dogmatic laissez faire. They claimed that their policy prescriptions had been deduced from a universal economic man and insisted that their political program enjoyed the support of an objective science of economics. Sympathetic students of deductive economics, both at the time and more recently, have rightly pointed out that classical economics had not been opposed to all social reform. Indeed, classical economists had often been the proponents of enlightened state intervention. Nonetheless, it is necessary to recall that classical economists argued for only limited schemes of state intervention and then only as exceptions to a general policy of laissez faire. Their ideal remained a market economy that championed the ideal of individual competition, and they did not allow their suggestions for state intervention to alter their general theoretical framework. This tradition of advocating state intervention as exceptions to a largely self-regulating capitalism was continued by the neoclassical economists. Moreover, the neoclassicists' concern with making microeconomic theory the center of economic studies initially decreased orthodox economics' emphasis on broad issues of national economic policy. Before World War I, for example, neoclassicism's support for the labor movement was certainly neither wholehearted nor central to its theoretical analysis. Likewise, during the vociferous debate on tariffs during the first decade of the twentieth century, neoclassical orthodoxy valiantly upheld the theory of free trade but failed to come to terms with Britain's declining industrial future. To argue, therefore, that the critique of laissez faire by the historical economists was largely misplaced, as many have done, is to overlook the very limited vision of reform and the narrow theoretical framework suggested by the main tradition of classical and neoclassical economics. As critics of a dominant orthodoxy, the historical economists often used excessive rhetoric against the classical views. Such rhetorical flourishes would have been more appropriate if they had been specifically directed toward the dogmatic and shallow views of popular laissez-faire economics. Nevertheless, a good deal of the substance of their criticism was justly aimed at the work of the great classical economists.

The historical economists often invoked the memory of Adam Smith to demonstrate that they remained within the central tradition of British economics. They did not emphasize, however, the Adam Smith of natural law or Smith as the originator of central theories of classical economics. Instead, they pointed to his historical and inductive work, his concern with issues of national economic development, and his persistent call for a political economy capable of solving contemporary problems. On the key issue of free trade, they pointed out Smith's willingness to make numerous exceptions in order to promote power as well as plenty. As the brilliant theoretical innovations of Ricardo hardened into early nineteenth century classical orthodoxy, nationalist critics, such as List and Carey, began to contest the increasingly deductive and absolutist free trade direction of classical economics. This protest was especially effective in America and Germany, where English classical economics was much more easily seen as the intellectual underpinning of making England the workshop of the world. During the 1840s, German economists shaped List's polemical historical and nationalist economics into an academic orthodoxy in which economic history was central. By the 1870s, the German Historical School would do much to fertilize and embolden the protest of English historical economists.

In England, Malthus dissented from the new orthodoxies of free trade and Say's Law. Indeed, he did so with what he perceived to be a historical method. His critique of industrial capitalism was profoundly conservative and agrarian. The encouragement that classical economics offered to England's industrialization and the extension of laissez faire capitalism even to agriculture were fundamental to historical economics. Richard Jones's early protest against classical economics and his encouragement of statistical and inductive research were especially directed at a critique of the classical teaching on population, diminishing returns in agriculture, and rent. The increasingly divergent views within classical economics during the middle of the century were muffled for a generation by Mill's broad synthesis and by his compassionate application of classical economics to contemporary social and economic problems. Mill, however, did not succeed in solving the growing contradictions between classical economic theory and the observable facts of the real world. His work has been seen as a "half-way house" toward the reconstruction of classical economic theory. His example of inductive research, especially on Ireland and the land question, his emphasis on the social application of economic study, and his historical vision of social theory as relative to a particular time and place served as a half-way house toward an English historical economics.

Mill's chief historical disciple in economics was Cliffe Leslie. Chiefly concerned with the problems of Ireland, Cliffe Leslie commenced a historical and comparative study of European land systems in order to demonstrate the insularity of both English economic policy and English classical economics. Cliffe Leslie's search for alternative policies and theories led him to continental critics of English economics. It also convinced him that a history of British economic thought would demonstrate the existence of alternative British economic thinkers who had been neglected by the advance of Ricardian orthodoxy. Leslie's critique ultimately found him questioning Say's Law. His call for the creation of a historical economics, which would combine economic history, applied economics, the history of economic thought, and economic theory, became the model of subsequent English historical economists. His early death, his failure to complete his projected economic history of Britain, his belief that massive inductive research was a prerequisite to sketching an alternative economic theory, the continuing prestige of classical economics in a Britain at the height of its power, his emphasis on Irish and agricultural issues, his lack of wealth and social status, and the unavailability of suitable academic posts within English universities, where economic studies were but poorly developed during his lifetime, combined to keep him from establishing a school of historical economics in England, such as the one that existed in Germany. Schools of economic thought, even more so than economic theories, are not merely the consequence of intellectual innovations, but products of complex historical circumstances.

Cliffe Leslie's critique of orthodoxy, though the most intellectually sophisticated, was not the only assault upon the classical economic tradition during the 1870s. Another Irishman, J.K. Ingram, produced an immensely popular history of economic thought that was unfortunately mired in his excessive adherence to a doctrinaire Comtean Positivism. Thorold Rogers's monumental history of prices pointed to the development of economic history as one outcome of the historical critique of economic orthodoxy. Rogers's checkered academic career, his preference for solitary and quantitative research, his vocal adherence to the increasingly unpopular laissez faire tenets of Gladstonian liberalism, and his continued emphasis on agricultural issues in an industrial England also did not produce a flock of students who rallied to his banner.

During the 1870s and 1880s a wide-ranging public debate ensued that increasingly turned to such industrial issues as the rise of the labor movement, pressure for further government intervention in such areas as education, sanitary reform, and municipal services, and even demands for "Fair Trade" legislation. Such statistical economists as Leone Levi, Robert Giffen, and A.L. Bowley employed inductive tools to provide a historical foundation for the principles of free trade and individual competition. Although their studies demonstrated the decline of Britain's staple industries and its increasing reliance upon invisibles to balance its international accounts, they remained committed to the wisdom of both free trade theory and policy. A new generation of historical economists, however, employed the historical method to question the beneficial effects of free trade and individual competition on Britain's continued existence as a great power and on the well being of its industrial working classes.

This new generation of historical economists, however, could no longer content itself with attacking classical economics. They now had to face the formidable challenge of the marginalist reformulation of classical theory that had also arisen out of the crisis of the 1870s. Both Jevons and Marshall were much impressed by the historical criticism of orthodoxy, but both sought to solve the controversies in economics with a value theory grounded in the principle of utility. Jevons boldly attempted to preempt the methodological debate by suggesting the division of economic study into a rigourous deductive science of economic theory, an inductive economic history, and a more eclectic applied economics. This solution would ultimately triumph. It was Marshall, however, who created a "school" of English neoclassical economics. He did so with his brilliant *Principles*, which became the central tool box of English economics, and he embodied his vision of economic theory in the new Cambridge economics curriculum at the turn of the century and employed his considerable personal influence to secure the success of his program beyond his lifetime. Twentieth century English economics is still recognizable as the child of Marshall. This success, however, should not blind us to the historical reality that Marshall's victory was won in the face of serious opposition even in England.

The potential for the creation of a school of historical economics seemed to exist at late-nineteenth-century Oxford. Oxford was at the forefront of the transformation of history into an academic discipline. Critics of utilitarianism, such as Jowett and Green, provided a hospitable environment for an attack on a utilitarian-based economic theory. Oxford's religious enthusiasm was well suited to those committed to moderate and Christian currents of reform. In Arnold Toynbee, the university possessed a brilliant young economic historian and critic of classical economic theory who employed his history of the industrial revolution to repudiate the very ideal of unfettered competition and offered a severe critique of Ricardo. Although Toynbee died very young, he was a powerful inspiration to the young Oxford economists of the late nineteenth century. After the death of Thorold Rogers, Oxford's professorship in Political Economy went to the mathematical economist and ally of Marshall, Edgeworth. Of the young Oxford economists, only

L.L. Price remained at Oxford to fight a long and lonely battle to improve the lowly position of economic studies at the university. Just after WW I, his efforts were rewarded by the creation of the PPE degree that provided Oxford economics with a solid foundation of inductive study.[2]

Inspired by Toynbee and guided by the scholarship of the German Historical School and American critics of orthodox theory, Ashley was the true English socialist of the chair and the most likely creator of a school of historical economics in England. In his economic history, he set out to find patterns in Britain's economic evolution and to discover inductively a new economic theory appropriate to a particular time and place. Abandoning the historicist hopes of his youth, he came closest to providing a stage theory of English economic history. With his eyes firmly on such contemporary developments as trusts, labor unions, and Britain's declining industrial position, he spoke to the broad economic issues of nationalism and neomercantilism that were at the heart of the debate on public policy in the early twentieth century. Even Ashley, however, was unable to create a school of historical economics in England. In Canada he laid the foundation for the Toronto school of economic history. At Harvard he firmly established the study of economic history on a professional basis. In England, however, he employed his energies to create a business economics at the Birmingham Faculty of Commerce. Although the latter effort was prophetic of the direction of economic study later in the twentieth century, it brought him little prestige among contemporary economists.

At Cambridge, Cunningham and Foxwell fought a rear-guard action against Marshall's dominance at the university. The brilliant but eccentric Foxwell was ill-suited for this battle, even though his suggestions for countercyclical state intervention based on inductive research were a pioneering effort during the 1880s. Cunningham, after bitter controversies with Marshall, abandoned theory to concentrate on economic history and insisted that the lessons of history pointed to the end of laissez faire and the necessity of neomercantilism. Cunningham did produce students, such as Lilian Knowles, the first full-time economic historian at the LSE. However, they were students devoted to economic history who had little interest in Cunningham's pleas on behalf of historical economics.

With the creation of the London School of Economics in 1895, the historical economists appeared to have finally found an institutional base for their approach to economics. Indeed, before World War I, the LSE became the chief source of opposition to Marshall's Cambridge in British economics. To it flocked the dissidents in English economics. Its curriculum was heavily inductive. It proved to be a fertile ground for the development of both economic history and applied economics. The Webbs, who were the school's founders and its chief sustainers in its early years, produced a large body of work that can be variously categorized as sociology, social history, economic history, applied economics or as historical economics. Beatrice Webb's early research, in particular, owed a large debt to the work of the historical economists. Although the Webbs ultimately incorporated marginalist theory into their plans for a socialist society, their views at the turn of the century were broadly compatible with those of Ashley on both public policy and the utility of economic theory. Hewins, however, directed the LSE's early curriculum. He moved rapidly from a primary interest in the social question to a fervent commitment to imperial integration, imperial preference, and tariffs. He laid aside his promising work in economic history for a life of administration and politics. This emphasis greatly diminished his personal intellectual influence, but it assured the early recognition of economic history as an independent discipline at the London School. It was above all Hewins who brought historical economics into politics, and he did so on behalf of an attack on free trade.

Generalizations about English historical economics are endangered by more than the usual difficulties of oversimplification. The economists were too diverse a group to constitute themselves into a school of economics. Their various interests, the early death of some, the eccentric personalities of others, the diffculty of finding suitable academic positions while criticizing established academic and economic policy, and especially the very nature of their enterprise, which emphasized the historical criticism of economic theories rather than their construction, led to their failure to produce an acknowledged leader, a central theory, a sacred text, or a dominant intellectual center around which economists could rally. There was, however, the common proposition, increasingly acknowledged by Marshall and his followers, that economic theory and policy must be relative to a particular time and place. By continually reminding economists of the hypothetical nature of economic theory, the historical economists deserve a prominent place in the history of economic thought. The historical economists, however, did more. They enlarged and enriched the field of economic study through their creation of the discipline of economic history.

The legacy of historical economics to the new professional economic history

Between the1880s and 1926, economic history not only became an independent academic discipline that exerted a considerable influence on economic theorists, but also played a major role in the wide-ranging discussion of public policy. Indeed, during this period, the studies of the historical economists focused attention on such important topics of public debate as the problem of monopolies, the emergence of organized labor, the degree of free competition in the economy, the likelihood of economic equilibrium, pressing issues of international trade policy, the structure of modern capitalism, and the direction of social evolution. The success of the historical economists in focusing attention on these fundamental issues was partly a result of the neglect of these matters by the neoclassical economists. Moreover, the years of high theory made theoretical analysis increasingly more technical and thus less accessible to a wider public. Finally, they continued to emphasize microeconomics. It was not until the 1930s, under the leadership of J.M. Keynes, that a number of English neoclassical economists rejected many of the classical assumptions and built a new framework of macroeconomic analysis that could be used as an effective tool with which to address these contemporary problems.

Meanwhile, the new subject of economic history attempted to grapple with the broadest of subjects, such as the "stages of economic development." During the formative years of economic history as an independent discipline, the historical economists had bequeathed the subject with a historiographical tradition that emphasized a pessimistic interpretation of the social consequence of the Industrial Revolution, rehabilitated both the medieval and mercantilist regulation of the economy, and suggested that the purpose of free trade had been essentially similar to that of mercantilism. Their economic history was, like that of Marx, a critique of nineteenth century laissez faire capitalism, but as nationalists and imperialists, their economic history owed more to List than to Marx. They could agree with both, however, that economic history was not merely a search for intellectual truth as an end in itself, but was a scholarly activity that sought a lasting influence on the formulation of public policy.

Although a full treatment of the economic historians of the interwar period is beyond the scope of this study, a sketch of some of the aims of several of the most important of the first generation of professional economic historians, a good deal of whose work was published or commenced before 1926, is essential in order to appreciate the influence of the historical economists on the historiography of professional economic history. The most important among the first professional economic historians were J.H. Clapham, George Unwin, Ephraim Lipson, and R.H. Tawney, as well as the non-university-based social historians John L. and Barbara Hammond. Securely installed in chairs of economic history and possessors of their own journal, the first generation of professional economic historians showed far less interest in engaging the economic theorists in overt methodological debate, although they continued to snipe at the theorists' "empty economic boxes." Instead, they concentrated on testing the broad generalizations inherited from the historical economists. With the exception of Lipson, they were far less conservative and neomercantilist than the previous generation of historical economists. However, they continued to see economic history as a more useful contribution to a broad debate on public social and economic policy than deductive economic theory.

Marshall's student, J.H. Clapham, succeeded Cunningham as the preeminent economic historian at Cambridge. In his inaugural address as the first Cambridge Professor of Economic History in 1929, Clapham declared that the *Methodenstreit* was dead. Even at Cambridge, the "economist and economic historian are at peace. We know our limitations. We can sit happily side by side under Adam Smith's great umbrella."[3] As he had done with the first volume of his economic history, he dedicated the Cambridge chair to both Cunningham and Marshall. He went on to praise Marshall, noting that he "was a greater economic historian than he had let the world know." Although Clapham also generously praised Cunningham, he declared that the aim of the German Historical School had been "to dissolve economics in history." Happily, he continued, this goal had long ago been given up by the English historical economists and had been shown to be a failure even in Germany.[4] Clapham's own account of the rise of economic history granted but a meager contribution to the work of the English historical economists. Previous contributors, he declared, had given the subject breadth and power; the contemporary task of economic history was to give precision to the discipline through quantitative research.[5]

Clapham's economic history consisted primarily of the rise of individual industries. One of its main themes was opposition to Toynbee's interpretation of the Industrial Revolution, which had been made more persuasive by the documentation of the Hammonds.[6] Clapham was not a critic of contemporary industrial and capitalist society. He did not disparage the ideal of individual competition and applauded free trade as one of the key forces in securing Britain's industrial success. Further, free trade and competition were the best solutions to the problem of poverty. Although he was rarely tempted to expand conclusions in his economic history into "the lessons of history," he left no doubt of his enthusiastic support of a capitalist civilization driven by competition as "not more threatening to the peace of the world than that centralized, impersonal, property-controlling or property-owning state selfishness which shows signs of succeeding it for a time."[7]

Despite his fundamental disagreements with the historical economists and his staunch defense of Marshall, even Clapham played a minor role in the intermittent *Methodenstreit* that continued to trouble English economics occasionally, despite pious declarations by everyone to the contrary. A.C. Pigou, Marshall's disciple and successor, was far less careful than his predecessor in reminding his readers of the tentative and hypothetical nature of economic theory. He declared that his deductive welfare economics could be employed as an applied economics while still retaining its scientific power. This claim to authority for deductive economics was a sufficient challenge to the teaching of economic history that Clapham felt compelled to respond. In 1922 Clapham declared that such categories as diminishing returns and increasing returns to scale, which Pigou wielded so confidently, were in fact "empty economic boxes." Clapham warned that statistical verification had lagged behind the formulations of economic theory. Unless this situation was altered, he continued, he saw "a grave danger to an essentially practical science such as economics in the elaboration of hypothetical conclusions about . . . human welfare and taxes."[8] Pigou replied that economic history could greatly benefit by paying more attention to economic theory. Clapham responded that economic theorists could learn much from economic history.[9] It was Clapham's last foray into public methodological debate and boundary disputes.

To George Unwin, who was appointed professor of Economic History at Manchester in 1909, belonged the distinction of holding the first such appointment in economic history in Britain. He devoted a considerable portion of his energies to reasserting Adam Smith's criticism of mercantilism against Cunningham's praise of the system. Reared in the tradition of the Mechanic Institute, the Wesleyan Sunday School, and the Unitarian Church, deeply steeped in the thought of Ruskin and T.H. Green, trained at Oxford and by Schmoller in Germany, associated with J. S. Nicholson's Edinburgh and the historical tradition of the LSE, and encouraged in his research by the Webbs, Unwin might have been expected to become a strong advocate of historical economics. Ideologically, however, Unwin vigorously dissented from Schmoller's glorification of the state. At a time when many of the historical economists were still active, he saw himself as the first of a new generation of professional economic historians and consciously distanced himself from the pioneers of the discipline. He told an Edinburgh audience in 1908: "Economic history owes more to the science of history than to the science of economics."[10] As a professional economic historian, he had little interest in quarreling with economists. He believed that the *Methodenstreit* had produced little of value. Even though agreeing that neoclassical economic theory had slight utility for explaining the past, he saw it as a useful tool for interpreting modern economic activity.

Unwin, however, was more philosophically inclined than Clapham. He believed that the great task of economic history was to determine the secret of economic progress. Was it to be explained by the rise of individual initiative and free association, as he believed Adam Smith had taught, or was it a consequence of the state direction of economic life, as List had argued? Unwin's economic history, which formed the foundation for a tradition of business history whose hero was the entrepreneur, was designed to document his interpretation of Adam Smith's conclusion that the secret of economic development was to be found in individual initiative, free competition, and free association.[11] Thus, the engine of economic progress was neither economic, as Marx had argued, nor political, as Cunningham had insisted, but could be accounted for by complex and essentially social forces.[12] Unwin argued that the development of free association among men – from tribes, to feudalism, to merchant towns, to nations with freely elected governments, and, ultimately, to a free world community – had liberated men from custom and authority.[13] His study of the sixteenth- and seventeenth-century British economy especially depreciated Cunningham's interpretation of the state's contribution to economic development.[14] Unwin's technical skill as a professional economic historian provided ample opportunity for his often strident attacks upon Cunningham's sweeping interpretations of economic history. There was also, however, a deep ideological difference between them. Both Unwin and Clapham remained cosmopolitan liberals who strongly objected to the social-imperialist and neomercantilist trends in early-twentieth-century British politics and historiography. Instead, their history sought to demonstrate the historical truth and continued relevance of the liberal creed.[15]

The first editors of the *Economic History Review* were two younger economic historians, R.H. Tawney and Ephraim Lipson. The latter was the most important successor to Cunningham in the economic history of mercantilism. Lipson, who taught economic history at Oxford, subscribed to a pessimistic interpretation of the social consequences of the Industrial Revolution, but did not blame the economic system of capitalism per se. Rather, he argued that the condition of the working classes during the period was aggravated by an excessive devotion to laissez faire among the ruling classes and to the wholesale introduction of modern machine technology. With Unwin, Lipson did not point to the mercantilist state as the driving force behind Britain's early economic growth, but emphasized the contribution of free association within early modern capitalism as one of the sources of economic progress. Although critical of the state's clumsy attempts at industrial regulation during the mercantilist era, he praised its goal of providing social welfare and stability. The system, he insisted, had been falsely maligned by Adam Smith. Indeed, he held up its corporate and nationalist spirit as an ideal for a modern planned economy.[16]

During the Second World War, he restated many of the arguments of the historical economists for a new generation. He described modern statecraft as "neo-mercantilism."[17] National security, he argued, demanded the provision of a wide system of social security, a commercial policy without dogma, a broad scheme of public services to enhance the quality of life, a rationalized economy, consisting of a partnership between large corporations, organized labor, and government, and a national planning mechanism. Lipson believed that Adam Smith's adage that defense was more important than opulence should be understood to mean that defense in a modern democratic state required a system of national welfare so that the working classes would have a stake in society. Neoclassical economic theory, he argued, offered little guidance to the creation of such a balanced and planned economy. Despite the criticism of several generations of historical economists and economic historians, it continued to be dominated by a deductive method, the hypothetical conclusions of which were of little practical value in the shaping of public policy. Although the economic theorists claimed to be defending the values of a free economy and society, they offered only a world of hypothetical free competition that corresponded to neither historical nor to contemporary reality. The real choice, he concluded, was between a planned economy dominated by corporate vested interests, and a planned economy directed by a democratic state.[18]

Tawney, who was one of the founders of the Economic History Society, was the most penetrating voice of the new social-democratic vision in British economic history after the Great War. A student of history and economics at Oxford, Tawney spent most of his career at the LSE, which in 1931 provided him with a personal chair in economic history. In his inaugural address, he located the origin of the writing of British economic history among the mercantilists, Adam Smith, List, and the German and English historical economists. He was also the first English economic historian who credited Marx with being the greatest and most dynamic force behind the study of both economics and history. Although Tawney's vision of economic history was much closer to history than to economics, he called for a "sociological interpretation of economic development which would find room in it for both."[19]

Despite his praise of Marxist economic history, Tawney's view of social evolution was anything but materialist. His greatest work, *Religion and the Rise of Capitalism*, exuded the spirit of Toynbee, Green, and the Christian Socialists. He saw the sixteenth- and seventeenth-century secularization of Christian values as the first step on the road to what he saw as the world of unbridled individual acquisitiveness that had been justified by the theories of the classical economists. He believed that their policy of laissez faire was now passing and that a more humane, democratic, and socialist Britain would take its place. Tawney's writings were a major force in British historiography. At least as influential was his personal influence on historians, political scientists, and economists. He called on academics to be advocates of social-democratic and ethical ideals in their scholarship, as well as to labor for these ideals by taking an active part in the reform of society. Although the historical economists had emphasized the need to provide for the economic education of the middle classes, Tawney especially placed his hopes for a just society on the education of the working class.[20] During the 1920s, Tawney was a major force in the Workers' Education Association, which was the successor to the university extension movement of the prewar period in promoting adult education. Economic history was to be a key component of this popular adult education, for it taught the evolutionary nature of society, demonstrated the birth of the new society, and could serve as a guide and inspiration for developing society along egalitarian lines of social development. The most popular subject was economic history, and the WEA played the chief role in disseminating English economic and social history to a wide segment of the population during the interwar period.[21]

The most widely read works in social and economic history during the early twentieth century were those of John L. and Barbara Hammond. Although they were avid antiimperialists and have been called the chief historical voices of the new liberalism that became social democracy, their work owed much to that of the historical economists.[22] In the face of severe criticism from Clapham and other academic economic historians, their personal blend of social, political, and economic history ensured that the Toynbean interpretation of the Industrial Revolution would remain a persistent historiographical tradition that continues to influence economic study down to the present.[23] The Hammonds did not hold academic appointments. They were journalists, civil servants, and publicists who used their scholarship as the foundation for their schemes of social reform.[24] Nonetheless, their scholarship was accepted as a professional contribution to social and economic history.

In 1911 they published their first influential study, *The Village Labourer*, which traced England's agrarian transformation from the enclosure movement of the eighteenth century to the rural risings of 1830.

Tawney observed that the careful and original research of the Hammonds had documented Toynbee's charge that political causes had been at the root of the creation of Britain's system of large scale agriculture.[25] Heavily indebted to classical scholarship, the Hammonds did not fully accept the desirability of making England primarily an industrial nation. Indeed, reiterating many of J.S. Mill's arguments, they called for the recreation of a species of peasant proprietors designed to revitalize the countryside, promote personal and family development, and bring a new sense of stability and permanence to the countryside. They next turned their attention to an account of the effects of modern industry upon the traditional artisans of the towns. *The Town Labourer*, first published in 1917, told of the rise of a "new Civilization" that had added "the discipline of a power driven by a competition that seemed as unhuman as the machines that thundered in the factory and shed" to the poverty of the old domestic system. They concluded that this revolution had "raised the standard of comfort of the rich," but had "depressed the standard of life for the poor."[26] Moreover, they declared that the dislocation brought by the rise of modern industry had been made harsher by the ruling class's fear of social and political revolution. This fear, stimulated by evangelical religion, had added intensity to the war of the ruling classes on the workers' efforts on behalf of political and social redress.

The Hammonds argued that classical political economy had richly deserved its reputation as the "dismal science." Their criticism of Ricardo was that of the historical economists. Moreover, it was contained in one of the most widely read works of social and economic history published in the twentieth century:

Ricardo's brilliant and rather labyrinthine deductive reasoning has led later students to the most diverse conclusions. . . . But of the character of his immediate influence there can be no doubt . . . [it was] to create the impression that every human motive other than the unfailing principle of self-interest might be eliminated from the world of commerce and industry; that the forces of supply and demand settled everything; that the laws governing profits and wages were mechanical and fixed.[27]

The Hammonds' interpretation of social and economic history was rooted in their rejection of the politics and culture of what the historical economists had called the age of laissez faire. They concluded that the economic man of classical economics had not been "a mere nightmare of the new textbooks," but had become an "omnipotent force in a world existing for a single purpose."[28] In his own scheme for social reconstruction after the Great War, one of John Hammond's central themes was his criticism of orthodox economics as too fatalistic and determinist. He urged that economics adopt a more complex human psychology, rooted in history and the new social sciences, that recognized the drive for cooperation and public welfare in human affairs.[29]

Their tradition of social and economic history, and the criticism of classical economic theory it contained, was continued by such post–World War II historians as E.P. Thompson and E.J. Hobsbawm and placed squarely in a Marxist framework.[30] In a recent comment on the standard-of-living controversy, R. M. Hartwell declared that his more optimistic conclusion on the social consequences of the Industrial Revolution should not be seen as politically motivated, since "my intentions and methods are clearly non-ideological."[31] Hartwell's claim to objectivity, rooted in his quantitative approach, contains its own ideological assumptions. Further, it suggests a very different role for the social scientist than that which the Hammonds envisioned.

The historiography of such issues as the social consequences of the Industrial Revolution and the merits and demerits of mercantilism have been questions of such continued relevance to the discussion of social and economic policy that their interpretation by historians, economic historians, and economic theorists could not easily escape their contemporary implications.[32] Keynes used his own rehabilitation of mercantilism in the *General Theory* as a weapon with which to attack economic orthodoxy. He noted that the dominance of the orthodox school in his youth had been so pervasive that "we were brought up to believe that it [mercantilism] was little better than nonsense." This may have been the view of his teachers, but in Keynes's youth there already existed a large body of economic history that argued that mercantilism had been an appropriate policy for the time and was relevant to policy debates in the twentieth century. In his own brief for managing the economy, he added: "It should be understood that the advantages claimed are avowedly national advantages and are unlikely to benefit the world at large."[33] During the nineteenth century, the essentially national framework of liberal economic theory had often given way to the ideals and theories of a cosmopolitan liberalism, especially in abstract analysis. Such a system was poorly equipped to deal with the realities of class, race, gender, and especially nations that were characteristic of the twentieth century. Even Keynes did not fully appreciate the difficulty of forging a theory that paid more careful attention to the nature of economic behavior in a particular time and place.

Building on the foundation laid by the historical economists, the early-twentieth-century economic historians shaped their research program in order to suggest a historical framework that provided a wider and more complex understanding of economic behavior. Tawney and the Hammonds were especially active in promoting their social-democratic visions beyond the academy; Clapham, Unwin, and Lipson more closely confined themselves to advancing their views as the "lessons of history" in a suitably academic fashion. None, however, could resist an occasional reference to the *Methodenstreit*. Faithful to the legacy of the historical economists, the first generation of professional social and economic historians believed that the lessons of history were far more useful in framing public debate on the broad issues of social and economic policy than were the theories of the neoclassical economists. Indeed, the economic historians' faith in the practical utility of social science has continued.[34]

Historical economics and politics: social imperialism and neomercantilism, 1900–32

From the professors' manifesto in 1903 to the adoption of a general tariff in 1932, a major debate took place in Britain concerning the wisdom of a continuing adherence to free trade as compared to the adoption of neomercantilist policies. During the nineteenth century, classical economic theory constituted a critical component to England's liberal ideology. Its attack upon the inefficiency and corruption of mercantilism, its criticism of the landed interest, its praise of individual competition and free trade, and its often fatalistic certainty were useful tools for advancing the economic and political interests of the emerging industrial and commercial classes. By the 1880s, liberalism was slowly being transformed into a more positive doctrine that culminated in the years immediately prior to WW I in the liberal social reform program of Lloyd George. The collapse of the Liberal Party in the postwar period has produced a large literature. Part of the crisis of interwar liberalism was the inability of neoclassical economics to offer a coherent intellectual economic framework for twentieth century liberalism. Although J.M. Keynes announced the death of laissez faire in 1926 and the descendants of Marshall offered far-ranging proposals for a government role in the economy during the 1920s, it was not until Keynes's brilliant theoretical synthesis in the 1930s that a new and coherent intellectual framework was forged for a liberal social-democratic creed. By this time British socialists had also created a viable and cohesive alternative theory.[35]

In the meantime, historical economics, and the economic history it spawned, offered itself as an alternative intellectual basis for shaping a new economic ideology. The social-democratic side of this has been best remembered. However, the work of the more conservative historical economists was at least equally influential at the time. Their ideas were an essential framework for a vocal minority within conservatism, both before and after the Great War, who pursued schemes of imperial development, industrial rationalization, cooperation between big business and labor unions, alternatives to the gold standard, countercyclical public expenditures, some nationalization, much state regulation, and even state planning. The end of formal empire and the coming of the mixed economy after WW II have made their social imperialism archaic to postwar Britain. The twentieth century, however, is a world far more of nationalism and corporatism than of the ideals of even a modified liberalism.[36] Although the free market of classical and neoclassical economics lives on in the world of economic theory and political slogans, it bears increasingly less resemblance to reality. The historical economists, despite their many shortcomings, saw this better than most, and they saw it earlier.

Even before World War I, the practice of laissez faire was but a memory. The historical economists laid the groundwork for its intellectual repudiation. Their goal was the creation of a balanced national economy capable of achieving both power and plenty. They agreed with the socialists that the inherent weaknesses of capitalist society would lead to its evolution in a more collectivist direction. Like many socialists, they were often unsympathetic to the materialism and competitiveness of modern industrial capitalism. They also saw themselves as an intellectual vanguard that hoped to convince the public to embrace a more cohesive form of social organization. Often deeply motivated by religious sentiments, convinced of the evolutionary rather than the revolutionary nature of social change, sometimes distrustful of a thorough egalitarianism, adherents of an organic vision of society, and believers in the efficacy of a regulated private property, these academic offspring of the new nationalism did not seek to destroy capitalism nor the British Empire. Rather, they hoped to transform both through integration, organization, and federation. In the language of the time, their vision was both neomercantilist and social imperialist.

One of the chief intellectual, social, and finally political issues of the period 1885 to 1914 was the rise of a social-imperialist ideology. Cunningham, Hewins, Ashley, and the Webbs, as we have argued, played a leading role in the articulation of its ideas. It also drew heavily on the Social Darwinism of Benjamin Kidd and Karl Pearson, the historical geography of Mackinder, and the ideas and politics of such men as Joseph Chamberlain, Alfred Milner, the Earl of Rosebery, and R.B. Haldane. In the years before the Boer War, most social imperialists were politically associated with the Liberal Party. Such political figures as Haldane and Rosebery, as well as the rising Lloyd George, advanced a liberal social-imperialist vision that remained firmly tied to free trade. The Webbs, who ultimately shied away from tariffs and imperial preference, were, for a time, closely associated with liberal social imperialism. From the Boer War to the collapse of the Lloyd George coalition in 1922, there was a good deal of talk about the creation of a unified social-imperialist Center Party. On the right, it would repudiate the landed and church interests of the diehard Tories, while on the left, it would jettison those liberals still committed to internationalism. At the same time, the Center Party hoped to capture a majority of the working classes through social reform and Imperial enthusiasm. It was a frankly counterrevolutionary scheme, designed to outflank both revolutionary socialism and a more moderate independent Labour Party.[37]

The key issue that divided the social imperialists was tariff reform. The liberal social imperialists had toyed with the idea of imperial preferences during the 1892–5 Liberal government, but had rejected it. Tariff reform was also the issue which doomed the Webbs' hopes of forging a unified social-imperialist movement. By 1902, Rosebery had succeeded in making a liberal social imperialism the dominant creed of a rejuvenated Liberal Party. The liberal imperialist analysis of Britain's difficulties was not altogether different from that of the conservative social imperialists. Their program was one of national efficiency that included education, temperance, housing, support for the labor unions, increased defense expenditures, Poor Law reform, and, a few years hence, a program of unemployment insurance, old age pensions, and national health insurance. Close to the interests of the City, they believed that Britain's economic problems must be solved while safeguarding its preeminent financial position, its insurance business, and its carrying trade. In addition to the traditional liberal fear that protection would bring corruption, they remained firm in their support of cheap imported food and became prisoners of the tensions between the cosmopolitan and national frameworks of liberal theory. Hard work, thrift, temperance, and competition would make British industry more viable. To this they added political imperial integration, imperial defense, and a dose of state chivalry for improving the lives of the working classes. Their program was to be funded by increases in direct taxation and through a final assault on the wealth of the landed classes. They too embraced the tools of the new social sciences and became increasingly empirical and historical in the intellectual justification of their program. Despite increasing political difficulties, the liberal imperialists retained political power in the decade before WW I.

In the postwar period, however, the Conservatives dominated politics. It is difficult to overemphasize the importance of the tariff issue in the history of the Conservative Party from 1903 to 1932. It was the key question on which Conservative leaders were judged. By 1906, there were only eleven Conservative members of Parliament who still declared themselves for free trade.[38] As Ashley and Hewins understood, this did not mean that Conservative politicians had also accepted their broader social-imperialist program. After 1905, when Chamberlain's illness made it impossible for him to lead the Unionist cause, the political heir apparent to the conservative social-imperialist program was Alfred Milner. Milner's ideas were deeply indebted to those of the historical economists. Raised in both Germany and England, he was much influenced by German scholarship. He attended Jowett's Balliol and became a close personal and intellectual friend of Toynbee and Ashley.[39] During the 1880s, Milner gave a series of lectures on socialism and economics, but he rapidly turned away from the possibility of a teaching career in favor of a distinguished career as an imperial civil servant. In 1903, he aligned himself with Chamberlain's tariff reform cause. He was prodded by L.S. Amery and other social imperialists to succeed Chamberlain as tariff reform's political leader. But, as he himself admitted, he was not well suited to lead a political party.[40] In 1917, he urged Lloyd George to transform the war coalition into a permanent social-imperialist Center Party that he believed would transcend traditional party politics.[41]

Milner's provocative ideas on economic policy were an important challenge to the postwar Conservative Party's inclination to adopt major components of late-nineteenth-century liberal economic policy. Milner first articulated his ideas in lectures on socialism delivered at Toynbee Hall in 1882. They were very close to the ideas Ashley expressed during the same period. Milner argued that the widespread misunderstanding of socialism derived from both fear and an undue reverence for the orthodox "laws of political economy."[42] In a Toynbean fashion, he traced the origin of modern socialism to the political repression, social trauma, rapid economic change, and widespread poverty of the Industrial Revolution. Although he found much to praise in collectivist ideas, he found the socialism of Marx and Lassalle excessively devoted to Hegel, to a determinist view of history, and especially to Ricardian economic theory.[43] He criticized the latter for infecting classical English political economy with the "exclusive use of deductive reasoning, the excessive value attached to abstract arguments, and the narrow range of observations with regards to matters of fact." They were obsessions, he continued, "which the late Mr. Cliffe Leslie has done so much to remove."[44] He especially faulted the Manchester School for opposing state sponsored social reform. However, the work of Mill, Leslie, and Toynbee showed signs of a more positive attitude on the part of English economists toward organized labor and state intervention, while In Germany the economists had already embraced state socialism. In these early lectures, Milner already suggested a measure of nationalization. In any case, he noted that the corporations and the trade unions were already creating the outlines of a new economic order.[45] He concluded that, although Mill's economic theory began with the principle of freedom and then provided exceptions for state intervention, Milner concluded the modern principle ought to be the socialist theory of state intervention "constrained by caution and incompetence."[46]

Milner's mature ideas were a logical extension of these early reflections. In 1923 he surveyed the wreckage of brave reconstruction plans after WW I. He confronted a Britain beset by unemployment, social tension, and lost overseas markets. He concluded that the chief postwar problem was that "production has outstripped effective demand."[47] Emphasizing the importance of the home market, he urged the effective utilization of Britain's industrial capacity through government management of private investment, state regulation, and direct government investment in housing, schools, public transport, and even in public industry. Through a joint public and private board, investment was to be concentrated in such new industries as aviation and automobiles. For older industries, such as railways and coal mining, he urged outright nationalization, and he offered government-induced and regulated rationalization for others. He urged tariffs to protect the old staple industries, to spur rationalization, and to develop new industries. Moreover, tariffs would allow the implementation of a system of imperial preference designed to encourage imperial economic integration. For the dependent empire, he suggested a large scale imperial development scheme. In order to reduce social tensions at home and to increase efficiency, he became a vigorous advocate of trade unions that would work with the large corporations and public industrial councils to promote productivity and stability. Further, the state would guarantee a minimum standard of life through a comprehensive system of social security. Finally, he was a lifelong advocate of the revitalization of British agriculture, which he saw as both a key element in the revival of the home market and as a source of national stability. He termed his approach one of "national economics."[48] Although he failed to convert the Conservative Party to his creed, Milner's ideas of the 1920s for national reconstruction were a productive expansion of those of the historical economists into a cohesive and dynamic expansionary program that was prophetic of later developments.

Milner's protege, L.S. Amery, was the most effective younger spokesman of the social-imperialist and neomercantilist program during the

1920s.[49] Amery's constant fear was that the Conservative Party would pursue a mere "negative *laissez faire* anti-Socialism."[50] Amery was, like Milner, educated both in Germany and in England. At Oxford, he studied politics, philosophy, economics, and history. He later pointed to Mackinder, the historical geographer, as a vital shaper of his ideas. He claimed that his methodological approach to economics was both historical and biological.[51] Although he freely used the methodological arguments of the historical economists in his work, he rarely acknowledged his debt to them. He was, in fact, highly resentful that his work was neglected by academic economists of whatever persuasion.[52] Although a founder of the Oxford Fabian Society, Amery found his political home in the Unionist Party. As a publicist, Amery was close to Maxse and Garvin. The latter, the editor of the *Observer*, spent a lifetime promoting the social-imperialist cause.[53] Amery saw his prewar writings on the tariff problem as a "fundamental criticism of the whole orthodox economic theory and, for that matter, also of its offspring, Marxian Socialism."[54] In truth, they were largely a repetition of the neomercantilist views of the historical economists.

During World War I, the adoption of the McKenna duties, a revenue tariff that allowed for a small measure of imperial preference, gave hope to the tariff reformers. When Hewins lost his position as Under-Secretary for the Colonies in 1918, he was replaced by Amery, who expanded Hewins's scheme of imperial integration into a broad program of colonial development and settlement. Amery's larger imperial vision ran up against domestic opposition to food taxes, the financial community's refusal to submit investment capital to public direction, and the alternative development plans of the components of the empire.[55] His plea for Commonwealth and European integration during the 1950s continued to employ List's call for a balanced economy and Cunningham's analysis of free trade imperialism. This time, however, the danger came from a free trade United States.[56]

Milner and Amery's efforts to convert the Conservative Party to an ideology of neomercantilism and social imperialism were no more successful than the efforts of the historical economists. Balfour, who was sympathetic to their cause, never became a forthright supporter of social imperialism and even Hewins supported his ouster from the leadership in 1911.[57] Bonar Law, who succeeded to the leadership, was born in Canada and imperial integration remained critical to his political make-up. His maiden speech in Parliament was in support of a revenue duty on wheat and included a broad attack on the theory of free trade.[58] Liberally supplied with arguments and statistics by Ashley, Hewins, and Amery, Law laced his speeches with references to the historical economists' approach to economics.[59] Law's program, however, contained little social reform and amounted to a claim that tariffs would decrease unemployment and imperial sentiments would heal class antagonism.[60]

With the end of the Lloyd George coalition in 1922, Stanley Baldwin became the Conservative leader. Though Baldwin had studied under Cunningham, he did little serious academic work. His visit to America in 1890 had a greater impact than academic arguments on his tariff views. He was deeply impressed by the size of its large protected home market and the scale of its firms. In anticipation of the party's electoral victory in 1923 on a tariff platform, the Conservatives created the Tariff Commission to frame a general tariff. It counted Hewins, Milner, and Amery among its members. Baldwin's election address, framed by Amery, bore the trademarks of historical economics. It defended tariffs on the basis of protecting domestic productive capacity, the reduction of unemployment, the integrated economic development of the empire, and the funding of an extensive scheme of social security.[61] The Conservatives, however, lost the election to a free trade Labour Party. When they returned to power in 1924, Baldwin abandoned his plans for a general tariff and concentrated instead on the passage of safeguarding legislation for specific industries. Although Baldwin continued to claim that he was a disciple of Toynbee and Milner, he did little to advance Milner's social-imperialist cause and pursued an unimaginative policy of deflation during the 1920's.[62]

As the economic landscape was altered by the reverberations of the failure of the international economy, Baldwin announced that the Conservatives would no longer regard safeguarding as an exceptional policy, but would generalize it into a broadly protectionist system. With Britain's abandonment of gold in 1931, the tariff issue was finally settled. In a historic moment, Neville Chamberlain introduced tariff legislation in 1932. Later that year, Britain agreed to imperial preference.[63] With both Ashley and Hewins now dead, it was left to Amery to lament that the great historical change had come about under the peculiar circumstances of the world economic crisis rather than from a firm commitment to the social-imperialist cause.[64] In retrospect, the adoption of a tariff did achieve the symbolic significance Amery sought. For forty years, a powerful tradition of economic history and applied economics had hailed a return to neomercantilism as a historic British policy of state intervention. The unequivocal acceptance of tariffs and the abandonment of the gold standard meant that imperial preference, industrial rationalization, quotas, marketing boards, and other nationalist economic measures could now be adopted without first debating the issue as a departure from principle.

In 1931, J.M. Keynes publicly suggested that a revenue tariff would relieve pressure on the budget, increase business confidence, and provide more domestic employment.[65] Lionel Robbins assumed the role of spokesman for the free traders. He was particularly incensed that Keynes had used his academic authority to attack the theory of free trade. Reminiscent of the professor's manifesto of 1903, he asserted that nearly all economists opposed tariffs. Keynes observed that the old ideal of free trade was a utopian hope. He urged that the needs of the hour demanded a new and national approach to economic policy. He observed that Joseph Chamberlain's tariff campaign had originated during a period of falling prices and that one of the aims of his expansionist policy had been to raise the price level.[66] The debate became increasingly vituperative and took on shades of the old *Methodenstreit*. Keynes objected to the "*odium theologicum*" of free trade.[67] Robbins finally commented that Keynes's arguments had given comfort to the discredited historical economists: "The shades of a million dead parrots – the much bewhiskered *historismus* of the past – rise up and hail him as brother, 'recognized at last,' they cry. 'The clever one always thought us stupid, and now the cleverest one of all has come to show us how right we really were.' "[68]

Robbins was quite wrong in linking Keynes to historical economics, though in the heated atmosphere of the time some of his positions were identified with those of the historical economists. Keynes's intellectual ancestry was overwhelmingly neoclassical. A student of Marshall and Pigou, Keynes had become increasingly dissatisfied with aspects of neoclassical economics after WW I. In an essay on Malthus, first written in 1922 but not published until 1933, he aligned himself with Malthus against Ricardo. In the process, he repeated many of Foxwell's arguments on the abstractions that Ricardo had brought to economics.[69] He later reiterated his view of Malthus in his *General Theory*. Although there were significant differences between Keynes's embrace of Malthus and the earlier historical economists' view of him, Keynes's criticism of the abstract equilibrium analysis of Ricardo contained many similar conclusions. It was a major break with one of the sacred truths and conventions of Marshallian economics.

In 1926 Keynes published a critique of laissez faire. He argued that the popularizers rather than the classical economists had made a plausible idea into a dogma. He warned, however, that contemporary economists were still too much wedded to the presumption of laissez faire. Pointing to the differences between contemporary large corporations and the individually owned and directed firms of classical economic theory, the reality of labor unions, and the growing capacity of the state to direct the nation's well-being, Keynes called for the forging of a new partnership among corporations, labor, and the state.[70] This line of argument had been suggested by the historical economists before the turn of the century. Keynes's critique of laissez faire, however, was not meant as a brief for social imperialism. He had few illusions about the social, political, economic, or racial possibilities offered by this school of thought. Instead, his purpose was to reform capitalism with a "New Liberalism." Within the context of the Great Depression, even Keynes declared himself in favor of "national self-sufficiency."[71]

Ironically, the Keynesian revolution in economic theory would provide a convincing theoretical case that could be used to promote the adoption of neomercantilist economic policy, whether conservative or social democratic. The lack of such a theoretical explanation of national development, capable of yielding immediate and specific government policies to manage the economy, was a central weakness of the neomercantilist program of the historical economists. In a wider sense, however, any theory of economic management must operate in a larger scheme of social and political goals that transcend economic theory. Such goals cannot be articulated out of abstract theory, but are rooted in a society's historical vision of itself. The historical economists understood that the future is shaped out of the past. Their development of economic history was designed to place the study of the economic life of the past on a scholarly foundation and to mold it into a usable past. If many of their ideas and policies seem archaic or socially and politically distasteful, at least they understood that economic thought and policy must be relative to a particular time and place. The true importance of the historical economists was their insistence on the necessity of inductive research and the continual need for cross-fertilization between economic theory and economic history in the education of those who study economics.

Notes

Introduction

1 William James Ashley, "The Place of Economic History in University Studies," *Economic History Review*, I (January 1927), 4.

2 Jevons had already suggested such a division during the 1870s. W. Stanley Jevons, *Theory of Political Economy* (5th ed. New York, 1957), xv–xxvii.

3 According to Joseph Schumpeter, the historical economists failed to form a school "in the sense of a scientific party committed to fighting for a distinctive program," *History of Economic Analysis* (New York, 1954), 822. On schools and subdisciplines, see Joseph V. Remenyi, "Core Demi-core Interaction: Toward a General Theory of Disciplinary and Subdisciplinary Growth," *History of Political Economy*, 11 (Spring 1979), 30–63.

4 A. W. Coats, "The Historist Reaction in English Political Economy, 1870–1890," *Economica*, N. S., 21 (May 1954), 143–53. See also H. S. Foxwell, "The Economic Movement in England," *Quarterly Journal of Economics*, II (October 1887), 84–103; A. W. Coats, "Sociological Aspects of British Economic Thought," *Journal of Political Economy*, 75 (October 1967), 706–29; John Maloney, *Marshall, Orthodoxy & The Professionalization of Economics* (Cambridge, 1985); Alon Kadish, *The Oxford Economists in the Late Nineteenth Century* (Oxford, 1982).

5 The first full-time lectureship in economic history was established in 1904 at London University, The second was founded at Manchester in 1905. The third was created at Oxford in 1907, the fourth at Edinburgh in 1908, and the fifth at Belfast in 1910. The first chair of economic history in England was established at Manchester in 1910 and the second at London in 1921. Chairs in the subject were not founded at Cambridge and Oxford until 1928 and 1931. See N. B. Harte, "Introduction," *The Study of Economic History: Collected Inaugural Lectures, 1893–1970* (London, 1971); N.S.B. Gras, "The Rise and Development of Economic History," *Economic History Review*, I (June 1927–28), 12–34; Sir Frederic Rees, "Some Trends in Economic History," *History*, XXXIV (1949), 1–14.

6 The society was especially the work of Ephraim Lipson and R. H. Tawney. See T. C. Barker, "The Beginnings of the Economic History Society," *The Economic History Review*, Second Series, XXX (February 1977), 12.

7 See, for example, the subject index of the Kress Library of Business and Economics, Harvard University.

8 J. W. Burrows, *Evolution and Society: A Study in Victorian Social Theory* (Cambridge, 1966); Reba N. Soffer, *Ethics and Society in England: The Revolution in the Social Sciences, 1870–1914* (Berkeley, 1978).

9 J. W. Burrow, *A Liberal Descent: Victorian Historians and the English Past* (Cambridge, 1981); G. P. Gooch, *History and Historians in the Nineteenth Century* (Boston, 1959); M. D. Knowles, "Some Trends in Scholarship, 1868–1968, in the Field of Medieval History," *Transactions of the Royal Historical Society*, 5th Series, 19 (1969), 139–58; Herbert Butterfield, "Some Trends in Scholarship, 1868–1968, in the Field of Modern History," *Transactions of the Royal Historical Society*, 5th Series, 19 (1969), 159–84.

10 L. L. Price, "Free Trade and Protection," *Economic Journal*, 12 (September, 1902), 314. Harry C. Johnson has also employed the term in this broad fashion in "Mercantilism: Past, Present, and Future," *The Manchester School*, 42 (March 1974), 1–17.

11 The crisis of classical economics took place during the late 1860s and early 1870s, T. W. Hutchison, *On Revolutions and Progress in Economic Knowledge* (Cambridge, 1978).

12 F. M. L. Thompson, *English Landed Society in the Nineteenth Century* (Toronto, 1963).

13 Derek H. Aldcroft and Harry W. Richardson, *The British Economy, 1870–1939* (London,1969); Phyllis Deane and W. A. Cole, *British Economic Growth, 1688–1959* (Cambridge, 1969); H. J. Habakkuk, *American and British Technology in the Nineteenth Century* (Cambridge, 1962); A. L. Levine, *Industrial Retardation in Britain, 1880–1914* (New York, 1967); Benjamin H. Brown, *The Tariff Reform Movement in Great Britain, 1881–1895* (New York, 1943).

14 Henry Pelling, *Origins of the Labour Party*, (2nd ed. Oxford, 1965).

15 Peter Stansky, ed., *The Victorian Revolution: Government and Society in Victorian Britain* (New York, 1973).

16 Helen Lynd, *England in the Eighteen-Eighties: Toward a Social Basis for Freedom* (London, 1945); Albion Small, *The Origins of Sociology* (Chicago, 1924); Melvin Richter, *The Politics of Conscience: T. H. Green and His Age* (Cambridge, Massachusetts, 1964).

17 Michael Freedan, *The New Liberalism: An Ideology of Social Reform* (Oxford, 1978); Bernard Semmel, *Imperialism and Social Reform: English Social-Imperial Thought, 1885–1914* (London, 1960); Robert J. Scally, *The Origin of the Lloyd George Coalition: The Politics of Social-Imperialism, 1900–1918* (Princeton, 1978); G. R. Searle, *The Quest for National Efficiency: A Study in British Politics and British Political Thought, 1899–1914* (Berkeley, 1971).

Chapter 1

1 Political Economy Club, *Revised Report of the Proceedings of the Dinner of 31st May 1876* (London, 1876), 5.

2 Coats, "Sociological Aspects of British Economic Thought (c. 1880–1920),"

Journal of Political Economy, (1967), 706–29; S.G. Checkland, "The Advent of Academic Economics in England," *Manchester School*, XIX (January 1951), 43–70; W.J. Reader, *Professional Men: The Rise of the Professional Classes in Nineteenth Century England* (London, 1966).

3 Political Economy Club, *Proceedings* (1876), esp. 8–12, 20–21.

4 Lowe reiterated these views two years later, "Recent Attacks on Political Economy," *The Nineteenth Century*, IV (November 1878), 858–68. On English popular economics, see W.D. Grampp, *The Manchester School of Economics* (Stanford, 1960) and *Economic Liberalism*, 2 vols. (New York, 1965).

5 Political Economy Club, *Proceedings* (1876), 30.

6 Ibid., 45.

7 Ibid., 24–25, 29–31.

8 Ibid., 33, 37.

9 T.W. Hutchison first drew attention to this document, *A Review of Economic Doctrines, 1870–1929* (Oxford, 1966), 1–5.

10 Walter Bagehot, *Economic Studies*, (R.H. Hutton, ed. Stanford, 1953), 5.

11 William Cunningham, "Political Economy as a Moral Science," *Mind*, III (July 1878), 369.

12 Bonamy Price, *Chapters on Practical Political Economy* (London: 1878), 5–7.

13 "Proceedings of the Forty-third Anniversary Meeting of the Royal Statistical Society, September 1877," *Journal of the Royal Statistical Society*, XL (September 1877), 342–50.

14 London Industrial Remuneration Conference, *The Report of the Proceedings and Papers* (London, 1885).

15 Quoted by Hutchison, *Revolutions and Progress* (1978), 58.

16 Political Economy Club, *Minutes of Proceedings* (London, 1860) II, III, IV, V.

17 Mill explained that it had been written in eighteen months, J.S. Mill, *Autobiography* (New York, 1960), 164–65.

18 J.S. Mill, *Principles of Political Economy; With Some of Their Application to Social Philosophy*, I, *The Collected Works of John Stuart Mill*, J.M. Robson, ed. (Toronto: 1965), II, xci–xcii. Subsequent references will be to this edition and will be cited as *Principles* volumes I or II.

19 Henry Fawcett, *Manual of Political Economy*, 8th ed. (London, 1907). Mill supported Fawcett in the latter's election to the Cambridge post; see Leslie Stephen , *Life of Henry Fawcett*, 5th ed. (London, 1880), 117–22.

20 The legacy of Adam Smith versus that of Ricardo was central to the English *Methodenstreit*; see Hutchison's excellent account, *Revolutions and Progress* (1978); and Donald Winch, *Adam Smith's Politics, An Essay in Historiographical Revision* (New York, 1978).

21 Hutchison, *Revolutions and Progress* (1978); S.G. Checkland, "Economic Opinion in England as Jevons Found It," *Manchester School*, XIX (May 1951), 143–69.

22 W. Stanley Jevons, *Theory of Political Economy*, 5th ed. (New York, 1957), 276–77.

23 Schumpeter, *History of Economic Analysis*, 578–88.

24 William Newmarch, "Condition of Political Economy," *Journal of the Statistical Society*, XXXIV (1871), 477.

25 Mark Blaug, *Ricardian Economics: A Historical Study* (New Haven, 1958), 167. See also John Robson, *The Improvement of Mankind: Social and Political Thought of J.S. Mill* (Toronto, 1968); and Bernard Semmel, *John Stuart Mill and the Pursuit of Virtue* (New Haven, 1984).

26 Schumpeter's comment on Mill as a "half-way house" specifically referred to his value theory *History of Economic Analysis*, 613. Jacob Viner saw Mill's methodology as inconsistent; "Benthem and J.S. Mill: The Utilitarian Background," *The Long View and the Short: Studies in Economic Theory and Policy* (Glencoe, Illinois, 1958). See also D.P. O'Brien, *The Classical Economists* (Oxford, 1975), 72–74; Pedro Schwartz, *The New Political Economy of J.S. Mill* (London, 1968), 59–61. Alan Ryan has argued that Mill was an inductive philosopher, *John Stuart Mill* (New York, 1970), xi.

27 Schumpeter, *History of Economic Analysis*, 452.

28 Mill, *Autobiography*, 110–13.

29 J.S. Mill, *Essays on Some Unsettled Questions of Political Economy* (London, 1948), 138–39. "On the Definition of Political Economy; and the Method of Investigation Proper to It," was first published in 1836 and republished in *Unsettled Questions* in 1844.

30 Ibid., 144–45, 150, 152–55, 158–59.

31 Mill, *Autobiography*,. 146.

32 J.S. Mill, *A System of Logic*, 8th ed. (London, 1967), 574–80.

33 J.S. Mill, *Auguste Comte and Positivism* (London, 1865), 89.

34 Mill, *Logic*, 583.

35 Ibid., 585–87.

36 Mill, *Autobiography*, 147.

37 Mill, *Comte*, 80.

38 Ibid., 81.

39 Mill, *Principles*, I, xci.

40 Ibid., 199.

41 Ibid., 21. Italics added.

42 Ibid., 199. Italics added.

43 Mill, *Autobiography*, 165–66.

44 Mill, *Principles*, II, 456. See also Blaug, *Ricardian Economics*, esp. 175; Schumpeter, *History of Economic Analysis*, 613; and Alfred Marshall, "Mr. Mill's Theory of Value," *Memorials of Alfred Marshall*, A.C. Pigou, ed. (New York, 1956), 119–34.

45 Mill, *Principles*, I, Bk. I, chapters 2 and 3, esp. 78–88.

46 See especially Mill's brilliant theory of international values in *Unsettled Questions*.

47 Mill, *Principles*, I, 158–59.

48 Ibid., 155.
49 Ibid., 164.
50 Blaug, *Ricardian Economics*, 120–27.
51 Mill, *Principles*, I. 338.
52 Hutchison, *Economic Doctrines*, 113–14; Schumpeter, *History of Economic Analysis*, 661–67; Blaug, *Ricardian Economics*, 120–27; S.G. Checkland, *The Rise of Industrial Society in England, 1815–1885* (London,1964), 414–16; T.V. Clements, "British Trade Unions and Popular Political Economy," *Economic History Review*, 2nd Series, XIV (No. 1, 1961), 93–104.
53 J.S. Mill, "Thornton on Labour and its Claims" (1869), *Collected Works*, V, 646.
54 Ibid., 662.
55 Mill, *Principles*, II, 929. In 1871, John Wilson argued that as a consequence of Mill's recantation, he should also have accepted Longfield's argument that demand determines supply, "Economic Fallacies and Labour Utopias," *Quarterly Review*, CXXXXI (July 1871), 236–42.
56 Mill, *Principles*, II, 731–32.
57 Ibid., 752.
58 Hansard's Parliamentary Debates, 3rd Series, 190 (12 March, 1868), 1525.
59 Lionel Robbins, *The Theory of Economic Policy in English Classical Political Economy* (London, 1952); D.M. Macgregor, *Economic Thought and Policy* (London, 1949); Scott Gordon, "The Ideology of Laissez Faire," in A.W. Coats, ed., *The Classical Economists and Economic Policy* (London: 1971), 180–205; O'Brien, *Classical Economics*.
60 Mill, *Unsettled Questions*, p. 45; Bernard Semmel, *The Rise of Free Trade: Imperialism; Classical Political Economy, The Empire of Free Trade and Imperialism* (Cambridge, 1970).
61 Mill, *Principles*, II, 921. On Carey and List, see below Chapter 2.
62 Mill, *Principles*, II, 918.
63 Cobden Club, ed., *John Stuart Mill and the Protection of Native Industry* (Westminster, 1911), 16–18, 23.
64 Mill, *Unsettled Questions*, 21.
65 Ibid., vi, 30–32; *Principles*, II, 856.
66 Mill, *Collected Works*, V, 750–51.
67 Mill, *Principles*, I, 239.
68 Ibid., II, Chapter 7.
69 See Mill's "Chapters on Socialism" (1879), *Collected Works*, V, and *Principles*, I, 203–14.
70 Adelaide Weinberg's, *John Elliot Cairnes and the American Civil War* (London, 1970) reveals Cairnes's deep anxieties and his Calvinist view of God and man, which help to explain his fundamentally pessimistic views. Cairnes wrote an influential historical work on the American South, *The Slave Power* (London, 1862). See also Leonard Courtney's obituary of Cairnes," *The Fortnightly Review*, N.S., XVIII (1875), 149–54; and T.A. Boylan and T.P. Foley, "John Elliot Cairnes, John Stuart Mill and Ireland," in Antoin E. Murphy, ed. *Economists and the Irish Economy* (Dublin, 1984), 96–119.

71 J.E. Cairnes, "New Theories in Political Economy," *The Fortnightly Review*, N.S., XI (January–June, 1872), 72.

72 J.E. Cairnes, *The Character and Logical Method of Political Economy*, 2nd ed. (New York. 1965; reprint of 1888 edition), vii.

73 Blaug, *Ricardian Economics*, 215.

74 J.E. Cairnes, *Essays in Political Economy* (New York, 1975; reprint of 1873 ed.), 252.

75 Ibid., 257.

76 Cairnes, *Character and Logic*, 22.

77 Cairnes, *Essays in Political Economy*, esp. 313–14, 316–19, 333–34; Frédéric Bastiat, *Economic Harmonies*, W. Hayden Boyers, transl., George B. de Husyar, ed. (Princeton, 1964).

78 Cairnes, *Character and Logic*, 84; see also "Mr. Comte and Political Economy" (1870), *Essays in Political Economy*.

79 Cairnes, *Character and Logic*, 180.

80 For Cairnes on Malthus, see *Character and Logic*, 169–70. Cairnes's essays on the gold question have been printed in *Essays in Political Economy*. See his triumphant defense of Ricardo's abstractions as brilliantly practical in *Some Leading Principles of Political Economy Newly Expounded* (New York, 1967), 315. See Michael D. Bordo, "John E. Cairnes on the Effects of the Australian Gold Discoveries, 1851–73: An Early Application of the Methodology of Positive Economics," *History of Political Economy, 7*, No. 3, (Fall, 1975), 336–59.

81 Cairnes, *Character and Logic*, iv-v; *Essays in Political Economy*, 76.

82 Cairnes, *Leading Principles*, 218–29.

83 Ibid., 176–78.

84 Ibid., 263, 265, 272–73, 280–94; his essay on cooperation is in his *Political Essays* (New York, 1967).

85 Cairnes, *Leading Principles*, 95, 388–406, and "Colonization and Colonial Government," *Political Essays*.

86 Jevons, *Theory of Political Economy*, esp. 1, 36, 77. See also Hutchison, *Revolutions and Progress*, 86; and the articles by Mark Blaug, Donald Winch, and A.W. Coats on the "marginal revolution," *History of Political Economy*, 4, No. 2 (Fall, 1972).

87 Jevons, *Theory of Political Economy*, ii–iii.

88 W. Stanley Jevons, *Letters and Journal*, Harriet A. Jevons, ed. (London, 1886), 154, 329, 332, 334, 342, 344, 419. See R.D.C. Black, "Jevons and the Economists of His Time," *Manchester School*, XXX (September 1962), 203–23; Rosamond Konekamp, "William Stanley Jevons, 1835–1882. Some Biographical Notes," *Manchester School*, XXX (September 1962), 251–75; Rosa M. Robertson, "Jevons and His Precursors," *Econometrica*, 19 (July 1951), 219–49; Lord Robbins, "The Place of Jevons in the History of Economic Thought," *Manchester School*, VII, No. 1 (1936), 1–17.

89 W. Stanley Jevons, *The Coal Question* (London, 1865).

90 W. Stanley Jevons, *Investigations in Currency and Finance* (New York,

1964). J.M. Keynes emphasized Jevons' contribution to inductive work in economics, *Essays in Biography* (New York, 1951), 278.

91 H.S. Foxwell, "Introduction," Jevons, *Investigations*, xxv.

92 Jevons, *Theory of Political Economy*, xv–xvii, 3, 16, 22; "The Future of Political Economy," *Principles of Economics* (New York, 1965), 191–200; *The Principles of Science: A Treatise on Logic and the Scientific Method* (New York 1958), pp. 760–61. *State in Relation to Labour* (New York, 1968), first published in 1882, was his contribution to the social application of economics.

93 Alfred Marshall, "Autobiographical notice for Eckstein's compilation of 'Portraits and Short Lives of Leading Economists,' " published in *History of Economic Thought Newsletter*, No. 8 (Spring 1972), 15–16.

94 J.K. Whitaker, *The Early Economic Writings of Alfred Marshall, 1867–1890* (New York, 1975), I, 9.

95 Alfred Marshall, "Method and History of Economics," lecture notes of the early 1870s, Marshall Papers 5, 1, f., Marshall Library, Cambridge.

96 Mary Paley Marshall, *What I Remember* (Cambridge, 1947), 23–24.

97 Black, "Jevons and the Economists of His Time," *Manchester School* (1962), 212.

98 Whitaker, *Early Economic Writings of Marshall*, I, 12, 50; Marshall, "Notes for Eckstein," *Economic Thought Newsletter* (1972), 15.

99 Mary Paley Marshall, *What I Remember*, 20.

100 Whitaker, *Early Economic Writings of Marshall*, I, 52.

101 See his notes on economic history: "Some Features of American Industry," Marshall Papers, 6(7); "The State in Relation to Land," Marshall Papers, 5(1)d; "A Notebook on India," Marshall Papers, 5(6–7); "Notebooks on Economic History," Marshall Papers, 5(8–9). On his theory of economic history and its place in the universities, see below Chapter 7.

102 Alfred Marshall and Mary Paley Marshall, *The Economics of Industry* (London, 1879), 2.

103 Mary Paley Marshall, *What I Remember*, 22

104 Alfred Marshall, "The Laws of Political Economy," letter to the *Beehive*, April 18, 1874, Marshall Papers, 9(2).

105 Marshall and Marshall, *Economics of Industry*, 3; see also his notebook on method, Marshall Papers, 9(2), 7.

106 Whitaker, *Early Economic Writings of Marshall*, I, 110; "Alfred Marshall: The Years of 1877 to 1885," *History of Political Economy*, 4 (Spring 1972), 51–53.

107 Marshall's comments at the London Industrial Remuneration Conference, *Report of Proceedings* (1885), 173–83.

108 Press reports of the Progress and Poverty Lectures given at Bristol in 1883, Marshall Papers, 5(1)g; notes on "The State in Relation to Land," Marshall Papers, 5(1)d.

109 Industrial Remuneration Conference, *Report of Proceedings* (1885), 173.

Chapter 2

1 It was published by the Carey Publishing Company of Philadelphia. The 1885 London edition was followed by a second English edition in 1928, translated by Sampson S. Lloyd, with an introduction by J.S. Nicholson. All references are to this last edition. On list in America, see Joseph Dorfman, *The Economic Mind in American Civilization* (New York, 1946–59), II, 578–84; W. Notz, "Friedrich List in America," *American Economic Review*, 16 (June 1926), 249–65.

2 List, *National System*, xxxiv–xliv; Bk. I.

3 Ibid., 295.

4 Ibid., 93.

5 Ibid., 208.

6 Ibid., 108, 127, 129, 142, 145–46, 253.

7 Alfred Marshall, *Principles of Economics*, 8th ed. (London, 1968), 633.

8 See, for example, List, *National System*, 106.

9 See especially William Cunningham and J.S. Nicholson, below Chapter 8. For a critical contemporary view of List's influence in England, see Margaret E. Hirst, *Life of Friedrich List and Selections from His Writings* (London, 1909).

10 Henry Charles Carey, *Principles of Social Science* (Philadelphia, 1873; first published, 1857–58), 3 vols. On Carey, see Dorfman, *American Economic Mind*, II,. 789–805; Paul K. Conkin, *Prophets of Prosperity: America's First Political Economists* (Bloomington, Ind., 1980), 263–307.

11 Carey, *Principles*, I, 9–40.

12 Ibid., 192–97.

13 Ibid., 324.

14 Ibid., 321–66.

15 Ibid., 97–98.

16 William Burton Cherin, "The German Historical School of Economics: A Study in the Methodology of the Social Sciences," Ph.D. Dissertation (Berkeley, 1933), 6.

17 On the Younger German historical school, see Chapter 5.

18 William James Ashley, "Historical School of Economics," R.H. Inglis Palgrave, ed., *Dictionary of Political Economy*, 2nd ed. (New York, 1963), II, 310–14; Gustav Cohn, "Political Economy in Germany," *Fortnightly Review*, N.S., XIV (June–December 1873), 337–50. See also Henry William Spiegel, *The Growth of Economic Thought*, revised ed. (Durham, N.C., 1983) and its excellent bibliography; Bert F. Hoselitz, *Theories of Economic Growth* (New York, 1960), 193–238.

19 W.J. Ashley translated the Preface to the *Grundriss* as "Roscher's Program of 1843," *Quarterly Journal of Economics*, 9 (October 1894), 110.

20 Ashley, "Historical School of Economics," Palgrave, Dictionary, II, 311; Schumpeter, *History of Economic Analysis*, 809.

21 Cherin, "German Historical School," 18, 37, 53–56.

22 Blaug, *Ricardian Economics*, Chapters 5 and 8; S.G. Checkland, "The Advent of Academic Economics in England," *Manchester School*, (1951), 43–70.

23 F.Y. Edgeworth, "Richard Jones," Palgrave, *Dictionary of Political Economy*, II, 490.

24 Alfred Marshall, "The Old Generation of Economists and the New," *Quarterly Journal of Economics*, XI (January 1897), 117. See also W.J. Ashley, "Historical School of Economics," Palgrave, *Dictionary*, II, 310; Karl Marx pointed to Jones as the last representative of the "true science of political economy," quoted by H. Grossman, "The Evolutionist Revolt Against Classical Economics, Part II, In England," *Journal of Political Economy*, 51, No. 6 (943), 509; Salim Rashid, "Richard Jones, William Whewell and the Inductive Political Economy," 1975 meeting of the History of Economics Society.

25 See below Chapter 3.

26 Richard Jones, *An Essay on the Distribution of Wealth and the Sources of Taxation* (New York, 1956), xiv–xv; see also xxxviii–xxxix; *Literary Remains: Lectures and Tracts on Political Economy*, William Whewell, ed.; first published in 1859, (New York, 1964), 536–37.

27 On population, see Jones, *Essay on Distribution*, xvii; *Literary Remains*, 465–79; on diminishing returns *Literary Remains*, 584–89 and *Essay on Distribution*, xv–xvi. His classification of rents constitutes the bulk of the last work. See also M.L. Miller, "Richard Jones' Contributions to the Theory of Rent," *History of Political Economy*, 9 (Fall, 1977), 146–65.

28 Jones, *Essay on Distribution*, xv. Jones decried the insularity of English economics in *Literary Remains*, 1.

29 Jones, *Essay on Distribution*, xxii–xxiii.

30 Jones, *Literary Remains*, 291–339. J.S. Nicholson later warmly praised Jones' early work on mercantilism, "The Balance of Trade," Palgrave *Dictionary of Political Economy*, I, 84.

31 J.S. Mill, "Leslie and the Land Question," *Essays in Economics and Society, Collected Works*, 5, 672.

32 Schumpeter, *History of Economic Analysis*, 823; T.W. Hutchison, *A Review of Economic Doctrines*, 19–21.

33 Mill, *Works*, 5, 671.

34 Ashley, "Historical School of Economics," Palgrave, *Dictionary*, II, 313.

35 L.L. Price, "The Study of Economic History," *Economic Journal*, 16 (March 1906), 13.

36 See Ingram's preface to T.E. Cliffe Leslie, *Essays in Political and Moral Philosophy* (London, 1879), ix; see also 411; J.K. Ingram to Cliffe Leslie, 7 Nov. 1878, Stirling Library, London University. The letters from Leslie to Ingram during the 1870s make clear that Leslie encouraged Ingram's heterodoxy and that he was very fond of his foreign connections. J.K. Ingram Papers, Public Record Office of Northern Ireland, D 2808/43/1–64. Another historical economist who objected to orthodox economics from the outside, and one who was in limited contact with Leslie, was the Aus-

tralian protectionist, David Syme; see his *Outlines of an Industrial Science* (London, 1876) and "On the Method of Political Economy," *Westminster Review*, N.S., 40 (July 1871), 206–18; J.A. La Nauze, "David Syme," *Political Economy in Australia: An Historical Study* (Melbourne, 1949), 96–136.

37 Leslie was prominently mentioned in German and French dictionaries of Political Economy during the period. Joseph Dorfman has argued that articles by Leslie and about Leslie first stimulated American interest in historical economics, *The Economic Mind in American Civilization*, vol. 3, 88–89; "The Role of the German Historical School in American Economic Thought," *American Economic Association: Papers and Proceedings*, No. 45 (May 1955), 19–22; Emile de Laveleye, "The New Tendencies of Political Economy," *Banker's Magazine and Statistical Registry* (Baltimore), 33 (February–March 1879), 601–09, 698–706, 761–67; Maurice Block, "The Two Schools of Political Economy," *Banker's Magazine* (London), 38 (January–December 1878), 168–87.

38 Leslie examined for the Indian and Civil Service Exams, the Society of Arts, the Home and Colonial Offices, and the City of London College; see Leslie to Ingram, 21 November 1878, and Leslie to Ingram, n.d., Ingram Papers, D2808/43/45.

39 In addition to the *Essays in Philosophy* of 1879, see his *Essays in Political Economy*, 2nd ed. (London, 1888 and *Land Systems and Industrial Economy of Ireland, England, and Continental Countries* (London, 1870). Other notices of Leslie are: *Atheneum*, "Cliffe Leslie," No. 2832 (4 February 1882), 158; *Times*, 28 January 1882, 7; R.D.C. Black, *The Statistical and Social Inquiry Society of Ireland: Centenary Volume, 1847–1947* (Dublin, 1947), 75–77.

40 Leslie, *Essays in Philosophy*, 155; see also 148–66.

41 Leslie, *Essays in Political Economy*, 137–38; *Essays in Philosophy*, 156–57.

42 Ibid., 161.

43 Leslie, "On the Philosophical Method of Political Economy," *Essays in Philosophy*, 230. This article was originally published in *Hermathena*, No. 4 (1876), 265–96.

44 Leslie, *Essays in Philosophy*, 228.

45 Ibid., 230.

46 Ibid., 231–34, 399.

47 Leslie to Ingram, 28 October 1878(?), D 2808/43/34, Ingram Papers.

48 Leslie, *Essays in Philosophy*, 390.

49 Ibid., 394.

50 Ibid., 385; *Essays in Political Economy*, 233.

51 Leslie, "The History and Future of Interest and Profit," *Essays in Political Economy*, 243–68.

52 Leslie, *Essays in Philosophy*, 402.

53 Ibid., 233.

54 Ibid., 244.

55 Ibid., 246.

56 Ibid., 221.

57 F.S.L. Lyons, *Ireland Since the Famine* (London, 1971), 22–59, 135–36, 156–69; Patrick Lynch and John Vaisey, *Guinness's Brewery in the Irish Economy* (Cambridge,1960), 9–36, 161–76. R.D.C. Black, *Economic Thought and the Irish Question, 1815–1870* (Cambridge, 1961), 3–11, 235–38.

58 Ibid., 239–42.

59 Hansard's Parliamentary Debates, 3rd ser. 190 (12 March 1868), 1489.

60 Ibid., 1493.

61 Ibid., 1525. See also Mill, "Leslie on the Land Question," *Works*, 5, 672.

62 Mill, *Principles*, I, 230; see also 142–52, Book II chaps. 6–10. Even in *England and Ireland* (London, 1868) Mill did not support land nationalization. See also Black, *Economic Thought and the Irish Question*, 31, 53–55; E.D. Steele, "Ireland and the Empire in the 1860s; Imperial Precedents for Gladstone's First Land Act," *Historical Journal*, 11,(No. 1, (1968), 64–83, and "J.S. Mill and the Irish Question: The Principles of Political Economy, 1848–1865," *Historical Journal*, 13 (June 1970), 216–36.

63 J.E. Cairnes, *Political Essays* (New York, 1967), 136–37.

64 Cairnes, "Fragments on Ireland," *Political Essays*, 127–98.

65 Leslie's role as a critic led Jevons to suggest him as a correspondent for Léon Walras, Leslie replied to Walras's inquiry: "Pour moi, nous n'avons pas même atteint aux inductions necessaires: et l'Economie politique manque beaucoup de recherches inductives avant de pouvoir devenir une science deductive," William Jaffe, ed., *Correspondence of Léon Walras and Related Papers* (Amsterdam, 1965), I, 395.

66 "Political and Economical Heterodoxy: Cliffe Leslie," *Westminster Review*, N.S., 64 (October 1883), 494. The article's author was probably Emile de Laveleye. See also Leslie's bitter comments on Cairnes to Ingram, 19 October 1878(?), Ingram Papers, D2808/43/32.

67 See Leslie's letters to Mill in the Mill Collection at John Hopkins University.

68 See J.S. Mill to Cliffe Leslie, 14 November 1863, *The Later Letters of J.S. Mill, 1849–73, Collected Works*, 15, 899. See also Mill to Leslie, 20 December 1861, 756–58.

69 See, for example, Mill to Leslie, 8 February 1869, *Works*, 17, 1557–58; Mill to Leslie, 8 May 1869, 17, 1599–1601; Mill to Henry Reeve, 1 May 1861, 15, 725–26; Mill to John Chapman, 13 May 1861, 15, 727.

70 Mill to Cairnes, 23 July 1867, *Works*, 16, 1294; see also Mill to Cairnes, 30 July 1867, 16, 1295.

71 Mill to Cairnes, 15 May 1872, *Works*, 17, 1895. See also Mill to Cairnes, 2 August 1872, 17, 1903; Mill to George Croom Robertson, 23 May 1872, 17, 1889–90. John Morley, the editor of *The Fortnightly Review*, also asked Mill for support in his own candidacy. Mill encouraged Morley not to compete since he had endorsed Leslie, Mill to Morley, 1 May 1872 and 11 May 1872, *Works*, 17, 1889, 1892.

72 Speaking of Leslie, Cairnes told Courtney: "I dare say you may have gath-

ered that I had not particular admiration or liking for him," 4 August 1867, Courtney Collection, British Library of Political and Economic Science.

73 Leslie to Ingram, 23 May, 1878 (?), Ingram Papers, D2808/43/24.

74 Leslie to Ingram (n.d.), Ingram Papers, D2808/43/42.

75 Leslie to Ingram, 24 November 1879 (?), Ingram Papers, D2808/43/33. See also Leslie to Ingram, 23 March 1868 (?), D2808/43/24 and n.d., D2808/43/51.

76 Leslie to Ingram, 24 November 1879 (?), Ingram Papers, D2808/43/36.

77 Leslie to Rogers, 24 April 1879, Rogers Papers, Ramsden.

78 Leslie to Ingram, 26 March 1878 (?), Ingram Papers, D2808/43/23.

79 Leslie to Ingram, 21 November 1878 (?), Ingram Papers, D2808/43/35.

80 Leslie to Ingram (n.d.), Ingram Papers, D2808/43/60.

81 R.D.C. Black noted that in methodology their "outstanding characteristic" was "their predilection for an inductive approach," "Economic Studies at Trinity College, Dublin," Part I, *Hermathena*, 70, No 1 (1947), 69.

82 R.D.C. Black, "Trinity College, Dublin, and the Theory of Value," *Economica* n.s. 12 (August 1945), 140–48, and "Economic Studies at Trinity College, Dublin," *Hermathena*, 70, 73–80; S.G. Checkland, "The Advent of Academic Economics in England, *Manchester School* 19 (January 1951), 43–70.

83 R.D.C. Black, "Economic Studies at Trinity College, Dublin," Part II, *Hermathena*, 71 (May 1948), 54–55; Isaac Butt, *Protection to Home Industries; Some Cases of the Advantages Considered* (Dublin, 1846).

84 "Cliffe Leslie," *Westminster Review* (1883), 492.

85 Leslie to Ingram, 25 June, 1879(?), D2808/43/19, 24 December 1878 (?) D2808/43/40; and n.d. D2808/43/50, Ingram Papers.

86 Leslie, *Essays in Philosophy*, vi.

87 Leslie, "Maine's Early History of Institutions," *Essays in Philosophy*.

88 George Feaver, *From Status to Contract: A Biography of Sir Henry Maine, 1822–88* (London, 1969); Kingsley B. Smellie, "Sir Henry Maine," *Economica* 8 (March 1928), 64–94.

89 Sir Henry Maine, "The Effects of Observation of India on Modern Economic Thought," *Village Communities*, 4th ed. (London, 1881), 203–40: "The Early History of Price and Rent," *Village Communities*, 175–201.

90 Walter Bahegot, *Economic Studies*, Richard Holt Hutton, ed. (Stanford, Cal., 1953), esp. 7–8, 19–20, 23–26.

91 Maine, *Village Communities*, 197.

92 This is one of the major themes of the correspondence between Leslie and Ingram, see for example, Leslie to Ingram, 19 August, 1878, Ingram Papers, D2808/43/28.

93 "Cliffe Leslie," *Westminster Review* (1883), 492.

94 Leslie to Ingram, 4 January 1878 (?), Ingram Papers, D2808/43/17.

95 Leslie to Ingram, 23 May, 1878 (?), Ingram Papers, D2808/43/24. Paul Adelman has pointed to the role of Frederic Harrison and Positivism in the origin of English historical economics in "Frederic Harrison and the 'Positivist' Attack on Orthodox Political Economy," *History of Political Econ-*

omy, 3 (Spring 1970), 170–89. Harrison's views owed a great deal to Mill, see esp. his article, "The Limits of Political Economy," *Fortnightly Review* I (May-August 1865), 356–76.

96 Leslie to Ingram, n.d., Ingram Papers, D2808/43/45.

97 Leslie, *Essays in Philosophy*, 83, 92–93; "The Future of Europe Foretold in History," 94–110; "Nations and International Law," 111–27.

98 Ibid., 145.

99 Ibid., 51–52.

100 Ibid., 36. See also "Utilitarianism and the Summum Bonum," *Essays in Philosophy*, 30–50.

101 Leslie, "The Distribution and Value of the Precious Metals in the Sixteenth and Seventeenth Centuries," *Essays in Philosophy*, 264–95; "The New Gold Mines and Prices in Europe in 1865," 296–325.

102 Leslie, *Essays in Philosophy*, 331; see also "Economic Sciences and Statistics," 375–82.

103 H.S. Foxwell commented on the Kress Library's copy (Harvard) of Leslie's *Trades Unions and Combinations in 1853* (Dublin, 1853), that Leslie "shows his usual good sense in strong contrast to the abstract economists." Compare Leslie, *On the Self Dependence of the Working Classes under the Rule of Capitalism* (Dublin, 1851).

104 For a recent statement of Leslie's very argument on wages, see E.J. Hobsbawm, "Custom, Wages, and Work Load," *Labouring Men: Studies in the History of Labour* (New York, 1967), 405–35.

105 Leslie, *Land Systems*, 360.

106 Ibid., 360, 364; *Essays in Philosophy*, esp. 193, 371–74.

107 In any case, deterministic explanations of Leslie's economic thought as rooted solely in the problems of Ireland would have to explain why Cairnes, who came out of the same Trinity College tradition and also dealt with the economic problems of Ireland, became such a staunch defender of orthodoxy.

108 Compare H.C. Carey's discussion of Ireland as an agricultural colony under free trade, *Principles of Social Science*, I, 320–37.

109 Leslie, *Land Systems*, 11–13, 16–18, 31, 50–56.

110 Ibid., 128; also 117, 121–29.

111 Leonce de Lavergne's *Essai sur l' économic rurale de l' Angleterre, de l'Ecosse et de l'Ireland* (1854) was Leslie's model for his own work on comparative land systems: see Leslie, "Leonce de Lavergne," *Essays in Political Economy*, 101–25. Leslie was also a student of the Belgian protectionist and bimetallist, Emile de Laveleye; see Leslie, "M. de Laveleye on Primitive Property," *Essays in Philosophy*, 435–47. Leslie corresponded with Laveleye; see Leslie to Ingram, 24 December, 1878, Ingram Papers, D2808/43/40. See also Paul Lambert, who viewed Laveleye as a socialist of the chair, "Emile de Laveleye, 1822–1892," *History of Political Economy* 2 (Fall, 1970), 263–83.

112 Leslie, *Land Systems*, 262–63.

113 Ibid., 29.

114 Ibid., 73–74.

115 Ibid., 116.

116 Ibid., 238, 253, 264, 270, 280.

117 Bernard Semmel, *The Rise of Free Trade Imperialism: Classical Political Economy, The Empire of Free Trade and Imperialism, 1750–1850* (Cambridge, 1970), chaps. 4 and 5.

118 Leslie, *Land Systems*, 184

119 Ibid., 187.

120 On Irish national economics, see Black, "The Irish Experience in Relation to the Theory and Policy of Economic Development," in A.J. Youngson, ed., *Economic Development in the Long Run*, (London, 1972) 201–06.

121 Leslie, *Land Systems*, 36.

122 Ibid., 35–36, 48–52; and "Cliffe Leslie," *Westminster Review* (1883): 474.

123 Schumpeter, *History of Economic Analysis*, 823 n., Ashley in Palgrave, *Dictionary*, 2nd ed., II, 313.

124 Gustav Cohn, "Political Economy in Germany," *Fortnightly Review* n.s. 14 (June–December 1873): 337–50. In a similar article thirty years later Cohn mentioned that it had been Leslie who had asked him to familiarize English readers with German economics, "Political Economy in Germany," *Economic Journal* 15 (December 1905), 600. Leslie himself wrote a review of William Roscher's *Principles of Political Economy*, in his *Essays in Political Economy*, 95–100.

125 Leslie to Ingram, n.d., Ingram Papers, D2808/43/51.

126 Leslie, *Land Systems*, 89.

127 J.K. Ingram, *History of Political Economy* (New ed. with a supplementary chapter by William A. Scott; Introduction by Richard T. Ely: London, 1923). All references are to this edition. It was first published as an article for the *Encyclopedia Britannica*. A much expanded version was published in Edinburgh in 1888. Enjoying an immense popular success, the work went through numerous printings and was translated into German, French, Polish, Russian, Swedish, Czech, Serbian and Dutch.

128 Schumpeter, *History of Economic Analysis*, 538 n.

129 Ashley to W.A.S. Hewins, n.d., but probably 1888, Hewins Papers, 41/269, Sheffield University; W.J. Ashley to E.R. Seligman 15 September, 1889 and ll March, 1890, Seligman Collection, Columbia University.

130 On Ingram, see T.W. Lyster, *Bibliography of the Writings of J. Kells Ingram, 1823–1907* (Dublin 1907–08); C.L. Lytton Falkiner, "Memoir of the Late John Kells Ingram," *Journal of the Statistical and Social Inquiry Society of Ireland*, Part LXXXVIII (1908), 105–24; F.Y. Edgeworth, "J.K. Ingram," *Economic Journal* 7 (June 1907), 299–301; Black, *Irish Statistical Society*, 63–66, includes a portrait.

131 Black, *Irish Statistical Society*, 1–6, 64; Falkiner, "Memoir of Ingram," *Journal of the Statistical Society of Ireland* (1908), 108–13. On the statistical societies, see below Chapter 3.

132 J.K. Ingram, "Considerations on the State of Ireland," *Journal of the Statistical and Social Inquiry Society of Ireland*, Part XXVL (1864–65), 26.

133 J.K. Ingram, "The Organization of Charity and the Education of the Children of the State," *Journal of the Statistical and Social Inquiry Society of Ireland*, Part XLVIII (December 1875), 470.

134 His warnings on violence are in a letter to his publisher, reprinted in his obituary, *The Times*, May 4, 1907, 10, f.

135 In addition to his inductive studies, cited above, see Ingram's "Additional Facts and Arguments on the Boarding Out of Pauper Children," *Journal of the Statistical and Social Inquiry Society of Ireland*, Part XLIX (February 1876): 503–24; "A Comparison Between the English and Irish Poor Laws," *Journal of the Statistical and Social Inquiry Society of Ireland*, Part XXVI (May, 1864), 43–61.

136 J.K. Ingram, "On the Present and Future Prospects of Political Economy," *Journal of the Statistical and Social Inquiry Society of Ireland*, Part LIV (August 1878), 1–28. All references are to this edition, which was reprinted as a pamphlet with the same pagination. It was simultaneously published in the *Journal of the Royal Statistical Society* and in the *Report of the Forty-Eighth Meeting of the British Association for the Advancement of Science*.

137 Ingram, "Present Position and Future Prospects of Political Economy," 6–7.

138 Ibid., 14.

139 Ibid., 15.

140 Ibid., 18.

141 Ibid., 25.

142 Ibid., 19.

143 J.K. Ingram, *Outlines of the History of Religion* (London, 1900), 20.

144 Ingram, *Sonnets*, especially the poem to Comte, 45. His popular Positivist works included: *Outlines of the History of Religion: The Final Transition: A Sociological Study* (London, 1901); *Passages from the Letters of August Comte* (London, 1901); *Practical Morals: A Treatise on Universal Education* (London, 1904). On Positivism, see Walter Michael Simon, *European Positivism in the Nineteenth Century* (Ithaca, NY. 1963) and "Auguste Comte's English Disciples," *Victorian Studies* 8 (December 1964), 161–72.

145 J.K. Ingram, "Positivism and Mr. Chamberlain's Scheme," *Positivist Review*, No. CXXXV (March 1904), 52; *Work and the Workman: Being an Address to the Trades Union Congress, Dublin, September, 1880* (London, 1884); *The Final Transition*, 2, 8, 48, 50–53, 60.

146 Ingram wrote articles for the ninth edition of the *Encyclopedia Britannica* on such individuals as Ricardo, Say, Senior, Quesnay, Rau, Turgot, Petty, and Young. See also his articles on Leslie, Lassalle, and Marx for J.H. Inglis Palgrave, ed., *Dictionary of Political Economy* (London, 1894–99).

147 Ingram, *History of Political Economy*, 34–57.

148 Ibid., 58–68.

149 Ibid., 104.

150 Ibid., 112.

151 Ibid., 134.

152 Ibid., 151–52.

153 Edgeworth, "Ingram," *Economic Journal* (1907), 301.

Chapter 3

1 Michael Cullen, *The Statistical Movement in Early Victorian Britain: The Foundations of Empirical Social Research* (New York, 1975), 10–11.
2 See above chapter 2.
3 Blaug, *Ricardian Economics*, 87.
4 H.S. Foxwell, "The Economic Movement in England," *Quarterly Journal of Economics*, 2 (October 1887), 87, 95.
5 O.J.R. Howarth, *The British Association for the Advancement of Science: A Retrospect, 1831–1921* (London, 1922), p. 87.
6 Royal Statistical Society, *Annals of the Royal Statiical Society, 1834–1934* (London, 1934), 6.
7 R.L. Smyth, "The History of Section F. of the British Association, 1834–1972," in Nicholas Kaldor, ed., *Conflicts in Policy Objectives* (New York,1971), 156–75; A.W. Coats, "The Origin and Early Development of the Royal Economic Society," *Economic Journal*, 78 (June 1968), 349–71.
8 *Annals of the Royal Statistical Society* (1934) 22.
9 Ibid., 52, 56, 82–83, 105, 111–12, 144–45, 151, 166–67, 178–80. At the 1885 Jubilee festivities of the Society, the economists who spoke – Giffen, Marshall, and Edgeworth – confined their remarks to mathematical problems of statistics; London Statistical Society, *Jubilee Volume of the Statistical Society* (London, 1885).
10 T.S. Ashton, *Economic and Social Investigation in Manchester, 1833–1933* (London, 1934); Black, *The Irish Statistical Society*.
11 G.R. Porter, *The Progress of the Nation* (London, 1836), I, 203.
12 Ibid., 2.
13 Thomas Tooke and William Newmarch, *The History of Prices and the State of the Circulation*, 8 vols.,(London, 1838–57). On Tooke and Newmarch, see Paul J. Fitzpatrick, "Leading British Statisticians of the Nineteenth Century," *Journal of the American Statistical Asociation*, 55 (March 1960), 38–70; Sir Athelstone Baines, "History of Statistics in Great Britain and Ireland," John Koren, ed., *The History of Statistics* (New York, 1918), 363–90.
14 William Newmarch, "Condition of Political Economy," *Journal of the Statistical Society* (1871), 476–80. See also Tooke and Newmarch, *History of Prices*, I, 5–6; II, 1–2; IV, 419; VI, 232–35, 238; William Newmarch, *In Memoriam* (London, 1882).
15 W. J. Ashley, "James E. Thorold Rogers," *Political Science Quarterly*, IV (September 1889), 382–83.
16 Ibid., 389.
17 W. Tuckwell, *Reminiscences of Oxford* (London, 1900), 100, 103.
18 His frequent attacks on the Oxford establishment culminated in his, "Oxford Professors and Oxford Tutors," *Contemporary Review*, 56 (November 1889), 926–36. To this the School of Modern History angrily responded:

"Here in Oxford...we are well accustomed to Mr. Rogers' inaccurate statements, his sweeping, ill founded, and often ill natured criticism," *Contemporary Review*, 57(1890), 454–55, On Rogers's career, see the article by W.A.S. Hewins, *Dictionary of National Biography*.

19 J.E.T. Rogers, *The Economic Interpretation of History* (New York, 1888), ix. On the election, see N.B. De Marchi, "On the Dangers of Being too Political an Economist: Thorold Rogers and the 1868 Election to the Drummond Professorship," *Oxford Economic Papers*, 28, No. 2 (November 1976), 364–80.

20 L.L. Price, "Memoir and Notes on British Economists, 1881–1947." unpublished ms., Royal Statistical Society, London, 30.

21 The Rogers papers, Magdalan College, Oxford, contains much material on politics. His "Scrapbook," at the Bodleian, has biographical material.

22 *Hansard's Parliamentary Debates*, Third Series, 252 (May 24, 1880), 347–51.

23 Ibid., 293 (November 6, 1884), 1164.

24 Rogers, *Economic Interpretation of History*, x.

25 Gladstone asked Rogers to write a popular account of the Irish Union as it bore upon the contemporary controversy; W.E. Gladstone to Rogers, July 7, 1886, Rogers Papers.

26 J.E.T. Rogers, *A Manual of Political Economy* (Oxford, 1868), v.

27 Ibid., 231.

28 Ibid., 149–50, 153–55.

29 Ibid., v, 125–56.

30 J.E.T. Rogers, ed., Adam Smith, *An Inquiry into the Nature and Causes of the Wealth of Nations* (Oxford, 1869), I, xli.

31 J.E.T. Rogers, *A History of Agriculture and Prices in England* (Oxford, 1866–1902), II, xi.

32 William Newmarch to Rogers, October 11, 1882, Rogers Papers.

33 See G.D.H. Cole's Introduction to J.E.T. Rogers, *Six Centuries of Work and Wages* (London, 1949), v.

34 Rogers, *A History of Prices*, I, vii.

35 Rogers, *The Economic Interpretation of History*, (New York, 1888), 2.

36 Ibid., 272–73.

37 Rogers, *Six Centuries of Work and Wages*, 301.

38 Rogers, *Economic Interpretation of History*, 165.

39 Rogers, *Six Centuries of Work and Wages*, 8.

40 Rogers, *The Industrial and Commercial History of England*, (New York, 1892), 457.

41 Rogers, *Economic Interpretation of History*, viii.

42 Rogers, *History of Prices*, I, ix.

43 J.E.T. Rogers, "Review of Cliffe Leslie's *Essays in Philosophy*," *The Academy*, No. 370 (June 7, 1879), 489–91; see also his review of "William Cunningham, *The Growth of English Industry and Commerce*," *The Academy*, No. 524 (May 20, 1882), 351–52.

44 Rogers, *History of Prices*, IV, xii.

45 Ibid., v; see also, *Economic Interpretation of History*, 6, 8.

46 Rogers, *Six Centuries of Work and Wages*, 435.

47 Ibid., 69, 84–85, 173–326.

48 Ibid., 398.

49 Ibid., 6, 398–400; *Economic Interpretation of History*, 21–23, 40, 46, 240–41.

50 Rogers, *History of Prices*, I, viii.

51 Rogers, *Industrial and Commercial History*, 318.

52 Rogers, *Six Centuries of Work and Wages*, 400–01, 523; *Industrial and Commercial History*, 162–83; *Economic Interpretation of History*, vii, ix, 307–16.

53 Ibid., 161–62, 227–31.

54 Ibid., 48–51, 172, 174, 181; "The History of Rent in England," *Contemporary Review*, 37 (April 1880), 673–90.

55 J.E.T. Roger, "English Agriculture," *Contemporary Review*, 35 (May 1879), 323; *Cobden and Modern Political Opinion* (London), 1873): 74–108; *Industrial and Commercial History*, 237–45, 369; *Six Centuries of Work and Wages*, 518; *Hansard's Parliamentary Debates*, 260 (May 2, 1881), 1606–10; 265 (January 10, 1881), 407–08.

56 Rogers, ed., *Wealth of Nations*, xxvi–xxvii; *Historical Gleanings* (London, 1869), 125.

57 Rogers, ed., *Wealth of Nations*, I, 29; *Industrial and Commercial History*, 191–204, 365–67.

58 J.E.T. Rogers, *The Relations of Economic Science to Social and Political Action* (London, 1888), 10.

59 Rogers, "English Agriculture," *Contemporary Review* (1879), 303–23; *Industrial and Commercial History*, 62–63, 291, 341–43.

60 Ibid., 225.

61 Rogers, *Six Centuries of Work and Wages*, 475.

62 J.E.T. Rogers, "Contemporary Socialism," *Contemporary Review*, 47 (January 1885), 54–57; *Wealth of Nations*, 152.

63 Rogers, *Economic Science and Political Action*, 27; see also *Wealth of Nations*, 37, 170; "The Colonial Question," *Cobden Club Essays*, Second Series (London, 1871–72), 447–48.

64 J.E.T. Rogers, "Lessons from the Dutch Republic," in E. Magnuason et al., *National Life and Thought* (New York, 1891), 247–48.

65 Rogers, *Economic Interpretation of History*, 318.

66 Rogers, *Industrial and Commercial History*, 32–33, 394–99, 402–05.

67 Rogers, *Cobden and Modern Political Opinion*, 18–19, 230.

68 Rogers, *Economic Interpretation of History*, 394–95; *Industrial and Commercial History* 111–12, 409–10; "English Agriculture," *Contemporary Review* (1879), 303–04, 3ll; "Colonial Question," *Cobden Club Essays*, 407. On the revival of protectionism, B.H. Brown, *The Tariff Reform Movement in Great Britain, 1881–95* (New York, 1943).

69 J.E.T. Rogers, "British Finance: Its Present and Future," *Contemporary Review*, 34 (January 1879), 301–03; "Colonial Question," *Cobden Club Essays*, 403–59; *Cobden and Modern Political Opinon*, 134–37, 243–48.

70 Ashley, "Rogers," *Political Science Quarterly* (1889), 382–84, 391–93.

71 William Cunningham, "Why Had Roscher So Little Influence in England?" *Annals of the American Academy of Political and Social Science*, 5 (November 1894), 324.
72 Rogers, *History of Prices*, III, xi.
73 William Cunningham, *Hints on the Study of Economic History* (London, 1919), 10.
74 James McMullan Rigo, "Leone Levi," *Dictionary of National Biography*; Leone Levi, *The Story of My Life: The First Ten Years of My Residence in England, 1845–55* (London, 1888).
75 Leone Levi, *The History of British Commerce and of the Economic Progress of the British Nation, 1763–1878*, 2nd ed., (London, 1888), Preface.
76 Levi, *The History of British Commerce and the Progress of the British Nation, 1763–1870* (London, 1872), viii.
77 Levi, *History of British Commerce* (1872 ed.), 443; (1888 ed.), 498–502, 531–37.
78 Ibid., (1872 ed.), 27.
79 Rogers, *Economic Interpretation of History*, 6. On Giffen, see F.Y. Edgeworth, "Sir Robert Giffen," *Economic Journal*, XX (June 1910), 318–21; L.L. Price, *A Short History of Political Economy in England*, 15th ed. (London, 1937), 244–48.
80 Robert Giffen, *Economic Inquiries and Studies* (London, 1904), I, 380.
81 Robert Giffen, *Essays in Finance*, First Series, 4th ed. (London, 1886), Preface; *Statistics*, Henry Higgs, ed., (London, 1913), 14.
82 Giffen, "The Progress of the Working Class in the Last Half Century," *Essays in Finance*, Second Series (London, 1886), 360, 406–07.
83 Ibid., 403.
84 Ibid., 414–15.
85 On Toynbee and the Hammonds, see below chapters 4 and 9.
86 Giffen, *Essays in Finance*, 1890 ed., 392.
87 Robert Giffen, *The Recent Rate of Material Progress in England* (London, 1887); see also his articles on foreign trade in *Essays in Finance*, various editions.
88 Robert Giffen, *The Growth of Capital*, reprint of 1889 ed., (New York, 1970), 113.
89 Giffen, *Economic Inquiries*, I, 344.
90 Ibid., II, 159.
91 Ibid., I, viii; see also II, 240–41, 387–88; "Imperial Policy and Free Trade," *The Nineteenth Century and After*, No. CCCXVII (July 1903), 1–2, 7–8, 14–15.
92 Giffen, *Statistics*, 97.
93 Arthur L. Bowley, *A Short Account of England's Foreign Trade in the Nineteenth Century*, rev. ed. (London, 1905), 108–09. On Bowley, see Agatha H. Bowley, *A Memoir of Professor Sir Arthur Bowley (1869–1952) and His Family* (Petworth, 1972).
94 Bowley, *England's Foreign Trade*, 134.
95 Ibid., 16.

96 Ibid., 132–33.
97 T.S. Simey, *Charles Booth: Social Scientist* (London, 1960), 250–52.
98 Ibid., 47–50; Mary Booth, *Charles Booth: Memoir* (London, 1918), 8–9.
99 Simey, *Booth*, 68.
100 Ibid., 68, 91; see Booth's letter to Beatrice Webb, 77.
101 The final volume of Booth's *The Life and Labour of the People of London* (London, 1902–03) was a summary of the preceeding sixteen. Booth never, however, succeeded in that "focusing" that Marshall had urged upon him, Simey, *Booth*, 156. See also B. Seebohm Rowntree's study of York, *Poverty, A Study of Town Life* (London, 1901).
102 Booth, *Life and Labour*, Second Series, V, 308.
103 Charles Booth, "Inaugural Address as President of the Royal Statistical Society," *Journal of the Royal Statistical Society*, LV, Part IV (December 1892), 554.
104 Simey, *Booth*, 96.
105 He also conducted a very substantial study of the poverty of the old, Charles Booth, *The Aged Poor in England and Wales* (London, 1894). See also Charles Booth's popular tract, *Pensions for All in Old Age* (London, 1899). On tariff reform, see Booth, *Memoir*, 36.
106 Booth, *Life and Labour*, Second Series, 5 (1902–03), 70.
107 Arthur L. Bowley, *The Mathematical Groundwork of Economics: An Introduction* (Oxford, 1924); F.Y. Edgeworth, *Papers Relating to Political Economy*, 2 vols. (New York, 1963).

Chapter 4

1 On Cunningham, Foxwell, and Marshall at Cambridge, see chapters 6 and 7. On the intellectual revitalization of Oxford, see A.J. Engel, *From Clergyman to Don: The Rise of the Academic Profession in Nineteenth Century Oxford* (Oxford, 1983).
2 On Ashley, see chapter 5. On Hewins, see chapter 8.
3 See Introduction.
4 See Melvin Richter, *The Politics of Conscience: T.H. Green and His Age* (Cambridge, Mass., 1965) and Lynd, *England in the Eighteen-Eighties* (1945).
5 Alfred Milner, "Reminiscence of Arnold Toynbee," Arnold Toynbee, *Lectures on the Industrial Revolution of the Eighteenth Century in England* (London, 1913), xiv.
6 L.L. Price, *A Short History of Political Economy*, 184, and Marshall's comments, 186; W.J. Ashley, "Arnold Toynbee," *Surveys, Historic and Economic*, reprint of 1900 ed. (New York, 1966), 428.
7 Toynbee, *Industrial Revolution*, 249–66, 269, 273.
8 Ashley, *Surveys*, 429–30.
9 Toynbee took part in Ruskin's work projects, designed to teach Oxford's undergraduates the nobility of manual labor, see, F.C. Montague, *Arnold*

Toynbee in *Johns Hopkins University Studies in Historical and Political Science* (Baltimore, 1889).

10 Toynbee, *Industrial Revolution*, especially the chapters describing England in 1760 and chapters 8 and 9. On the Hammonds, Chapter 9.

11 Toynbee, *Industrial Revolution*, 6.

12 Ibid., 35. His methodological comments are chiefly on 2–7.

13 Ibid., 64.

14 Ibid., 143.

15 Ibid., 109, 113–14, 125–26, 138–40.

16 Ibid., 65, 85–96.

17 Ibid., 66.

18 Ibid., 190.

19 Ibid., 269.

20 Bonamy Price, *Chapters on Practical Political Economy*, (1878), 1.

21 Bonamy Price, "Free Trade and Reciprocity," *Contemporary Review*, XIII (January-March, 1870), 321–45.

22 Alon Kadish, *The Oxford Economists in the Late Nineteenth Century* (Oxford, 1982).

23 Quoted in Marshall's Preface to L.L. Price, *Industrial Peace: Its Advantages, Methods and Difficulties, a Report of An Inquiry Made for the Toynbee Trust* (London 1887), vi.

24 On Marshall and the *Economic Journal*, see Chapter 6.

25 Economic Review, I, No. 1 (1891), 2.

26 A.W. Coats, "The Origins and Early Development of the Royal Economic Society," *Economic Journal*, 78 (June 1968), 349–71.

27 Marshall to J.N. Keynes, 30 January 1902, Marshall Papers, Marshall Library, Cambridge.

28 W.J. Ashley to T.F. Tout, April 16, 1891, Tout Papers, 1/37/1–16, John Rylands University Library, Manchester. On the election, see Kadish, *Oxford Economists*, see Chapter 6.

29 L.L. Price, "Memories and Notes on British Economists, 1881–1947," 37, Ms, Royal Statistical Society, London.

30 Another Oxford economist, Edwin Cannan, joined the LSE upon its formation and charted there an independent criticism of Marshall and Cambridge economics, see Chapter 8.

31 On Price, see A. Petridis, "Bilateral Monopoly, Tariff Reform, and the Teaching of Economics: the neglected contribution of Langford Price (1862–1950)," *History of Political Economy*, ll (Spring 1979), 94–116, and the obituary in *The Times*, 28 (February, 1950), 5. See also his own notes for an autobiography, "Memories and Notes," Royal Statistical Society, London, and his "Miscellaneous Reminiscences," Oriel College, Oxford.

32 L.L. Price, *The Present Position of Economic Studies in Oxford: A Letter to the Vice Chancellor of the University*, 14 January, 1902, The Bodleian, Oxford, *Miscellaneous University Papers, 1900–1902*, 159. See also L.L. Price, "Economics and Commercial Education," *Economic Journal*, 11 (December 1901) 520–36.

33 H.S. Holland, L.L. Price, and W.G.S. Adams, *The Oxford Diploma in Economics and Political Science* (Oxford, 1913). See also the *Report of the Committee on a Proposed Degree in Economics* (Oxford, 1915) to the Hebdomadel Council; *Report of the Committee for a Proposed Degree in Economics* (Oxford, 1915); *Wanted a New School at Oxford* (Oxford,1909); T. H. Penson, *A Plea for Greater Recognition of Economics at Oxford* (Oxford, 1920); and the Reports of the Board of Studies for Philosophy, Politics, and Economics, Bodleian Library, Oxford.

34 L.L. Price, "The Relations of Economic Science to Practical Affairs," Presidential Address to Section F. of the British Association (1895), *Economic Science and Practice; or Essays on Various Aspects of the Relations of Economic Science to Practical Affairs* (London, 1896), 166.

35 L.L. Price, "The Practial Aspects of Economics," *Economic Journal*, 19 (January 1909), 173–89.

36 Price, *Economic Science and Practice*, 285.

37 Ibid., 297.

38 Ibid., 308-09.

39 Ibid., 211–44.

40 Price, "Miscellaneous Reminiscences," 47. Oriel College.

41 L.L. Price, *A Short History of English Commerce and Industry* (London, 1900), 6–9; "The Study of Economic History," *Economic Journal*, 16 (March 1906), 22–23.

42 L.L. Price, "Review of J.S. Nicholson, *Principles of Political Economy*, I," *Economic Journal* 3 (December 1893), 658–64; compare his less critical "Review of J.S. Nicholson, *Principles of Political Economy*, III," *Economic Journal*, 12 (March 1902), 50–56.

43 Price to Cannan, 23 April 1931, Cannan Papers, British Library of Political and Economic Science.

44 Price, "Memories and Notes on British Economists," Royal Statistical Society, 14.

45 Price, "The Study of Economic History," *Economic Journal* (1906), 21.

46 Price, *Economic Science and Practice* (1896), 3.

47 Ibid., 120.

48 W.J. Ashley, "Review of L.L. Price, *Industrial Peace*," *Oxford Magazine*, VI (1 February, 1888), 201–02; Edwin Cannan, "Our Reviewer Reviewed," *Oxford Magazine*, (8 February, 1888), 217–18.

49 Price, *Industrial Peace*, 107–08, 127.

50 Price, *Economic Science and Practice* (1896), 203.

51 The early essays can be found in Price's *Economic Science and Practices* (1896); the later work is in *Cooperation and Copartnership* (London, 1914). Compare the later work to Beatrice Webb's views on cooperation in Chapter 8.

52 Price, *Cooperation and Copartnership*, 7–10; and Introduction to J.A. Estey, *Revolutionary Syndicalism: An Exposition and Criticism* (London, 1913), xxlii.

53 Price, *Cooperation and Copartnership*, 45.

54 Ibid., 52, 55.

55 Ibid., 75.

56 See Price's section on Bagehot, *Short History of Political Economy*.

57 L.L. Price, *Money and Its Relations to Prices*, 2nd ed., (London, 1900), 53, 59.

58 Price, *Economic Science and Practice*, 245–72; "Reconstruction and Monetary Reform," *Economic Journal*, 32 (March 1922), 45–52.

59 Price, "Miscellaneous Rminiscences," Part IV, chapter III, 17, Oriel College.

60 Price, *A Short History of Political Economy* (1891), chapter 1; "Adam Smith and Recent Economics," (1892), *Economic Science and Practice*, 290-94.

61 Price, *English Commerce and Industry* (1900), 165–66, 182–83.

62 L.L. Price, "Some Economic Consequences of the South African War," *Economic Journal*, 10 (September 1900), 335.

63 L.L. Price, "Free Trade and Protection," *Economic Journal*, 12 (September 1902), 310; he praised J.S. Nicholson in 1906 for his interpretation of the context of the English corn laws and alluded to its interpretation, popularized by Cunningham, as the imperialism of free trade, "Economic History," *Economic Journal* (1906), 32.

64 Price, "Free Trade and Protection," *Economic Journal* (1902), 317.

65 The Manifesto was published in *The Times*, 15 August 1903, 4. On the economists and tariff reform during the period, see A.W. Coats, "Political Economy and the Tariff Reform Campaign," *Journal of Law and Economics*, 11 (April 1968), 181–229; and Semmel, *Imperialism and Social Reform*, especially chapters 4 and 5. For the responses of the other historical economists, see the following, passim.

66 Price to Edgeworth, 5 August 1903, published in *The Times*, 15 August, 1903, 4.

67 L.L. Price, "The Economic Possibilities of an Imperial Fiscal Policy," *Economic Journal*, 13 (December 1903), 486–504; and "An Economic View of Mr. Chamberlain's Proposals," *Economic Review*, 14 (April 1904), 129–44.

68 L.L. Price, "Economic Theory and Fiscal Policy," *Economic Journal*, 14 (September 1904), 375.

69 L.L. Price, "Review of A.C. Pigou, *The Riddle of the Tariff*," *Economic Review*, 14 (April 1904): 233. There was a reply by Pigou and a counterreply by Price, *Economic Review*, 16 (July 1906), 328–34. See also Alfred Marshall, "Current Topics," *Economic Journal*, 14 (September 1904), 483–84.

Chapter 5

1 Anne Ashley, *William James Ashley: A Life* (London, 1932).

2 Semmel, *Imperialism and Social Reform*, chapter 11; Schumpeter, *History of Economic Analysis*, 822–23.

3 Ashley quoted Wagner in support of his own position: "These references of Wagner's ought to make our friend Marshall very uncomfortable; he has so long told us how much he reveres him!" Ashley to Bonar Law, 6 November, 1905, Bonar Law Papers, House of Lords Record Office.

4 James J. Sheehan, *The Career of Lujo Brentano; A Study of Liberalism and Social Reform in Liberal Germany* (Chicago, 1966); Henry William Spiegel, *The Growth of Economic Thought*, rev. ed. (Durham, N.C., 1983), chapter 18. See also Schumpeter's more critical views, *History of Economic Analysis*, 803–05, and *Economic Doctrine and Method*, 154–80; and Ashley's accounts in Sir Robert Palgrave, ed., *Dictionary of Political Economy* (London, 1925–26), "Historical School" and "Socialists of the Chair."

5 Ashley, *Surveys*, 5.

6 Anne Ashley, *Ashley*, 144–47. In addition to his published work, a good deal of his correspondence consisted of information on German historical economics. He corresponded regularly with Lujo Brentano and more sparingly with Schmoller and others in Germany.

7 Janet L. MacDonald, "Sir William Ashley (1860–1927)," in Bernadotte E. Schmitt, ed., *Some Historians of Modern Europe* (Chicago, 1942), 20–40; Anne Ashley, Ashley, 20, 22–23; J.H. Clapham, "Sir William Ashley," *Economic Journal*, 37 (December 1927), 679; A.P. Usher, "William James Ashley: A Pioneer in the Higher Education," *Canadian Journal of Economics*, 4 (May 1938), 155; W.R. Scott, "Sir William Ashley," *Economic History Review*, 1 (January 1928), 319.

8 Ashley, *Surveys*, 431; "Comparative Economic History and the English Landlord," *Economic Journal*, 23 (June 1913), 165.

9 Ashley to Brentano, 16 October, 1890, in H.W. McCready, "Sir William Ashley; Some Unpublished Letters," *Journal of Economic History*, 15, No. 1 (1955), 35.

10 W.J. Ashley, *The Early History of the English Woollen Industry, Publication of the American Economic Assoc.*, II, No. 4 (September 1887), 8.

11 W.J. Ashley, *The Economic Organization of England: An Outline History* (London, 1926), 168.

12 Anne Ashley, *Ashley*, 19, 79; W.J. Ashley, *The Christian Outlook; Being the Sermons of an Economist* (London,1925), esp. 14, 24–25, 44–45, 67–74; "The Pilgrim Fathers and Their Place in History," *Quarterly Review*, 234 (October 1920), 278–79.

13 Ashley to Seligman, 20 January, 1887, Seligman Collection; Ashley to Richard T. Ely, 20 January, 1887, Ely Papers, State Historical Society, Madison, Wisc. On the Oxford Economic Society, see Cannan Collection, vol. 905, British Library of Political and Economic Science. On the AEA, see A.W. Coats, "The First Two Decades of the American Economic Association," *American Economic Review*, L (September 1960), 555–74.

14 Ashley to Seligman, n.d., Seligman Collection.

15 Ashley to Seligman, 3 November, 1890, Seligman Collection; see also Ashley to Brentano, 16 October, 1890, McCready, "Ashley Letters," *Journal of Economic History* (1955), 35–36; Ashley to Goldwin Smith, 12 May, 1890, Goldwin Smith Papers, Cornell University.

16 Ashley to Seligman, December 30, 1890, Seligman Collection. See also his letters to Tout, Tout Papers, John Rylands University Library, Manchester, 1/37/1-16. Ashley's Testimonials are at the Bodleian Library.

17 Ashley to Bonar Law, November, 6, 1905, Bonar Law Papers.
18 Ashley was succeeded at Toronto by James Mavor in 1897. The Toronto School reached maturity in the work of such scholars as Fay, Innis, and Bladen; see Crauford D.W. Goodwin, *Canadian Economic Thought: The Political Economy of a Developing Nation, 1814–1914* (Durham, N.C., 1961), 159–61, 175–9. Ashley's "Original Minute Book of the Economics Seminary" is at the University of Toronto Library.
19 Arthur H. Cole, "Economic History of the United States: Formative Years of a Discipline," *Journal of Economic History*, XXVIII (December 1968), 558–60; Warren Samuels, "Ashley and Taussig's Lectures in the History of Economic Thought at Harvard," *History of Political Economy*, 9 (Fall 1977), 384–411.
20 Ashley to Brentano, 11 December, 1893, McCready, "Ashley Letters," *Journal of Economic History* (1955), 38–39.
21 Ashley's *English Woollen Industry* was published in America and especially exhibits deference to American views. On American economic thought of the period, see especially A.G. Gruchy, *Modern Economic Thought: The American Contribution* (New York, 1947); Dorfman, *The Economic Mind in American Civilization*, 3; and Joseph Dorfman, ed., *Institutional Economics: Veblen, Commons, and Mitchell Reconsidered* (Berkeley, 1963); Spiegel, *The Growth of Economic Thought* has a superb bibliography.
22 Anne Ashley, *Ashley*, 35–36.
23 W.J. Ashley, *What is Political Science?* (Toronto, 1888).
24 Ashley, *Christian Outlook*, 92–93; "Evolutionary Socialism," *Birkbeck College Centenary Lectures* (London, 1924), 37.
25 Ashley, *English Woollen Industry*, p. 9.
26 Ibid., 11.
27 W.J. Ashley, *An Introduction to English Ecnomic History and Theory*, 2nd. ed. (New York, 1893), I, xi–xii.
28 Ashley, *What is Political Science?* 10.
29 See, for example, M.M. Postam, *Fact and Relevance: Essays in Historical Method* (Cambridge, 1971).
30 W.J. Ashley, "Review of L.L. Price, *Industrial Peace*," *Oxford Magazine*, VI (1 February, 1888), 201.
31 Edwin Cannan, "Our Reviewer Reviewed," *Oxford Magazine*, VI (8 February, 1888), 217–18; Ashley to Seligman, 15 September 1889, Seligman Collection. During a controversy about their opposite fiscal views in 1903, Ashley criticized Cannan's anti-Semitic statements, Ashley to Edwin Cannan, 27 September 1903, Cannan Collection.
32 See Appendixes D and L of Marshall's *Principles*.
33 W.J. Ashley, "The Rehabilitation of Ricardo," *Economic Journal*, I (September 1891), 477.
34 See Chapter 7.
35 Ashley to Seligman, 3 January 1892, Seligman Collection. On the Cunningham-Marshall exchange, see Chapter 7.
36 Ashley to Seligman, 15 September 1889, Seligman Collection.

37 Ashley,"The Study of Economic History," (1893), *Surveys*, 7.
38 Ibid., 4; *English Economic History*, II, xi.
39 W.J. Ashley, "On the Study of Economic History After Seven Years," (1889), *Surveys*, 22.
40 Ashley to Seligman, 27 August, 1901, Seligman Collection. See the account of the founding of the Birmingham Faculty of Commerce by J.H. Muirhead in Anne Ashley, *Ashley*, esp. 91–4; Ashley to Brentano, 19 September 1901, McCready, "Ashley Letters," *Journal of Economic History* (1955), 41: University Collection, University of Birmingham; and Barbara Smith, "Education for Management: Its Conception and Implementation in the Faculty of Commerce at Birmingham Mainly in the 1900's," Research Memorandum, No. 37, October 1974, Center for Urban and Regional Studies, University of Birmingham.
41 W.J. Ashley, *Commercial Education* (London, 1926), 103.
42 W.J. Ashley, *The Universities and Business, Excerpts of Proceedings of the Staffordshire Iron and Steel Institute* (Dudley, April 4, 1903), 158.
43 Ibid., 161. As early as 1891, Ashley was already urging Manchester to become more of a "Professional School" and to encourage Commercial Education, Ashley to Tout, April 16, 1891, Tout Papers, John Rylands University Library, Manchester.
44 W.J. Ashley, *The Faculty of Commerce and the University of Birmingham* (Birmingham, 1912), 2.
45 Ashley, *Commercial Education*, 151; "The University and Training for Commerce," n.d. and "A Science of Commerce and Some Prolegomena" (1906), University Collection, Birmingham. A new curriculum required new textbooks and Ashley wrote several: *Business Economics* (London, 1926); (ed.) *British Industries; A Series of General Reviews for Businessmen and Students* (London, 1903); (ed.) *British Dominions; Their Present Industrial and Commercial Conditions* (London, 1911). On the LSE, see, Chapter 8.
46 Ashley, "Past History and Present Position of Political Economy" (1907), in Smyth, ed., *Essays in Economic Method*, 233.
47 On Pigou and his selection as Marshall's successor, see Chapter 6.
48 H.S. Foxwell to W.R. Scott, 18 November, 1927, Foxwell Papers, Kress Library of Business and Economics, Harvard University.
49 Ashley to Alfred Milner, 4 February 1907, Milner Papers, Bodleian Library, Oxford. His social background had kept him off the Balliol rowing team; *Birmingham Gazette*, February 3, 1912.
50 W. J. Ashley, "The Place of Economic History in University Studies," *Economic History Review*, I (January 1927), 3.
51 Ibid., 4.
52 J.H. Clapham believed that Ashley's *The Economic Organization of England* was the best introduction to English economic history; Clapham, "Ashley," *Economic Journal* (1927), 680–81.
53 Anne Ashley, *Ashley*, 33.
54 Ashley, *Surveys*, 16, 20, 38, 213.
55 Ashley, *English Economic History*, I, 42–43, 137–40, 176–77.

56 W.J. Ashley, ed., Fustel de Coulanges, *The Origin of Property in Land*, tr. Margaret Ashley (London, 1927), xiii, xxxi, xliv; *Surveys*, 1–24.

57 Ashley, *Economic History*, II, 169; see also *Economic Organization of England*, 39–43, 95–118.

58 Ibid., 139; see also 6–7, 56–57; "Comparative Economic History of the English Landlord," *Economic Journal* (1913), 178, 181.

59 Ashley to the editor of the *Bystander*, 17 May, 1890, Goldwin Smith Papers, Cornell University; see also *Economic Organization of England*, 159–62.

60 Ashley, *English Economic History*, II, 381.

61 Ibid., 379–81, 387–88.

62 Ashley, *Surveys*, 368–403, 311.

63 Ashley, "Evolutionary Economics," *Birkbeck College Lectures*, 38. When entrusted with the student edition of Mill, he assured Seligman, "I shall not 'temper with the sacred text,' " Ashley to Seligman, June 17, 1909, Seligman Collection.

64 Ashley, "Evolutionary Socialism," *Birkbeck College Lectures*, 42.

65 Ashley to Seligman, 8 April, 1903 and 27 August, 1901, Seligman Collection.

66 W.J. Ashley, "The Enlargement of Economics," *Economic Journal*, 18 (June 1908), 189.

67 Ashley, *Christian Outlook*, 28.

68 W.J. Ashley, "Bolshevism and Democracy," *Quarterly Review*, 237 (January 1921), 159, see also "Methods of Industrial Peace," *Economic Review*, II (July 1892), 297–317; "Present Position of Social Legislation in England," *Economic Review*, XVIII (October 1908), 391.

69 Ashley, "The Canadian Sugar Combine," (1889), *Surveys*, 373.

70 Ashley, "American Trusts," (1899), *Surveys*, 383–85.

71 Ashley, *Economic Organization of England*, 189.

72 Ashley to Brentano, 9 February 1892, McCready, "Ashley Letters," *Journal of Economic History* (1955), 37.

73 W.J. Ashley, "The Railroad Strike of 1894," *Publications of the Church Social Union*, Series A, No. 1 (April 1895), 8–12.

74 Ashley, *Economic Organization of England*, 174–80; "Cooperative Production in England," (1899), *Surveys*, 399–400; *The Adjustment of Wages: A Study in the Coal and Iron Industry of Great Britain and America* (London, 1903), 12–21, 54–56, 159–83. Ashley urged Bonar Law to include support for trade unionism in the Unionist program; Ashley to Law, 21 December 1904, Bonar Law Papers. He also urged Milner to support the creation of Wages Boards, Ashley to Steel-Maitland, 31 July, 1908, Milner Papers. See also his correspondence with Ramsey MacDonald, University Collection, Birmingham. During the war he served on the Labour Council, Ashley, Add. ms., British Museum.

75 W.J. Ashley, *Gold and Prices* (London, 1912); *The Rise of Prices and the Cost of Living* (London, 1910). Ashley served on the 1916 committee on prices and a 1918 committee on the cost of living, see Ashley Add. ms., British Museum.

76 W.J. Ashley, *The Tariff Problem*, reprint of 1920 ed. (New York, 1968), 68–92.

77 Ibid., 112; see also 111–14, 211–14, 226, 228–37; "The Argument for Preference," *Economic Journal*, 14 (March 1904), 7.

78 Ashley, *Tariff Problem*, 25–26; see also 119–20; "Political Economy and the Tariff Problem," *Compatriot Club Lectures*, First Series (London, 1905), 242.

79 W.J. Ashley, *The Progress of the German Working Classes in the Last Quarter of the Century* (London, 1904), 140–41; see also *The Tariff Problem*, 169, 177, 187–92. He returned to the issue of the staple food of the English worker after his retirement in *The Bread of Our Forefathers; An Enquiry in Economic History* (Oxford, 1928).

80 Ashley to Brentano, 25 March, 1913, McCready, "Ashley Letters," *Journal of Economic History* (1955), 43.

81 Ashley to Graham Wallas, 22 July, 1897, Wallas Collection, British Library of Political and Economic Science.

82 Quoted in Coats, "Political Economy and the Tariff Reform Campaign," *Journal of Law and Economics* (1968), 222.

83 See the correspondence between Ashley and Chamberlain and between J.C. Garvin and Chamberlain in Julian Amery, *Joseph Chamberlain and the Tariff Reform Campaign*, V (London, 1969), 289–92; Anne Ashley, *Ashley*, 134–35; W.J. Ashley, *The Tariff Problem*, iii, v, ix.

84 Ashley to Bonar Law, 12 December, 1904, Bonar Law Papers.

85 Anne Ashley, *Ashley*, 111–17, 126–29; J.W. Hills, W.J. Ashley, Maurice Woods, *Industrial Unrest: A Practical Solution, The Report of the Unionist Social Reform Committee* (London, 1914). The report was written by Ashley. The Webbs sent him an advance copy of the minority report on the Poor Law, suggesting he review it favorably; see S. Webb to Ashley, 23 January, 1909, University Collection, Birmingham.

86 Ashley to Bonar Law, 7 December 1904, Bonar Law Papers. See also Ashley to Alfred Milner, 21 December, 1905, Milner Papers; G.B. Shaw to Ashley, 19 November, 1903, University Collection, Birmingham.

87 Ashley to Bonar Law, 7 December, 1913, Bonar Law Papers. On Ashley's service to these committees, see Ashley, Add. ms., 42, 243–56, British Museum.

88 See, for example, his comment on the General Strike of 1926, Anne Ashley, *Ashley*, 168.

89 Ibid., 108.

90 Ashley, "Political Economy and the Tariff Problem," *Compatriot Club Lectures*, 244–45, 256; "A Retrospect of Free Trade Doctrine," *Economic Journal*, 34 (December 1924), 501–39.

Chapter 6

1 As noted by A.W. Coats, "The Appointment of Pigou as Marshall's Successor: Comment," *The Journal of Law and Economics*, 15 (October 1972), 489. On Cunningham, see Chapter 7.

2 A.L. Bowley, "Herbert Somerton Foxwell," *Dictionary of National Biography, 1931–40*, 294.

3 On Marshall's early career, see Chapter 1.

4 H.S. Foxwell, *Syllabus of Lectures: Political Economy and Democracy* (Cambridge, 1884). J.M. Keynes maintained that Foxwell had been greatly influenced by F.D. Maurice at Cambridge in "H.S. Foxwell," *Economic Journal*, 46 (December 1936), 593. Compare Melvin Richter, *The Politics of Conscience*; Sheldon Rothblatt, *The Revolution of the Dons: Cambridge and Society in Late Victorian England* (London, 1968); and C.J. Dewey, " 'Cambridge Idealism': Utilitarian Revisionists in Late Nineteenth Century Cambridge," *Historical Journal*, 17 (March 1974), 63–78.

5 On Foxwell, see the excellent article with a bibliography by J.M. Keynes, previously cited; James Bonar, "H.S. Foxwell," *Journal of the Royal Statistical Society*, 99 (Part IV, 1936), 837–41; Audrey G.D. Foxwell, "Herbert Somerton Foxwell: A Portrait," Kress Library of Business and Economics Publication No. 1 (Boston, 1939), 3–30; "H.S. Foxwell" (obit.), *The Eagle*, XLIX, No. 218 (1937), 274–6.

6 Application and Testimonials of Herbert Somerton Foxwell (1881), 9, Foxwell Papers, Kress Library of Business and Economics, Harvard Graduate School of Business Administratrion. On Marshall's disenchantment with the history of economic thought, see Marshall to J.N. Keynes, 6 February, 1902, quoted in R.H. Coase, "The Appointment of Pigou as Marshall's Successor," *Journal of Law and Economics*, 15 (October 1972), 478.

7 Applications and Testimonials, 7.

8 Ibid., 9.

9 Coats, "Sociological Aspects of British Economic Thought," *Journal of Political Economy* (1967), 706–29. On the Cambridge Tripos, see this chapter.

10 H.S. Foxwell, "The Economic Movement in England," *Quarterly Journal of Economics*, 2 (October 1887), 84–103.

11 Ibid., 92.

12 Alfred Marshall, "The Old Generation of Economists and the New," *Quarterly Journal of Economics*, 11 (January 1897): 115–35.

13 Foxwell, "Economic Movement," *Quarterly Journal of Economics* (1887), 85.

14 Foxwell, *Syllabus of Lectures*, Foxwell Papers, Kress Library.

15 See, for example, his critique of Christian Socialism, Marshall to Bishop Westcott, 20 January, 1901, in *Memorials of Alfred Marshall*, A.C. Pigou, ed. (London, 1925), 392. See also his defense of competition in *Principles of Economics*, 8th ed. (London, 1920), Book I, chapters 1 and 4; and Rita McW. Tullberg, "Marshall's 'Tendency to Socialism,' " *History of Political Economy*, 7 (Spring 1975), 110.

16 H.S. Foxwell, *Irregularity of Employment and the Fluctuations of Prices* (Edinburgh, 1886), 12.

17 Ibid., 16.

18 Ibid., 18.

19 Ibid., 19, 21–22, 96; see also Foxwell's Introduction to Anton Menger, *The Right to the Whole Produce of Labour*, reprint of 1899 ed. (New York, 1962), xv.

20 Foxwell, *Syllabus of Lectures*.
21 Foxwell, *Irregularity*, 58, 67, 96.
22 Ibid., 78, 80–82.
23 H.S. Foxwell, *Papers on Current Finance* (London, 1919), 88.
24 Ibid., 264.
25 Ibid., 85–86, 89; Alfred Marshall, *Industry and Trade*, 3rd ed. (London, 1921), 578–84, 633–34, 650–55.
26 Foxwell, *Papers in Current Finance*, 277; see also his Introduction to Menger, *Whole Produce of Labour*, cix–cx.
27 Foxwell to W.R. Scott, 15 April, 1930, Foxwell Papers, Kress Library.
28 H.S. Foxwell, "The Monetary Question," Parts I and III, Unpublished Lectures, Foxwell Papers, Kress Library; *The International Monetary Conference of 1892* (London, 1895); *Certain Misconceptions in Regard to the Bimetallic Policy of the Fixed Ratio* (Manchester, 1888); and *A Criticism of Lord Farrer on the Monetary Standard* (London, 1895). Marshall called his solution symetalism. See his evidence before the royal commissions of 1886, 1887, and 1889 in Alfred Marshall, *Offical Papers*, J.M. Keynes, ed. (London, 1926), chapters 1 and 2; Marshall to Foxwell, 5 May, 1901, and 10 May, 1901, Marshall Papers, Marshall Library. Foxwell told H.R. Beeton that Marshall "knowing nothing of English bi-metallists, he is filled with suspicion of them. In fact he regards them as unmitigatedly soft money men, most unfairly of course"; Foxwell to Beeton, April 1894 (?); and see also, 24 April, 1894, 21 May, 1894, Miscellaneous Letters, Marshall Library.
29 Foxwell, "Monetary Question," Part I, 34–37, Kress Library; *Misconceptions*, 18; *Irregularity*, 47–48. Marshall was less optimistic on the preferability of inflation over deflation, see *Official Papers*, 9, 19.
30 Foxwell, *Irregularity*, 24–25, 32–33, 36–42, 46–53. Foxwell's thesis on the politics of bimetallism suggests an interesting comparison with Bernard Semmel's argument on the politics of tariff reform, *Imperialism and Social Reform*, especially 131–56.
31 H.S. Foxwell, "The Pound Sterling," *Institute of Bookkeepers Journal*, 2 (December 1922), 149–50.
32 Marshall to L.L. Price, 19 July, 1892, in Pigou, ed., *Memorials*, 379.
33 The Kress Library's copies of David Ricardo, *On the Principles of Political Economy and Taxation* (London, 1817); and Robert Malthus, *An Essay on the Principle of Population*, 2nd ed. (London, 1803).
34 Marshall to Foxwell, 28 February, 1899, Foxwell Papers, Kress Library.
35 Foxwell, Introduction to Menger, *Whole Produce of Labour*, xxv–xxvii, xl–xlii, lxxii–lxxiii.
36 H.S. Foxwell, "A Letter of Malthus to Ricardo," *Economic Journal*, 17 (June 1907), 273.
37 Foxwell, "Economic Movement in England," *Quarterly Journal of Economics* (1887), 85.
38 Foxwell to E.R. Seligman, 24 November, 1895, Seligman Collection, Columbia University.
39 Foxwell to E.R. Seligman, 23 June, 1909, Seligman Collection.

40 H.S. Foxwell, "Review of the Duke of Argyll's *Unseen Foundations of Society: An Examination of the Fallacies and Failures of Economic Science Due to the Neglected Elements,*" 7; see also the original manuscript, 5–6, 11, Foxwell Papers, Kress Library. The review was published in the *Manchester Guardian*, 21 February, 1893.

41 On Cairnes's methodological position, see Chapter l.

42 J.N. Keynes, *The Scope and Method of Political Economy*, 4th ed. (New York, 1964), 8–9. See also Henry Sidgwick, "The Scope and Method of Economic Study," (1885), in R.L. Smyth, ed., *Essays on Economic Method: Selected Papers Read to Section F. of the British Association for the Advancement of Science, 1860–1913* (London, 1962), 73–97; Henry Sidgwick, *The Principles of Political Economy*, 3rd ed. (London, 1901), chapters 2 and 3.

43 Keynes, *Scope and Method*, 211, see also 227–36.

44 Ibid., 60–63.

45 Ibid., 64–65, 76–78.

46 Ibid., 279.

47 Ibid., 318.

48 J.M. Keynes, "Foxwell," *Economic Journal* (1936), 593n. Foxwell's correspondence with J.N. Keynes demonstrated that despite methodological differences their relations were cordial.

49 Marshall's views on methodology are scattered throughout his writings. See especially "The Old Generation of Economists and the New," Pigou, ed., *Memorials*, 295–311; *Industry and Trade*, vi and appendix A; *Principles*, appendix D; the accounts of Marshall's Bristol Lectures of 1877 in J.K. Whitaker, "Alfred Marshall: the years 1877 to 1885," *History of Political Economy*, 4 (Spring 1972), 51–53; and Mary Paley Marshall, *The Economics of Industry* (London, 1879), 2–5. See also H.M. Robertson, "Alfred Marshall's Aims and Methods Illustrated from His Treatment of Distribution," *History of Political Economy*, 2 (Spring 1970), 1–64; Donald Winch, *Economics and Policy: An Historical Study* (New York, 1969), 28–46; and R. H. Coase, "Marshall on Method," *Journal of Law and Economics*, 18 (April 1975), 25–31.

50 J.M. Keynes, "Foxwell," *Economic Journal* (1936), 603.

51 Foxwell to J.N. Keynes, 6 October, 1900, J.N. Keynes Letters, Marshall Library. Foxwell's complaints about Marshall are a frequent theme of this correspondence, culminating in his comment of 6 February 1912: "I believe he has in his inner feelings a very honest contempt; and at any rate, he has left me in no sort of doubt as to the value he sets on any service it is in my power to render."

52 Quoted in Coats, "Sociological Aspects," *Journal of Political Economy* (1967), 713. See also Marshall's letters to Hewins concerning the LSE in A.W. Coats, "Alfred Marshall and the Early Development of the London School of Economics: Some Unpublished Letters," *Economica*, N.S. (October 1967), 408–17. On discussions between Marshall and Foxwell con-

cerning the curriculum and the latter's teaching, see Marshall to Foxwell, 2 February, 1897; 29 January, 1902; 14 February, 1902; 18 February, 1902; and 23 February, 1902, Marshall Papers, Marshall Library. See also Marshall to Foxwell, 4 February, 1899; 27 March, 1899; and 12 February, 1901, Foxwell Papers, Kress Library. On the Tripos, see Alfred Marshall, *Plea for the Creation of a Curriculum in Economics and Associated Branches of Political Science* (Cambridge, 1902); and *The New Cambridge Curriculum in Economics* (London, 1903).

53 Foxwell to Leonard Courtney, 14 April, 1902, Courtney Collection, British Library of Political and Economic Science; Foxwell to James Bonar, 15 December, 1900; and Edwin Cannan to Foxwell, 12 October, 1900, Foxwell Papers, Kress Library.

54 Quoted in Keynes, "Foxwell," *Economic Journal* (1936), 591–92. Although he expressed regret that he had failed to win the post, Foxwell nonetheless noted: "I am thankful to be allowed to remain in my congenial surroundings," Foxwell to Seligman, 6 January, 1902, Seligman Collection.

55 Foxwell's letter to *The Times*, 20 August, 1903, 10. Marshall's position was cautious and complex, though staunchly free trade. It must also be recalled that his opposition to tariff reform went virtually unexplained until his "Memorandum on the Fiscal Policy of International Trade," which was not published until 1908, *Official Papers*, 365–420; *Industry and Trade*, rev. ed. (London, 1923), appendixes B and E. See also J.C. Wood, "Alfred Marshall and the Tariff Reform Campaign of 1903," *Journal of Law and Economics*.

56 Foxwell to James Bonar, 22 November 1903, Foxwell Papers, Kress Library. Balfour was himself a critic of classical economics.

57 Discussing German competition after the war, Foxwell criticized the City for its lack of interest in domestic investment as it lavished funds abroad, *Papers in Current Finance*, 110–11, 129. Although Marshall's defense of free trade was an attack on the imperialist economics of the tariff reform historical economists, it has also been characterized as a defense of imperialism—the imperialism of free trade. See Bernard Semmel, *The Rise of Free Trade Imperialism*, 226.

58 See especially Foxwell's letter to his student, Clara Collett, 8 June, 1908, quoted in Coats, "Appointment of Piguo," *Journal of Law and Economics* (1972), 493–94.

59 Marshall to J.N. Keynes, 13 December, 1908, Marshall Papers, Marshall Library. Marshall's letters to Foxwell discussed their differences on a variety of issues, including Marshall's criticism of Foxwell's teaching, 8 February, 1906; 12 February, 1906; 24 February, 1906; and Marshall's painful letter of 5 May, 1908, telling Foxwell the result of the election, Marshall Papers.

60 Foxwell to W.R. Scott, 24 November, 1926 and 28 November, 1927, Foxwell Papers, Kress Library.

61 See Foxwell's own account of the Goldsmith Library, which later caused

him much anguish, in Palgrave, *Dictionary of Political Economy*, 2nd ed.; and the account by a fellow collector, Keynes, "Foxwell," *Economic Journal* (1936), 598–608.

62 Foxwell to Scott, 16 March, 1929, Foxwell Papers, Kress Library; see Henry Higgs, "Professor Foxwell," *Cambridge Review*, 58 (October 1936), 8.

63 Sheldon Rothblatt, *Tradition and Change in English Liberal Education: An Essay in History and Culture* (London, 1976).

64 The Times, "Obituary of H.S. Foxwell," 4 August, 1936.

65 Keynes, "Foxwell," *Economic Journal*, 593.

Chapter 7

1 On Clapham, see Chapter 9.

2 W.J. Ashley, "Cunningham's *Growth of English Industry and Commerce*," *Political Science Quarterly*, 6 (March 1891), 152–61; W.A.S. Hewins, "Review of Cunningham's *The Growth of English Industry and Commerce*," *Economic Journal*, 2 (December 1892), 694–700. See Cunningham's testy reply to criticism even from those who were sympathetic to his views, "Dr. Cunningham and his Critics," *Economic Journal*, 4 (September 1894), 508–16.

3 H.S. Foxwell, "Archdeacon Cunningham," *Economic Journal*, 29 (September 1919), 384–85. See also Semmel, *Imperialism and Social Reform*, chapter 10.

4 Quoted by Audrey Cunningham, *William Cunningham: Teacher and Priest* (London, 1950), 14. There is a partial bibliography of his writings in William Cunningham, *The Progress of Capitalism in England* (Cambridge, 1916).

5 William Cunningham, *Christianity and Politics* (New York, 1915), 87; see also 62–87, 90, 115, 123; *Politics and Economics: An Essay on the Nature of the Principles of Political Economy, Together with a Survey of Recent Legislation* (London, 1885), 43–46; *Christianity and Economic Science* (London, 1914), 58–75.

6 Ibid., 19–20, 35–36, 84; Cunningham, *Christianity and Politics*, 15–25, 30–63; *Making the Most of Life* (London, 1920), 27–30, 50–51; *Christianity and Social Questions* (London, 1910), 175–76.

7 William Cunningham, *The Secret of Progress* (Cambridge, 1918), 3–4, 168; *Making the Most of Life*, 75–78; *Christ's Kingliness* (Sermon preached at Great St. Mary's, Cambridge, 27 June, 1901); *Christianity and Social Questions*, 20. On the Church Social Union, see Maurice Beckett, *Faith and Society* (London, 1932), chapter 3; Peter d'A. Jones, *The Christian Socialist Revival, 1877–1914: Religion, Class, and Social Conscience in Late Victorian England* (Princeton, 1968), chapter 6. On Maurice, see Clive J. Brose, *Frederick Denison Maurice: Rebellious Conformist* (Athens, Ohio, 1971).

8 Quoted by A. Cunningham, *Cunningham*, 50.

9 Cunningham, *Christianity and Economic Science*, 95–97; *Politics and Economics*, 135–37; *Christianity and Social Questions*, 48, 53–55. See his phil-

osophical study, *The Influence of Descartes on Metaphysical Speculation in England* (London, 1876).

10 A. Cunningham, *Cunningham*, 10, 12, 22.

11 Ibid., 102–04, 115, 120.

12 Ibid., 34.

13 William Cunningham, "Political Economy as a Moral Science," *Mind*, 3 (July 1878), 372.

14 See, for example, William Cunningham, *Political Economy Treated as an Empirical Science: A Syllabus of Lectures* (Cambridge, 1887); for a full discussion, see later in this chapter.

15 William Cunningham to an anonymous correspondent, 22 February, 1919, quoted by N.S.B. Grass, "The Present Condition of Economic History," *Quarterly Journal of Economics*, 34 (February 1920), 211.

16 Cunningham, *Hints on the Study of English Economic History* (London, 1919), 20.

17 He reported on this thirty years later; William Cunningham, Presidential Address to the Historical Society, "Sir Francis Bacon and the Office of History," *Royal Historical Society Transactions*, 3rd series, 4 (1910), 6; A. Cunningham, *Cunningham*, 38–41; and his contemporary account, "Letters from India," *Cambridge Review*, February 8, 15, 22, and March 1, 8, 15 (1882).

18 William Cunningham, *The Growth of English Industry and Commerce* (Cambridge, 1882), vii. His intellectually more radical, but personally kinder, attack upon Rogers is in his criticism of Marshall, "The Perversion of Economic History," *Economic Journal* (1892), especially 498–502, 505–506. See also his critique of Rogers's statistical method, "On the Value of Money," *Quarterly Journal of Economics*, 13 (July 1899), 370–85.

19 Cunningham, *Growth* (1882), 8; see also 14, 387–89.

20 Ibid., 88–89, 170, 180–81.

21 Ibid., 301–08, 319, 324.

22 Ibid., 375.

23 Ibid., 389.

24 Ibid., 386–400, 404–10.

25 Ibid., 411–13, 420–23; *Politics and Economics*, 76–78, 80, 100–04, 124.

26 John Maloney, "Marshall, Cunningham, and the Emerging Economics Profession," *Economic History Review*, 2nd series, 29 (August 1976), 440–51; A. Cunningham, *Cunningham*, 63–68.

27 William Cunningham, "The Comtist Criticism of Economic Science," (1889), in Smyth, ed., *Essays on Economic Method*, 99; see also *The Use and Abuse of Money* (New York, 1891), 10; Foxwell, "Cunningham," *Economic Journal* (1919), 388.

28 William Cunningham, "Plea for Pure Theory," *Economic Review*, 2 (January 1892), 20; see also "Why Had Roscher so Little Influence in England?" *Annals of the American Academy of Political and Social Science*, 5 (November 1894), 392.

29 Cunningham, "Plea for Pure Theory," *Economic Review* (1892), 33.

30 Ibid., especially 30–31, 36–38.
31 Cunningham, "Roscher," *Annals of the American Academy of Political and Social Science* (1894), 320–21.
32 Ibid., 330; see also 322–26.
33 Cunningham, *Progress of Capitalism* (1916), 7–8, 12, 90–91.
34 Cunningham, *Political Economy Treated as an Empirical Science* (1887), 8.
35 Ibid., 15.
36 Cunningham, *Politics and Economics* (1885), 12.
37 On Nicholson, see later in this chapter.
38 "The British Economic Association," *Economic Journal*, 1 (March 1891), 4. On the *Economic Review*, see Chapter 4.
39 "British Economic Association," *Economic Journal* (1891), 7.
40 The Marshall Papers contain his copious notes on economic history; see Chapter 1.
41 William Cuningham, "The Perversion of Economic History," *Economic Journal*, 2 (September 1892), 491.
42 Ibid., 492.
43 Ibid., 491.
44 On J.N. Keynes's criticism of historical economics, see Chapter 6.
45 Marshall's letters to Brentano, in H.W. McCready, "Alfred Marshall and Tariff Reform: Some Unpublished Letters," *Journal of Political Economy*, 63 (1955), 259–67. See also John Cunningham Wood, *British Economists and the Empire* (London, 1983), 121–132.
46 Alfred Marshall, "A Reply," *Economic Journal*, 2 (September 1892), 518–19. Cunningham's repeated criticisms were in "On the Comtist Criticism of Economic Science" (1889) in Smyth, ed., *Essays in Economic Method*, 96–111; "What Did Our Forefathers Mean by Rent?" *Lippincott's Magazine* (February 1890), 278; "Presidential Address to Section F.," *Report of the 61st Meeting of the British Association for the Advancement of Science, Cardiff, 1891* (London, 1892), 729.
47 Marshall, "A Reply," *Economic Journal* (1892), 518.
48 Ibid., 512.
49 William Cunningham, *Hints on the Study of English Economic History*, 27. Cunningham's counter reply, "The Perversion of Economic History," is in *The Academy*, No. 1065 (1 October 1892), 288.
50 Bruce Glassburner, "Alfred Marshall on Economic History and Historical Development," *Quarterly Journal of Economics*, 69 (November 1955), 593. See also R. L. Andreano, "Alfred Marshall's *Industry and Trade*: A Neglected Classic in Economic History," in R.L. Andreano, ed., *New Views on American Economic Development* (Cambridge, 1965), 317–29.
51 Cunningham, "Why Had Roscher so Little Influence in England?" *Annals of the American Academy of Political and Social Science* (1894), 327.
52 Ibid., 322.
53 Jean O. McLachan, "The Origin and Early Development of the Cambridge Economic Tripos," *Cambridge Historical Journal*, 9 No. 1 (1947), 93.

54 A. Cunnigham, *Cunningham*, 63–68.

55 William Cunningham, et al., *Methods of Economic Teaching in This and Other Countries: Report of the Committee for Section F. of the British Assocation* (London: 1894). Henry Higgs (1865–1940), an historical economist, studied economics under Foxwell and was associated with the effort to make Toynbee Hall into a center for the study of historical economics. Primarily a civil servant, Higgs conducted a major study of the Physiocrats, aided Foxwell in compiling a bibliography of economics, lectured on finance and national economics at University College, London, and wrote numerous articles for the *Dictionary of Political Economy*. See C.E. Collett, "Henry Higgs," *Economic Journal*, 50 (December 1940), 546–55; and J.M. Keynes, "Henry Higgs," *Economic Journal*, 555–58.

56 Marshall to Foxwell, 4 February, 1899, Foxwell Papers, Kress Library.

57 Cunningham, "Plea for the Study of Economic History," *Economic Review*, IX (January 1899), 67.

58 William Cunningham, "The Teaching of Economic History," in W.A.J. Archbold, ed., *Essays on the Teaching of History* (Cambridge, 1901), 42.

59 Ibid., 48.

60 William Cunningham and J. Ellis McTaggart, fly sheet to Senate, 26 May, 1903, Cambridge, University Library; and the fly sheet of 4 February, 1903, to the Economics Syndicate.

61 Alfred Marshall, "The Proposed New Tripos," fly sheet, 5 June, 1903, Cambridge University Library.

62 Marshall, *The Cambridge Economics Curriculum*, 23, 27–28.

63 F.W. Maitland, "Economics and History," fly sheet, 2 June, 1903, Cambridge University Library.

64 In Marshall Papers, Large Brown Box (21), Marshall Library.

65 On Marshall's preference for Clapham, see his letter to J.N. Keynes, 13 December, 1908, J.N. Keynes Letters, Marshall Library. On Clapham, see Chapter 9.

66 Quoted by McLachlan, "The Historical Tripos at Cambridge," *Cambridge Historical Journal* (1947), 104.

67 Cunningham, Growth, (1882), 9.

68 Hewins, "Review of the *Growth of English Industry and Commerce*, Vol. II," *Economic Journal*, 2 (December 1892), 696.

69 Cunningham, *Growth*, II, 2nd ed. (1890–92), 331–32; see also 415, 417, and I, 427.

70 Ibid., II, 17.

71 William Cunningham, *An Essay on Western Civilization in its Economic Aspects* (New York, 1913), I, 68–70, 175–94; II, 190, 204, 213, 215.

72 William Cunningham, "English Imperialism," *Atlantic Monthly*, 84 (July 1899), 1–7; "The Prospects of Universal Peace," *Atlantic Monthly*, (August 1899), 236–41; "The Good Government of the Empire," *Atlantic Monthly*, (November 1899), 654–60.

73 The publication history of *The Growth of English Industry and Commerce* was complicated by his method of publishing each volume separately as it

was completed. Thus the third edition was published in 1896 and 1903. It was the second volume, published in 1903, that called for tariff reform.

74 Cunningham, *Progress of Capitalism*, 133.

75 Cunningham, *Case Against Free Trade*, (London, 1911) 37; see also 18, 25, 31, 34; *Growth*, II, 5th ed., 876.

76 William Cunningham, *The Rise and Decline of the Free Trade Movement* (Cambridge, 1905), 45, 86–90; *Progress of Capitalism*, 120; *Growth*, II, 5th ed., 867–69.

77 Cunningham, *Rise and Decline of Free Trade*, 158; see also 12–20, 85–95, 159–63.

78 Ibid., 108; see also, 104–22, 137–44.

79 Ibid.,153; see also *Growth*, 5th ed., II, 869–70.

80 Ibid., 858–61; *Rise and Decline of Free Trade*, 155–57; *The Wisdom and the Wise: Three Lectures on Free Trade Imperialism* (Cambridge, 1906), 54, 89–90.

81 William Cunningham, "Economic Problems After the War," in Kirkaldy, ed., *Credit, Industry, and War*, 264–65; *Case Against Free Trade*, 4, 10, 15, 17.

82 Cunningham, "Tariff Reform and Political Morality," *Compatriot Club Lectures*, 310–17; *Wisdom and the Wise*, 105; "The White Man's Burden" was the last lecture of his life, *Making the Most of Life*.

83 Cunningham, "Progress of Socialism in England," *Contemporary Review* (1879), 247.

84 William Cunningham, "The General Election: Prospects of Social Legislation," *Economic Review*, 5 (October 1895), 515.

85 Cunningham, *Christianity and Social Questions*, 149; see also 25–26; *Making the Most of Life*, 8–9; *Christianity and Economic Science*, 12; "The Church's Duty in Relation to the Sacredness of Property," *Publications of the Church Social Union* (Boston), series B, No. 2 (May 1895), 1–10.

86 Cunningham, *Causes of Labour Unrest and the Remedies for It: The Draft of a Report* (London, 1912), 8–20.

87 Cunningham, *Causes of Labour Unrest*, 21–22; *Christianity and Social Questions*, 118–25; *Wisdom and the Wise*, 52–53. On his inability to fully accept the trade union movement, compare the 1882 edition of *Growth*, 418, and the 5th ed., II, 878–80.

88 Cunningham, "Francis Bacon and the Office of History," *Royal Historical Society Transactions* (1910), 18.

89 See, for example, Charles Wilson, Introduction, William Cunningham, *Alien Immigrants in England* (London, 1969), v.

90 See, for example, Cunningham's praise of Nicholson's work in a letter to the *Cambridge Daily News*, 11 September, 1910; Cunningham, "Why had Roscher so Little Influence in England?" *Annals of the American Academy of Political and Social Science* (1894), 333; *Growth*, 5th ed., II, 878; *Wisdom and the Wise*, 26–28; *Christianity and Economic Science*, 15–19; "Economic Problems after the War," in Kirkaldy, ed., *Credit, Industry, and the War*, 264.

91 W.R. Scott and Henry Higgs, "Joseph Shield Nicholson," *Economic Journal*, 37 (September 1927). 495–502.

92 Coats, "Political Economy and the Tariff Reform Campaign," *Journal of Law and Economics* (1968), 214; J.S. Nicholson, *The Tariff Question With Special Reference to Wages and Employment* (London, 1903).

93 Nicholson to J.N. Keynes, 26 August, 1889; 29 August, 1889; 17 September, 1889; 16 July, 1890; and 2 November, 1890, J.N. Keynes Letters, Marshall Library.

94 Nicholson to J.N. Keynes, 27 July, 1890, J.N. Keynes Letters, Marshall Library.

95 Nicholson to Edwin Cannan, 27 December, 1918, Cannan Collection, British Library of Political and Economic Science. On Cannan, see Chapter 8.

96 For a statement of Nicholson's methodological views, see his preface to *The Effects of Machinery On Wages* (London, 1892). His opposition to socialism can be found in *Historical Progress and Ideal Socialism*, 2nd ed. (London, 1894) and *The Revival of Marxism* (London, 1920). Nicholson's economic views of trade unions have been discussed by A. Petridis, *The Economic Analysis of Trade Unions by British Economists, 1870–1930* (Duke University Dissertation Abstract, 1974), chapter 4.

97 For Price's review of Nicholson, see Chapter 6; and "Memories and Notes on British Economists," Royal Statistical Society, London, 25–26.

98 See especially J.S. Nicholson, "The Reaction in Favour of Classical Political Economy," (1893), in Smyth, ed., *Essays on Method*; Nicholson, *Principles of Political Economy* (London, 1893–1901), I, v–vi, 4, 16–20, 23–31, 59–60, 229–31, 268–69; III, iii–iv.

99 J.S. Nicholson, *A Project of Empire; A Critical Study of the Economics of Imperialism, With Special Reference to the Ideas of Adam Smith* (London, 1910), especially xii–xvi; 5–6, 39, 44–60, 79–81, 90, 92–95, 128, 159, 174, 207, 232–35. It was originally published in 1900, three years before the tariff controversy erupted. See also his edition of Adam Smith, *An Inquiry into the Nature and Causes of the Wealth of Nations* (London, 1895), Preface; *Principles*, II, 322–27.

100 J.S. Nicholson, "Friedrich List: The Prophet of the New Germany," *Economic Journal*, 26 (March 1916), 92–97; Introduction, List, *National System* (1928 edition).

Chapter 8

1 W. A. S. Hewins, "The Teaching of Economics," *Journal of the Society of Arts*, XLV, No 2298 (4 December 1896), 47.

2 The phrase was used by Alon Kadish, *The Oxford Economists in the Late Nineteenth Century*.

3 W. A. S. Hewins, *The Apologia of an Imperialist: Forty Years of Empire Policy, 1889–1929* (London, 1929), I, 15. On Hewins, see L. L. Price, "W.A. S. Hewins," *Economic Journal*, 42 (March 1932), 151–55.

4 Hewins, *Apologia*, I, 19.

5 Hewins Papers, Vol. 204, Sheffield University Library.

6 Hewins, "Teaching Economics," *Journal of the Society of Arts* (1896), 46.

7 Hewins, *Apologia*, I, 23; Hewins's testimonials from Charles Gore and C.H. Firth are in the Hewins Papers, 43/58–59, Sheffield. I have not been able to trace his plan for economics at King's College.

8 Hewins to his mother, 15 May, 1898, Hewins Papers; Tout to Hewins, Tout Papers, 1/517/1–4.

9 Hewins Diaries, 5 August, 1882, Hewins Papers, 195/11.

10 Hewins, *Apologia*, I, 40–42.

11 Hewins Diaries, 1882–1904, Hewins Papers, 195/23.

12 Hewins to his mother, 19 July, 1895, Hewins Papers.

13 Hewins, *Apologia*, I, 21–22.

14 Ibid, I, 4.

15 Hewins Papers, Boxes 138 and 141.

16 Hewins Papers, 185/380–81; see also "The Wrought Nail Trade," Hewins Papers, 518/335–56. Very few of Hewins' manuscript lectures can be dated precisely.

17 Hewins Papers, 158/307–08.

18 Hewins Papers, Vol. 205 contains his ideas for worker education.

19 Hewins, "Pol. Economy and the Scientific Method" (1888?), Hewins Papers, 14/141–42.

20 Ibid., 14/147.

21 Ibid., 14/151.

22 Price, "Hewins," *Economic Journal*, (1932), 152.

23 Hewins, "Pol. Economy and the Scientific Method," Hewins Papers, 14/153.

24 Ibid., 14/157.

25 Ibid., 14/158.

26 Hewins, "The Industrial Employment of Women," (1893), Hewins Papers, 158/380.

27 Hewins, "The Practical Value of Economics," Hewins Papers, 141/165–66.

28 W.A.S. Hewins, "Review of Thorold Rogers, *The Industrial and Commercial History of England* (1892)," *Economic Journal*, II (September 1892), 520–22.

29 C. H. Firth to Hewins, n.d., Hewins Papers.

30 W.A.S. Hewins, "Review of William Cunningham, *The Growth of English Industry and Commerce in Modern Times* (1892)," *Economic Journal*, II (December 1892), 695.

31 Hewins, *Apologia*, I, 23.

32 Hewins, "Early History of the Corn Laws," Hewins Papers, 158/288.

33 W.A.S. Hewins, *English Trade and Finance, Chiefly in the Seventeenth Century* (London, 1892), 127.

34 W.A.S. Hewins, "English Early Economic History," Palgrave, ed., *Dictionary of Political Economy*, I (1894), 723–24. See also his "The Early History of Free Trade," *Dictionary of Political Economy*, 146 and the manuscript in the Hewins Papers, 158/315–16.

35 W.A.S. Hewins, "Mercantile System," in Palgrave, ed., *Dictionary of Political Economy*, II (1896), 727. He would later quote this very statement in his autobiography and employ it in many of his articles and lectures, *Apologia*, I, 35.

36 F.A. Hayek, "The London School of Economics, 1895–1945," *Economica*, N.S., 13 (February 1946), 4. See also Gerard M. Koot, "An Alternative to Marshall: Economic History and Applied Economics at the Early L.S.E.," *Atlantic Economic Journal*, X (March 1982): 3–17.

37 Collett, "Foxwell," *Economic Journal* (1936), 617–19.

38 Janet Beveridge, *The Epic of Clare Market: Birth and Early Days of the London School of Economics* (London, 1966), 11–14.

39 Ibid., 29, 34. See R. L. Smith, "The Teaching of London: A Scheme for Technical Instruction," *Contemporary Review*, 61 (May 1892),741–53.

40 See Chapter 7.

41 For a detailed account of the Hutchinson Trust and the founding of the LSE, see Sir Henry Caine, *The History of the Foundation of the London School of Economics and Political Science* (London, 1963). See also the Hutchinson Trust Minute Books, British Library of Political and Economic Science, London.

42 Beatrice Webb, *Our Partnership*, Mary Barbara Drake and Margaret Cole, eds. (New York, 1948), 86.

43 Ibid., 93.

44 Sidney Webb to Hewins, 24 March, 1895; 29 March, 1895; and Hewins to Sidney Webb, 30 March, 1895, Hewins Papers, 43/127–28, 131–35.

45 B. Webb, *Our Partnership*, 87.

46 Hewins, Diary, 1882–1904, Hewins Papers, 195/26.

47 B. Webb, *Our Partnership*, 87–88.

48 Beatrice Webb, MS Diary, 9 April, 1895, Passfield Papers, 15/71, London School of Economics and Political Science.

49 W.A.S. Hewins, *Trade in the Balance*, (London, 1924), 9.

50 Cunningham to Hewins, 14 April, 1895, Hewins Papers.

51 W. Smart to Hewins, 30 August, 1895, Hewins Papers.

52 Foxwell, to Hewins, 13 August, 1895, Hewins Papers.

53 Ashley to Hewins, 29 September, 1895, Hewins Papers.

54 W. Bauer to Hewins, 14 May, 1895, Hewins Papers.

55 Marshall's attitude can be followed in Coats, "Alfred Marshall and the Early Development of the London School of Economics: Some Unpublished Letters," *Economica* (1967), esp. 411–12. See W.A.S. Hewins, "The London School of Economics and Political Science," in Michael E. Sadler, ed., *Special Reports on Educational Subjects*, (1898), 76–98, Command Paper, 8943. See also Hewins's account of Marshall, *Apologia*, I, 26–27.

56 The Prospectus is in the Hewins Papers, 14/65.

57 Cannan desrves a study. He made an important independent contribution to the history of economic thought; see *A History of the Theories of Production and Distribution in English Political Economy, from 1776 to 1848*

(London, 1893). See also his *An Economist's Protest* (London, 1927). His views on the method and purpose of economics is summarized in his "The Practical Usefulness of Economic Theory," in Smyth, ed., *Essays in Economic Method* (1962). See his interesting review of Ashley, "Our Reviewer Reviewed," *Oxford Magazine*, VI (February 8, 1888), 218 and his "Alfred Marshall, 1842–1924," *Economica*, VI, No. 12 (1924), 257–61. See his comments on the practical purpose of economic history, *A History of Local Rates in England in Relation to the Proper Distribution of the Burden of Taxation*, 2nd ed. (London, 1912), 1. On Cannan, see Lionel Robbins's notice in the *D.N.B.*; Hugh Dalton, "Professor Cannan's General Contribution," and T.E. Gregory, "Professor Cannan and Contemporary Monetary Theory," in T.E. Gregory, ed., *London Essays in Economics in Honor of Edwin Cannan* (London, 1927), 3–68; Charles Ryle Fay, "Edwin Cannan: The Tribute of a Friend," Cannan Papers, 1969, British Library of Political and Economic Science, abridged version in *Economic Record*, III (June 1927), 1–21.

58 B. Webb, *Our Partnership*, 94, July, 14, 1896.
59 S. Webb, "Brief Account of the Work of the School During Michaelmas and Lent Terms, 1895–96," Passfield Papers, X, 2, (i)9. See also Webb's reports in the Hutchinson Trust Minute Books and "Reminiscences of Former Students," British Library of Political and Economic Science. The faculty and program of studies can be studied in the annual LSE *Calendar* and its *Register, 1895–1932* (London, 1934). Lilian Knowles served as Cunningham's research assistant at Cambridge. She joined the staff of the LSE, first as a substitute lecturer for Hewins, then as a lecturer, reader, and finally as the professor of Economic History in 1924. Her work concentrated on the nineteenth century and drove home Cunningham's thesis that laissez faire had been but a temporary aberration, which, owing to Britain's industrial preeminence, would have to be abandoned. See, Sir William Beveridge, "Professor Lilian Knowles," and Graham Wallas, "Professor Lilian Knowles," *Economica*, 6 (June 1926): 112–22; T.E. Gregory, "Professor Lilian Knowles," *Economic Journal*, 36 (June 1926), 317–20; C.M. Knowles, "Memoir," in Lilian Knowles, *The Economic Development of the British Overseas Empire*, 2 vols. (London, 1928–30); *The Industrial and Commercial Revolutions in Great Britain During the Nineteenth Century* (London, 1921).
60 Hewins, Diary, Hewins Papers, 195/23. See Hewins's letters to S. Webb concerning the LCC's attack on the school, 30 May, 1898; 27 July, 1898; 17 October, 1898, Passfield Papers, 2(i).
61 Hewins, *Apologia*, I, 33.
62 Hewins, Diary, Hewins Papers, 195/25–26.
63 Hewins, *Trade in the Balance*, 9–10.
64 Hewins to S. Webb, 30 May, 1898, Passfield Papers, 2(i).
65 Hewins to his mother, 14 October, 1900, Hewins Papers.
66 See S. Webb's defense of his involvement with the LSE of 3 January, 1903, Caine, *Foundations of the L.S.E.*, 10–14.

67 S. Webb to Hewins, 30 May, 1903, Hewins Papers, 43/214–15; Hewins to S. Webb, 31 May, 1903 and 12 June, 1903, Passfield Papers, II,4,b.
68 Hewins to S. Webb, 19 November, 1903, Passfield Papers, II,4,b; see also Hewins to S, Webb, 18 April 1905, Passfield Papers, II,4,c.
69 B. Webb, *Our Partnership*, 195.
70 On Mackinder, see Semmel, *Imperialism and Social Reform*, chapter 8 and David Ronald Peirce, "Halford Mackinder: The Geography of Imperialism," Harvard Honor's Thesis, 1963, Widener Library, Harvard University. H.J. Mackinder, "On the Scope and Method of Geography," *Proceedings of the Royal Geography Society*, 9 (March 1887), 141–60; "The Geographical Pivot of History," *Geographical Journal*, 23 (April 1904), 421–37; *Money Power and Man Power: The Underlying Principles Rather Than the Statistics of Tariff Reform* (London, 1906); *Syllabus of Eight Lectures on Wealth and Wages* (Oxford, 1886).
71 S. Webb to Ashley, 23 January, 1909, University Collection, Birmingham.
72 Sir William Beveridge, *Power and Influence: An Autobiography* (London, 1953), esp. 175–76, 184, 274; Jose Harris, *William Beveridge: A Biography* (Oxford, 1977).
73 Winch, *Economics and Policy*, 189–98; A.W. Coats, "The Distinctive L.S.E. Ethos in the Inter War Years," and R. H. Coase, "Economics at the L.S.E. in the 1930's," *Atlantic Economic Journal*, X (March 1982), 18–30, 31–34.
74 Hewins to S. Webb, 22 September, 1898, Passfield Papers, 2(i), 81–82.
75 Hewins to S. Wcbb, 26 January, 1903, Passfield Papers, X,2(ii).
76 Joseph Chamberlain to Hewins, 5 February, 1900, Hewins Papers, 45/36.
77 Hewins, *Apologia*, I, 48. Schmoller set forth his own views on England's free trade imperialism in 1899, McClelland, *The German Historians and England* (1971), 203.
78 Hewins, "Imperialism and Its Probable Effect on the Commercial History of the United Kingdom," was largely reprinted in his *Apologia*, I, 50–57. It was also published as a pamphlet. See also his *Trade in the Balance*, 12.
79 Hewins, *Apologia*, I. 68.
80 See the press clippings of these articles, especially his letters to the *Times*, by an "anonymous economist," Box 35, and the Chamberlain-Hewins correspondence, Hewins Papers. See also Julian Amery, *Joseph Chamberlain and the Tariff Reform Campaign* (London, 1969), V, 288, 294; VI, 479, 530–32.
81 Ashley to Hewins, 21 November, 1903, Hewins Papers.
82 Hewins to S. Webb, 25 June, 1903, Passfield Papers, II,4,b; Hewins, *Apologia*, I, 163, 169–71, 189.
83 A.J. Balfour to Hewins, 22 November, 1904, Hewins Papers, 47/57.
84 Hewins to Baldwin, 2 November, 1923, Baldwin Papers, 26/252–53, Cambridge University Library; see also Hewins memorandum to Baldwin on the economic crisis, Hewins Papers, 88/234–48; and, still the dissenter, he recommended Lloyd George's economic program, Hewins to Baldwin, 29 April, 1929, Hewins Papers, 92/79.

85 Hewins, *Trade in the Balance*, 15.

86 Hewins, *Apologia*, I, 76.

87 Ibid., 150–61; see also 75–86. Boxes 18–40 of the Hewins Papers contain material on the Tariff Commission. See also the Tariff Commission Collection at the British Library of Political and Economic Science.

88 Hewins to Asquith, 23 March, 1916, Asquith Papers, 29/255, Bodleian Library, Oxford.

89 On Amery, see below Chapter 9.

90 Hewins, "Old Nations and the New Empire" (1910–11), Hewins Papers, 22/336. Ashley shared Hewins's frustration in providing conservatism with a social program, Ashley to Hewins, 4 January, 1906, Hewins Papers, 21/1. See also Hewins, Diary, 1925–29, 19, Hewins Papers.

91 Hewins, "The Relation of Economic Knowledge to Christian Charity" (1899), Hewins Papers.

92 Hewins, "The State Regulation of Wages," The National Liberal Club, Political and Economic Circle, *Transactions*, III (London, 1901), 137–38.

93 Hansard's Parliamentary Debates, 5th Series, 35, 21 March, 1912, 2116–20.

94 Hewins, Speech to the Norwich United Club, 18 November, 1913, Hewins Papers, 24/104.

95 Hewins, Diary, 1925–29, 14, Hewins Papers; see also Hewins, *Apolgia*, II, 188–90, 193–200.

96 Ibid., II, 283.

97 See, for example, Hewins' lectures: "How to Fight the Question of Tariff Reform" (1913), Hewins Papers, 24; "Free Trade, Its Principles, Objects and Results Decided by Logical Facts and Impartial Examination from a Workingman's Standpoint" (1910), Hewins Papers, 18; "Old Nations and New Empire" (a series of speeches, 1910–11), Hewins Papers, 72; *Trade in the Balance* (1924) and *Empire Restored* (London, 1927).

98 Semmel, *Imperialism and Social Reform*, chapters 3 and 6.

99 B. Webb, *Our Partnership*, 191–94, 203, 217, 219–20, 223–24.

100 Ibid., 267. The complex psychological relationship between Chamberlain and the Webbs can be followed in Norman and Jeanne McKenzie, eds., *The Diary of Beatrice Webb, I, 1873–1893 and II, 1892–1905* (London, 1982–83).

101 Sidney and Beatrice Webb, *The Decay of Capitalist Civilization* (New York, 1923), 232.

102 Beatrice Webb, *My Apprenticeship* (London, 1926), 182–83.

103 Ibid., 290.

104 B. Webb, "The History of English Economics" (1880), 8, Passfield Papers, VII, I, 3. The essence of her essay was published in her *My Apprenticeship*.

105 Ibid., 12–13.

106 B. Webb, Diaries, 21 June,1886, 10, 13–14, Passfield Papers, I.

107 B. Webb, "History of Political Economy," 24, Passfield Papers, VII, 1, 3.

108 B. Webb, "The Economic Theory of Karl Marx" (1886), Passfield Papers, VII, 1, 5.

109 B. Webb, "History of Political Economy," 39, Passfield Papers, VII, 1, 3.

110 Ibid., 40.

111 B. Webb, Diary, 14(1), 58, Passfield Papers, I.

112 Ibid., 16, 23, February, 1897, 77–78.

113 B. Webb, "History of Political Economy," 50, Passfield Papers, VII, 1, 3; see also Diary, 10, 21 June, 1886, 14.

114 Herbert Spencer to Beatrice Webb, 2 October, 1886, Diary, 10, 114; Mary Booth to B. Webb, September, 1886, Diary, 32; Charles Booth to B. Webb, 21 September, 1886, Diary, 24, Passfield Papers, I.

115 B. Webb, *My Apprenticeship*, 282. See G.D.H. Cole, "Beatrice Webb as an Economist," *Economic Journal*, 53 (December 1943), 422–38; R.H. Tawney, *Beatrice Webb* (London, 1943).

116 B. Webb, *My Apprenticeship*, 246.

117 Webbs, *Decay of Capitalist Civilization*, 10. See also B. Webb's earlier judgment, *My Apprenticeship*, 346.

118 Ibid., 395; see also 376–78, 381, 383–85, 391–94, 397.

119 S. Webb, "Lecture on Political Economy, Fragment," Workingman's College, London, October 1883, Passfield Papers, VI, 9, 10.

120 S. Webb, "On Economic Method" (1885), Passfield Papers, VI, 25, 5.

121 S. Webb, "Rent, Interest, and Wages; Being a Criticism of Karl Marx and a Statement of Economic Theory" (1889), Passfield Papers, VII, 1, 4:1; see also "The Economic Basis of Socialism" (1887), Passfield Papers, VI, 33.

122 S. Webb, "Economics as a Science" (1900?), Passfield Papers, VI, 64:42. See also "The Economic Function of the Middle Class," Lecture, February 1885, Passfield Papers, VI, 20.

123 S. Webb, "The National Dividend and its Distribution," in Sidney and Beatrice Webb, *Problems of Modern Industry*, new ed. (London, 1902), 209–28.

124 S. Webb, "The Rise and Fall of Feudalism" (1884), Passfield Papers, VI, 19, 3–4. The syllabus for the entire course is in Passfield Papers, VI, 16.

125 B. Webb, *Our Partnership*, 92; see also 43, 45.

126 Sidney and Beatrice Webb, *Industrial Democracy*, 1st ed. published in 1892 (New York, 1902), 653; see also 613–52.

127 Ibid., 795; see also 822.

128 B. Webb, *Our Partnership*, 147–52; see also R.H. Tawney, "In Memory of Sidney Webb," *Economica*, N.S., 14 (November 1947), 249.

129 Sidney and Beatrice Webb, *Methods of Social Study*, (London, 1932), esp. v and 8.

Chapter 9

1 Ashley, "The Place of Economic History in University Studies," *Economic History Review*, I (1927), 4.

2 See the new study by Chester Norman, *Economics, Politics, and Social Studies in Oxford, 1900–1985* (London, 1986).

3 J. H. Clapham, *The Study of Economic History: An Inaugural Lecture* (Cambridge, 1929), 32.

4 Ibid. 8–30.

5 Compare J. H. Clapham, "Economic History: Survey of Development to the Twentieth Century," *Encyclopedia of the Social Sciences* (1935 ed.) and Rees, "Recent Trends in Economic History," *Journal of the Historical Association* (1949): esp. 1–2; and Gras, "The Rise and Development of Economic History," *Economic History Review* (1927–28), esp. 19–22.

6 J. H. Clapham, *An Economic History of Modern Britain* (Cambridge: 1950–52), I, vii.

7 Ibid., III, 518. On Clapham, see W. H. B. Court, "Sir John Clapham," *Scarcity and Choice in History* (London: 1970), 141–50; A. P. Usher, "Sir John Harold Clapham and the Empirical Reaction in Economic History," *Journal of Economic History*, II (No. 2, 1951), 148–50; M. M. Postan, "Sir John Harold Clapham (1873–1946)," *Economic Journal*, 56 September 1946), 499–507.

8 J. H. Clapham, "On Empty Economic Boxes," *Economic Journal*, XXXII (September 1922), 312.

9 A. C. Pigou, "On Empty Economic Boxes: A Reply," *Economic Journal*, XXXII (December 1922), 458–65; J.H. Clapham, "The Economic Boxes: A Rejoinder," *Economic Journal*, XXXII (December 1922), 563.

10 George Unwin, "The Aims of Economic History," R. H. Tawney, ed., *Studies in Economic History: The Collected Papers of George Unwin* (London, 1958), 28. See also Tawney's memoir of Unwin affixed to this edition.

11 The model of this economic history, which came to include work by T. S. Ashton, G. W. Daniels, and C. Gill, was Unwin's local study, *Samuel Oldknow and the Arkwrights: The Industrial Revolution in Stockport and Marple*, 2nd ed. (New York, 1968).

12 George Unwin,"Some General Fallacies in Economic History," Tawney, ed., *Collected Papers of Unwin*, 5.

13 George Unwin, "The Aims of Economic History," *Collected Papers of Unwin*, 36.

14 George Unwin, *Industrial Organization in the Sixteenth and Seventeenth Centuries* (London, 1951); *The Gilds and Companies of London* (London, 1908). See also W. R. Scott's more moderate interpretation, *The Constitution and Finance of English, Scottish and Irish Joint-Stock Companies* (Cambridge, 1910–12). Scott was sympathetic to historical economics. He did important work in the history of economic thought and was closely associated with H. S. Foxwell and Ashley. He succeeded Ashley as President of the Economic History Society.

15 R. H. Tawney, "Memoir of George Unwin," *Collected Papers of Unwin*, lxii. See especially Unwin's attack on Cunningham's interpretation of Edward III's economic policies, "The Economic Policy of Edward III," *Collected Papers of Unwin*, 117–32.

16 Ephraim Lipson, *The Economic History of England*, II, *The Age of Mercantilism* (London, 1956). esp. lxxxviii, cxliv, cxxxvi.

17 Ephraim Lipson, *A Planned Economy or Free Enterprise: The Lessons of History* (London, 1944), 8.

18 Lipson, *A Planned Enconomy*, esp. 13–14; *Reflections on Britain and the United States, Mainly Economic* (London, 1959).

19 R. H. Tawney, "The Study of Economic History," (1932), Harte, ed., *The Study of Economic History*, 95.

20 J. D. Chambers, "The Tawney Tradition," *The Economic History Review*, Second Series, XXIV (August 1971), 355–70; Ross Terrill, *R. H. Tawney and His Times: Socialism and Fellowship* (London, 1974).

21 The role of the WEA in disseminating economic ideas deserves a study. See R. H. Tawney, *The W.E.A. and Adult Education* (London, 1953); A. J. Alloway, "Adult Education in England," *Vaughan College Papers*, No. 1, rev. ed., 1957; Alan John Corfield, *Epoch in Workers' Education: A History of the Workers' Educational Trade Uniuon Committee* (London, 1969); Mary Stocks, *The Workers' Educational Association: The First Fifty Years* (London, 1953).

22 Clarke, *Liberals and Social Democrats*.

23 J. L. Hammond, "The Industrial Revolution and Discontent," *Economic History Review*, II (January 1930), 220.

24 See, for example, Jason [John L. Hammond], *Past and Future* (London, 1918). On the Hammonds, see R. H. Tawney, "J. L. Hammond," *Proceedings of the British Academy* XLIV (1960), 267–93; Henry Winkler, "J. L. Hammond" in Hans A. Schmitt, ed., *Historians of Modern Europe* (Baton Rouge, 1971), 95–119; Gilbert Murray, "J. L. Hammond," *DNB* (1941–50), 350–52.

25 J. L. and Barbara Hammond, *The Village Labourer, 1760–1832: A Study in the Government of England* (New York, 1970). See also R. H. Tawney, *The Agrarian Problem in the Sixteenth Century* (New York, 1967); first published in 1912.

26 J. L. and Barbara Hammond, *The Town Labourer: The New Civilization, 1760–1832* (New York, 1968). Their indictment of the social consequences of the Industrial Revolution was made more specific in *The Skilled Labourer: 1760–1832* (New York, 1970); first published in 1919.

27 Hammonds, *Town Labourer*, 176; see also, 170–86.

28 J. L. and Barbara Hammond, *The Rise of Modern Industry*, 9th ed. (London, 1966), 158l first published in 1925.

29 Jason (Hammond), *Past and Future*, esp. 22–26. On Keynes in this connection, see Clarke, *Liberals and Social Democrats*, 271 and the suggestive comments by Semmel, *J. S. Mill and the Pursuit of Virtue*, 186–98.

30 E. P. Thompson, *The Making of the English Working Class* (New York, 1963); E. J. Hobsbawm, *Labouring Men: Studies in the History of Labour* (New York, 1964); E. M. Hartwell, "The Standard of Living: An Answer to the Pessimists" and "The Making of the English Working Class?" in *The Industrial Revolution and Economic Growth* (London, 1971).

31 Hartwell, *The Industrial Revolution and Economic Growth*, xiii.

32 Eli F. Heckscher, *Mercantilism*, 2nd rev. ed., 2 vols. (London, 1955); Ja-

cob Viner, *Studies in the Theory of International Trade* (New York, 1937) and "Power versus Plenty as Objectives of Foreign Policy" in D. C. Coleman, ed., *Revisions in Mercantilism*, (London, 1969), 61–91; Charles Wilson, *Profit and Power: A Study of England and the Dutch Wars* (London, 1957) and *Economic History and the Historian: Collected Essays* (New York, 1969).

33 J. M. Keynes, *The General Theory of Employment, Interest and Money* (London, 1936), 335.

34 See especially the inaugural lectures of Eileen Power, G. N. Clarke, W. K. Hancock, M. M. Postan, and Sidney Pollard in Harte, ed., *The Study of Economic History* and the important study by M. M. Postan, *Fact and Relevance: Essays in Historical Method* (Cambridge, 1971).

35 See the recent discussion by Elizabeth Durbin, *New Jerusalems: The Labour Party and the Economics of Democratic Socialism* (London, 1985).

36 Nigel Harris, *Competition and the Corporate Society: British Conservatism, the State, and Industry* (London, 1972).

37 Semmel, *Imperialism and Social Reform* (1960); Scally, *The Origin of the Lloyd George Coalition* (1975); Searle, *The Quest for National Efficiency* (1971); and H. C. G. Mathew, *The Liberal Imperialists* (1973).

38 T. F. Lindsay and Michael Harrington, *The Conservative Party, 1918–1970* (New York, 1974), 16.

39 Alfred Milner, "Reminiscences" in Toynbee, *Lectures on the Industrial Revolution*.

40 Alfred Milner, "A Political Ishmaelite"(1906) *The Nation and the Empire* (London, 1913).

41 On Milner, see John Marlowe, *Milner: Apostle of Empire* (London, 1976); A.M. Gollin, *Proconsul in Politics: A Study of Lord Milner in Opposition and in Power* (London, 1964); and Vladimir Halperin, *Lord Milner and the Empire: The Evolution of British Imperialism* (London, 1952).

42 Viscount Milner, "Lectures on Socialism," *The National Review*, XCVI (January 1931), 36. They were not published until 19?1, but his earlier notes are in the Milner Papers, Bodleian Library, Oxford.

43 Milner, "Lectures on Socialism,: *The National Review* XCVI (February 1931), 186 and *The National Review* XCVI (March 1931), 347, 352.

44 Milner, "Lectures on Socialism," *The National Review* XCVI (April 1931), 494.

45 Milner, "Lectures on Socialism," *The National Review* XCVI (June 1931), 765–66.

46 Ibid.:770–71.

47 Alfred Milner, *Questions of the Hour* (London, 1923), 15. Milner's notes refer to a volume entitled, "Reflections of an Economic Heretic," Milner Papers, 125. f. 33.

48 Milner, *Questions of the Hour*, vii.

49 Helperin, *Milner*, 208; see also Amery's Introduction.

50 L. S. Amery, *My Political Life* (London, 1953), I, 255.

51 Ibid., 50–51.

52 Ibid., 25.

53 J. L. Garvin, *The Economic Foundations of Peace* (London, 1919); "Principles of Constructive Economics as Applied to the Maintenance of Empire," *Compatriots Club Lectures*, First Series (London, 1905); [Calchas], "Cobdenism and Capital," *Fortnightly Review*, LXXIV, n.s. (July 1903), 19–34; [Calchas], "Imperialist Democracy and Socialist Revision," *Fortnightly Review*, LXXXI, n.s. (March 1907), 375–91.

54 Amery, *My Political Life*, I, 247; see his *Tariff Reform: The Great Question* (London, 1909) and *Fundamental Fallacies of Free Trade* (London, 1906).

55 Ian M. Drummond, *Imperial Economic Policy, 1917–1939* (London, 1974)

56 L. S. Amery, *A Balanced Economy* (London, 1954)

57 A.M. Gollin, *Balfour's Burden: Arthur Balfour and Imperial Preference* (London, 1965).

58 Robert Blake, *Independent Tory: The Life and Times of Andrew Bonar Law, 1858–1923*, (New York, 1956), 45.

59 See, for example, Bonar Law's speech of 1910, which reflected Ashley's views, Bonar Law Papers, Cambridge University Library, 19/1–2.

60 Blake, *Independent Tory*, 109.

61 Amery, *My Political Life*, II, 279–80.

62 Stanley Baldwin, "Lord Milner and Arnold Toynbee," *On England and Other Addresses* (London, 1926), 181–84; Keith Middlemas and John Barnes, *Baldwin: A Biography* (London, 1969); Deryck Abel, *A History of British Tariffs, 1923–1942* (London, 1945).

63 Abel, *History of British Tariffs*; Drummond, *Imperial Economic Policy*; Keith Feiling, *The Life of Neville Chamberlain* (Hamden, Conn., 1970).

64 Amery, *My Political Life*, III, 95.

65 J.M. Keynes, "Proposals for a Tariff," *The New Statesman and Nation*, I, n.s. 2 (March 7, 1931), 53–54).

66 J.M. Keynes, "Letter," *The New Statesman and Nation* (March 21, 1931), 142; L. Robbins, "A Reply to Mr. Keynes," *The New Statesman and Nation* (March 14, 1931), 99–100.

67 J. M. Keynes, "Economic Notes on Free Trade, III," *The New Statesman and Nation*, (April 11, 1931), 243.

68 L. Robbins, "Letter," *The New Statesman and Nation* (April 18, 1931), 279–80; (March 28, 1931), 178–79; (April 4, 1931), 214–16. During the 1930s, Robbins and Hayek defended the orthodox, individualist and deductive tradition at the LSE; F.A. von Hayek, "The Trend of Economic Thinking," *Economica*, XIII (May 1933), esp. 125–26.

69 J. M. Keynes, "T. R. Malthus," *Essays in Biography* (New York, 1963), esp. p. 98.

70 J. M. Keynes, "The End of Laissex Faire," *Essays in Persuasion* (New York, 1963), 288–89.

71 J. M. Keynes, "National Self-Sufficiency," *Yale Review*, 22 (June 1933), 758. As Secretary to the Cambridge Free Trade Association in 1910, he had objected to Cunningham's interpretation of Nicholson's *Project of Empire* as giving comfort to protectionists; letter to the *Cambridge Daily News* 13 January, 1910, Elizabeth Johnson, ed., *The Collected Works of John Maynard Keynes* (London, 1971), 15, 43.

Selected bibliography

Manuscripts

W.J. Ashley. Original Minute Book of the Economics Seminary, University of
Toronto.
Ashley, Add. ms. British Museum.
Baldwin Papers. University Library, Cambridge.
Cambridge University Archives. University Library, Cambridge.
Cannan Collection. British Library of Political and Economic Science.
Courtney Collection. British Library of Political and Economic Science.
Ely Papers. State Historical Society, Madison, Wisconsin.
Foxwell Papers. Kress Library of Business and Economics, Harvard
University.
Goldwin Smith Papers. Cornell University.
Hammond Papers. Bodleian Library. Oxford.
Hewins Papers. Sheffield University Library.
Hutchinson Trust Minute Books. British Library of Economic and Political
Science.
Ingram Papers. Public Record Office of Northern Ireland.
Ingram-Leslie Letters. Stirling Library, London University.
J.N. Keynes Letters. Marshall Library, Cambridge.
Bonar Law Papers. House of Lords Record Office.
Manchester University Archives. Manchester.
Marshall Papers. Marshall Library, Cambridge.
John Stuart Mill Collection. Johns Hopkins University.
Milner Papers. Bodleian Library, Oxford.
Miscellaneous Letters. Marshall Library, Cambridge.
Miscellaneous University Papers, 1900–1902, The Bodleian Library, Oxford.
Passfield Papers. London School of Economics and Political Science.
L.L. Price. Memoir and Notes on British Economists, 1881–1947. Royal Sta-
tistical Society, London.
L.L. Price. Miscellaneous Reminiscences. Oriel College, Oxford.
Rogers Papers. Magdelan College and Bodleian Library, Oxford.
Seligman Collection. Columbia University.
Tariff Commission Papers. British Library of Political and Economic Science.
T.F. Tout Papers. John Rylands University Library. Manchester.
Wallas Collection. British Library of Political and Economic Science.

260

Primary sources

Amery, L.S. *A Balanced Economy*. London: Hutchison, 1954.

Amery, L.S. *My Political Life*. London: Hutchinson, 1953, 3 vols.

Ashley, W.J. *The Economic Organization of England: An Outline History*. London: Longmans, Green, and Co., 1926.

Ashley, W.J. *An Introduction to English Economic History and Theory*, 2nd ed. New York: G.P. Putnam, 1893, 2 vols.

Ashley, W.J. "The Place of Economic History in University Studies," *Economic History Review*, I (January 1927), 1–11.

Ashley, W.J. "The Rehabilitation of Ricardo," *Economic Journal*, 1 (September 1891), 474–89.

Ashley, W.J. *Surveys, Historic, and Economic*. New York: A.M. Kelley, 1966.

Ashley, W.J. *The Tariff Problem*. New York: A.M. Kelley, 1968.

Ashley, W.J. *What is Political Science?* Toronto: University of Toronto, 1888.

Bagehot, Walter. *Economic Studies*. R.H. Hutton, ed. Stanford: Academic Reprints, 1953.

Booth, Charles. *The Life and Labour of the People of London*. London: Macmillan and Co., 1902–3, 17 vols.

Bowley, Arthur L. *A Short Account of England's Foreign Trade in the Nineteenth Century*. Rev. ed. London: S. Sonnenschein and Co., 1905.

Cairnes, J.E. *The Character and Logical Method of Political Economy*. 2nd ed. New York: A.M. Kelley, 1965.

Cairnes, J.E. *Essays in Political Economy*. New York: A.M. Kelley, 1975

Cairnes, J.E. *Political Essays*. New York: A. M. Kelley, 1967.

Cairnes, J.E. *Some Leading Principles of Political Economy Newly Expounded*. New York: A.M. Kelley, 1967.

Cannan, Edwin. *An Economist's Protest*. London: P.S. King and Son, 1927.

Cannan, Edwin. *A History of Local Rates in England in Relation to the Proper Distribution of the Burden of Taxation*. London: P.S. King and Son, 1912.

Cannan, Edwin. *A History of the Theories of Production and Distribution in English Political Economy, from 1776 to 1848*. London: Percival and Co., 1893.

Carey, Henry Charles. *Principles of Social Science*. Philadelphia: Lippincott, 1873. 3 vols.

Clapham, J.H. *An Economic History of Modern Britain*. Cambridge. Cambridge University Press, 1930–32. 3 vols.

Clapham, J.H. *The Study of Economic History: An Inaugural Lecture*. Cambridge: Cambridge University Press, 1929.

Coats, A.W. "Alfred Marshall and the Early Development of the London School of Economics: Some Unpublished Letters," *Economica*, N.S. 34 (October 1967), 408–17.

Cole, G.D.H. *Some Relations Between Political and Economic Science*. London: Macmillan, 1934.

Cunningham, William. *Christianity and Economic Science*. London: John Murray, 1914.

Cunningham, William. *Christianity and Politics*. New York: Houghton Mifflin, 1915.

Cunningham, William. *The Growth of English Industry and Commerce*. Cambridge: Cambridge University Press, 1882.

Cunningham, William. *The Growth of English Industry and Commerce*. 2nd ed. Cambridge: Cambridge University Press, 1890–92. 2 vols. and subsequent editions.

Cunningham, William. *Hints on the Study of Economic History*. London: S.P.C.K., 1919.

Cunningham, William. "The Perversion of Economic History," *Economic Journal*, II (September 1892), 491–506.

Cunningham, William. "Plea for Pure Theory," *Economic Review*, 2 (January 1892), 25–41.

Cunningham, William. "Plea for the Study of Economic History," *Economic Review*, 9 (January 1899), 67–71.

Cunningham, William. "Political Economy as a Moral Science," *Mind*, III (July 1878), 369–83.

Cunningham, William. *Politics and Economics: An Essay on the Nature of the Principles of Political Economy, Together with a Survey of Recent Legislation*. London: Kegan, Paul, French, 1885.

Cunningham, William. *The Progress of Capitalism in England*. Cambridge: Cambridge University Press, 1916.

Cunningham, William. *The Rise and Decline of the Free Trade Movement*. Cambridge: Cambridge University Press, 1905.

Cunningham, William. "Why Had Roscher So Little Influence in England?" Annals of the American Academy of Political and Social Science, 5 (November 1894), 317–34.

Foxwell, Herbert Somerton. "The Economic Movement in England," Quarterly Journal of Economics, II (October 1887), 84–103.

Foxwell, H.S. *Irregularity of Employment and the Fluctuations of Prices*. Edinburgh: Cooperative Printing Co., 1886.

Foxwell, H.S. *Papers in Current Finance*. London: Macmillan, 1919.

Giffen, Robert. *Economic Inquiries and Studies*. London: Macmillan and Co., 1904. 2 vols.

Giffen, Robert. *Essays in Finance*. First Series. 4th ed. London: George Bell and Sons, 1886. Second Series, 1890.

Giffen, Robert. "Imperial Policy and Free Trade," *The Nineteenth Century and After*, No. CCCXVII (July 1903), 1–16.

Hammond, John L. *Past and Present*. London: Chatto and Windus, 1918.

Hammond, J.L. and Barbara. *The Village Labourer, 1760–1932: A Study in the Government of England*. New York: Harper and Row, 1970.

Hansard's Parliamentary Debates.

Harte, N. (ed.). *The Study of Economic History: Collected Inaugural Lectures, 1893–1970*. London: Frank Cass, 1971.

Hewins, W.A.S. *The Apologia of an Imperialist: Forty Years of Empire Policy, 1889–1929.* London: Constable & Co., 1929, 2 vols.

Hewins, W.A.S. *English Trade and Finance, Chiefly in the Seventeenth Century.* London: Methuen and Co., 1892.

Hewins, W.A.S. "The Teaching of Economics," *Journal of the Society of Arts*, XLV, No. 2 (4 December 1896), 42–52.

Hewins, W.A.S. *Trade in the Balance.* London: Philip Allan and Co., 1924.

Ingram, J.K. *History of Political Ecconomy.* New ed. London: A. & C. Black, 1923.

Jevons, W. Stanley. *Principles of Economics.* New York: A.M. Kelley, 1965.

Jevons, W. Stanley. *The State in Relation to Labour.* New York: A.M. Kelley, 1968.

Jevons, W. Stanley. *Theory of Political Economy.* 5th ed. New York: Kelley and Millman, 1957.

Jones, Richard. *An Essay on the Distribution of Wealth and the Sources of Taxation.* New York: Kelley and Millman, 1956.

Jones, Richard. *Literary Remains: Lectures and Tracts on Political Economy.* William Whewell, ed. New York: A. M. Kelley, 1964.

Keynes, J.M. *Essays in Biography.* New York: W.W. Norton and Co., 1951.

Keynes, J.M. *The General Theory of Employment, Interest, and Money.* London: Macmillan, 1936.

Keynes, J.N. *The Scope and Method of Political Economy.* 4th ed. New York: A.M. Kelley, 1964.

Leslie, T.E. Cliffe. *Essays in Political and Moral Philosophy.* London: Longmans, Green, and Co., 1879.

Leslie, T.E. Cliffe. *Essays in Political Economy.* 2nd ed. London: Longmans, Green, and Co., 1888.

Leslie, T.E. Cliffe. *Land Systems and Industrial Economy of Ireland, England, and Continental Countries.* London: Longmans, Green, and Co., 1870.

Levi, Leone. *The History of British Commerce and of the Economic Progress of the British Nation, 1763–1878,* 2nd ed. London: John Murray, 1888.

Lipson, Ephraim. *A Planned Economy or Free Enterprise: The Lessons of History,* London: Adam and Charles Black, 1944.

List, Fredrich. *The National System of Political Economy.* 2nd ed. Sampson S. Lloyd, tr. London: Longmans, Green, and Company, 1928.

Macmillan, Harold. *The Middle Way.* London: Macmillan and Co., 1938.

McCready, H.W. "Sir William Ashley: Some Unpublished Letters," *Journal of Economic History*, 15 (No. 1, 1955), 34–43.

Maine, Sir Henry. *Village Communities.* 4th ed. London: John Murray, 1881.

Marshall, Alfred. *Industry and Trade.* 3rd ed. London: Macmillan, 1921.

Marshall, Alfred. *Memorials of Alfred Marshall.* A.C. Pigou, ed. New York: Kelley and Millman, 1956.

Marshall, Alfred. *Principles of Economics*, 8th ed. London: Macmillan, 1968.

Marshall, Alfred and Mary Paley Marshall. *The Economics of Industry.* London: Macmillan, 1879.

Mill, J.S. *Autobiography.* New York: Columbia University Press, 1960.

Mill, J.S. *The Collected Works of John Stuart Mill*. J.M. Robson., ed. Toronto: Toronto University Press, 1965–67, Vols. 1–5.

Mill, J.S. *Essays on Some Unsettled Questions of Political Economy*. London: London School of Political Economy and Political Science, 1948.

Mill, J.S. *The Later Letters of J.S. Mill, 1849–73*. Francis W. Mineka and Dwight Lindley, eds. *Collected Works of J.S. Mill*. Toronto: Toronto University Press, 1972. Vols. 14–18.

Mill, J.S. *A System of Logic*. 8th ed. London: Longmans, Green, and Co., 1967.

Milner, Alfred. *The Nation and the Empire*. London: Constable and Co., 1913

Milner, Alfred. *Questions of the Hour*. London: Hodder and Stoughton, 1923.

Nicholson, J.S. *Principles of Political Economy*. London: Macmillan, 1893–1901. 3 vols.

Nicholson, J.S. *A Project of Empire: A Criticial Study of the Economics of Imperialism, With Special Reference to the Ideas of Adam Smith*. London: Macmillan, 1910.

Nicholson, J.S. *The Revival of Marxism*. London: John Murray, 1920.

Nicholson, J.S. *The Tariff Question With Special Reference to Wages and Employment*. London: A.C. Black, 1903.

Palgrave, J.H. Inglis. *Dictionary of Political Economy*. London: Macmillan, 1894–9; 2nd ed. 1925–6. 3 vols.

Political Economy Club. *Revised Report of the Proceedings of the Dinner of 31st May 1876*. London: Political Economy Club, 1876.

Price, L.L. *Cooperation and Copartnership*. London: Collins, 1914.

Price, L.L. *Economic Science and Practice; or Essays on Various Aspects of the Relations of Economic Science to Practical Affairs*. London: Methuen and Co., 1896.

Price, L.L. "Free Trade and Protection," *Economic Journal*, 12 (September 1903), 305–19.

Price, L.L. *Industrial Peace: Its Advantages, Methods and Difficulties, A Report of An Inquiry Made for the Toynbee Trust*. London: Macmillan and Co., 1887.

Price, L.L. *A Short History of English Commerce and Industry*. London: E. Arnold, 1900.

Price, L.L. *A Short History of Political Economy in England*, 15th ed. London: Methuen and Co., 1937.

Rogers, J.E.T. *The Economic Interpretation of History*. New York: G. Putnam's Sons, 1888.

Rogers, J.E.T. *A History of Agriculture and Prices in England*. Oxford: Clarendon Press, 1866–1902. 7 vols.

Rogers, J.E.T. *The Industrial and Commercial History of England*. New York: G. Putnam's Sons, 1892.

Rogers, J.E.T. *A Manual of Political Economy*. Oxford: Clarendon Press, 1868.

Rogers, J.E.T. *The Relations of Economic Science to Social and Political Action*. London: Swan, Sonnenschein, 1888.

Rogers, J.E.T. *Six Centuries of Work and Wages*. London: Allen and Unwin, 1949.

Royal Statistical Society. *Annals of the Royal Statistical Society 1834–1934*. London: The Royal Statistical Society, 1934.

Smyth, R.L., ed. *Essays in Economic Method: Selected Papers Read to Section F. of the British Association for the Advancement of Science, 1860–1913*. London: Gerald Duckworth and Co., 1962.

Tawney, R.H. "J.L. Hammond," *Proceedings of the British Academy*, XLIV (1960), 267–93.

Tawney, R.H. *The W.E.A. and Adult Education*. London: Athlone Press, 1953.

Tawney, R.H. *The Webbs and Their Work: Webb Memorial Lecture*. London: Fabian Society, 1945.

Tooke, Thomas and William Newmarch. *The History of Prices and the State of the Circulation*. London: Longmans, 1838–57. 6 vols.

Toynbee, Arnold. *Lectures on the Industrial Revolution of the Eighteenth Century in England*. London: Longmans, Green, and Co., 1913.

Unwin, George. *Studies in Economic History: The Collected Papers of George Unwin*. R.H. Tawney, ed. London: Frank Cass, 1958.

Webb, Beatrice. *The Diary of Beatrice Webb*. Vol. I, *1873–1892*, Vol. II, 1892–1905, Norman and Jeanne Mackenzie, eds. London: Virago, 1982–83.

Webb, Beatrice. *My Apprenticeship*. London: Longmans, 1926.

Webb, Beatrice. *Our Partnership*. Mary Barbara Drake and Margaret Cole, eds. New York: Longmans, Green, and Co., 1948.

Webb, Sidney and Beatrice. *The Decay of Capitalist Civilization*. New York: G. Allen and Unwin, 1923.

Webb, Sidney and Beatrice. *Industrial Democracy*. New York: Longmans, Green, and Co., 1902.

Webb, Sidney and Beatrice. *Problems of Modern Industry*. London: Longmans, Green, and Co., 1902.

Secondary sources

Amery, Julian. *Joseph Chamberlain and the Tariff Reform Campaign*. London: Macmillan and Co., 1969. 2 vols.

Ashley, Anne. *William James Ashley: A Life*. London: P.S. King, 1932.

Barker, T.C. "The Beginnings of the Economic History Society," *Economic History Review*, Second Series, XXX (February 1977), 1–19.

Beveridge, Janet. *Epic of Clare Market: Birth and Early Days of the London School of Economics*. London: G. Bell and Sons, 1960.

Black, R.D.C. *Economic Thought and the Irish Question, 1815–1870*. Cambridge: Cambridge University Press, 1961.

Blaug, Mark. *Ricardian Economics: A Historical Study*. New Haven: Yale University Press, 1958.

Boylan, T.A. and T.P. Foley, "John Elliot Cairnes, John Stuart Mill and Ireland," Antoin E. Murphy, ed., *Economists and the Irish Economy*. Dublin: Irish Academic Press, 1984, 96–119.

Brown, Benjamin H. *The Tariff Reform Movement in Great Britain, 1881–1895*. New York: Columbia University Press, 1943.

Burrow, J.W. *Evolution and Society: A Study in Victorian Social Theory*. Cambridge: Cambridge University Press, 1966.

Burrow, J.W. *A Liberal Descent: Victorian Historians and the English Past*. Cambridge: Cambridge University Press, 1981.

Caine, Sir Sidney. *The History of the Foundation of the London School of Economics and Political Science*. London: London School of Economics and Political Science, 1963.

Chambers, J.D. "The Tawney Tradition, *Economic History Review*, 2nd. Series, XXIV (August 1971), 355–70.

Checkland, S.G. "The Advent of Academic Economics in England," *Manchester School*, XIX (January 1951), 43–70.

Clarke, Peter. *Liberals and Social Democrats*. Cambridge: Cambridge University Press, 1978.

Coats, A.W. "The Historist Reaction to English Political Economy," *Economica*, New Series, 21 (May 1954), 143–53.

Coats, A.W. "The Origin and Early Development of the Royal Economic Society." *Economic Journal*: 78 (June 1968), 349–71.

Coats, A.W. "Political Economy and the Tariff Reform Campaign," *Journal of Law and Economics*, 11 (April 1968), 181–229.

Coats, A.W. "Sociological Aspects of British Economic Thought," *Journal of Political Economy*, 75 (October 1967), 706–29.

Cole, Margaret. *The Life of G.D.H. Cole*, London: Macmillan, 1971.

Court, W.H.B. *Scarcity and Choice in History*. London: Edward Arnold, 1970.

Cunningham, Audrey. *William Cunningham: Teacher and Priest*. London: S.P.C.K., 1950.

De Marchi, N.B. "On the Dangers of Being Too Political an Economist: Thorold Rogers and the 1868 election to the Drummond Professorship," *Oxford Economic Paper*, 28 (November 1976), 364–80.

Engel, A.J. *From Clergyman to Don: The Rise of the Academic Profession in Nineteenth Century Oxford*. Oxford: Clarendon Press, 1983.

Feaver, George. *From Status to Contract: A Biography of Sir Henry Maine, 1822–88*. London: Longmans, 1969.

Freedan, Michael. *The New Liberalism: An Ideology of Social Reform*. Oxford: Clarendon Press, 1978.

Gollin, A.M. *Balfour's Burden: Arthur Balfour and Imperial Preference*. London: Anthony Blond, 1965.

Gras, N.S.B. "The Rise and Development of Economic History," *Economic History Review*, I (June 1927–28), 12–34.

Harris, José. *William Beveridge: A Biography*. Oxford: Clarendon Press, 1977.

Harris, Nigel. *Competition and the Corporate Society: British Conservatives, the State, and Industry*. London: Methuen, 1972.

Hayek, F.A. "The London School of Economics, 1895–1945," *Economica*, N.S. 13 (February 1946), 1–31.

Hutchison, T.W. *A Review of Economic Doctrines, 1870–1929*. Oxford: Clarendon Press, 1966.

Hutchison, T.W. *On Revolutions and Progress in Economic Knowledge*. Cambridge: Cambridge University Press, 1978.

Kadish, Alon. *The Oxford Economists in the Late Nineteenth Century*. Oxford: Clarendon Press, 1982.

Lynd, Helen. *England in the Eighteen-Eighties: Toward a Social Basis for Freedom*. London: Oxford University Press, 1945.

McClelland, Charles E. *The German Historians and England: A Study in Nineteenth Century Views*. Cambridge: Cambridge University Press, 1971.

Maloney, John. *Marshall, Orthodoxy and the Professionalization of Economics*. Cambridge: Cambridge University Press, 1985.

Marlowe, John. *Milner: Apostle of Empire*. London: Macmillan, 1976.

Meek, Ronald L. "The Decline of Ricardian Economics in England." *Economica*, N.S., XVII (February 1950), 43–62.

O'Brien, D.P. *The Classical Economists*. Oxford: Oxford University Press, 1975.

Petridis, A. "Bilateral Monopoly, Tariff Reform, and the Teaching of Economics: The Neglected Contribution of Langford Price." *History of Political Economy*, 11 (Spring 1979), 165–98.

Postan, M.M. *Fact and Relevance: Essays in Historical Method*. Cambridge: Cambridge University Press, 1971.

Richter, Melvin. *The Politics of Conscience: T.H. Green and His Age*. Cambridge Mass.: Harvard University Press, 1964.

Robbins, Lionel. *The Theory of Economic Policy in English Classical Political Economy*. London: Macmillan, 1952.

Scally, Robert J. *The Origin of the Lloyd George Coalition: The Politics of Social-Imperialism, 1900–1918*. Princeton: Princeton University Press, 1978.

Schumpeter, Joseph. *History of Economic Analysis*. New York: Oxford University Press, 1954.

Schwartz, Pedro. *The New Political Economy of J.S. Mill*. London: Weidenfeld and Nicolson, 1968.

Searle, G.R. *The Quest for National Efficiency: A Study in British Politics and British Political Thought, 1899–1914*. Berkeley and Los Angeles: University of California Press, 1971.

Semmel, Bernard. *Imperialism and Social Reform: English Social-Imperial Thought, 1885–1914*. London: Allen and Unwin, 1960.

Semmel, Bernard. *John Stuart Mill and the Pursuit of Virtue*. New Haven: Yale University Press, 1984.

Semmel, Bernard. *The Rise of Free Trade Imperialism: Classical Political Economy, The Empire of Free Trade and Imperialism, 1750–1850*. Cambridge: Cambridge University Press, 1970.

Small, Albion. *The Origins of Sociology*. Chicago: University of Chicago Press, 1924.

Smyth, R.L. "The History of Section F. of the British Association, 1834–1972" in Nicholas Kaldor, ed. *Conflicts in Policy Objectives*. New York: A.M. Kelley, 1971, 156–75.

Soffer, Reba N. *Ethics and Society: The Revolution in the Social Sciences, 1870–1914*. Berkeley: University of California Press, 1978.

Spiegel, Henry William. *The Growth of Economic Thought*. Revised ed. Durham, N.C.: Duke University Press, 1983.

Terrill, Ross. *R.H. Tawney and His Times: Socialism as Fellowship*. Cambridge: Harvard University Press, 1973.

Usher, A.P. "Sir John Howard Clapham and the Empirical Reaction in Economic History," *Journal of Economic History*, II, No. 2 (1951), 148–53.

Whitaker, J.K. *The Early Economic Writings of Alfred Marshall, 1867–1890*. New York: Royal Economic Society, 1975. 2 vols.

Winch, Donald. *Economics and Policy: An Historical Study*. New York: Hodder and Stoughton, 1969.

Wood, John Cunningham. *British Economists and the Empire*. London: Croom Helm, 1983.

Index